DECISION-MAKING

DECISION-MAKING

Its Logic and Practice

John D. Mullen
and
Byron M. Roth

ROWMAN & LITTLEFIELD PUBLISHERS, INC.

ROWMAN & LITTLEFIELD PUBLISHERS, INC.

Published in the United States of America
by Rowman & Littlefield Publishers, Inc.
8705 Bollman Place, Savage, Maryland 20763

British Cataloging in Publication Information Available

Library of Congress Cataloging-in-Publication Data

Mullen, John Douglas.
  Decision-making : its logic and practice / John D. Mullen
and Byron M. Roth.
    p.   cm.
  Includes bibliographical references and index.
  1. Decision-making.   I. Roth, Byron M. (Byron Mitchell)
  II. Title.
BF448.M84   1990
153.8'3—dc20   90–19313 CIP

ISBN 0–8476–7619–6 (alk. paper)

5   4   3   2   1

Printed in the United States of America

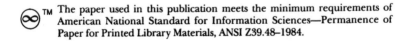 TM The paper used in this publication meets the minimum requirements of
American National Standard for Information Sciences—Permanence of
Paper for Printed Library Materials, ANSI Z39.48–1984.

for
Doris E. Roth
and
Constance H. Mullen
with all our love

Contents

Preface

This is a book about how to improve your thinking and reasoning in that broad area of human life known as decision-making. Decisions are not the products only of thinking. They derive as well from will, occasionally courageous, and from character or personality, often secure and stable but sometimes not. Still we firmly believe that reasoning about choices can be significantly enhanced by mastering, through study and practice, a set of patterns or tactics with which to approach decision problems. In the same way that studying logic or critical thinking (as generally conceived) will benefit reasoning about what to believe, and studying statistics will supply tactics for handling and understanding quantitative data, so studying decision-making will improve our attempts to make serious personal and professional choices as well as decisions concerning political and social policy.

The tactics and strategies that we present in these chapters were not invented *de novo,* but derive from a vast interdisciplinary literature called *decision theory.* A brief check of this literature will reveal contributions from a variety of disciplines—economists, psychologists, philosophers, logicians, political scientists, management specialists, and others. Despite this broad range of disciplines, there has been a remarkable consistency of language and orientation in the area, an orientation that has often been, unfortunately, more concerned with elegance of form than with practical application. There have been exceptions, of course, but these tend either to lack the specificity to generate concrete solutions, or they presuppose a level of mathematical and theoretical expertise beyond what it would be useful for most to achieve.

Yet this literature is, despite its penchant for formalization, a gold mine of interesting and practical techniques and strategies for solving decision problems. This book, a survey of much of the results of this literature, always has two things in mind: ease of understanding, and practical applicability. Although formatted as a textbook for classroom use, the book could profitably be read by anyone who is serious about improving his or her decision-making effectiveness. This includes managers in business, government, or education; attorneys whose practices take them to the negotiating table; counselors whose clients bring to therapy questions about how to handle their everyday decision problems; and many others.

As a textbook, it is appropriate for: introductory courses in decision-making; for courses in logic or critical thinking, as an extension from the logic of belief to the logic of action, what Aristotle called the practical syllogism; for those courses in psychology that include discussions of decision theoretic models of behavior; for courses in political science that focus upon models of political decision-making; for courses designed to train managers; and for courses in ethics that intend a rigorous approach to social and political issues.

In our own case, we began teaching an elective course titled, "Critical Thinking for Decision-making" in 1985. Its clientele represents a spectrum of day and evening students, recent high school graduates and adults attending evenings after work, men and women, and students with majors as diverse as aeronautics, psychology, business, and education. This course, and the text that it produced, was the result of a long, cooperative effort on both of our parts. Roth's interests in decision-making, initially awakened by the lucidity and beauty of the work of von Neumann and Morgenstern, developed under the guidance of Professor Martin Shubik of Yale University. Mullen was introduced to the decision-making literature by Professor Michael Martin of Boston University, at first struggling with the ground-breaking work of Frank Plumpton Ramsey, and later enjoying the many elegant papers of Patrick Suppes. As a team over the last twenty years, we have taught the philosophy of psychology, negotiated faculty labor agreements, taught decision-making to public school teachers as part of a critical thinking project, remodelled Mullen's house, conducted decision-making workshops at critical thinking conferences, and fought about this book. It is said that writing a book together is rather like being married. But that can't be so, because if marriages were anything like this, then both of ours, each now approaching twenty-five years, would have dissolved long ago.

In addition to the thanks that each of us owes Professors Shubik and

Martin mentioned above, we are grateful also to Professor David M. Messick of the University of California at Santa Barbara for his kind assistance in pointing us to some very interesting literature in decision-making, and for his general encouragement. We acknowledge the support in funds and time from Dowling College to carry out the writing of this book. Most of all we are indebted to the students of Dowling who taught us so much about how to teach decision-making, and by extension, how to write a text about it. They taught us that it's uninteresting to be able to solve a decision matrix for the minimax regret solution unless you can structure the problem in the first place; that learning Bayes' theorem is less important than being able to avoid the gambler's fallacy; that numbers should be introduced to represent phenomena only if there's a believable problem whose elements are represented; and that it's best not to demonstrate iterations of the prisoner's dilemma by dividing the group between men and women. They demanded that we not use the classroom as a vehicle for our own appreciation of formal elegance, and that demand has taken root in this text. "Keep it practical," they said in so many ways, and that's what we have tried to do. Despite all these debts, any mistakes, missteps, or misjudgments that are found in the following pages are entirely our responsibility.

John D. Mullen
Byron M. Roth

Chapter 1

Introduction

This is a book about decision-making, and about how to improve the way you think about decisions. To improve how you think about something means, in its broadest sense, to change your habits of thought to better accomplish your goals. Some thinking has as its purpose whether or not to believe something, without implying any particular course of action. An example of this could be investigating whether there is intelligent life beyond the earth. This could be called *thinking toward belief*. The techniques of effective thinking toward belief are the focus of most of what is found in books on logic. Most thinking, though, is directed not only toward arriving at beliefs about what the world is like, but also toward the selection of some course of action. This could be called *thinking toward decision-making*. It seems clear that thinking toward belief is one element of thinking toward decision-making. This is true because effective decision-making requires that our beliefs about the world are accurate. But the principles of effective decision-making go far beyond the principles of logic as commonly understood. You can know all you need to know about your world and still not know what to do, which choices to make. This book introduces some common and useful logical techniques and principles to enhance effective thinking toward belief. But it goes beyond logical reasoning as commonly understood to emphasize some of the most effective techniques to enhance thinking toward decision-making.

Elements of a Decision Problem

Before discussing the various types of investigations that are relevant to the improvement of decision-making, let's look at a very broad outline of the elements involved in the making of decisions. These elements are presented sequentially, although in actual choice, selection of the order is often different.

Step One: Problem Recognition and Values Analysis

While it may seem obvious that decision-making begins with problem recognition, what is not obvious is that accurate problem recognition demands a clear analysis of values. All important decisions arise in the middle of living one's life in which there already is a "present course" that has been challenged (Janis and Mann 1977). This present course would include a set of more or less routine actions, as well as some very well established values and goals. Decision situations begin with some information indicating that to continue the present course of behavior unchanged will involve some sort of loss. The loss may be of something that we now have and that we value, as for example, when we discover that we have a serious illness and must choose a treatment. Or the loss may be of an opportunity, something that we could have if we choose correctly. This is the case, for example, when we are offered a new job and must choose to accept or reject. This information must be evaluated as true or false, relevant or irrelevant.

Part of this evaluation is determining very precisely which of our goals and objectives that are part of our present course are challenged by the threat to the status quo. Unless we have a clear idea of the goals that we are now trying to achieve, we cannot accurately appraise the nature of a problem. This may seem obvious, but in actual situations it is often less clear. For example, people often confuse goals and means. Frank fails to get accepted to the MBA program at Harvard, so his goal of earning a Harvard MBA is shattered, and so is he. On further analysis, his real goal was to succeed in the securities business, and the Harvard MBA was only one means to do this. Also necessary for a clear goals analysis is the identification of the stakeholders in the problem, the people or institutions whom the decision is meant to benefit (Edwards and Newman 1982). In cases where the decision-maker is a fiduciary for others, particularly in the decisions of professionals such as lawyers, consultants, negotiators, doctors, corporate managers, etc., this is often a very complex problem. These issues will be taken up in Chapter 3. Accurate and relevant information of this nature provides the incentive for step two. It has shaken our confidence in the "present course."

Step Two: Generating Alternative Choices

This involves the gathering of new information concerning possible alternatives to the present course. These new alternatives will be called *choices*. They are entertained as actions leading to the achievement of the goals and objectives reviewed in step one. This search is usually done grudgingly since changing an already decided on course of action involves extra effort and costs, and threatens the comfort of the behavioral inertia established by the efficiency of past routines. It is necessary to seek choices that meet the challenge of step one without imposing costs that exceed the losses which that challenge threatens. Step two ends with the narrowing of the field of choices to a set that can be effectively evaluated against each other, or against some set of external criteria. This step can be thought of as a preliminary scanning of alternatives, but it is very important to generate the maximum number of possibly effective choices, even including some that seem outlandish. Step two will be ineffective unless the values and goals of step one are very clear, including the proper identification of means and ends.

Step Three: Evaluating Choices

The first item of business in step three is to decide whether one wants to identify the best possible choice, or merely find a choice that satisfies some external criteria. In the former case, one is said to be *optimizing,* and in the latter case one is *satisficing* (Simon, 1957). What gets evaluated (if one is optimizing) are the costs and benefits of each alternative choice. These options are evaluated against each other to determine which choice has the most beneficial or the least detrimental outcome. In the case of satisficing, we evaluate choices against some external criteria that we have developed to identify choices that are acceptable. The evaluation continues only until we arrive at one that fulfills the criteria of acceptability. We stop there and select that choice. Evaluating alternatives involves assessing what the *outcomes* of our choices will be. An outcome of a choice is not the same as an *effect* of the choice. An outcome of a choice is any effect that the choice has on the fulfillment of our goals. Thus, an accurate goal assessment is a necessary condition for knowing what each choice's outcomes could be. One *effect* of my deciding upon a surgical procedure is to increase the wealth of the hospital. But this is not an *outcome* of my choice, since the wealth of the hospital is not one of my goals, and so the hospital is not a stakeholder in my choice.

Often we can't know for certain what the outcomes of our choices will be, since the outcomes will depend upon matters beyond our control. These matters beyond the control of our choices, but that affect the outcomes of choices, are called *states of the world* (or just *states*). In formulating a decision problem in which there is uncertainty, the identification of the states often gives us the greatest difficulty. It demands that our decision-making be outcome oriented, and that we have the habits of thought and the ability to predict the cause and effect sequences that are likely to be initiated by our choices. If, for example, we are weighing the benefits of medical choices to treat a disease, we have to consider such factors as the probabilities of our body's reacting adversely to the treatment, of the treatment interfering with our life and work, of the surgeon succeeding in the procedure, etc. Step three will therefore often involve the calculation of the probabilities of the states. This can be done without numbers (using words like "probable," "very probable," "almost certain," etc.), or it can be done with numbers (the probability is three in ten). In many cases, reliable numerical probabilities can be arrived at, and will be found to be essential to a proper decision. We will also find it useful to be able to represent the values of the outcomes numerically. Procedures for both of these measurement problems will be discussed.

Finally, we have to decide upon a *decision rule,* and use it. A decision rule is a way of integrating the information that we have gathered concerning goals, choices, states, probabilities of states, outcomes, and values of outcomes. This is done in such a way as to indicate what choice is best, or which choice(s) meet the satisficing criterion. The decision rule may be very simple, such as "Assume the worst will happen and select the choice that avoids it," or the rule could be a very complex decision strategy involving many steps and innumerable calculations.

Step Four: Binding the Will and Ignoring Sunk Costs

Decisions take time to implement. During this time, things do not always go well. Information is almost always received that tends to call for a course of action different from that which was chosen. This situation is similar to step one, and yet is not the same. In step one, the present course had been given a "fair test," whereas in step four the new course has not yet been sufficiently tested. Thus, there is a need for some "will power" in the face of initial disappointment. This is best accomplished by building some incentive into the decision to ride out the inevitable early disappointments.

On the other hand, when it should have become clear that the decision was wrong, we have to be prepared to cut the losses and return to step one. This move demands that we avoid the trap of deciding the future on the basis of what we have "sunk" into the past. Again, there are ways to prepare for this difficult decision of when to stick it out, and when to cut and run. When step four is completed, if the choice works out, then it has become the "present course," and remains so until step one begins again.

Process vs. Outcomes

It is not difficult to convince you that making decisions is something that you do all the time. Sometimes you do it well, and sometimes you don't. When you do it well the decisions are likely to turn out well, though not always. Sometimes when you make a decision in a slipshod way, with little thought or analysis, it turns out well. That's when you thank your lucky stars. More often than not, decisions that are made badly produce bad results. This points up the fact that there is a difference between the *process* of making a decision and whether or not the decision produces favorable *outcomes*. When we say of a decision that it was smart, or reasonable, or rational, we should be referring to the thinking that went into the decision, not to its favorable outcomes. A novice who enters the stock market with his life's savings, refuses expert advice, and refuses to learn any of the principles of fundamental or technical analysis, is acting foolishly. Yet it's possible for him to do very well, at least over the short run. Despite the success, however, it was still foolish of him to risk his savings in that way. He has displayed many of the features of poor decision-making. Success over a *long* run, on the other hand, may suggest that there is "a method to the madness." In this case, we will want to investigate the seemingly foolish method to find its hidden rationale. But we should be very reluctant to judge effective decision-making on consequences alone. The basic principle here is that there are procedures for making various kinds of decisions well, and the better your decision-making procedures are, the more likely you will be to achieve favorable outcomes. This is one good reason for studying decision-making, to make you more aware of how you make decisions, and to suggest some strategies for improved decision-making.

Normative Decision Theory

If we were interested in improving our own decision-making, what exactly would we study in addition to logic as usually understood? There are two areas of research that are relevant to this. One is called normative decision theory. This is a body of research and theory that seeks to prescribe or recommend how decisions ought to be made. To make a normative statement is to tell a person what he *ought* or *should* do. In contrast to normative decision theory, there is empirical decision theory that seeks to describe how people *actually do* make decisions, warts and all. To make a descriptive statement is to tell a person how things actually are, rather than how they should be. Let's look at some examples that illustrate this:

> Frank has a tumor adjacent to a sensitive area of the spine. There is no way to tell if it is malignant except by removing it. Such a procedure is likely to be successful, but is very expensive. Frank has no medical insurance. His doctor tells Frank that there is a one in one hundred chance that the tumor is malignant. If it is malignant and not removed Frank will certainly die, and if it is not malignant and is left alone it will disappear on its own. Frank has the money saved, but it was designated to pay for the Ivy League educations of his four very bright children.

It is a question for normative decision theory to determine how Frank should go about making this decision. There are rational ways to approach a problem like this, and there are less than rational ways. Again, the idea is that the rational ways are more likely to result in favorable consequences than the others. The above problem is a case of decision-making under risk because Frank is uncertain what the results will be whether he chooses to have the operation or chooses not to have it. The problem that Frank faces is one of developing a proper balance between the goals that he wants to achieve with his financial resources, his own personal goals, the probability that the tumor is malignant, and the probability that if the tumor is malignant the operation will succeed. He wants to maximize his expectation of success. Yet these factors are quite a lot to keep in mind and balance off against each other, without some procedures for structuring the problem to achieve such a balance. Normative decision theory supplies just such procedures.

It is important to note that it is not a part of normative decision theory to tell Frank which decision to make. This is a matter that depends upon Frank's own values, upon how much Frank values his children's expensive educations, for example. However, there is a part of normative decision theory which has as its major focus the proper analysis of values, that is, of goals and objectives, and of how to develop priorities among goals and objectives.

There are types of decision problems in which you know exactly what you will get when you select any one of your potential choices. These types of choices are called decisions under certainty. In these situations, there are no probabilities involved. The only remaining difficulty is to determine exactly what goals and objectives you want the outcome of your choice to fulfill, and which outcome will provide the maximum fulfillment. Consider the following:

> Jane is a traveling sales representative for an electronics firm. She needs a new vehicle. It is important that it be fuel efficient since she pays for her gas. It is also important that it be able to carry large quantities of cargo, but also that it be presentable for clients she takes to lunch. Finally it must be easily accessible for loading and unloading in order to prevent Jane's back problem from getting worse. Jane's options are: Buick station wagon, Chevrolet Chevette hatchback, Toyota van, Olds Cutlass sedan.

Which vehicle will best fulfill Jane's needs? Note that the attributes that Jane wants from a vehicle tend to work against each other. She wants cargo size, yet she wants fuel efficiency; ease of access, yet style. This problem is called a multi-attribute decision problem. It calls for a balancing of factors on Jane's part. There is a body of normative theory that recommends to Jane the proper way to do the balancing, given what Jane wants from the choice.

Some of our most difficult and important decision problems involve trying to be rational in interaction with other people who are themselves trying to be rational. Each one is trying to maximize what is best for himself or herself. Think about the following:

> Sue and Harry are caught by the police as they are preparing to rob a jewelry store. The chief immediately separates them. Knowing that his case is weak without a confession, he makes the same offer to each. If one confesses and the other does not, the one who confesses goes free.

If both confess they both get put away for ten years. If one confesses and
the other doesn't, then the one who doesn't gets fifteen years hard labor.
Each knows that if neither confesses both will get two years on reduced
charges.

If you were Sue, what would you do? Is keeping silent in your best
interest? What if Harry confesses? If you confess and Harry does not,
then you go free, but if Harry confesses also, then you get ten years.
This situation is called the *prisoner's dilemma* and was first formulated
in 1950 by Melvin Dresher and Merrill Flood of the Rand Corporation
(Rapoport and Chammah 1969; Hofstadter 1983). Situations resem-
bling the prisoner's dilemma occur often in our everyday lives. For
example, Pete and Mary decide after much thought to get a divorce.
To preserve their limited resources and to stay friends they decide to
avoid using lawyers. On the other hand, each could secretly seek legal
advice and so advance his or her position in the settlement. But if both
do this, and it becomes known, the situation would deteriorate to the
point where both would lose. What should Pete do if he were concerned only with advancing his interests in the settlement?

The body of theory that deals with rational behavior when you are
faced with rational opponents is called game theory (von Neumann
and Morgenstern, 1947). The word "game" in the title is an unfortunate one, because the nuclear arms race is a classic example of a game
theoretic problem. The prisoner's dilemma is but one type of strategic
situation. In the case of Sue and Harry, you might recommend that
they negotiate. This is a good idea, except that there is nothing to
ensure that either will keep any of the bargains that were struck with
the other. Double-cross in this case would be a very effective strategy.
Another kind of a decision problem involves the determination of *fair*
and *rational* solutions to conflicts of interest. These are negotiation or
bargaining problems. Think about the following:

Raoul and Canarsie have been in the printing business for ten years, and
now can't get along with each other. When they began the business they
had decided that if it was sold Raoul would get 40% and Canarsie the
rest. It's now worth $800,000, but Raoul does not agree to the old
arrangement since he believes that he has put more into the business over
the ten years. He threatens to get his uncle, a very tough lawyer, to bring
suit. If he sues, and Canarsie does not contest it, then he believes that he
could get $500,000, minus $40,000 in lawyer fees. Canarsie gets the rest.
But if both sue then Raoul's uncle would increase his fee by $10,000, but

Canarsie's lawyer would charge $90,000, and if both sued the courts would be likely to split the value of the business 50/50. Canarsie knows that if he sues and Raoul does not it will probably come out the same as if neither sued, except that he would have to pay $50,000 in lawyer fees.

What do you think that a rational settlement would be from the standpoint of each of the parties? In addition, what do you think that a fair settlement would be like? What reasoning led to your settlement? There are some fairly well worked out procedures for deciding which solutions would be rational in cases like these, and which would be fair as well.

Empirical Decision Theory

Normative decision theory seeks to recommend the way you ought to go about making decisions when faced with the various types of decision situations. Empirical decision theory, often called *behavioral* decision theory, seeks to discover how people actually do make the decisions that they do. One way to engage in empirical or behavioral decision research is to test to see how closely people approximate making their decisions in the way that the normative theory would tell them to make them. For example, suppose you were offered a choice:

You could choose either to receive $100 outright, or you could choose to take a wager on a coin toss in which you receive $300 if the coin comes up heads and zero if it comes up tails.

One type of normative theory would recommend that you choose the wager, since the value of the wager, measured in the way that decision theorists tell us to measure it, is $150. And $150 is more desirable than a mere $100. Research would show, however, that most people would take the $100 (Kahneman and Tversky 1979). It seems that most people are averse to risk in these types of situations. Even though the wager is worth more than the sure thing of $100, the fact that there is risk in the wager deters people from choosing it.

Let's look at another example. One of the key ingredients in making effective decisions with risk is to know something about probabilities and about sampling. It is not at all necessary to have depth of knowledge about these things, but it is important to avoid certain obvious errors. Suppose you were betting on tosses of a coin. As it happens, the coin has come up heads on the last four tosses. What is it more likely to come up on the next toss? Most people in betting situations would bet on tails, arguing that the coin was "due" to come up tails. This is not true. The coin has no memory. Each toss is a fifty-fifty chance. The response of most people is called the gambler's fallacy or the Monte Carlo fallacy. There is considerable research in the area of behavioral decision theory to discover the degree to which the attitudes and choices of individual people conform to what probability theory and statistics recommend (Kahneman, Slovic, and Tversky 1982). In the area of the prisoner's dilemma, there is a great deal of research concerning strategies that people adopt in *sequences* of prisoner's dilemma situations (Rapoport and Chammah, 1969). There is also a large body of research into the ways in which stress interferes with proper decision-making. We will be looking at some of that in the next chapter.

Interdependence of the Normative and the Empirical

What are the relationships between the normative and the empirical studies of decision-making? What is clear is that they are not done independently of one another. For example, suppose that you were interested in creating a normative theory of decision-making in some sort of situation. One of the concerns you would have is whether or not humans actually *could* follow the recommendations of your theory. It makes no sense to recommend that people act in ways that are beyond their abilities. Thus you would need to know the limits of human capacities, which is an empirical question. In addition, you would want to know whether the decision processes that you recommend actually did conform to the decisions of people whose decision-making you respect, the experts in the field. Thus you would research decisions already taken, an empirical question. In constructing your theory of rational decision-making you would rely upon your own "intuitions" concerning what is and is not rational. But if you found through behavioral research that very few others shared your intuitions, you would have to re-think your premises. Thus, empirical research into the behavior of decision-makers is entirely relevant to normative theory.

The reverse is also true. We have already noted that much empirical research is driven by the desire to determine the extent to which actual behavior conforms to the normative recommendations. But it is also true that the carrying out of empirical research is itself a series of decision problems. The research itself can be done well or not. Thus, the basic principles governing good vs. bad research are themselves part of a general theory of rational choice. To put it bluntly, without a normative theory of decision-making, there could be no such thing as scientific research. Tarot cards, astrology, and organic chemistry would be on the same footing. The image of the behavioral scientist (or any other kind of scientist for that matter) as the impartial collector of "facts," committed to no value system, is not only a myth but a logical impossibility. Science is a human institution governed, as are all human institutions, by a set of values and goals that define such normative concepts as objectivity, appropriate evidence, adequate controls, well supported inference, satisfactory confidence intervals, rational theory choice, and many more. It is the shared understanding of these normative concepts that generates judgments about whether a piece of research is good science or not, as well as the choice as to whether it should be further pursued or abandoned. Decision research is one of those areas in which the lines between behavioral scientist, philosopher, statistician, logician, economist, and historian, all disappear. This is due to the pervasive nature of the subject under discussion—human decision-making.

Agency and the Fiduciary Role

Many of the decisions that we make are not made to further our own personal interests directly, but involve the various roles we have adopted and groups to which we belong. We make decisions for our families, our children, our clients, employers, the stockholders, our patients, students, elderly parents, club members, in addition to ourselves. In these cases where others are the proper beneficiaries of our choices, we are acting as trustees or "fiduciaries." When acting only for ourselves we have a perfect right to be sloppy in thought, negligent in the analysis of goals, or haphazard in the evaluation of outcomes. Such freedom is intolerable, however, when one is acting in a fiduciary capacity. This point should not be confused with the fact that most of our decisions will affect others. The fact that the lives of others are touched by our choices does not in itself imply that we should consider that fact in the selection of our choices. When deciding to purchase an automobile, it is unnecessary to consider the financial well-being of the auto dealer. But when we have freely adopted a fiduciary role, we have taken on the obligation to further the interests of another to the best of our abilities. This obligation is a moral one, and sometimes a legal one as well, as when a trustee must observe the "prudent man rule" in preserving the best interests of the estate's beneficiaries.

The point here is not the obvious one that in your role as fiduciary you ought to put the interests of the beneficiaries above your own. The point is rather to remind you that many, and perhaps most, of your actions are explicitly taken for the benefit of others, and that you have agreed to this. In these situations you will be held accountable for your decisions, for providing a rationale that shows that you acted prudently and with seriousness. Bosses demand this of their subordinates, the law demands it of trustees, the voters demand it of their elected officials, clients demand it of those whom they hire, and so forth. This is an important reason to follow guidelines for the making of the decisions, rather than relying upon intuitive choices or holistic evaluations.

Does Decision Theory Require Selfishness?

The point about the fiduciary nature of much of our decision-making suggests the question of whether decision theory as a normative inquiry requires that we be selfish in the living of our lives. It is certainly true that decision theory arose historically out of the classical liberal economic tradition that emphasizes the maximization of one's own happiness (Stigler 1968). It is also true that decision theory is *results oriented,* requiring that we think very clearly about the outcomes of our choices. And it is true that most of the decision rules that we discuss will aim at maximization, that is, at selecting the choice that accomplishes more than any rival choice. However, there are at least three reasons why what follows is not a prescription for selfishness. First, decision theory does not recommend that the decision-maker maximize any particular quantity. The grandparent of decision rules requires that we maximize "utility," but the modern concept of utility is not to be equated with any particular quantity such as happiness, pleasure, or the like. As a concept, utility simply represents the degree of fulfillment of our goals. Second, the goals that we adopt as decision-makers may be the satisfaction of our own wants and needs, or those of others. There is no principle of decision-making that either states or implies that the choice to fulfill your own needs is more rational than the choice to fulfill the needs of another. You can be as rational as an altruist as you can be as a selfish egoist.

The third reason brings us to the question of the relations between decision theory and ethical theory. Decision theory recommends ways to solve problems. Ethical theory recommends ways to solve specifically moral problems. The principles in both cases are normative. The defining characteristic of a moral principle is that it tells you what you should do *regardless of what you want*. The physician's recommendation that you take your acne medication is normative, but purely practical. It has no force, and so no reason to be followed, if you have no desire to have smooth skin. The prescriptive that parents should protect the interests of their young children, is normative and moral. The parents are not let off the hook by ceasing to want the child protected. Moral philosophy involves the study of what we ought to do whether we want to or not.

There are two competing traditions in moral theory. One tradition focuses upon the consequences of an action to determine its moral status. An action is morally correct if its net positive consequences are better by some standard than those of its alternatives. The most thoroughgoing example of this tradition is the utilitarianism of John Stuart Mill who claims that we are required in all our actions to promote the greatest possible happiness, and that we are not allowed to prefer any one person's happiness over any other's (Mill 1882). In general, this tradition is referred to as "consequentialism." The competing tradition emphasizes that there are certain types of actions that are morally prohibited no matter what overall beneficial consequences flow from them. Slavery is wrong not because the overall balance of happiness produced by it will be negative. In some instances, the happiness of the many free citizens may, in fact, outweigh the unhappiness of the few slaves. But slavery remains a moral evil because it is a violation of basic rights or, in the view of Immanuel Kant, it is treating another person as a means only (Kant 1985). This is referred to as the "deontological" tradition after the Greek *deon* meaning "rule." It is the view that there are moral rules that must be respected regardless of the consequences.

While it is important for moral theorists to continue the attempt to work out pure theories of either kind, in practice our actual moral reasoning uses both approaches. In fact, some of our most difficult moral questions involve balancing the loss of basic rights against great potential consequences. While it is our right to demand that government protect our individual liberty, that same government is justified in taking away that liberty by ordering conscription in times of national peril.

There is no question that decision theory is more at home in the

consequentialist framework. However, there is no reason why deontological considerations cannot be inserted into the steps of a decision
problem to exclude the selection of potential choices that would violate
some moral rule. On the surface this may seem to be the insertion of
irrational elements into the decision procedures in order to accomplish
moral ends, but that is so only on the surface. It may well be that being
morally correct in our decision-making is itself one of our goals, or
that if it is not, it should be. And it may also be true that in the long
run, making morally appropriate choices is in our best interest, even in
the most crudely practical sense.

The question of the relationships between the practical and the
moral goes back to the analysis of justice in Plato's *Republic*. We will
not attempt to resolve it here. It is our view that a work that recommends procedures for decision-making ought to recognize the obvious
fact that in most of our choices moral considerations play an important
role. This is especially true in those many cases in which we are
fiduciaries for the interests of others. As a result, in most of the
decision-making procedures that follow, we have included as a step in
the evaluation of alternative choices the consideration of moral excluders. We have not attempted to provide a system for the development
of such excluders. That would be for a work on moral theory to
accomplish.

To Quantify or Not to Quantify

In the area of decision research, there are those who believe that
formulating decisions quantitatively by use of a mathematical language, is crucial to thinking clearly and rigorously. There are others
who believe that most decision problems are too complex to be usefully
formulated mathematically. This issue is sometimes formulated in
terms of "hard" vs. "soft" science, with the quantitative types describing themselves as doing the hard science. We do not see it that
way. There is research in the field that is rigorously experimental, but
in which the overarching theory is non-quantitative. The research on
attribution theory is a very good example of rigorous science that is
not based upon any quantitatively formulated paradigm. The nonmath-
ematical theorists sometimes claim that the important factors involved
in decision-making cannot be measured, and so any numerical formulation will represent an overly simplified decision environment. This
view we believe is also mistaken. In the appendix on measurement, we

point out that any quantitative property, anything that you can describe as being more or less, can be measured. The question is whether the measures can be valid and reliable enough to serve the needs of some situation. This is a purely empirical question that we believe has been sufficiently decided by the successful applications of quantitative analysis to the areas of decision research. The early theoretical work of Davidson, Suppes, and McKinsey (1957) as well as the later work of Kahneman and Tversky especially on prospect theory (1979) are excellent examples. The applied work in decision analysis, the technology of decision theory, also makes the point that the numerical formulation of decision problems provides very distinct advantages (Raiffa 1968; Edwards and Newman 1982).

In the following pages, we describe procedures for the formulation and solution of various types of decision problems. It is our view that a numerical formulation of decision problems is an important element of any successful normative approach. But quantitative methods by themselves provide no guarantee of objectivity or sophistication. The numbers are only as accurate or objective as the thought that went into the framing of the problem, including the measurement procedures that resulted in the application of the numbers. Decision theory does not and could never provide algorithms for decision-making that would replace the expertise and mature judgment of the decision-maker. This point is argued very strongly by the brothers Herbert and Stuart Dreyfus (Dreyfus and Dreyfus 1986). In the following pages, we place great emphasis upon the difficulties involved in the proper structuring of decision problems. In these discussions, it will be clear why mature and expert judgment can never be replaced by mechanical procedures. But saying this in no way diminishes the importance or applicability of the results of decision theory, nor of the practice of representing decision problems quantitatively. To suggest that one should either rely upon mathematics and exclude expertise, or one should fall back upon pure intuition is to create a false dilemma of the worst kind.

Finally a word about mathematics. We have all read introductions to texts that stated emphatically that no mathematical expertise is required. We then turned the page to find that the rest of the text seemed to contain only intermittent English words scattered through hundreds of pages of formulae. Part of the problem here is that mathematical expertise is not only the ability to apply specific mathematical techniques, it is also a facility, arrived at through practice with formalizations in general. It involves the ability to be comfortable with symbolic ways of presenting ideas, even simple or trivial ideas. This facility is in no way mysterious, and it is certainly not restricted to geniuses. As with all abilities, it comes with practice. What follows requires only that you be able to add and multiply numbers, including fractions. We will not assume that you are comfortable with symbolic formulations, and so we keep them to an absolute minimum. Where symbolic formulations are irresistable but not necessary, they will be included in the appendices, and occasionally in optional sections.

The Purpose of What Is to Follow

When all is said and done, the purpose of mastering the material that follows is to become a more intelligent person in the way you live your life. This needs some clarification, especially concerning the meaning of intelligence. When we say of a person that he or she is *intelligent,* we can mean one or more of three different things (Perkins 1987). On the one hand we can think of intelligence as a kind of "mental power." This is what we are referring to when we say of someone that he has a high IQ. It is the ability to deal swiftly with complex abstractions. Such people learn quickly, especially when it comes to abstract and symbolic material such as mathematics and theoretical science. Mental power of this sort is relatively fixed, and it is unclear what anyone can do to improve his or her IQ. What is clear is that people with strong powers of this sort are not always "intelligent" in other ways. For example, some people are intelligent because they know a great deal. This is a *content* kind of intelligence. A person who knows a great deal about history, science, literature, baseball, electronics, wines, and auto repair deserves to be called intelligent even if he or she got a C + in calculus. There is much that we can do to improve the extent of our content knowledge, but this takes a great deal of time. It is not merely memorizing "facts" as one would do to prepare for a quiz show. It is the development of a comprehensive and interrelated understanding of important areas of knowledge. Formal education is the most efficient, though not the only, way to become content intelligent.

Finally there is the person who is intelligent by virtue of being a practical problem-solver. This is the person you ask when you want something to get done, the intelligent person who is an effective tactician. It is intelligence as *tactics.* What this person has is an arsenal of tactics that can be used to approach and solve problems, as well as the ability to decide which tactics apply to which types of situations. In this sense, a tactic is a more or less routine set of steps leading from problem recognition to problem solution. It is in this sense that the materials of this book are intended to improve your intelligence, since tactics can be learned relatively quickly in a way that power and content cannot.

To learn tactics is to go through a set of stages. First the tactic is described and applied to simple and admittedly artificial problems. Second, you practice applying the tactic to new and different, but still simple, problems. Third, the problems get more and more complex and similar to "real life." As you practice on these, the principles and steps of the tactic are internalized and become "second nature." Finally, you apply the tactic to actual problems in some area of life without being conscious of using the skill at all. Examples of these steps would be learning arithmetic, a foreign language, learning to ski, or to solve word problems in algebra (Perkins 1987). Each of the chapters of this book will deal with tactics that can be used in some sort of decision situation. At the end of the chapter, there are problems to be solved using the techniques that the chapter described. Practice is as important in this situation as it is in learning to ski.

The problems that are created in the following chapters for you to practice upon are from all areas of life. The explicit study of decision-making is most common in the contexts of the training of managers in business and tacticians in the military. Some of these types of problems are included here. However, the making of decisions constitutes a large part of what makes all areas of human life both difficult and interesting. It is unfortunate, then, that what has been learned about effective decision-making has not been more widely disseminated. This is one of the goals of this book. Particularly important are problems of social and historical analysis, such as whether to legalize drugs, to distribute free needles to addicts, to support the Contras in Nicaragua, or to have dropped the atom bombs on Japan. Equally important are problems of personal analysis, such as how to choose a college, whether to have surgical procedures of various types, or how to make career choices.

There is another goal in presenting the materials that follow. The study of human decision-making is an area that is interesting in and of itself. It is an area of knowledge in the same way that chemistry, ethics, history, or music are areas of knowledge. Some study music to become more accomplished musicians. Some study it because they find it interesting. The same is said for decision research. It is our hope that some of the excitement we experience in this research will also be felt by our reader. Thus, the following will provide a broad introduction to a large chunk of decision research.

Important Concepts

Process of decision-making

Normative decision theory

Multi-attribute decision problem

Game theory

Reasoning toward decision

Prisoner's dilemma

Consequentialism

Practical rule

Outcomes of decisions

Empirical decision theory

Decision-making under risk

Reasoning toward belief

Fiduciary role

Intelligence

Deontologism

Moral rule

Chapter 2

Psychological Impediments to Sound Decision-Making

Most conceptions of rational decision-making assume that a person knows what he wants. Most conceptions also assume that one has acccurate information about one's own abilities, as well as about the world. It is assumed that with this knowledge a person can, as indicated in Chapter 1, begin to develop effective means to achieve goals and objectives.

As a first step in clarifying goals and values, it is a good idea to develop some sort of *value hierarchy* in which goals are formulated and priorities set. This is true whether the decision involves some personal matter, the activities of a firm, or the policies of a government agency.

Such a value hierarchy could have a pyramidal form. At the top will be those few, stable long-term goals and values that are the guiding principles for an individual, organization, or society. For an individual, these might include the goals of physical and psychological well-being, satisfying family relationships, achieving social respect, or living in accordance with a moral code, among others. For a firm, these might include the goal of increased profits, or maintaining customer and employee satisfaction. For a society like our own, they are embodied in our Constitution and in such widely shared values as equality of opportunity, the desire to improve our standard of living, and preserving democracy.

In the middle range of the hierarchy will be the goals and objectives that we have chosen as ways to best further our longer-range objectives. For an individual, these might include success on one's current

19

job, keeping a place of residence, or desirable skills and tastes. These can be variable over time and are likely to change as circumstances require.

At the base of the pyramid will be the various short-run activities designed to assure the attainment of the goals and objectives of the middle range.

Organizations generally have an organizational hierarchy mirroring the value hierarchy, with those higher up assigned the task of monitoring the long-range values and those lower down implementing choices made in the middle range.

When we talked of the *present course* in Chapter 1, we were referring, in a different way, to the current make-up of one's value hierarchy. A challenge to the present course is clearly a challenge to an important value or to the way we have been attempting to satisfy that value. As such, every decision will be located somewhere in the hierarchy, and every decision involves some adjustment in the hierarchy.

In general, we will be confronted with a range of possible ways to achieve some end or goal, and we must decide which one of these best suits the purpose of those goals. Once a choice is made however, say of a career, that choice becomes relatively fixed and in turn becomes a goal to be achieved by choices at a lower level. In other words, the goals at one level are always the means for satisfying the goals of a higher level, with the exception of the values at the very top, which are, in effect, ends in themselves.

Most of the material in this book covers decisions in the middle range. In the next chapter we will discuss at length the way one goes about developing a *goals and objectives tree,* and means of evaluating choices in terms of those goals and objectives. Those techniques can be applied at any level, although it may be overly time-consuming to apply them at the lower levels of the hierarchy. It is important to stress that decision-making techniques are designed to help you arrive at the best possible choice that satisfies the higher order values and goals that YOU have selected. What those higher order values should be is the stuff of your family upbringing, religious faith, and philosophical commitments. Once you have established those higher level values, the application of decision-making techniques aids greatly in the rational choice of lower level goals and objectives.

This all seems fairly simple. All you need to do is sit down and figure out your basic values and then start to build the value hierarchy. If you can do that, you should be able to live a coherent and rational life, or plot sound business strategy, or devise rational social policy.

But, alas, things are not so simple. We make mistakes, we have accidents, the world changes, we change, other people change, we overestimate our abilities or our patience, our values may be challenged and changed, to name but a few of the things that can make our best laid plans go awry.

Other sorts of problems can also arise. Sometimes our need to satisfy some shorter-term goal may end up in conflict with some longer-term value. Goals may come to contradict each other in ways we hadn't foreseen. For example, a person's desire to provide a comfortable income for his or her family may make it difficult to spend adequate time building the sort of family life that was the reason they wanted the income in the first place. Attempting to find ways to sort out such dilemmas is another, important task that will occupy us in later chapters.

Many problems arise, however, simply because we are not perfectly rational computing machines but highly complex human beings whose needs and desires are not always easy to formulate. We are driven by biological desires that can sometimes seem overwhelming. Our ability to sort through the complexity of our own desires and abilities, and the complexities of the world is often inadequate. And, like most creatures, when we find ourselves in danger we may, under stress, react in automatic and sometimes destructive ways. In addition, each of us is an individual, a separate creature, different in important ways from every other human being. In our attempt to get a handle on things, we cannot always look to the experience of others. What works for them may not work for us. Because we are unique, much of what we know about ourselves must be learned through the actual experience of living, and the lessons we learn may be confusing and not always helpful. We have, in short, all sorts of personal biases and prejudices, well established habits, and very personal ambitions that guide our behavior in important ways and that were, in no sense, rationally chosen.

Much of modern social science has cautioned us that success at rational action is, at the least, problematic. We have been taught to be wary of unconscious fears and desires. We know how habits can be blindly built up by subtle rewards, or reinforcements. Our economic and social position, our gender, race, and ethnic background can distort our understanding. The task seems so formidable that some have suggested that human decision-making is inherently flawed and that human beings are simply incapable of rational choice.

It is our position that, despite all of the above, it is nevertheless possible for people to deal effectively and rationally in the world. Many of the topics we will cover are specifically designed to help us overcome some of these weaknesses. And while it is true that we are individuals, we nevertheless operate in ways that are sufficiently similar to each other that general guidelines can be drawn to enable us to avoid some of the more obvious pitfalls. Indeed much psychological research in the past half century has uncovered some striking regularities in the sorts of errors people make. In this chapter, we will cover some of this psychological research. We will, in general, limit ourselves to those topics about which there is widespread agreement, and which relate directly to the quality of our judgment in decision-making.

There are four broad classes of problems that cause us difficulty in decision-making and that merit discussion. One set of problems arises because we are social creatures and very much dependent on the aid and goodwill of others. We belong to groups and communities that demand loyalty in matters of action and belief, and whose opinions matter to us. A second group of problems arises when important values and goals are threatened. When so threatened we often find ourselves in a state of stress, which if it becomes intense can be extremely unpleasant and lead us to seek quick solutions to decrease the stress. Under such circumstances we are prone to various distortions and errors that can act as powerful barriers to rational thought. Third, difficulties arise from our need to have a coherent and consistent view of the world and our place in it. When we discover inconsistencies in our understanding, we may engage in irrational attempts to preserve our original understanding rather than struggle to develop new ones. Last, problems arise in our attempt to structure a decision problem in a meaningful and useful way. Most problems have more complications than we can possibly take into account, and so we need to find ways to represent our problems in some more simple and abstract form. We need to simplify and abstract, and in doing so we are prone to a variety of errors.

There are a number of other systematic errors highlighted by decision research, especially in the way we treat probabilities and causal relations. These will be taken up in later sections.

It is important to emphasize that all of the biases under discussion are the products of predispositions and tendencies that, on the whole, are valuable guides to action. Many are based on the evolutionary development of the human species, which, to now, has been quite successful. Many are based on the collective wisdom of thousands of years of human experience and passed on in cultural values and mores. In general, we are born with and are taught some very valuable tendencies and predispositions, which are usually helpful to us in making decisions. It is because most of these predispositions are so fundamentally sound that it is difficult for us to see how they can at times get us into trouble. In general, the best antidote for such difficulties is a clear understanding of these human predispositions and a familiarity with the ways they can lead us astray.

Conventional Wisdom and Conformity

Much of our activities in new situations are guided by past experience. Humans are, as most animals, quick to form habits and tend to do things in ways that have worked in the past. In other words, we generalize from past experience. What, however, are we to rely upon in situations unlike any we have confronted before, or in cases where past experience seems inadequate. In general, our initial tendency is to look to others to see what works for them in such circumstances. The ability to learn from imitation is a capacity possessed by very few species, and only humans can learn by symbolic instruction. These abilities set us apart in the animal kingdom and are probably the most important reasons for our success as a species. In most cases it is just plain good sense to look to others for advice and counsel, and this is one of the reasons we tend to respect conventional wisdom and majority judgment.

Our tendency to look to others also satisfies another, equally important function, namely our need for self-assessment and our desire for social approval. To operate successfully in the world, each of us has to ask (like New York City Mayor Ed Koch) "How'm I doin' ". Very often we can judge the effectiveness of our behavior or the rightness of our conduct without any outside help, but just as often we need such help and certainly feel better when it is approving. We are, of course, more likely to receive approval if we conform to communal expectations. Children expect such appraisal, and their development is seriously imperiled if they fail to get it. As we grow into adults, we need less guidance, but we never completely outgrow the need for it; nor do we ever quite outgrow the desire for the appraisal to be positive and approving. This is especially so since our lives are so much affected by our being acceptable members of our families and communities. If we fail to exhibit acceptable tastes and goals or use acceptable means to achieve our ends, or in other ways exhibit disloyalty to group values and interests, we face almost certain rejection and ridicule. A human being deprived of the support of some social group is a sorry creature indeed. Most of us, quite sensibly, are loathe to deviate from the norm, except for very pressing reasons.

For all of the above reasons, we are generally willing to conform our behaviors, our ideas, and even our principles to the expectations of others. Solomon Asch, in a classic group of experiments, demonstrated that people will acquiesce to majority judgment even in such seemingly innocuous tasks as judging the lengths of lines (Asch 1955). In Asch's experiment, subjects were asked to state which of three lines on a card was closest in length to another standard line. When confronted with "social pressure" from seven other group members (who were accomplices of the experimenter) to answer wrongly, only 20% gave the obviously correct answer on all trials. On the other hand, and equally important, was the finding that if the subject had only one ally who agreed with him, such conformity was totally eliminated.

If we are prone to conform to the expectations of others, we are equally likely to do so when that other is an authority figure who we assume is in a position to represent community standards. Stanley Milgram demonstrated that people will often violate personal principles (such as those that require that we do no intentional harm to others) if pressured to do so by an authority figure (Milgram 1974). In a very controversial set of experiments, he tricked subjects into thinking that they were administering electric shocks for legitimate experimental purposes to other people, who were, in fact, actors hired by Milgram. He would explain and then insist that the shocks be administered "for the good of the experiment," and that the voltage be increased to apparently dangerous levels. While this was happening the subjects could hear increasingly loud screaming from the actors impersonating the subjects in the "experiment." Milgram had little trouble inducing the subjects to administer what they believed to be painful and dangerous levels of electric shock. Happily Milgram's study is not the last word on the power of authorities. Gamson, Fireman, and Retina (1982) found a much reduced rate of compliance if subjects were part of a group. As in Asch's research, the presence of an accomplice seems to increase our resistance to the tyranny of the group or to an authority figure. It is when we are alone that we are most readily swayed.

Even if we acknowledge that the above experiments are somewhat contrived and artificial, they nevertheless highlight our pervasive tendency to conform to group standards, to go along with the prevailing wisdom. And, while we maintain that this predilection to conformity is generally prudent, we must at the same time admit that such tendencies often interfere with sound judgment. This is particularly true if the groups and communities to which we belong are provincial or out of touch with reality. Adolescent subcultures are a case in point, but teenagers are hardly alone in this.

If the communities to which we belong are, in fact, out of touch or provincial, and we conform our beliefs and values to them, we will be making decisions with inadequate data, guided by values inconsistent with our own. Irving Janis (1972) has written extensively on the phenomena of *groupthink,* the tendency for decision-making groups to form sets of collective perceptions and values and to exclude members who deviate. In such groups, the desire for unanimity of opinion and group acceptance can override the need for realistic and careful consideration of alternatives. Even highly respected individuals with little to fear from deviation are prone to "go along" with majority opinion, especially in times of crisis.

The danger here is that the majority may be wrong. Thoughtful and serious dissent from majority opinion is important and, in serious decision-making groups, minority voices should be cultivated and not squelched. One is reminded of the philosopher Socrates who, at being condemned to death by Athenians, announced that they would suffer far more from his death than he. Who would replace him as gadfly, pricking their consciences and questioning their assumptions? Who would be the force to move them along the road to the truth? While individual dissent can sometimes interfere with carrying out actions already decided upon, it is usually invaluable in coming to sound decisions as to what actions should be taken in the first place. Most would agree that thoughtful whistle-blowers and other serious dissenters should be protected from retaliation, but all too often we see them as threats to accomplishing the goals we have set and that seem, at least to us, so *obviously* correct.

In organizations, special techniques are often necessary to overcome this impediment to sound decision-making. In the *delphi technique,* individuals write an anonymous analysis of a problem, which is passed around to other members of the group for anonymous comments. The initial comments are then revised, and finally the group meets to discuss the problem collectively. The point is to avoid the premature squelching of potentially sound, but deviant, positions. *Brainstorming* is sometimes used with the same intention. By setting ground rules in which whatever idea is thrown out is temporarily accepted without judgment, it is hoped that people will overcome their reluctance to offer a suggestion that might appear foolish, thereby depriving the group of potentially useful ideas.

Dissent has its rewards as well as its risks, especially if the dissenter is correct and can, with sound reasoning and persistence, turn the group away from faulty actions. It takes time, energy, persistence, and sometimes courage to adopt the minority opinion. But it should be recalled that much of what we take for granted as truth today was, in the past, looked upon as foolish and dangerous dissent. In the final analysis, the serious and thoughtful dissenter is as valuable to the group as the "team player."

Because of our inclination to conform, we often forget that we are distinct individuals with our own concerns, abilities, and values. A little personal assessment now and then is usually worth the effort. Are you going along with the other committee members because you agree, or because it seems awkward to disagree? Have you given up a particular activity because you no longer enjoy it, or because it has become something of an embarrassment to you?

Very generally we conform because it is prudent to do so. Doing things differently from the way they are generally done involves risk. We also conform so as to avoid group rejection and ridicule, or to obtain admiration. It is, after all, sensible to "have a healthy respect for the opinions of mankind." Deviation has its risks and costs, but so does blind conformity. As a practical matter it is extremely important that we balance the advantages of conformity with its costs. We must be clear in our own minds about which personal goals and values are so crucial to us that to betray them in the face of group pressure is to redefine who, in some fundamental sense, we are. We must draw a line, as it were, that must not be crossed in our day-to-day affairs, because to do so would require a total reevaluation of our long-term goals and values. Short of that imaginary line our conformity should derive from a conscious evaluation of costs and benefits. It hardly needs saying that a knee-jerk nonconformity can be as counterproductive as a knee-jerk conformity.

Decision-Making and Stress

Human beings are, as all members of the animal kingdom, provided with innate predispositions and automatic responses that help them survive. For that reason, when biological needs, such as hunger or sexual arousal, become acute, there is a tendency for them to take precedence over our longer-term goals and needs. In such cases, biology imposes its own priorities on us, because evolution has seen to it that our bodies place a very high priority on survival and reproduction. Stress is an important example of this evolutionary predisposition.

When confronted with imminent harm, we are thrown into a state of physiological alert and arousal to deal with the danger. We experience this reaction as stress. Unlike most animals, however, we can anticipate dangers to our well-being that are not immediate and physical, so that even things such as threats to self-esteem can induce fairly strong stress reactions.

This is normally all to the good. Stress, which involves autonomic arousal, is a normal and often valuable reaction to any threat to our well-being. It is part of the *fight or flight* mechanism that enables us to take strenuous action in dangerous situations and as such is helpful to us. On the other hand, it is a primitive reaction we share with other animals and is designed, primarily, for physical action of some sort (fight or flight). In moderate amounts, stress heightens our awareness and makes us more alert: in excessive amounts, it may, because of its normal bias to induce "action," make reflective thought difficult. Also, since excessive stress is unpleasant we are strongly inclined to reduce it. In attempts to do so, we may take actions that provide the short-term advantage of stress reduction at the expense of our long-term goals. For these reasons, stress is often counterproductive in situations where calm reflection is required.

Kurt Lewin (1935) in a now classic analysis described some very general situations that cause stress because they involve threats or possible losses. They are interesting to us because these conflicts arise in almost all decision-making situations. Lewin conceptualized an individual as possessing a *cognitive field* of his environment composed of positive and negative elements. An individual's actions and decisions in this view are determined by the shape of this cognitive field, which may be more or less related to the real world. Lewin's view is often contrasted to the behaviorist position in that, in his view, a person's behavior is dependent not so much on the environment per se, but rather on a person's cognitive representation of the environment. Three basic conflict situations are outlined below:

A. Approach-Avoidance Conflict

In this case, something in our environment or psychological field both attracts us and repels us at the same time. For example, we are attracted to a business proposition for its potential profits, but repelled by its potential losses. We are sorely tempted by the chocolate cake, but upset at the thought of breaking our diet. We would love to get to know the stranger across the hall, but are afraid of rejection. We are anxious that a child should visit her grandparents, but are fearful of putting her on an airplane.

In all such cases we are likely to vacillate, taking a step forward and then a step back, all the while anguishing over our inability to act. Hamlet's behavior is a classic example. What we eventually do is a function of the relative strengths of our desires and of our fears. The strength of these opposing tendencies can change over time as a result of events in the world, or the way we look at a problem. Sometimes we want to do something so badly that we overcome our fear by *steeling* ourselves and rushing ahead blindly to "take a leap in the dark" and thereby take an action from which we cannot turn back. Sometimes, on the other hand, the trip to grandma and grandpa is put off until the child is older.

The source of the stress in these conflicts is the potential danger that hangs over us until a decision is taken and the threat has passed.

B. Approach-Approach Conflict

In this case we are confronted by two equally desirable but mutually exclusive courses of action. Trying to decide what to select at a good restaurant is an example. Selecting a college or an automobile, or choosing a CD in a bank are other examples. Whether to marry one of two desirable suitors is another. When the choices are valuable and practically equal, we have the most trouble. Typically, such situations produce hesitation and postponing of the decision. We often act as if waiting for something new to come to light to make the decision easier. We say we are not ready to order when the waiter asks what we desire, but after he has gone around the table, we probably are still undecided. At that point, since we have no basis upon which to make a decision, we usually decide arbitrarily. We order what someone else has ordered, or what we usually order, or alternatively, we choose what no one else has ordered, or what the waiter suggests. In such situations, it often seems best simply to flip a coin just to get the decision over with.

The stress in these cases arises because of our desire to avoid regret. Before we make any decision, our future is bright, since we can bask in the good luck of having so many desirable alternatives. However, once we have chosen one of those options is gone, is lost to us. We fear that we will be unhappy with the choice made, and will suffer the pain of regretting that we didn't choose the alternative. In essence we are torn between the present state of anticipation and the future state where we have acted and may be disappointed.

C. Avoidance-Avoidance Conflict

In this circumstance we are confronted with a Hobson's choice of having to choose the lesser of two evils. We can fail the course or cheat on the exam. We can live with a bad marriage or go through with a painful divorce. We can sell the stock now and take a large loss, or hold on and lose even more. We can undergo disk surgery or endure the pain of a bad back. The stress in these cases comes from the danger that confronts us, and with which we must deal no matter which action we take.

When faced with such situations we quite naturally attempt to *flee the field*. If this is practically impossible, we may attempt to flee or withdraw psychologically through denial, sometimes aided by drugs. We may, on the other hand, become ritualistically preoccupied with manageable, but often trivial details, or engage in other forms of denial and withdrawal.

Counter-Productive Approaches to Decisional Stress

In many cases of decision-making, the outcomes may appear trivial and the stress induced minimal. As the stakes rise so too does the likelihood of stress reactions. Stress is a two-edged sword in such cases. On the one hand it can be a motivating factor for our responding to challenges. As such it is a necessary ingredient of human living. On the other hand stress is an important factor predisposing us to engage in poor strategies of decision-making if it fosters poorly thought through or counterproductive attempts to reduce the stress without eliminating the real problem.

Janis and Mann (1977) in their exhaustive treatment of this topic outline some of the more common reactions in such circumstances. In most cases this involves imposing a new frame of reference on the problem, a restructuring of the cognitive field as it were. Janis and Mann use the term "defensive avoidance" to refer to the sort of distortions of fact, or the distortions of important values that we sometimes engage in to avoid or reduce the stress induced by a pending decision. Such distortions of fact or value can seriously impair our judgment.

One common reaction when confronted by a serious threat is simple denial and maintenance of the status quo in what Janis and Mann refer to as *unconflicted adherence*. We avoid the stress of making a decision by denying that any decision needs to be made. One can deny the seriousness of the threat, or the significance of what is threatened, or both, and thereby avoid any action. Suppose a teacher receives information that she has received poor teaching evaluations from her students, she may deny or downgrade the significance of student opinion. Or she may begin to reevaluate the value of teaching as a career. By this sort of restructuring, the discomfort of stress is avoided but only by a distortion of what she has good reasons, upon calm reflection, to believe.

Janis and Mann (1977) describe research on cancer patients and patients experiencing the early signs of heart attacks that show that, in both cases, there is a denial of the validity of the early signs, resulting in a delay of treatment.

Another common way of avoiding the need to make a decision is to procrastinate by convincing ourselves that no decision is currently necessary. We can also postpone a decision by downgrading its importance relative to other problems requiring our attention. Thus it results in pushing the problem out of one's mind in favor of other less stressful activities or problems. You busy yourself arranging the deck chairs on a sinking ship. Or, more likely, instead of immediately responding to a request for an evaluation of a colleague, you decide that you first need to put your desk in order. Procrastination of this sort relieves the stress since the mind is busy elsewhere.

Because we know from past experience that the stress of uncertainty will end once we have taken some course of action, we are often tempted to blindly choose one of the available alternatives without making any serious attempt to evaluate which is best. One is so anxious to "get it over with" that one avoids the time necessary to find the better course. Stress is avoided, but at the cost of reasoned decision-making?

It should be noted that in approach-approach conflict such an action may be quite rational if one decides that the time lost vacillating over a decision is worth more than the difference in value between the various alternatives. But such "unconflicted change" (Janis and Mann

1977) can be quite dangerous if the difference among the options (especially if all are negative) is great and we are merely acting to eliminate the stress of the decision process. As we shall see, one additional consequence of such hasty decisions is that we are often tempted to *bolster* our decision by convincing ourselves that the action taken was really the rational one. This can be dangerous because it interferes with our ability to learn from our errors.

A common form of *defensive avoidance,* according to Janis and Mann, is to shift responsibility by "passing the buck," pretending to oneself and others that the responsibility belongs to someone else. This also allows one to get on to other, less troubling and less stressful matters. Much experimental work has been performed in an attempt to determine the factors that influence people's willingness to help others in distress (Latane and Darley 1970). This work on *bystander intervention* is interesting at this juncture because of one consistent finding that people are less likely to offer assistance if they believe others are likely to help. When a large number of people are available to aid the person in distress, a sort of *diffusion of responsibility* takes hold in which each individual takes the attitude "Why get involved if I am not needed." One possible consequence of this phenomenon is that you are more likely to be offered assistance if your car breaks down on an isolated country road than on a crowded superhighway. It also helps explain part of the groupthink effect. When a situation is threatening and we are not sure what to do, why not let those who seem confident take the responsibility?

If the stress involved in some decision becomes extreme and there seems insufficient time to search for better alternatives, Janis and Mann suggest that *hypervigilance* may take hold. This involves an extreme fixation on the immediate details of the situation with an attendant failure to think clearly about various courses of action. Such hypervigilance sometimes afflicts students during examinations. They become so fearful that they cannot concentrate on answering the questions. Hypervigilance often involves a frantic search pattern among the more obvious choices accompanied by high levels of anxiety. With no time to think, the autonomic nervous system takes over and the fight or flight impulse gains ascendance. In extreme cases, panic ensues. The individual who believes he is trapped in a burning theater blindly runs to the nearest exit (a simple and obvious choice) and begins to claw at those already there. In panics, one may simply do what everyone else is doing, also a simple and obvious choice.

Stock and other market panics (and crazes) are obvious examples of such hypervigilant and panic-driven conformity.

If there is nowhere to run and all possible flight is blocked (as in some test situations), a panic reaction may create a frozen immobility; one is "scared stiff." Stage fright is a common example of this reaction. Obviously it is wisest to so structure your world so as to avoid such extreme cases by, for instance, installing more than enough exits in theaters. Also, one can reduce such reactions and develop "poise" by familiarizing yourself with threatening situations through practice. In some cases it may be wise to reduce the possibility of such panic reactions by taking out insurance policies, if possible, for particularly damaging possibilities. Automatic stop-loss orders are common practice among stock investors as a way of avoiding undue stress. No decision is required when panic might ensue, because the decision was made beforehand in a period of calm reflection.

Decision Skill as an Antidote to Stress

Making decisions about important matters is a stressful business, but stress, in and of itself, does not necessarily lead to faulty decision-making, even in high stakes situations. One powerful antidote to the tendency to make errors under stress is to have available various decision tools to aid in such circumstances. If one knows how to approach a decision and has had practice with the various tools of decision-making, then most decisions can be transformed into problems or puzzles that need working out, rather than threats to our well-being that require avoidance. To the extent that such problems are seen as puzzles that can be rationally solved, there is usually a great deal less stress involved and therefore less need to engage in neurotic stress reduction.

Those involved in the training of soldiers, fire fighters, emergency room personnel, and others who may be confronted with extreme stress, know full well the advantage of well-practiced emergency procedures. These are routines that experience has shown to be the most useful in a limited variety of emergency situations. The more those procedures are rehearsed, the more they become routine and the less likely are personnel to panic or freeze. Well-designed courses in first aid are effective because they teach us what to do and because they help us to avoid the inaction caused by panic or a frantic attempt to do anything, even the wrong thing.

Intuitive Science and Its Limitations

As we discussed earlier, most situations are simply too complicated to deal with in total. For that reason, it is necessary for us to simplify most decision problems. We need to abstract out the critical elements of the situation so as to come up with a model or *theory* that enables us to deal effectively with the problem. In truth we are doing such abstracting or theorizing all the time. There is simply too much going on in our world and in our own lives to take everything into account. Consequently, we are all amateur or *intuitive scientists* attempting to build a clear, consistent, and coherent image of the world and of our place in it. Part of that task involves building the value hierarchy, which is a theory of what is important to us and how we are most likely to achieve our ends. Similarly we develop through schooling and from personal experience an understanding of how the world operates. This is what is meant by Lewin in his notion of a cognitive map. Rational conduct is impossible without such a coherent understanding of ourselves and the world and is problematic if our understanding is flawed.

Cognitive Dissonance

We are usually troubled or disturbed when we come upon inconsistencies in our understanding. Social psychologist Leon Festinger (1957) has coined the term *cognitive dissonance* to describe this distress. Notice that the term is used to denote inconsistencies in our cognitive maps or theories, and these are not always the same as logical inconsistencies. Many logical inconsistencies are not psychologically disturbing at all, while on the other hand we may be deeply troubled by apparent contradictions that are not, on the surface, logically inconsistent. In general, cognitive dissonance arises when an inconsistency is perceived and threatens some long-term value or desire, not least of which is the desire to maintain a positive self-image. If the threat is serious, such dissonance can generate considerable stress.

Suppose, for example, Joan is told that her trusted friend and confidant, Mary, has been making jokes at her expense to a mutual friend. All of a sudden Joan is confronted with a contradiction that she can not let stand. But why? There is no logical contradiction in a friend making fun of us, unless of course our theory of friendship excludes that act.

How can Joan resolve her feeling of discomfort? She could reject the information and (displaying unconflicted adherence) deny any threat to her well-being. She could, on the other hand, accept the information and change her definition of friendship. Or she could conclude that she was mistaken about Mary.

Festinger suggests that in such cases we are tempted to choose the most psychologically acceptable alternative. Freud was making the same point in his notion of *rationalization*. Festinger found that people will sometimes go to extraordinary ends by often very illogical means to resolve the cognitive dissonance that can arise in everyday affairs.

The most practical solution in Joan's case is to postpone judgment until she can talk to Mary. But if she talks to Mary there is always the risk that she will make the painful discovery that Mary is not a true friend. One way to avoid that risk, at least temporarily, is for Joan to deny the troubling information by discrediting the informant; either the informant misunderstood, or is malicious, or both. If Joan finds that she is getting angry at this third party and thinking of what an unpleasant and malicious person she is, then Joan is probably rationalizing.

We can all sympathize with Joan's dilemma. Friends are important to us for a number of reassons, not least of which is that they help define who we are and how we feel about ourselves, so that their opinions matter to us. The betrayal of a close friend is a serious blow to our self-regard. No wonder we look for ways to avoid having to admit such a betrayal.

Consider another example. John, who has always been a good student and thinks of himself as a fairly bright fellow, has decided to pursue a career in electrical engineering. Unfortunately, he is failing calculus in his first semester at college. He might conclude that his difficulty suggests poor high school preparation. That is not an unreasonable possibility, but what does that imply about his grades in high school and his expectation of doing well in college? Perhaps his high school record is less impressive than he'd like to admit. That would be a reasonable premise, which he could easily verify, but doing so might be painful. John, however, has compared notes with his roommate and has concluded that his teacher is simply unreasonable, and has therefore decided to drop the course. If his teacher really is unreasonable then the action might make sense, but there is a big "if" there. What if he didn't drop the course but started cutting classes on the grounds that calculus is a dumb subject, and if engineers have to know that kind of stuff he would just as well do something else with his life. But won't cutting classes make him more likely to fail? Perhaps John would rather admit to poor attendance than deal with the possibility that he isn't as bright as he thought he was.

Cognitive dissonance creates problems when we adopt less than rational ways of eliminating it, for example trying to eliminate the dissonance without eliminating the contradiction. One way for John to eliminate his dissonance would be to "bite the bullet" and honestly admit that he is less capable than he had come to believe, and that he must work harder in the future to do well. Another way is to lie to himself, to rationalize. When we rationalize we distort known facts or long-held values in order to reduce cognitive dissonance. Is John's judgment that the fault lies with the teacher an honest assessment, or is he lying to himself about the facts? Is his decision that engineering is "not so great" an honest appraisal or is he lying about his values? A crucial question is whether or not he would hold these judgments if he were not failing the course. If he would not, then clearly he is lying to himself to reduce cognitive dissonance.

On a practical level, if you are experiencing conflict about images of yourself or things that matter a great deal to you, and find that you are "rethinking" some known facts or established values, there is a good chance that you may be rationalizing in the face of cognitive dissonance. It is not always easy to determine whether you are rationalizing, but a good signal to look for is psychological distress. If there is a lot of it, be careful. It is usually best at this point to face the situation, accept the discomfort, and move ahead. From the standpoint of good decision-making, you cannot decide important issues rationally if you have distorted the facts or altered the true values that you place on things.

Confirmation Bias and the Halo Effect

Cognitive dissonance concerns the ways we deal with the stress that contradictory information causes us, but as discussed earlier it only comes into play when contradictions threaten important values and are brought to our attention. Many inconsistencies in our intuitive understanding are never brought to our attention. One reason is due to what is known as the *confirmation bias* (Ross and Anderson 1982, p. 149–51). This refers to the fact that once we have developed our model or theory about some phenomenon, we are far more likely to accept information that is consistent with our hypothesis (and therefore confirms or bolsters it) than information that discredits it. We are particularly unlikely to engage in an active search for disconfirming evidence. In other words, in building our intuitive explanations for everyday events, we often accept the first one that comes along that enables us to get on with our business, rather than continuing to search for the truest explanation. Clearly, we can live with such false or *superstitious* explanations for years before some event forces us to reconsider our beliefs.

Attribution theory refers to the body of experimental work that explains the errors we make as intuitive scientists, especially in our interpretations of people's behavior. All of us, including those with specialized training in the social sciences, are prone to such errors. One common bias is the confirmation bias discussed above, a variant of which is known as the *halo effect*. It arises because we are used to experiencing things in clusters of properties. The woman who drives an expensive car also wears expensive clothes and is well-spoken. The house that is well-kept outside is neat as a pin on the inside. The man who reads Camus is nonviolent in his personal life and discriminating about his friends. As a shorthand to drawing conclusions about people, we identify specific properties as signals or indicators of the presence of the other characteristics in the cluster. These indicator properties cast a "halo" over the whole cluster. The defense lawyer dresses his client in a business suit hoping that the jury will be unable to imagine a man so properly dressed mugging an elderly lady in the park. When the new acquaintance with whom we have spent time discussing Camus is accused of child abuse, we feel it must be an error. When the hobo recites Shakespeare in the park, we think he must have memorized some lines while he was in prison. When the applicant shows up for a job interview in blue jeans with impressive credentials and a fine work history, we search particularly hard for signs of instability.

The problem with such confirmation biases is that they often make it difficult for us to evaluate information fairly, especially if such information suggests a change in our current way of doing or seeing things. As such it is another factor contributing to our tendency to deny the existence of dangers in the present course, above and beyond our desire to avoid the stress that evidence of such dangers induce.

The Self-Serving Bias

Much work in attribution theory involves the way we understand the causes of people's behavior; i.e., how we tend to attribute causation.

Under what circumstances, for instance, do we hold an individual personally responsible for his acts? Under what circumstance do we hold the environment responsible? One of the results of this research has been the identification of a *self-serving bias*. It will probably not surprise you that people generally attribute actions with desirable outcomes to themselves, and actions with undesirable outcomes to external causes (Brown 1986, p. 162–65). This result is perfectly consistent with, and predictable from, the theory of cognitive dissonance. It is also an amusing example of the halo effect; i.e., we have a generally good impression of ourselves, which we tend to confirm in explaining why the decisions we made come out as they did.

Interesting, and also consistent with dissonance theory, is the finding that people who hold negative self-images, as do many depressives, tend to be exceptions to the general rule; they are more likely to hold themselves responsible for negative outcomes (Anderson, Horowitz, and French 1983).

One danger of the self-serving bias is that we develop distorted estimates of our abilities. One remedy is to recall that it is rarely the case that any outcome is solely the responsibility of one person or of his environment. A simple antidote is to look to others when things turn out well, and turn our gaze inward when they turn out badly. This hurts in the short run, but avoids trouble over the long haul.

Post-Decisional Dissonance Reduction

Once we have made a decision, we have a psychological stake in its correctness that goes beyond the costs or benefits of the outcome. Our decisions reflect on us, our judgment, and our values. For example, when we buy a *lemon,* i.e. a car with an uncorrectable flaw, we are angry for our misfortune and tend also to feel embarrassed or foolish. This is a mistake in that we are confusing the quality of the outcome of a decision with the quality of the decision itself. The unhappiness we feel results, in part, from the dissonance created by the contradiction that "I am a thoughtful person," and, "My decision had a negative outcome." The dissonance is made worse if we were careless in the way we made the decision.

If we are experiencing such "post-decisional dissonance," we can reduce the discomfort by what Janis and Mann (1977) call *bolstering.* One can bolster a decision in a number of ways. Among the most common is the exaggeration of the benefits of the decision, minimizing the costs of the unfavorable outcome, or denigrating the value of the available alternatives. Suppose, for instance, that you bought a car whose air conditioner cannot be made to work properly. You can bolster your decision by stressing how well the car handles and how beautiful it looks. You can further note that driving with the windows open is the only way to get a real sense of the countryside; when the windows are up you can never really experience the exhilaration of the open road. Or you can dwell on the numerous friends whose cars also have problems and conclude that yours is minor by comparison.

Sunk Costs

In many cases, post-decisional bolstering is mildly amusing, but occasionally it can lead to serious errors of judgment. Such is the case when one sticks with a bad decision whose negative repercussions continue to mount. In such cases you find you are throwing "good money after bad," whereas you would be better to cut your losses and begin a more productive alternative.

Sometimes we make this error not so much because of a desire to bolster, but because we frame our decision in such a way as to distort the nature of sunk costs. *Sunk costs* are the costs in capital, time, and energy we have devoted to carrying out a decision that cannot be recovered. Once we have paid to rent a movie for our VCR, the $2.00 fee is gone whether we watch the movie or not. Once we have spent five hours writing the introduction to a term paper, the time is gone, whether we use what we have written or throw it in the waste basket. In such cases our judgment about the worth of watching the movie or of using the introduction should not be affected *at all* by a consideration of what is past, of the sunk costs.

Nevertheless it is not unusual to believe that we must continue on a course of action because of all that has been invested to the current point. Arkes and Blumer (1985) demonstrated that subjects presented with a hypothetical case thought it wise to continue an aircraft development project in which $9 million had been sunk, even in the face of very weak prospects for success, by spending the $1 million required for its completion. On the other hand, most subjects were against a $1 million initial investment to achieve a result with identical prospects if no money had already been committed to the project.

Similarly, research suggests that subjects who have gone through a difficult initiation to gain membership in an organization tend to value their membership more than those who had an easier time gaining entry (Aronson and Mills 1959).

There are of course powerful reasons why we dislike writing off past commitments. Not least of these is our general conviction that we ought to finish what we start, which is a good principle in light of our need to "bind the will" in difficult situations. Nevertheless, from a practical point of view every decision should be judged from the present moment. If it is still sound we should continue; if it is not we should let it go, regardless of what we have invested to that point. If the only reason we are sticking with something is to avoid acknowledging that our decision produced a negative outcome, it is probably just as well to make a clean break. This is much easier if the decision to take the action was well justified in the first place.

Binding the Will

If staying the course when we should abandon it is a problem, so is the opposite problem of failing to carry through a course of action because of a failure of will. Very often we make a decision that we know is right and good—to finish school, to break up a relationship, to stop smoking or lose weight, to get more exercise—but find that we fail to carry out the decision because we lack the willpower. This is often so because in mapping out and simplifying our problem, we have failed to anticipate the future difficulties that are likely to arise. Even when we do anticipate such difficulties, we often underestimate their force. This is not an altogether bad tendency. If in structuring our decision problem we devote too high a priority to anticipating difficulties, we might become so discouraged that we give up a useful goal. This error is taken up later under the heading of the *sour grapes phenomenon.*

In his book, *Ulysses and the Sirens,* Elster (1979) discusses the problem known as *binding the will* in depth. Ulysses, knowing that he would be sorely tempted by the Sirens, had himself bound to the wheel of his ship so that he could not succumb to their temptations. Thomas Schelling (1984) also treats this subject, and suggests that part of the problem is the fact that we cannot make legally binding contracts with ourselves. We cannot, for instance, under our legal system, contract with a second party to forfeit $100 every time we are detected smoking a cigarette. Such a no-smoking agreement would probably enable some of us to give up smoking more easily. Such an agreement would help us to substitute for a long-term consequence (getting sick), which we tend to discount, an immediate consequence (losing money), which is hard to discount.

As a general principle, if you think it may be difficult to adhere to a decision, you ought to think through, ahead of time, the difficulties you are likely to face and your strategies for dealing with them. Sometimes it will make sense to modify your environment to make things easier on yourself. There is little point trying to avoid eating ice cream in an attempt to lose weight if this is your favorite food and your freezer is stocked with eight varieties waiting to test your will. Sometimes enlisting the aid of outside parties will help you stick to the course chosen. Weight loss clinics are often helpful in this regard. If you have decided to leave an abusive spouse and are convinced the decision is right and proper, but suspect that you may back down when confronted by your temporarily contrite spouse pleading for forgiveness, it might be wise to hire a lawyer, who is unlikely to be moved because he is uninvolved. Automatic stop-loss orders enable an investor to bind his will beforehand. The penalties the government imposes on early withdrawals from IRA accounts have a similar effect, as do the penalties for the early redemption of bank CD's. We are more likely to save money if we have an automatic payroll deduction than if we have to decide each week how much to put aside.

The point is that once a decision is made and the more automatic becomes its execution, the less dependent you are on willpower. In general, you are more likely to carry through a decision if you have planned well for your own weaknesses and if you have, wherever possible, arranged your environment so that it is your ally rather than your enemy.

Fear of Failure and the Sour Grapes Phenomenon

Because most of us are well aware of cognitive dissonance and the pain caused by failing to achieve a goal in which we have devoted much time and energy, we are wary of striving for goals we do not believe we can obtain. Generally, this is a prudent course of action. The fact that this is sometimes referred to as a *fear of failure* should not blind us to the truth that failure is something to be feared. On the other hand, we should avoid the *sour grapes error* of devaluing a goal simply because we do not think it can be obtained (Baron 1988, p.

275). These are variants of cognitive dissonance in which we resolve the dissonance created by desiring something unattainable. We convince ourselves that we do not really desire the unattainable thing by distorting the value we originally assigned to the goal. The danger is that we may be wrong in our estimate of attainability. We may cease striving for important goals, such as an education, a happy marriage, a life without drugs, simply because we think we cannot achieve them. Once we give up the desire, we are very unlikely to make the necessary effort that might produce success. This is not to denigrate a certain stoicism, especially if our estimates of attainability are realistic. However, it is important that those estimates be realistic. Furthermore, people differ in the degree to which they are optimistic or pessimistic about their own abilities to effect change. For example, people from traditional cultures are often fatalistic because they assume that they can little affect what happens to them. People in modern societies generally err in the opposite direction. Remember the "little engine that could."

The antidote to the sour grapes error is to avoid confusing the likelihood of an outcome with its desirability, and to keep in mind that, while failing is painful, you cannot achieve much if you are unwilling to risk it on occasion.

Simplifying and Abstracting in Decision-Structuring

Recognizing the biases to which we, as intuitive scientists, are prone can certainly help us minimize their impact. But the need to simplify and abstract, and the dangers of doing so, cannot be avoided. When we attempt to formulate a problem in such a way that a sound decision can be made, we are attempting to attack our problem in the same way as is the scientist trying to understand some phenomenon. He must try to represent the phenomenon, whether it be the solar system or an atom, in a useful and manageable way. His model of atomic structure is not an atom per se, nor is it meant to be, but an abstraction in which much is left out. If his model is useful, it is because he has included enough information to enable him to answer his question, and has left out what would have been superfluous. Similarly a map of Spain is not Spain but a particular representation for a particular purpose, namely the purpose of getting around effectively.

When you think about a decision, you must "map out" or structure the problem in a simplified, abstract way; you have no other choice.

You have to build a model or theory of your problem that includes your goals, the relevant choices you can make in the world as you understand it, and take into account your abilities as you understand them. The model must also include your evaluation of the consequences of those choices. As you will see in the next chapter, how you structure your decision, what you include in your map or model, and what you exclude, will have a major impact on the choices you make and, by extension, on the likelihood that you will be satisfied with the outcome.

When we simplify we generally do so by limiting the time frame of our decision, its context, the number of people affected, the range of choices, and the range of values to take into account (i.e., how high up the goals and objectives hierarchy we look). We further simplify our task by generalizing from past experience or by conforming to conventional or popular understandings. We try to simplify the implementation of our task by using tried and true ways of doing things, rather than trying to reinvent the wheel for each occasion.

It is important to note that it is not only the extraordinary complexity of most situations that forces us to simplify. Even where it might be possible to do a more elaborate analysis, the cost and the time involved might not be practical given what is at stake. Herbert Simon (1957) suggested that human beings very often operate in terms of what he called *bounded rationality*. For example, people do not usually take the time and trouble to find the very best solution to a problem, but stop looking once they have found one that satisfies some minimal requirement. In such cases they are said to be *satisficers* rather than *optimizers*. Satisficing can be quite rational in the overall scheme of things, if the decision-making costs of an attempt to optimize would cancel out any gain that could be realized by a more thorough analysis.

Framing

Amos Tversky and Daniel Kahneman have engaged in an extensive experimental program designed to illuminate the sort of biases and the heuristics (or rules of thumb) that apply in decision-making. Some of their work will be discussed later. Their discussion of *framing effects* seems useful at this point.

Consider the following question which Tversky and Kahneman (1985) put to their subjects.

> Imagine that you are about to purchase a jacket for ($125) . . . and a calculator for ($15). . . . The calculator salesman informs you that the calculator you wish to buy is on sale for ($10) . . . at the other branch of the store, located 20 minutes drive away. Would you make the trip to the other store?

Two groups of subjects were presented with the above paragraph. One group saw it exactly as given. The other group had the price of the jacket and calculator reversed, with the calculator on sale at the other branch for $120. Most subjects thought the trip worthwhile when the calculator was priced $15, but not when it was priced at $125. Why should this be so? The result appears paradoxical, because the act of driving across town is identical and only the context in which it is undertaken differs, i.e. if $5 is worth a drive across town in the case of a $15 calculator, why isn't it worth the drive if the calculator costs $125? It appears that the context, or *frame of reference* in which the $5 is presented determines its worth.

Consider another problem presented by Tversky and Kahneman (1985), which further illustrates the effects of the way we think about or frame a decision.

> Imagine that you have decided to see a play where admission is $10 per ticket. As you enter the theater you discover that you have lost a $10 bill.
>   Would you still pay $10 to see the play?

They asked a second group of subjects:

> Imagine that you have decided to see a play and paid the admission price of $10 per ticket. As you enter the theater, you discover that you have lost the ticket. The seat was not marked and the ticket cannot be recovered.
>   Would you still pay $10 for another ticket?

In the first case, 88 percent of the subjects said they would pay the $10, whereas only 46% said they would in the second. Why should that be? Tversky and Kahneman believe that in the first case the subjects isolate the lost $10 in a mental account separate from the price of the ticket, whereas in the second they do not do this and in their accounting see the price of the play as having doubled to $20. From a purely rational perspective, the loss of $10 in cash is the same as the loss of a ticket worth $10 and should have no effect on how much the play is worth.

Such framing effects are difficult to avoid. Consider a person purchasing a car for $15,000 who decides to "throw in" leather seats for an additional $1,500. Would that same person be prepared to refinish his favorite chair at home in leather if it would cost $1,500 more than cloth? He might, but then again he might not. Perhaps the reason that $1,500 didn't appear excessive in the case of the car was because it was considered within the framework of the overall price of $15,000. A good idea in such cases is to try to set up separate mental accounts. In this case a separate account might be entitled "nice things I desire." Leather seats would certainly be included, but so might a trip to Florida, or a new stereo system. In this account, $1,500 spent on leather seats may, though it need not, seem foolish.

Such framing effects are very much related to the *law of diminishing marginal utility,* which is the economist's way of describing the fact that, with some exceptions, as we get more of something, whether it be apples, shoes, fame, or money, the less is each additional bit of it worth to us. Suppose your current job pays $10,000 a year after taxes, and you are offered a promotion to a job paying $20,000 (also after taxes), but only on condition that you spend three nights a week taking a year-long training course. Would you opt for the course? Now imagine that you are a successful securities broker earning $460,000 a year after taxes. Would you spend three nights a week to increase your after-tax salary to $470,000 a year? If you are like most people you would probably jump at the offer in the first case, and shrug it off in the second. But why? After all, $10,000 is $10,000.

While that may be so, under the principle of diminishing marginal utility a dollar is worth less (is said to have less utility) to a person who has many dollars than to one who has few. Robyn Dawes (1988) suggests that it is as if our "perception" of value follows the general perceptual principle known as the Weber-Fechner law in which the effect of a change in stimulus intensity is proportional to the intensity of the original. For example, a candle in a completely darkened room appears much brighter than it would if taken out into a well-lighted corridor.

In other words, we seem to operate under what we might call a *principle of proportionality* in which the value we attach to something or some activity is determined by the context or framework within which the thing or activity is embedded. In planning a wedding, for instance, it may seem foolish to quibble over one or two hundred dollars to get the flowers we want, and yet we may be annoyed with ourselves if we miscalculate and leave an extra fifty-cent tip at the lunch counter.

While the rule of proportionality can create some paradoxical findings and may get us into trouble (as when we go overboard on a big wedding), we think that, in general, it is a fairly sound principle. Suppose Tversky and Kahneman's subjects had been told that they could save $5 on an automobile worth $9,000 (rather than on a calculator selling for $125) by driving across town. In this more extreme case, one's reluctance to make the trip makes sense. Most of the time, when we are involved in a major transaction such as buying a car, we have a great many things to take into consideration, more than we can reasonably handle. We simplify the task by limiting ourselves to things of major concern, and $5 in such a context is simply not a major concern, nor in truth should it be. When a transaction doesn't involve much (buying a $15 calculator), $5 is given a higher priority, as it should be. Likewise, if we are earning $500,000, a change of $10,000 is unlikely to have a significant impact on anything we are concerned about, and for that reason we are justified in not wishing to devote much of our time or energy to obtain it. It is important to add that there are very wide individual differences here.

Since the rule of proportionality is such a natural principle, it is sometimes difficult to know when it is leading us astray. The only antidote is to stop and ask yourself if you have framed the decision in the appropriate way. Are there alternative ways of looking at things? If the problem were framed differently, would priorities change? Driving an extra five miles to save $5 on a box of computer paper probably makes sense in most cases, but might not in the middle of final exam week. Is forty dollars for wine an outrageous price given what you normally spend, or is it a reasonable complement to a fine, expensive dinner.

Time Frames

In general, what we include in our model of a problem will be critically dependent on the time frame we adopt. Our temporal perspective will determine how far up the value hierarchy we look, as well as how much detail we can include. Should we follow the advice of the saint and look upon every act in light of our eternal salvation, or should we follow the more practical advice of limiting ourselves to the here and now. Once again, it depends on the task at hand. Choosing a career is a powerfully consequential decision. A long time frame would seem appropriate, and fundamental values must be kept in mind. In choosing an elective course in college to satisfy the overall credit requirements, it would seem safe to merely consider such short-run concerns as ease of scheduling, whether the course will be fun, etc.

But there is danger here, and it arises from the fact that all acts have consequences, and consequences can snowball in ways often difficult to foresee. In the field of public policy this is known as the principle of *unintended consequences*. While most economists agree, for instance, that rent control will, at least initially, keep rents from rising, most also agree that such a policy has the consequence of creating housing shortages in the future, because people decline to invest in rental housing if they cannot make a profit. In general, when governments try to set prices, they drive sellers from *legitimate markets* into *black markets* where sellers can get the prices they demand. Such unintended consequences arise when decision-makers create too short a time frame and compound their error by forgetting how resourceful people can be in getting what they think they deserve. In other words, taking too short a time frame makes it difficult for us to sufficiently trace out the causal chain of events that an act sets in motion.

The problem is exacerbated by the all too human tendency to *discount the future*. In general, the further off in time something is the less we pay attention to it, and the less value we assign to it. And there is nothing irrational in such a discounting. A bird in hand may well be worth more than two in the bush. Such discounting can, however, cause us misery if we *overdiscount* the future out of a tendency to procrastinate, or as a form of psychological denial. Crossing bridges when you come to them may be sound advice, but depends on the bridges being there when you need them.

The problem is compounded because we are subject to what the psychologist Edward Thorndike called the *law of effect* in that we tend to repeat activities that bring us satisfaction. The proclivity to form habits is valuable and useful to us in most circumstances, but as B. F. Skinner has pointed out, the most powerful reinforcers of habits are those that follow quickly after our acts. Long-term consequences of our behaviors have no effect whatsoever unless we make a conscious effort to see that they do. Most people who smoke derive immediate social and physical gratification, while the dangers appear remote. Many new smokers imagine that they will smoke only for a few years, and discount the future, not only in terms of the danger, but also in terms of underestimating the difficulty they will have in breaking a well-established habit. The same principle holds on the other side of the coin in that we are likely to discount the future benefits to be gained by developing habits in the present such as wearing seat belts or saving money.

Taking the long-term view is not without costs. The longer the time frame, the further up the value hierarchy are we likely to look. Given our need to simplify and abstract, taking too long a view may interfere with our ability to deal effectively with the short-range goals that must be carried out. If our frame of reference is sufficiently broad and philosophically farsighted, nothing we do is of much significance. "In the long run," as economist John Maynard Keynes is said to have suggested, "we will all be dead."

Choosing the appropriate time frame is one of the most important elements in any decision, and in general it is probably wiser to err in the direction of taking the longer view. Also, it is well to remember that our biology, especially in times of duress or need, is likely to demand immediate gratification, and such pressures can get us into trouble unless restrained by a conscious effort to increase the salience of the long-run perspective. It is also well to bear in mind that, as a general principle, economic success is associated with the longer view and a willingness to *postpone gratification*. Needless to say, a person's age, social class and personal background can predispose him to taking a longer or a shorter view.

Framing and Social Comparison

Suppose you had the choice of being the highest paid member of one organization at a salary of $50,000 or the lowest paid member of another at $60,000. Which would you choose? If all that mattered to you were income, then of course you would choose the latter. But things other than income often matter to us a lot. Economist Robert H. Frank (1985) suggests that *relative standing* is one of those things that matter. His research suggests that the range of salaries in most organizations is usually smaller than could be explained on purely economic grounds. One of the reasons is that people at the top will often decline better paying jobs, because they would have to move into a new organization at a lower level. In a way, they are willing to subsidize the organization for the pleasures of maintaining their status as "big fish in little ponds."

This is clearly a problem of framing, but one that is fairly difficult to manipulate. Even though most of us would be considered phenomenally wealthy by the standards of our grandparents or of people in third-world countries, we find it difficult to avoid the conclusion that we are merely muddling through by current American standards.

Even if we cannot always adjust our frame of reference in these matters, we are almost always better off if we have thought clearly and honestly about them, especially about the price we are willing to pay for status. If we make a choice only or primarily for the status it will bring, we are probably skating on thin ice. Taking the longer view is usually helpful here. If going for the more prestigious job, or college, or car, or neighborhood is consonant with our long-term values, we are less likely to be disappointed than if such things are in conflict with those values.

Inappropriate or exaggerated concern with relative standing can lead to very serious difficulties when we engage in negotiations with others, as will become clear in our discussion of that topic.

Ethical Implications in Decision-Structuring

Many of the decisions we make, perhaps most, are not made in our own personal interests directly but involve the various organizations and social groups to which we belong. We make decisions for our families, our children, our students, our country, our employer. We are, in other words, often acting as fiduciaries and as such are confronted by a host of ethical questions.

One of the most difficult tasks of the decision-maker when structuring a problem is determining who should be taken into account. When deciding how to cast your ballot, should you be concerned with the effect of the outcome of the election on you, on your family, your city, your region, your country, the world? In deciding whether to support or oppose a nuclear power plant, should we be concerned only with the people in the immediate vicinity of the plant or should we take into account the nation's overall interests, and consider such things as the military and foreign policy implication of the nation's energy policies.

Even in what appears to be very private matters, our decisions affect others. When deciding on a school for my child, should I take into account that if I choose a private school I may be undercutting the possibility of a public school system of high quality.

There are no easy answers to such questions. A decision-maker is always acting in some degree as a fiduciary for the community at large and at the least should think through the consequences of his decisions, even though his analysis is unlikely to be complete. Every stone thrown in a lake sends ripples in all directions, and every decision has consequences that stretch beyond what the mind can encompass. Nevertheless, as moral beings we are obliged to consider the effects of our decisions as best we can. In the next section we will see that who we decide to take into account will greatly influence the way any decision is structured.

Another important ethical consideration concerns the range of possible means we consider to achieve our ends. We discussed this earlier in Chapter 1, but it is worth repeating here. We must be careful to identify those means that fall outside the range we believe to be morally acceptable and to rule them out. This is not always as easy as it sounds, especially when grappling with Hobson's choices—avoidance-avoidance conflicts where all the outcomes are unsatisfactory. For instance, we abhor torture and have vowed to oppose it categorically, but are confronted with a captured terrorist who we are sure knows about an upcoming attack on civilians. We are absolutely opposed to lying, but know that if we tell our employer about our homosexuality it will seriously and unfairly damage our prospects for advancement. We are opposed to the killing of civilians, but are convinced of the need to bomb a target where innocent victims will be killed, but believe that in the end more lives will be saved if we drop the bombs.

Do medical personnel act properly when they choose to administer a vaccine on a wide scale in order to save thousands of lives, but know that a certain number of innocent people will die from the adverse effects of the vaccine?

Such dilemmas are fairly common and when confronted by serious people are excruciatingly difficult. We can offer no moral principles here, but believe that the thoughtful analysis of such problems is absolutely essential if decisions are to be made in a responsible and ethical way. As thinking beings, we can never abrogate our ethical obligation to think about the consequences of our acts.

Because the way a problem is framed or structured has an important effect on how it is solved, framing can be used to rhetorical effect by politicians and salesmen, as well as by demagogues and rabble rousers of all stripes. Is a tax reduction relief for the working man or a boon to the rich? Are immigrants taking jobs from Americans or jobs that Americans don't want? Is the product dangerous or the consumer careless? Is abortion freedom of choice or the murder of the unborn?

The best antidote to becoming a victim of such rhetorical abuses is to take the trouble to structure all such questions for yourself, in your own terms. It may be time consuming, but it is time well spent.

Conclusions

It is well to keep in mind that most of the potential sources of error we have discussed are rooted in valuable human predispositions. As such, they can never be completely eliminated. As we said at the outset, we believe familiarity with these tendencies is the best antidote to the biases and distortions they can cause.

It is also well to keep in mind that when we are under stress we are more likely to make such errors. The more emotional stress that we experience, or the more our self-esteem is threatened, the less likely are we to perform the sort of thorough analysis necessary for sound decision-making. On the other hand, the more confident we are in our analysis of a decision problem, the less likely it is to induce stress in us. In that sense, decisional stress and decision-making confidence are contrary forces; the more confidence you have, the less will be your decisional stress.

It is our contention that the study of decision-making theory, and that experience and practice with its procedures, will have the effect of making it more likely that rational courses of action will be decided upon. Furthermore, given such study, we believe that the decision process will come to be seen more as a challenging search for opportunities, and less as a means of dealing with threats to be avoided. Clarity of thought in such matters is, therefore, the best antidote to the sorts of errors brought on by anxiety and despair.

Important Concepts

Value hierarchy	Unconflicted adherence
Present course	Unconflicted change
Groupthink	Hypervigilance
Brainstorming	Bystander intervention
Delphi technique	Diffusion of responsibility
Approach-approach conflict	Intuitive scientist
Approach-avoidance conflict	Cognitive dissonance
Avoidance-avoidance conflict	Rationalization
Fleeing the field	Confirmation bias
Decisional stress	Halo effect
Defensive avoidance	Self-serving bias
Fight vs. flight reaction	Sunk costs

Binding the will

Sour grapes phenomenon

Bounded rationality

Framing

Diminishing marginal utility

Unintended consequences

Rule of proportionality

Discounting the future

Law of effect

Problems for Analysis

Describe and explain the errors or biases in judgment that most likely are exemplified in the following situations. There may be more than one error in each example.

1. Mary had always done well in school, but lately she seems to have lost interest. In discussions with her guidance counselor, Mary's father found out that she has gotten a fairly low score on an IQ test. The guidance counselor reassured him not to worry, since this matter has already been discussed with Mary who seemed untroubled by it. Mary's father went to the schoolboard demanding that the guidance counselor be dismissed. On what psychological tendency do you think he based his argument?

2. Robert had spent six weeks trying to prove a mathematical theorem for his masters thesis. He has just just been directed to a recent paper, demonstrating that what he is trying to prove is mathematically impossible. Robert has decided, against the advice of his advisor, to continue with his efforts. What error does he seem to be making?

3. You and your wife have taken out your brother-in-law and his wife to dinner to celebrate your wedding anniversary. The dinner was expensive, but the food and service were excellent, well worth the cost. In leaving, you tip the young boy who parked your car $1. Driving away you feel awfully cheap about that. Why?

4. Janis and Mann (1977) discuss the fact that the military command in Pearl Harbor prior to World War II failed to take seriously reports that Pearl Harbor was a potential Japanese bombing target. Consequently, they took little defensive action. What error do you think they were illustrating by this example?

5. Your husband has purchased an extremely expensive sports car that has a top speed of 140 mph. Lately he has become an avid reader of car magazines and is always amazed at how slow most cars are. He

never seemed so interested in speed before. Why his current obsession?

6. Kitty Genevese was murdered in New York City. Many people heard her screams but nobody went to her assistance or called the police. What reasons did they give later to reporters for their inaction?

7. Your friend, who is very concerned about the homeless, is always pointing to poor people on the street as examples of the magnitude of the problem. You are troubled by this, since he has no way of knowing whether the people he points to are in fact homeless or not. How would you explain his behavior?

8. In discussing World War II with a veteran, you are surprised that he thinks it was right to drop the atom bombs on Hiroshima and Nagasaki, actions that you find morally repugnant. His main argument from what you can gather is that he thinks more people would have died if the bombs weren't used because of the need to invade Japan. You don't see the point. What principle would help explain your disagreement?

9. Mary is in the midst of an affair with the husband of her best friend Ethel. Lately she has come to wonder how she could have been so friendly with a woman like Ethel who is so cruel and unloving as to drive her husband into the arms of another woman.

10. John is a professsor of philosophy who really enjoys professional wrestling. At his promotion party to which all his colleagues were invited, his wife Jena-Lynn presented him with a gift of a video cassette player and a 3-cassette collection entitled "Best of Big Time Wrestling." John seemed unhappy and drank a lot more than usual. What did Jena-Lynn do wrong?

11. Alex was pretty good at pool as were most of the hoods at Squaresville High. At a party some nerd who always made the honor roll wanted to play a game with him. Alex, always mindful of an opportunity, bet the honor student ten dollars on the game. Alex lost. Where did he go wrong?

12. George has been married for twelve years. Lately his drinking has become a real problem for his wife and children, disrupting his family life and causing constant friction in his marriage. George's father was an alcoholic and he figures it's in his genes. He decides that his wife married him for "better or worse," and if she can't take his condition, maybe a divorce is best.

13. Mary had to stay late to put the finishing touches on a major brief. As she was walking toward her car, she became nervous and reproved herself for not calling a security guard to accompany her.

She noticed a man coming toward her and started running back to the office screaming for help. She was extremely embarrassed to discover that, when he finally caught up with her, the man was her boss. What was her mistake?

14. Jane always does well on standardized tests like the S.A.T. She really gets annoyed at people who claim the tests really don't measure anything significant. She's convinced they just bellyache so much because they don't study as much as she does. What error is she attributing to the complainers? It's the same error she may be making.

15. James was always very conservative when it came to the loans he would recommend for approval. The new management decides loans in committees. These people are very excited about the high interest rates they are able to get in loans to Central American firms. He initially felt like an outsider at these meetings, but over time began to see the need for high-yield risk in the newly competitive banking field. At the congressional hearing on his bank's failure, he explained that the new people had really made a sound, almost unbeatable case, which convinced him to adopt their policies. What did the committee members think?

Chapter 3

Evaluating Complex Outcomes

Introduction

A decision involves risk when there are factors that the decision-maker cannot entirely control (states), and that affect the outcomes of the decision-maker's choices. It follows then that where there is no risk, you will know with certainty what the outcomes of your choices will be. This decision situation is referred to as decision-making under certainty. Assuming that you have three choices, A, B, or C, it can be represented by the following simple tree diagram.

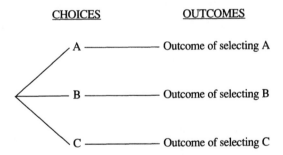

It may seem at first thought that decisions in which there is no risk must be particularly simple to make, and must fail to arouse the sort of decisional stress that was discussed in Chapter 2. It is true that, all other things being equal, if you can remove all risk from a decision you have simplified it considerably. What is particularly simple in this sort of situation is the decision rule that states:

Select the choice that leads to the outcome with the greatest value.

The only problem facing the decision-maker is to decide which outcome has the greatest value, or is most desirable, or has the greatest
utility. The terms "value," "desirability," and "utility," all mean the
same thing here. So the fundamental problem of decision-making under
certainty is one of how to go about *evaluating,* that is, placing value
upon, the outcomes that our choices bring about. While there is no
risk involved, given our definition of risk, there is still the possibility
of making a bad choice. This would be the case if you made a mistake
while determining the relative values of the outcomes. And with the
possibility of a mistake comes the possibility of regret, guilt, shame—
all those bad consequences of bad decision-making. You may be
tempted to doubt that a person can make a mistake when evaluating
the desirability of some situation since you may believe that value
judgments are just subjective tastes.

Are Values Subjective?

Aren't values subjective, just a matter of opinion? Isn't it true that
one person's value may not be another person's value? Aren't values
relative? And if the answer is "yes" to these questions, how can a
person be wrong when he decides upon the values of the potential
outcomes? As long as the decision-maker *thinks* that the outcome of
choice A is more desirable than the outcome of choice B, doesn't that
make it so? The answer to this last question is a definite "NO," and
there are many reasons for this. Let's look first at the more philosophical discussion about the relativity or subjectivity of values.

A value judgment is any claim, either explicit or implied, that
something is good or bad based upon some set of criteria, or that
something is better or worse than something else, based upon some
set of criteria. This is to be distinguished from an empirical claim about
how things are, were, or will be. To say that Greg Louganis was a
platform diver is an empirical claim, and is in fact a true one. The
evidence for the claim is abundant, and would include video tapes and
records of meets as well as the definition of "platform diver." Not
everyone who has dived from a platform is a "platform diver." To say
that Greg Louganis is a politician is a false empirical claim. To say that
in the 1988 Olympic Games, Greg Louganis dove better than any diver
in the bottom ten percent of the field is a value claim. It is a claim that
one thing is better than another. It is also a true value claim, and could
be easily shown to be true by an experienced judge, employing appropriate criteria and demonstrating with video-taped footage.

It is a mistake to confuse value claims with judgments of taste. Judgments of taste are simple statements that something is enjoyed, or is more or less enjoyed than something else. We use the word "good" to indicate a favorable judgment in both matters of taste and in value judgments. In matters of taste, "good" means "enjoyed." In matters of value judgments, "good" means "passes the test of appropriate criteria." You could easily have judged a film to be a masterpiece, and yet not enjoy seeing the film. Perhaps you were in a sour mood, or the topic of the film offended, saddened, or bored you. Perhaps it was the fourth film you had seen that day. Of course those who use taste as the only criterion for a value judgment can grow into more sophisticated critics. The novice who tastes two wines says, "I like this Burgundy better than that Burgundy." After extensive training, the novice turned expert says, "This Burgundy is a better wine than that Burgundy because of its body and bouquet."

It is a mistake to think that value judgments must be subjective. For a judgment to be subjective means that it is seriously influenced by the biases of the person who is making the judgment, that some unique feature of that person has influenced his judgment in a way that would not be the case with another judge. Both value judgments and empirical ones may be subjective in this sense, but neither is doomed to subjectivity. The consistency of judgment in the Olympic diving meets shows that the scores are not merely reflections of the judges' idiosyncrasies. Where the criteria are clear and well thought out, value claims can be as objective as any empirical claim.

It is a mistake to think that value judgments are mere opinions. A mere opinion is a claim that one cannot substantiate with good arguments. Some value claims have this status now, since they have not yet been resolved. One example is the claim that capitalism is a better economic system than socialism, or the more specific claim that socialism is the more just system. But it is just as common for empirical claims to have this status of mere opinion; for example, the empirical claim that there is intelligent life beyond the earth, or that reducing capital gains taxes will result in greater tax revenues. The opposite of an opinion is a well-reasoned claim, and there is no reason to think that, as a class, value claims cannot be well-reasoned. What diving judge would not argue rationally and successfully that Greg Louganis dove better than the competitor who finished last? This is certainly not a mere opinion. Let's conclude then that value claims need not be treated or understood as in any way inferior in their provability or potential credibility to any other type of claim. It follows from this that one can make mistakes when making value claims, and it is perfectly possible to demonstrate that such errors are mistaken.

Unidimensional vs. Multi-Attribute Value Judgments

So far we have argued against the idea that you cannot make mistakes in making value claims, since they are purely subjective, or purely matters of taste. It is also possible to argue directly that value claims can be mistaken. This can be done by explaining how mistakes arise in the making of a value claim. A value judgment is a claim that something is good, bad, better, or worse, based upon how it fulfills appropriate criteria. Some value judgments are based upon unidimensional criteria. This simply means that the object evaluated needs to fulfill only one criterion. If we are offered two jobs and are only concerned with salary, then we will judge the job with the greatest salary to be the better job. On the other hand, we could be interested in salary, commuting distance, benefits, prestige, and possibility of advancement. We will look at each of the two jobs based upon how it fulfills all five *attributes*. One job may have better salary, but less prestige, equal commuting distance but inferior possibility of advancement. This is multi-attribute evaluation.

Most important decisions concerning values are multi-attributed situations. We can evaluate these situations "holistically," as if they were unidimensional, or we can employ a method of evaluation that explicitly takes into account the fact that they are multi-attributed. This chapter describes a procedure for evaluating multi-attributed situations, those that are to be judged good, bad, better, or worse, based upon more than one criterion. It is a technique of divide and conquer in which each competing situation is broken down into its relevant attributes, each attribute is evaluated, and then the sum of each attribute's value provides a final value or utility for the whole complex situation. This final value or utility can then be compared to the utility of competing situations. Once each situation is evaluated, then you can select the choice that will produce the situation with the greatest value or utility.

One of the most common sources of error in making value judgments is an improper analysis of goals and objectives. Judgments of value (and thus choices) are often made on the basis of what feels right at the time, while later it is evident that the goals and objectives of the choice were far from satisfied. How many students choose a college because the admissions personnel made them feel comfortable, or one or two students on the campus during their campus visit were nice to them, or the dorms were clean and new, or the campus nightlife happened to be particularly active that weekend. Yet how many of those same students lived to regret the choice? The problem here is that none of the factors involved, friendliness of the admission staff or of the well-selected student guides, or the cleanliness of the dorms, is crucial to the question of which college serves a student's unique needs the best. Insisting that a student do a clear value analysis prior to any campus visits will insure that those visits focus upon attributes of the colleges that really matter. Without such an analysis, students and their anxious parents would do better to forego the famed campus visit entirely on the grounds that no information is often better than unreliable information.

Multi-Attribute Utility Analysis—A Case Study

Let us suppose that your local community organization assigns you the job of selecting someone to receive an award from the organization. This is a decision problem since the point is to choose someone to receive the award. It is a decision under certainty since you are sure what the outcome of selecting the winner will be. The outcome will be that this winner receives the award. If you are to give an award, it will be based upon some criteria that the competitors for the award must fulfill. It's reasonable to think that the criteria will be multiple.

At this stage, however, you are in no position to make a judgment, or even offer a helpful suggestion. What is missing is value analysis, a statement of the goals and objectives that are to be achieved by the giving of the award. Without this, there is no standard against which to judge the prospective recipients.

Establishing Goals and Objectives

The purpose of clarifying goals and objectives is to create a set of criteria with which to evaluate the outcomes of possible choices. In fact as we saw in Chapter 1, without a clear idea of the goals of a choice we cannot even identify the outcomes. We noted that there is a distinction between the *effects* of a choice, all the events that the choice caused to happen, and the *outcomes,* the degree to which the effects fulfill the goals and objectives of the choice. A consequence of taking a certain job is that my car will be in the parking lot of that company. This is not an outcome since it is irrelevant to any of my goals of salary, prestige, commuting time, etc. So an adequate analysis of the goals and objectives of a choice are necessary both to identify and to evaluate the outcomes of that choice.

The *goal* of a choice is the most general achievement or accomplishment that the decision-maker wants the consequences of the choice to fulfill. There can be more than one goal; though for the sake of arriving at something general enough, it is worth the effort to try to formulate just one. The *objectives* of a choice are all the important components of the goal. The point here is to find a set of categories that divides up the goal into logically distinct parts. Suppose that your local community organization has decided that the award should be a scholarship for the recipient, to the college of his or her choice. You will now need to establish the goal and objectives of the program. You could decide upon a goal such as the following:

GOAL: To foster scholarship and responsibility in the youth of the community through offering an award recognizing the "best graduating senior."

This may seem at first glance to be too obvious to mention, but that would be a mistake. One of the important reasons to establish a clear statement of the goal is to determine exactly who is the intended beneficiary or "stakeholder" of the choice. The stakeholder of a choice is anyone or anything in whose interests the decision is being made (Edwards and Newman 1982). In the decision problem above, the stakeholder could be the organization, it could be you as decision framer; it could be the leaders of the organization; it could be "the youth of the community"; or it could be some combination of these. If, for example, the intended beneficiary of the program were the organization itself, then it would make sense to adopt as a goal: "To give an award to the person who would most likely benefit the organization." In stipulating "the fostering of scholarship and responsibility in youth of the community" as the goal, you have ruled out all but "the youth of the community" as beneficiary of the program. It is often a very difficult and complicated matter to determine the decision's intended stakeholder, especially when the decision-maker is acting in a fiduciary role. In the case of a company president making decisions in response to a takeover bid, should the beneficiary be the corporation, the stockholders, the management team, the employees, the consumers, the industry, the president's own career, or some combination thereof? These are complicated and yet unavoidable questions.

Another purpose of thinking clearly about these very general goals is to avoid confusing ends and means, that is, avoid confusing what you want to accomplish with how you want to accomplish it. Take as an example a student whose ostensible goal is to be a psychologist. If he has been unable to gain admittance to a graduate program in psychology, it seems that he has failed to achieve his goal. But a thoughtful counselor may inquire as to why he wanted to become a psychologist in the first place. If the answer was that the young man wanted to work with troubled teenagers, then becoming a psychologist turns out to be only one among many means for achieving that goal. He could be a success as a social worker, coach, physical education teacher, policeman, probation officer, and so forth. The problem here was that he had not thought about his goals in general enough terms. When this happens we are tempted to give up important goals because one among many means to achieve them is closed to us.

In thinking about the goal then it is important to consider first who are to be the stakeholders of the decision, and second, what in general terms are the elements of the goal.

OBJECTIVES

    a. To reward excellent scholarship.

    b. To reward extra-curricular activities.

    c. To reward community service.

These objectives are in fact aspects of, or parts of, what "best graduating senior" means. In a sense, the statement of the objectives is a definition of the key concepts or aspects of the goal. As with any definition, it is important to use language and concepts that are different from those used to describe the goal. It is also important that the list of objectives be *exclusive* and *exhaustive*. The list is exclusive if the objectives do not overlap, if no features are counted more than once. The list is exhaustive if there are no other considerations that will go into the selection of the choice. The above can be represented on a rudimentary *value tree:*

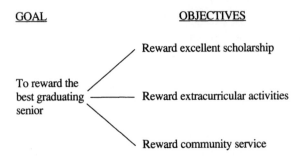

Compensatory vs. Noncompensatory Approaches

Systems of decision-making under certainty are often divided into *compensatory* vs. *noncompensatory* approaches (Green and Wind 1973). The compensatory approach allows that a potential choice that is weak in one area can compensate for that weakness by a strength in some other area. A noncompensatory approach does not accommodate such a trade-off, but contains criteria that, if not met, will rule a potential choice out of contention. Noncompensatory rules are said to be either *conjunctive* or *disjunctive*. A conjunctive rule will eliminate choices that do not have features *A and B and C,* or have these features at a specified level. For example, in the choice of a house we might stipulate that it must have two baths, four bedrooms, and one-half acre of land. A disjunctive rule stipulates that a choice must have *either D or E*. In the choice of a house one might stipulate that it must either be close to public transportation or less than ten miles from work (or both).

While the basic approach of this chapter, multi-attribute utility theory (referred to as MAUT), is compensatory, actual situations will almost always involve a combination of both compensatory and noncompensatory rules.

Preliminary Noncompensatory Criteria

The objectives that we have selected will be fulfilled only to a degree. Some students will be stronger on some, and weaker on others. The objectives will be treated, therefore, in a compensatory fashion. But it is useful at this stage to determine if there are any conditions that will rule out a potential choice regardless of his or her ranking on these objectives. These excluding conditions will not be on the value tree, since they cannot be compensated for and so will not carry any weighting. This is the point at which moral and other excluders may be introduced. In considering this question, it is decided to impose the following conjunctive rule:

Preliminary noncompensatory criteria: To be considered for the award the student must have no history of drug use, no arrest record, and no suspensions from school.

It is important to establish these preliminary noncompensatory criteria very clearly and exhaustively. One of the major strengths of this multi-attribute utility approach to decisions is that it provides a clear justification for our choices. Without clear noncompensatory criteria, we would find ourselves in the position of ruling out potential choices after they have proven themselves to satisfy the objectives of the decision. This is to put oneself in an untenable position in which our choices seem capricious and unjustifiable.

Establishing Priorities Among Objectives

Assuming that this is an exclusive and exhaustive set of objectives, there are several remaining problems. It is necessary in most cases to establish priorities among the goals (if there are more than one), and among the objectives. These priorities should reflect not only which are more important than which, but also *how much* more important. The easiest way to reflect both the order and the degree of importance among the goals and objectives is to use numbers. These numbers should, if possible, be "real interval numbers" as opposed to "ranking numbers." This distinction can be illustrated as follows.

Think of the way you would value the following objectives of a car purchase. The real interval numbers are on a scale of 1 to 10 (least to most desirable).

There is more information contained in real interval numbers than in mere ranking numbers. The ranking numbers give information as to

OBJECTIVES	REAL INTERVAL NUMBERS	RANKING WORDS	RANKING NUMBERS
ECONOMY	2	USEFUL	1 (least)
HANDLING	4	IMPORTANT	2 (middle)
PRESTIGE	9	ESSENTIAL	3 (best)

which objective is more important to which, but no information as to how great the difference is. The real interval numbers give all the information that the ranking numbers give, and also information about the distances between items.

Let's look more clearly at what is meant by "ranking numbers." What ranking numbers tell you is the *order of importance* of the objectives, the most important being given the number 3, the second most important being given a 2, and so forth. The higher the number, the greater the importance. The numbers indicate that the items are equally spaced; that is, the ranking numbers used must be adjacent whole numbers. This is not entirely realistic in most cases, but we should look at ranking numbers as approximations to real interval numbers. There is a point to remember. When using numbers to represent some phenomena (in this case, the importance of objectives), always be very certain exactly which features of the phenomena are being represented by the numbers, and which features are not being represented. This is crucial since, at some point, you will be making inferences on the basis of the numbers, and you want these inferences to be legitimate.

How are real interval numbers arrived at? There are a number of different techniques for this, each of which has its passionate defenders. Some of them will be discussed in the appendix on measurement and utility. The simplest method is the "direct rating technique" (von Winterfeldt and Edwards 1986). Suppose that you are interested in knowing Mary's priorities for career objectives. You ask her to rank the objectives:

OBJECTIVES	RANKING WORDS	RANKING NUMBERS
salary	second from the most	4
benefit	second from the least	2
prestige	most important	5
location	third from the most	3
travel	least important	1

Now ask Mary to give each of the potential objectives a number from 1 to 10, which will indicate not only which is more important than which, but will also represent how much more important. She does as we ask and produces the interval numbers below under the heading INTERVALS. But in the value tree we want all the objective weights to sum to "1." We accomplish this in the case of Mary's interval numbers by first adding them up (giving us 24) and then dividing the sum of 24 into each of the interval numbers. This gives us the "normalized" numbers under the right hand column below.

OBJECTIVES	INTERVALS	NORMALIZED
salary	6	.25
benefits	2	.08
prestige	10	.42
location	5	.21
travel	1	.04

This provides a set of real interval numbers and, in addition, numbers that sum to "1." Of course, we want to be sure that these numbers really do reflect the strength of the objective's importance (validity of measurement), and that this technique will produce similar numbers under similar circumstances (reliability of measurement). The more important the decision, and the closer together the choices, the more need there is for testing for validity and reliability. Remember that using this technique, you must be sure that all the numbers that you assign add up to the largest number on your scale range. This procedure will be refined in later sections, but since the number of objectives is not likely to be large, it should not cause difficulty. It is decided that the objectives above could be weighted as follows:

OBJECTIVE	0 to 1 scale	1 to 10 scale	1 to 100 scale
Scholarship	.6	6	60
Extra-curricula	.3	3	30
Community service	.1	1	10
SUMS TO	1	10	100

You could visualize the results of the weighting of the objectives on a value line such as the following:

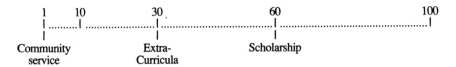

It's easy to see that it makes little difference which scale is chosen. We can now put the objective weights on the (partial) *value tree* below.

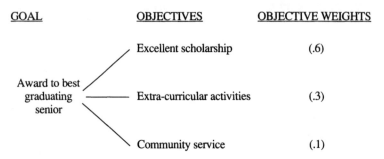

GOAL	OBJECTIVES	OBJECTIVE WEIGHTS
	Excellent scholarship	(.6)
Award to best graduating senior	Extra-curricular activities	(.3)
	Community service	(.1)

Measures of Satisfaction of the Objectives

The problem that we have now is to determine what exactly we are going to look at in the outcomes of choosing each candidate that will rate or measure the degree to which the objectives are fulfilled. How shall we determine "Excellent scholarship," "Community service," etc.? What is necessary is a set of *attributes* that the outcomes of selecting each candidate can be expected to have, and which can be used to measure how well those outcomes fulfill the chosen objectives. Thus for example, the objective of "scholarship" could be measured by the attributes "grade point average" or "SAT scores," etc. These are attributes of the choice outcomes that will serve as measures of satisfaction of the objectives. It should be emphasized that these attributes are observable characteristics of the *outcomes* of the choices. What are being evaluated are the outcomes of choices (choice outcomes) and not, initially, the choices themselves. We will use the evaluations of these *choice outcomes* to finally evaluate the choices, and to select the best choice. This distinction between evaluating outcomes and evaluating choices is easy to overlook in the riskless situation, since the outcomes follow with certainty from the choices, but it is necessary nonetheless to keep the two separate.

The set of attributes that we will select are given below on the (partial) value tree.

It is very important that the set of attributes be chosen carefully. The set should have the following properties:

(1) Each attribute should be operational, that is, measurable more or less directly through some sort of empirical procedure. This means

OBJECTIVES		ATTRIBUTES	RELATIVE ATTRIBUTE PRIORITIES
Scholarship	(.6)	Grade average	(.4)
		Class standing	(.3)
		Composite S.A.T. score	(.3)
Extra-curricular activities	(.3)	Number of terms of sports	(.3)
		Number of terms of non-sport clubs	(.3)
		Number of terms as officer or captain	(.4)
Community service	(.1)	Months working in charitable or religious organizations	(1)

that the attributes should be more or less observable characteristics of the consequences of choosing the candidate as the winner. It would not be helpful for example to use "feeling for his fellow citizens" as an attribute for the objective "community service." While these may be related, the problem is that "feeling for his fellow citizen" is as difficult to observe as "community service."

(2) Attributes are useful only if, when applied, some outcomes do better than others. In other words, each attribute must distinguish at least two candidates (Green and Wind 1973). This implies that each attribute must have a level of fulfillment such that it would select different choices if the level of fulfillment of all the other attributes were the same.

(3) The set of attributes must be exclusive or nonredundant, that is, no attribute should be logically or empirically implied by any other. This assures that no attribute will be counted more than once in the evaluation. Thus, if we choose "months of service" as a way of measuring "community service," then we should not insert "hours of caring for the sick" as an additional attribute (Keeney and Raiffa 1976; Green and Wind 1973).

(4) The set of attributes must be exhaustive in the sense that no other attributes will be involved in the evaluation of the choice outcomes. This is a crucial requirement since one of the most important benefits of the MAUT approach to decision-making is that it forces all relevant considerations out into the open, and suppresses irrelevant considerations. In this sense, the approach is a bias preventer in situations where bias can be a problem. If, for example, the choice that we are discussing was taking place in a town in which racial bias

might rule out minority candidates, this approach would make it very difficult to include race as a hidden variable in the selection.

(5) The set of attributes must be value independent, and therefore additive. This means that the value of some level of fulfillment of one attribute is in no way affected by the level of fulfillment of some other attribute (Hammond, McClelland, and Mumpower 1980). If the independence requirement is met then the value of some combination of two attributes will be equal to the sum of the value of each taken separately. This is a complicated characteristic, and presents some difficulties if not kept in mind. Suppose you compare the value of "only a nail" to "only a hammer" to "hammer and nail" to "only a tube of glue" as means of bonding two pieces of wood (Michalos 1967; Mullen 1970). On a scale of 1 to 10, you may give each of them something like:

Only a nail	——	1
Only a hammer	——	1
Hammer and nail	——	5
Only glue	——	7

Note in this case that the value of the whole "hammer and nail" is greater than the value of the sum of its parts "only a nail" and "only a hammer." The point here is that the hammer and the nail complement each other so that as a way of bonding wood the value of the whole is greater than that of the sum of the parts. Two quantities are additive if the measure of their combination is equal to the sum of their individual measures. The items above are not value independent, and consequently their utilities are not additive. On other occasions, the values of things may work against each other, as when your value of the taste of chocolates smeared with garlic is less than the sum of your value for the tastes of chocolates and of garlic eaten separately. It is important that the attribute of each objective be value independent in this sense, because the MAUT approach demands that the measures of the fulfillment of the attributes be additive. The conditions necessary to test value independence have been very elegantly investigated in a classic article by E. W. Adams and R. F. Fagot (1959). While it is important that the attributes are value independent, we should note that it is possible to have a system of evaluation that handles nonadditive measures (Hammond, McClelland, and Mumpower 1980). Such a system, however, is extremely complicated and in reality the problems created by complementary or competing attributes will not be sufficient to justify the added complexity.

Constructing the Value Tree

In determining the attributes, we focus on certain relevant and observable characteristics of the outcomes of the choices. The priorities given above for the attributes are *relative* priorities, that is, they are relative to their specific objectives. We would not want to use these numbers to rate the importance of the candidates since then "months in charitable and religious organizations" would be more important than "grade average." That cannot be right since "scholarship" has a much higher priority than "community service." What we need are "final attribute weights" (or priorities) that reflect how important each of the objectives are, as well as how important the attributes are. We get these "final attribute weights" by multiplying the weights of the objectives times the relative attribute weights. This gives us the following completed *value tree*. A completed value tree should state the goal, objectives, objective weights, attributes, relative attribute weights, and final attribute weights.

GOAL	OBJECTIVES		ATTRIBUTES		FINAL ATTRIBUTE WEIGHT
	Scholarship	(.6)	Grades	(.4)	(.24)
			Class	(.3)	(.18)
			S.A.T.	(.3)	(.18)
Award to best graduating senior	Extra-curricula	(.3)	Sports	(.3)	(.09)
			Nonsport	(.3)	(.09)
			Officer	(.4)	(.12)
	Community service	(.1)	Months	(1.0)	(.10)
	TOTAL	1.0			1.0

Final Noncompensatory Criteria

We are almost at the point where potential choice outcomes can be evaluated on the basis of our precise value analysis. It is important to remember that the only measures allowed at this point are the attributes we have delineated. Before doing this, however, it will usually be the case that we will set down some minimum level requirements, or *aspiration levels,* on one or more of the attributes that cannot be compensated for by strong scores on other attributes. This is a noncompensatory criterion that is restricted to the attribute levels. In the above case, we will stipulate the following criteria:

> *Final noncompensatory criteria:* To be considered for the award a candidate must have at least an A − average, and either have participated in at least one sport or have been an officer in at least one club.

The final noncompensatory rule will serve to very severely limit the field of possible choice outcomes. Suppose that the field had been narrowed in this manner to Pete, Sue, Leander, Cherise, and Linda. Then the choice problem looks like this:

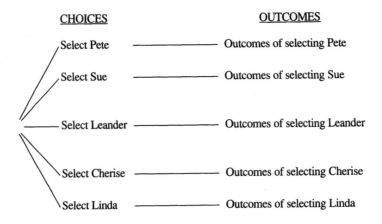

CHOICES	OUTCOMES
Select Pete	Outcomes of selecting Pete
Select Sue	Outcomes of selecting Sue
Select Leander	Outcomes of selecting Leander
Select Cherise	Outcomes of selecting Cherise
Select Linda	Outcomes of selecting Linda

Evaluate the Outcomes of the Choices

In the case of the selection of the prize winner, the difficult work has been completed. The establishing of a set of weighted attributes in order to evaluate the outcomes of choices is the part of any decision problem under certainty that demands serious brain power. The rest is rather mechanical. The remaining problem is to rate the outcome of each choice on some scale, 1 to 10, 1 to 100, −10 to +10, etc., *for each of the weighted attributes*. The principle behind the entire method that we are discussing is, "divide and conquer." The evaluation is divided into as many parts as possible, and each of these parts is evaluated independently. In the example we are discussing, the outcome of selecting each candidate will be evaluated by seven criteria. In fact, for the purposes of the decision, the outcome of each choice should be looked upon as an "attribute bundle" of seven attributes, and *only* seven attributes. These are the seven criteria that have been developed, and that are listed as attributes on the value tree. Since these criteria are not all of equal importance, they have been weighted. It may be that Cherise is very beautiful, and so a consequence of selecting Cherise would be to have a beautiful recipient. This, though, is not an outcome since "attractiveness" does not show up on the value tree. Thus Cherise's beauty is irrelevant, and will be excluded from the judgment. Note again that this type of analysis makes it very difficult to sneak in our biases, either consciously or otherwise.

It is important that each of the choice outcomes be evaluated against the other, attribute by attribute. This means that you will begin with the attribute "grade average" and evaluate all the choice outcomes; you will then move to the next attribute "class standing" and evaluate all the choice outcomes, until all the attributes have been used. While evaluating the choice outcomes on any one attribute, all the other attributes are to be ignored. This process is best accomplished through the use of a matrix such as the one below.

If we are to illustrate the selections process, we must know something about the candidates. Here is some information.

PETE: Excellent grades, 10th from top of class, 1200 combined SAT, no sports, very active in clubs and president of three of them, a little work with a church group.

SUE: Pretty good grades, 8th from top of class, 1100 SAT, four varsity sports, very active in clubs and president of three, four years as a hospital volunteer.

LEANDER: Slightly better grades than Sue, 6th from top of class, 1300 SAT, two varsity sports, no clubs, no officer, three and a half years as a camp big brother for the handicapped.

CHERISE: Superb grades, 3rd from top of class, 1200 SAT, no sports, active in clubs, president of one club, no charity work.

LINDA: Excellent grades, 6th from top of class, 1100 SAT, no sports, active in clubs, vice president of one, no charity work.

In the data summaries above, we have the information that we need to make an overall evaluation of each of the candidates for the award. Of course the candidates have many more features and aspects than those mentioned in the summary. But these other features can be safely ignored since we have a very clear idea of what it is that we are looking for as a result of our analysis of goals, objectives, and attributes. We have to recall, though, that not all the attributes that we will be looking at are of equal weight in assessing the candidates. The final attribute weights at the right hand side of the value tree tell us how important each attribute is in comparison to the others. We need then a way of comparing and evaluating each candidate's attributes in relation to the attributes of the others. The matrix that follows is a convenient way of summarizing this evaluation procedure.

The matrix below contains quite a bit of numerically formulated information. It is a summary of our evaluations of the outcomes of selecting each candidate for the award. It is important to think of each outcome of each choice as simply a bundle or collection of the weighted attributes. Thus for example, Linda is female and Pete is male, but that has no place in the decision problem since gender does not appear as an objective of interest. Cherise may be wealthy and Leander poor, but that too is irrelevant. What is being evaluated, once the value tree is completed, are the collections of attributes that result from each of the choices. We are not evaluating the choices themselves. We are evaluating the "attribute bundles" that result from the choices. We will then select the choice that will lead (with certainty in this case) to the "attribute bundle" that has the greatest value.

In the matrix we have listed the attributes along the top. Under each attribute is its final weight. Down the side we have listed the outcomes of each choice. In each cell of the matrix there are two numbers. The first is a whole number from one to ten. This is a *rating* number that measures the degree to which that choice outcome fulfills the attribute. The rating numbers are also referred to as *utility* numbers. Note that each one of the attributes has its own unique system of measurement, for example, grades, or months of service. Since the multi-attribute utility theory (MAUT) system is compensatory, it must be necessary to compare ratings between attributes. Thus it must make sense to say that Cherise's weighted score on SAT (1.08) is equal in value to Sue's weighted score on OFFICER (1.08). This is why we needed to translate

CHOICE OUTCOMES   WEIGHTED ATTRIBUTES   WEIGHTED SUM

	GRADES .24	CLASS .18	SAT .18	SPORTS .09	NON-SPORTS .09	OFFICER .12	MONTHS .10	WEIGHTED SUM
Outcome of Selecting Pete	7/1.68	5/.90	6/1.08	1/.09	8/.81	9/1.08	2/.20	5.84
Outcome of Selecting Sue	4/.96	6/1.08	5/.90	9/.81	8/.72	9/1.08	7/.70	4.99
Outcome of Selecting Leander	5/1.08	7/1.26	7/1.26	4/.36	1/.09	1/.12	6/.60	4.41
Outcome of Selecting Cherise	8/1.92	8/1.44	6/1.08	1/.09	5/.45	6/.72	1/.10	6.77
Outcome of Selecting Linda	7/1.68	7/1.26	5/.90	1/.09	5/.45	5/.60	1/.10	5.17 (dominated)

the original measures into utility numbers. One of the advantages of a noncompensatory system is that this translation is not necessary.

It is important that each attribute be considered one at a time. This means that in arriving at these rating numbers you should begin with the first attribute and go *down* the matrix until all choice outcomes have been rated. You then move to the next attribute, and so on. As an example, we begin with the attribute of "GRADES." Cherise's rating number is an "8," as opposed to Sue's, which is a "4." This reflects the information that we have that Cherise's grades were "superb" and Sue's grades were "pretty good." On the other hand in the category of "SPORTS" Sue receives an "8" since she engaged in four varsity sports, and Cherise receives a "1" since she had no varsity sports.

The second number in each cell is the weighted rating, which we got by multiplying the attribute weight listed at top times the 1 to 10 rating that the choice outcome got on that attribute. The seven weighted ratings for each choice outcome are then added, and the resulting sum is the final evaluation of the outcome of selecting that choice. The weighted sum decision rule stipulates that you should select the choice whose outcome has the greatest outcome value, where the outcome value is the weighted sum. In the above case, Selecting Cherise is the best choice because it has the greatest outcome value.

We can represent the problem on a decision tree as follows:

CHOICES	OUTCOMES	OUTCOME VALUES
Select Pete	Outcome of selecting Pete	5.84
Select Sue	Outcome of selecting Sue	4.99
Select Leander	Outcome of selecting Leander	4.41
Select Cherise	Outcome of selecting Cherise	6.77
Select Linda	Outcome of selecting Linda	5.17

Steps in Decision Problems Under Certainty

Step 1: Determine the overall goal of the selection of the choice. Stipulate clearly in the goal statement who the stakeholder(s) of the decision are to be.

Step 2: Break down the goal into important and relevant objectives, being careful that the list of objectives is exclusive and exhaustive.

Step 3: Stipulate any preliminary noncompensatory criteria. Include any moral excluders that may apply to the decision.

Step 4: Establish a priority among the objectives by weighting each from .99 to .01 in order of priority respectively, and in such a way that the total of all the objectives sums to 1.

Step 5: Survey the choice/outcomes concentrating on those attributes of the choice/outcomes that either fulfill the objectives or can serve as measures of the fulfillment of the objectives. Be sure that each attribute under an objective is value independent, operational, exclusive, and the list is exhaustive.

Step 6: Weight the attributes relative to each objective in the same manner that the objectives were weighted. This means that the weights of all the attributes for any one objective should sum to 1.

Step 7: Complete the value tree by multiplying the objective weight by each of its attribute weights to arrive at final attribute weights.

Step 8: Stipulate any noncompensatory aspiration levels on the attributes.

Step 9: Construct a matrix in which the weighted attributes are along the top, and the outcomes of each choice are down the sides.

Step 10: Evaluate the outcome of each eligible choice on a scale of -10 to $+10$, or 1 to 10 on each attribute, and fill in the results (the utility numbers) in the cells of the matrix.

Step 11: Eliminate any Dominated Choices. Choice A dominates Choice B if the outcome of A is at least as good as the outcome of B on every attribute, and better than B on at least one attribute. That is, B does not beat A on any attributes, and A beats B on at least one attribute. If a choice is dominated by even one other choice, then it should be eliminated. In the above example, Linda is dominated by Cherise and thus should be eliminated from consideration.

Step 12: Apply some decision rule to select the optimal Choice.

Weighted Sum Rule: Multiply the attribute weight by the utility number and add across the matrix to get the weighted sum for each choice outcome. Select the choice whose outcome has the greatest weighted sum.

Step 13: Review and re-evaluate the analysis. Check to see if it is consistent with initial preferences for choices. If it is not consistent, review the analysis checking to see if any objectives have been left out, or improperly evaluated. When initial estimates do not coincide with the results of a thorough analysis, it is often that the initial estimate overvalued something that, on reflection, is not so important, or that some objective is being used in the initial estimate that reflection forces the decision-maker to eliminate. It is interesting at this point to determine the degree of change in the numbers, for example the objective weights, that would result in the selection of a different choice. This process is called sensitivity analysis, since it seeks to determine how sensitive the decision is to changes in variables. Sensitivity analysis will be discussed in a later chapter.

Alternatives to the Multi-Attribute Utility Model

It may at first glance seem that the multi-attribute approach is overly complex. However, whether this is so depends upon what is at stake in the decision. If one is purchasing a watch for oneself, then the full procedure is too complex, but if one is purchasing 10,000 watches as part of a Navy procurement program this is the type of procedure one should use.

However, there are a number of simplifications that one could easily invent for this approach. We could decide not to weight the objectives or attributes. Or we could use a 0 to 1 scale for the utility numbers rather than the 1 to 10 scale. The 0 to 1 scale would amount to a judgment of unacceptable vs. acceptable. Or, we could use ranking numbers in place of the attributes weights and/or in place of the utility rating numbers.

One example of an alternative is a procedure used in baseball to determine its best hitter. Here, the attributes are unweighted and ranking numbers are used in place of utility ranking numbers. In that system, a matrix is constructed with unweighted attributes along the top. These attributes include "batting average," "on base percentage," "slugging percentage," "runs scored," "runs batted in," "home runs," "extra base hits," "times at bat," and "strike outs." Instead of utility numbers, ranking numbers are used. These ranking numbers are summed to give a total. Since the ranking numbers are reversed in the sense that the best is 1, the next best is 2, etc., the player with the smallest total is the best hitter. Over the 1983–1988 seasons, Don Mattingly received a total of 46, with his closest rivals Eddie Murray receiving 184 and Wade Boggs receiving 203. One noncompensatory criterion that is used is that each player must have averaged at least 400 times at bat per season over the period in question.

In Chapter 1, we drew a distinction betwen satisficing vs. optimizing models of decision-making. It should be clear that the MAUT approach is an optimizing approach. Many of the decisions under certainty that we make are satisficing in the sense that we have an established acceptability level, and will select the first choice that meets this set of criteria. This contrasts with the MAUT method in which we list all possible eligible choices, many of which may be entirely acceptable, and select the best of these. But the MAUT approach can easily be modified and simplified to account for this satisficing method. One way to do this is to construct the value tree and then stipulate a set of noncompensatory criteria that will be sufficient to select a choice. These criteria should be some combination of conjunctive and disjunctive standards. Having done that, one can being a relatively random search for choices, and select the first one that satisfies the noncompensatory set of criteria. In situations in which it is necessary to constantly replenish some sort of resource or supply, this method works well, for example in military recruitment, college "rolling admissions," or union hall hiring. In the purchase of an automobile, once it is determined that the car is acceptable if it gets better than 30 mpg, is under $15,000, and is manufactured in the United States, and has four doors, a stereo system, and air conditioning, the choice from among the candidates is likely to be relatively random with the first or second candidate reviewed being chosen.

One final simplified approach is the *elimination by aspects* method that Amos Tversky has found that many people actually use in an informal way (1972). This requires that the attributes be ranked in importance, and that in place of utility rating numbers, judgments of acceptable or unacceptable be made. The decision-maker then begins with the most important attribute and eliminates any choice outcomes that are unacceptable on that attribute. If there are more than one choice outcomes remaining, the decision-maker moves to the second most important attribute, and so on, until there is only one choice outcome remaining. The decision-maker then selects the choice with that remaining choice outcome. In order for this method to generate acceptable results, the list of potential choice outcomes would have to have been narrowed considerably by the use of additional noncompensatory criteria. No doubt many people select their presidential candidates in this way. They may begin with the issue of whether there ought to be a tax increase, eliminating any candidate who is in favor of an increase. For those who remain, the issue of gun control may be used to further narrow the field, etc., until there is only one candidate who remains.

The appendix that deals with alternative decision rules concentrates upon decisions with risk. However, many of the rules surveyed in that appendix can easily be adapted to the types of decisions that we have been investigating in this chapter.

Important Concepts

Decision under certainty	Decision under risk
Goals	Objectives
Attributes	Final attribute weights
Unidimensional	Multidimensional
Outcomes	Choices
Value tree	Decision tree
Weighted sum	Exhaustive
Compensatory	Noncompensatory
Additive	Value independent
Outcome value	Dominated choices
Ranking number	Weighted rating number
Relative attribute weights	Utility number
Aspiration level	Satisficing
Exclusive	Optimizing
Elimination by aspects	MAUT

Problems for Analysis

DIRECTIONS: Do a value tree for each of the following problems of evaluation. Include goal, objectives, objective weights, attributes, relative attribute weights, and final attribute weights.

1. Jack has to devise a grading system for the course he is about to teach called "Introduction to Writing and Literature." He decides that writing and literary appreciation should be equally weighted. Class

participation should be weighted half of what each of these are weighted. Writing should be divided into in-class writing and take-home work with the latter being about twice as important as the former. Class participation should be judged on attendance and speaking. The latter is about twice the former. Finally, literary appreciation should be two-thirds based on the term paper, and one-third on the tests.

2. Michael has to purchase a sailboat. Most of all by far he values sailing performance, though light wind performance is not as important as heavy wind performance. He also values comfort, both the comfort of the cockpit, by far the most important, but also the comfort of sleeping, and to a slight degree the comfort of the cooking spaces. Second only to performance is cost. Here, initial cost is not as important as yard up-keep.

3. Sue is put in charge of determining which ambulance company to recommend to the mayor as the company that the city should contract with. Although there are possibilities for Sue to make some side money and some useful friends based on her recommendation, she decides to recommend on the basis of what is best for the health of the city's people. She is interested in the condition of the vehicles of course, measured by their up-keep and much more importantly their age. But this is the least of her concerns. Foremost is the training of their staffs measured in courses completed and more importantly by far, their months of experience. Also important is their past performance. This she decides to measure by their average response time to the scenes and (equally important) their alive-on-arrival percentage.

4. Jane has wanted to be an elementary school teacher since she can remember. By the time she graduated from high school, the word was out that there were very few jobs in teaching, and that big-city cabs were filled with drivers who had prepared to be teachers. She has now just completed her junior year in college as a finance major, and is doing extremely well. All her professors predict a very successful (and very lucrative) career in finance, and the benefits of a very good salary are a close second in her set of priorities. The problem is that after a semester's internship in one of New York's largest firms, she still finds herself thinking about teaching. Her job volunteering to teach in her church school seems like her career to her. Career satisfaction is her number one priority. In addition, Jane now finds that a teacher shortage is just beginning, though teaching salaries will never approach those she is assured of in finance. She also is concerned about the fact that a career in finance will necessarily take her away from her home

town and from her mother to whom she is devoted. At very least, she would have to live in New York, where the pace of the environment is too quick for her to feel relaxed, and, much more importantly, she would get home only on weekends. Teaching jobs will be available within minutes of her home. On the other hand, for a time she was dating a very wealthy guy, Trevor, who has taken her on weekends to Paris and to Rio. She has found that she loves travel, especially when it is first-class. She knows that there will be only very little of this on a teacher's salary, especially since she has not been able to replace Trevor as easily as she thought she would when she dumped him. And she knows that the teacher's salary will not allow her to purchase the type of home that she dreams of when she ponders her career in finance. She admits that travelling is somewhat more important to her than luxury home ownership. One final concern that Jane has is for her health, in particular for her blood pressure, which inexplicably remains too high even now and would be worsened by the hectic environment of the large city. This is not really important since she can control this with medication, though there are irritating side effects. Jane's final concern is that she is anxious to get on with her life. She is unusual in that she actually is looking forward to being through with school. Should she choose teaching, she will need to put in one full year extra of schooling to make up the necessary courses. This is as important in her own mind as the financial rewards of her job.

5. You are in charge of site selection for your company's new bottling plant. You are a long-term and devoted employee, and so decide that the idea is for you to recommend to your boss a plant site that will most effectively contribute to the company's goals and objectives. Whatever site is chosen, you will become its manager, and so your recommendation will probably be followed. Your husband suffers from both arthritis and emphysema, and will likely die soon if not moved to a warm, dry climate. The company is interested in a good water supply. Most importantly, this means adequate volume, although purity is important too since filtration is costly. Your boss witnessed the hardship that bottlers experienced during the 1987 Pepsi bottlers' strike and so he is fanatical about the labor problem. First and foremost, you need a location with weak union traditions. After that, adequate water supply, and years of schooling are equal to each other. Finally, centrality is second in importance to the most important labor situation, and is more or less equally distant between the labor and the water issues. Centrality is measured by distance to major metropolitan areas, and by ease of access to interstate highways, though the highway

access is slightly more important. Finally, your company is led by a board that believes in corporate responsibility to its community. While this is the least important of the concerns, it means that the location should be in an economically depressed area measured by the rate of unemployment and, slightly less in importance, in one that is not effectively served by government programs. Lately your husband's health has been deteriorating rapidly, and he has been in a lot of pain. He's the one person in the world that you love.

6. You are put in charge of selecting a site for a stadium for a new baseball team that will be established in the metropolitan New York area in three years. Create a value tree describing the criteria that you will use to select such a site. Include goal, objectives, objective weights, attributes, relative attribute weights, and final attribute weights.

7. Formulate and solve Jeanine's decision problem under certainty given the information available about Jeanine's values, and about the (hypothetical) candidates. Include all the elements listed above for decision under certainty. It is September, 1992 and the U.S. presidential elections are in full swing. The Republicans have nominated BB, the Democrats have nominated KK, and JJ is running as an independent. Jeanine's eleventh grade social studies class has been using a decision analysis approach to the study of American history and politics. Jeanine has been given the task of presenting and justifying her selection of a candidate to her class. Jeanine asks her father, who responds "Pick KK, he's the Democrat." Her mother chooses BB since he favors school prayer. Jeanine leans toward BB, but is not sure why. Fortunately, her new training in decision analysis gives her a way of analyzing the problem, since it is a multi-attribute decision problem. Jeanine decides that the goal of her selection is to vote for the candidate who best fulfills the country's needs. This is a very general goal, but it does exclude certain considerations, e.g., being consistent with the views of her parents, voting for the candidate most likely to win (rejecting arguments to not "waste your vote"), voting for a local candidate because he is local, voting for a candidate who will do the most for her region. Jeanine thinks about what it is that a good president must do and must be, given the problems of today's world. She discovers that she is concerned above all about her country's foreign policy. She is also concerned with maintaining a kind of national pride and unity that she associates with leadership qualities of the President. She believes that leadership is most directly a function of the varieties of public service engaged in, but also to some lesser

degree of the length of service. Her view is that in nuclear arms control, the United States has not been accommodating enough with the Soviets; on the other hand she does not trust the Soviets "good intentions" in any way. She also favors all-out support for the "Contras" though this is not as important to her as arms reduction. In domestic policy, which to her is second only to foreign policy in importance, she is appalled by the gaps in income and quality of life that separate Americans. She is somewhat concerned that the present farm crisis will destroy the family farm (her grandparents' farm included). Pressed for time, Jeanine asks her brother to give her a summary of each of the candidates. He provides the following data.

BB   From the West; married; favors flat tax rate with 1970's system of deductions; immediate end to farm supports; delay arms agreement until United States has "star wars" and clear nuclear superiority; 18 years of public service including Congress, head of FBI, and as vice president; enjoys skiing, hiking; favors tripling aid to the "Contras"; is favored to win the election.

JJ   Marrried; from mid-West; favors steep graduated tax; steep increase in farm supports; served 12 years as head of a community organization; enjoys reading and jogging; favors aid to the Sandinista government; supports nuclear arms reduction relying upon CIA intelligence estimates of Soviet intentions; has no chance of winning.

KK   Divorced; from the East; favors a slightly graduated tax system with 1970's style deductions; served in Senate for 24 years; enjoys sailing and skiing; opposes aid to "Contras" favoring economic pressure on the Sandinistas to democratize; supports nuclear arms reduction assuming on-site inspection; could win in upset; on farm policy favors the status quo.

8. Design a tree stating goal, objectives, and attributes for the evaluation; establish relative weights for the objectives and attributes; and then final attribute weights. Construct a matrix of choices; and using what you know about the vehicles, fill in the matrix with utility numbers 1 to 10 from least to best. Eliminate any dominated choices. Use the weighted sum rule to select the optimal choice.

Jim is a traveling salesman and needs a new vehicle for work. He works for a small salary, plus commission and must pay all his expenses. He is reasonably successful at selling electronics parts. He must therefore travel with a large inventory, the larger the better, but must also occasionally take potential clients out to dinner to impress them with the success of his company and himself. This does not happen often. His territory is large, demanding long hours on the road.

He has for some time had a nagging, but not yet serious back problem. *Available Choices:* Chevette hatchback; Chevy deluxe diesel station wagon; Dodge Maxivan; Mercedes diesel wagon; Ford luxury two door sedan; Oldsmobile station wagon.

9. Following the directions for #8 above, analyze the following problem, eliminate dominated choices, use the weighted sum rule to select the best house.

Ed is a single parent who has decided that he needs a new home. The main impetus for the move is that the family is getting older so that his three children each need a separate room, and he certainly needs a second bathroom. In addition he has been commuting 37 miles to work for 12 years and would like to have a break from that. He has always lived in a ranch house, while admiring houses that are more modern in styling both from the interior and exterior point of view. Ed is very concerned with the education of his children, and so insists that the house be in a good school district, meaning in the top 40 percent academically in the state measured by percentage of Regent scholars from his school, as well as by the mean IQ of the student body. Ed has narrowed the choices to those listed below. The data has been provided by the real estate agent. All houses are in the same price range. The academic figures are a measure of the top percent in the state.

AVAILABLE HOUSES

	A	B	C	D	E
Lot size	1/2	1/4	3/4	1/2	1
Number of Bedrooms	4	3	5	4	4
Number of Bathrooms	2	2	2	2	2
Roof Type	flat	peek	mansard	peek	flat
Miles to Work	20	30	18	18	45
Roads to Work	highway	suburb	highway	city	highway
Rgts.Sch.(top)	20%	37%	15%	18%	20%
Mean IQ (top)	18%	32%	19%	22%	15%
Exterior Style	modern	colonial	split level	ranch	modern
Interior Style	modern	colonial	neo-suburban	colonial	modern

Time to work	20 minutes	55	18	22	48
Exterior siding	shingle	clapboard	aluminum siding	shingle	clapboard
Municipality	town	incorporated village	incorporated village	town	private association
Road of House	busy	dead end	quiet	cul de sac	quiet
Age of House	6 years	9	10	15	9
Number of owners	2	2	1	3	2

Chapter 4

Reasoning About Probabilities

What Is Probability?

We live in an uncertain world, a world of imperfect knowledge. For this reason, we often find ourselves stating, relying upon, and in general grappling with probabilities. What are probabilities? There are several philosophically respectable ways of interpreting exactly what we mean when we make the statement, for example, that there is a 40% probability of rain. For our purposes, it is most useful to think of probabilities as measures of the degree of confidence that we ought to have in the truth of some proposition, or in the occurrence of some event. If I show you a normal coin toss and then say, "It will come up heads," you say that there is a fifty-fifty chance that I am right. The "fifty-fifty," or the ".5" is a measure of the confidence that you as a rational person should have in my prediction. Similarly, I could show you an urn filled with balls in which 60 percent are white. The proposition, "The ball that I randomly draw from the urn will be white" should have a measure of confidence that is slightly higher than the proposition, "The coin toss will come up heads." The measure of the confidence that you should have in the selection of the white ball is ".6," or "sixty-forty." In the appendix on measurement, we note that measurement is only putting a number onto some value or attribute in order to be more precise in defining its degree—greater, less, or the same. In an uncertain world, propositions will have greater, or less, or the same credibility; they will be more, or less, or equal in the degree of confidence that they deserve. Probabilities allow us to state these levels of credibility more precisely than if we were restricted to saying "pretty sure," "beyond a doubt," "probably not," etc. Probability is

85

usually measured by a scale of either 0 to 100, or 0 to 1. Using the first scale, we say that there is a thirty percent chance of rain. Using the second scale, we say that the probability of the coin's being heads is .5, or 1/2. It makes little difference which scale is used.

You want two things from probability estimates: accuracy and reliability. An estimate of the probability of some event is accurate if the probability stated is the same as the actual relative frequency of that type of event. If I believe that the probability of having a car accident at a specific time on a specific road is .0001, that belief is accurate if, in fact, one out of every 10,000 people who are like me in relevant respects, and who travel that road at that time, are in accidents. Reliability means that a person will give the same estimate of the same event over time when his or her information remains the same. In striving for accuracy and reliability, the use of numerical measures of probability give us a great advantage.

There are some relatively effective techniques for "eliciting" reliable estimates of the probabilities of some sorts of events. These techniques rely upon the use of numerically measured probabilities, and would not be effective if we depended upon merely verbal statements of "very likely," "very unlikely," etc. In fact, research has shown that people have very different judgments concerning how the verbal estimates should be reflected by numerical values. When people were asked to give a numerical equivalent to some verbal reports of probabilities, the results were widely varied (Wright 1984). In other words, one person may say that "very probable" means 90 percent chance, while another believes "very probable" means 75 percent chance. One possible explanation for the lack of correlation between verbal reports and numerical estimates is that verbal reports such as "very probable" imply not only the pure "odds" that an event will occur, but also the seriousness with which the event's occurrence should be taken. Thus, a .2 probability of an accident at a nuclear power plant may be described as "probable," whereas a .2 chance that the Red Sox will win the next game may be described as "very improbable." The point is that verbal reports of probabilities are very unstable, and most likely very context dependent. Numerical reports are by no means absolutely stable and objective. And in fact one should always be warned against the assumption that because a report of any kind is stated in numerical terms, it must be objective or accurate. It has been said that there are three kinds of lies: "lies," "damned lies," and "statistics." But it remains true that numerical measures of probability make possible some effective procedures for more accurate and reliable probability estimates.

Let us agree then that a statement of probability is a claim about the degree of confidence that we should give to a proposition, or to the occurrence of an event. How are these probabilities determined? Here we must distinguish between the initial determination of the probabilities and the calculation of combinations of previously determined probabilities. The determinations of initial probabilities are most often, and most reliably, based upon evidence of the frequency with which some event or property has occurred in the past. This also carries the implication that this frequency will continue in the future under similar circumstances. For example:

1. The probability that the next child born in the United States will be a male is 1/2. Based upon evidence that under similar circumstances in the past and on into the future, the ratio of males born to children born is one in two.

2. The probability of getting into an auto accident over the fourth of July is 1 in 10,000. Based upon evidence that under similar circumstances in the past and on into the future, one car was and will be in an accident for every 10,000 cars driving.

3. The probability of throwing a five on one throw of a die is 1/6. Based upon evidence that similar dice in the past and on into the future that were thrown, one came and will come up with five on the long-term average of once in six tosses.

Accurate statements of initial probability are most often made on the basis of some past frequency and imply some future frequency if similar conditions hold. Of course there are other ways in addition to past frequencies to arrive at initial probabilities. In fact, we often place probabilities on events that have never occurred. We say for example, "The probability of a nuclear meltdown in the United States of America is now 1/2,000,000." While this cannot be based upon similar past events, it must be based upon some past experiences to have any standing. In the case of a throw of a die, we may conclude that the probability of the throw of a five is 1/6 on an inspection of the die showing it to be symmetrically constructed. But here again it is past experience, as well as some of our laws of physics, that allow us to conclude from the physical symmetry of the die to the equal probability that each of the sides will come up. In the case of the probability of a male child being born, our confidence that the probability is .5

depends not only upon past frequencies but also upon our understanding of the physical processes of reproduction. In point of fact, the probability of conceiving a male child is significantly larger than .5, the probability of giving birth to a male child is also larger than .5 though smaller than that of conceiving a male, but the probability that a randomly selected child from among all American ten-year-olds will be a male is just about .5.

In terms of the sequence of investigation, the observation of the frequency generally occurs first, giving rise to a probability estimate. This is followed by a theoretical explanation of the frequency, which strengthens the estimate. Knowing why a frequency is the way it is strengthens its power to justify a probability estimate.

The points to remember then are that a probability statement is a measure of the confidence that we should have in the truth of a statement, or the occurrence of an event. The premises that give reasons for the truth of the probability statement are most often statements about the relative frequency of some type of occurrence in the past, implying that the frequency will continue under similar conditions. Where frequencies do exist, and have been studied, and are available to us without undue effort, they should be used to justify our probability estimates. This will insure the maximum accuracy of those estimates. This may seem obvious, but as we shall soon see, people make probability estimates on the basis of reasoning that is often quite biased and inaccurate.

Combining Initial Probabilities

An example of determining initial probabilities is deciding the probability that a male of sixty living in Florida will live to be seventy, or determining that a male of seventy living in Florida will develop skin cancer. An example of combining probabilities would be to take those two initial probabilities and determine the combined probability that a male of sixty living in Florida will develop skin cancer at age seventy. This, if treated as a problem of estimating initial probabilities, could become the focus of a research project, but there is an easier way of doing combining probabilities. What is needed is a set of rules for the combining of initial probability statements. This set of rules is called the mathematics of probability, or the calculus of probability. It is a calculus not because it has anything in common with that dreaded branch of mathematics called "calculus," but rather because it is a system of calculating. We have little need to get very involved in this system of calculating. Only a few of its most basic rules are important for us. If fact, for now we will need only three combining principles.

PRINCIPLE 1: The probability of a statement that is certain to be true = 1, and the probability of a statement that is certain to be false = 0. Thus, if it is certain that either A or B will occur, and if both A and B cannot occur together, that is, if A and B are exclusive and exhaustive, then:

a. $PROB(A) + PROB(B) = 1$
so, b. $PROB(A) = 1 - PROB(B)$

Examples: i. What is the probability that the card you select from a deck is either red or black?
ii. What is the probability that on one roll of a die you get either an even or an odd number?
iii. If the probability of getting a one on a roll of a die is 1/6, what is the probability of getting a two through six?
iv. If there is a 99% chance of living to fifty if you are forty what is the probability of dying between forty and fifty?

Let's look at number iii above. Here is how you should do it.

Let A = getting *either* a two, three, four, five, *or* six on a single roll of a die.
Let B = getting a one on a single roll of a die.
When you roll a die it is certain that you will get either A or B, and you can't get A and B, so:

$PROB(A) + PROB(B) = 1$
and $PROB(A) = 1 - PROB(B)$

We are given $PROB(B)$ as 1/6, so:

$PROB(A) = 1 - 1/6$
or $PROB(A) = 5/6$

You could have done all that in your head perhaps, but this illustrates the principles that justify all that work that your head so easily did for you. We will see that on a decision tree whenever the tree branches out for states the sum of the PROBS of all of the branches must equal

1, and if you know the probabilities of all but one of the branches, you will be able to calculate the probability of the remaining branch using PRINCIPLE 1.

> PRINCIPLE 2: THE MULTIPLICATION RULE: The probability that two events will *both* occur is calculated by multiplying the PROB of the first times the PROB that the second will occur *given that* the first has occurred.

c. PROB(*A* and *B*) = PROB(*A*) × PROB(*B* given *A*)

Examples: i. I flip a coin then roll a die. What is the PROB of heads then a three?
           ii. I flip a coin four times. What is the PROB of the sequence HTHH? What is the PROB of TTTT?
          iii. I have an urn of 5 black and 5 white balls. I randomly select one ball and do not replace it, then I randomly select another. What is the PROB that I have selected two black balls?
          iv. Suppose that the PROB of a newborn American living to be 90 is 1 in 10, and that the PROB that a 90-year-old being in an auto accident is 2 in 10. What is the PROB of a newborn American being in an auto accident at age 90?
          v. As an entering freshman the probability that I will be assigned to Professor Sadism's English comp class is 1 in 20. The PROB of my failing Professor Sadism's class if I am put in it is 1 in 5. What is the PROB that I will be one of Professor Sadism's victims?
          vi. When a child is born in the United States of America, the PROB that it is either a boy or a girl is 1. If I randomly select one birth for each day of a week, and then repeat the process several times later, which is the more probable selection sequence?

	MON	TUES	WED	THURS	FRI	SAT	SUN
Sequence week A:	G	B	B	G	G	B	G
Sequence week B:	G	G	G	G	B	B	B
Sequence week C:	B	B	B	B	B	B	B

Let's look at number iii above. Here is how you should do it.

Let A = Selecting a black ball on the first selection.
Let B = Selecting a black ball on the second selection.
PROB(A) = 1/2
PROB(B given A) = 4/9 (since there are only 9 balls left and 4 are black).
Note that I cannot say what PROB(B) is since that depends upon what occurs in the first selection. I can only say, therefore, what PROB(B given A) is.

PROB(A and B) = PROB(A) × PROB(B given A)
PROB(A and B) = 1/2 × 4/9
$\qquad\qquad$ = 4/18
$\qquad\qquad$ = 2/9

So, the probability that I will select a black ball and then another black ball when I did not return the first is 2/9. This implies that the black and black sequence should occur *on average* two times out of every nine times that we make the double selections. The phrase "on average" is important. It means that if we did such double selections many times over, the overall ratio of black and black selection pairs to all selection pairs would be 2/9. For every 9,000 selection pairs, there should be approximately 2,000 black and black pairs. As the number of selection pairs increases, this fraction will get closer and closer to 2/9.
On a decision tree if there is a branching out with stated PROBS from a previous state branch that itself has a PROB, then we will calculate the PROB that the final branch will occur by using PRINCIPLE 2 and multiplying through the tree.

PRINCIPLE 3: THE ADDITION RULE: The probability that either one event or another event will occur when they cannot both occur is calculated by adding the PROB of the first to the PROB of the second.

d. PROB(either A or B) = PROB(A) + PROB(B)
$\qquad\qquad$ where A and B are exclusive.

Examples:$\quad$ i.$\;$ What is the probability that one thrown die will come up either a six or a three?
$\qquad\qquad$ ii.$\;$ If 33 percent of the workers are Polish born and 20 percent are Italian born, what is the probability that a randomly selected worker will be either Polish or Italian born?

iii. If on a decision tree the probability that outcome 3 will result from choice *A* is 1/3, and the probability that outcome 2 will result from choice *A* is 1/4, and if there are only three outcomes of choice *A*, what is the probability that choice *A* will result in outcome 1?

Fallacies in Combining Probabilities

It is important to avoid pitfalls in the calculation of combined probabilities. There has been some interesting work done on ways that people typically go wrong in these types of cases. We think of these as fallacies since they are ways of reasoning that lead us astray. Below are some of these fallacies.

The Gambler's Fallacy: In probability theory two events are said to be *independent* if the occurrence of one does not affect the probability of the other. Thus *A* and *B* are independent when PROB(*B*) = PROB(*B* given *A*). Randomly selected events are independent in this sense. The gambler's fallacy is the treating of independent events as if they were not independent. It is the belief that the occurrence of one event will affect the probability of some other independent event. In the movie, *The World According to Garp*, Garp is looking at a house with the idea that he might purchase it. Suddenly a small plane crashes into the front of the house. "I'll take it!" says Garp. "It's been pre-disasterized." Separate plane accidents are independent in this sense, so the fact that a plane has already crashed into Garp's house does not lessen or affect in any way the probability that it will or will not happen again. In Monte Carlo in 1913, a roulette wheel came up red an incredible 26 straight times. By the 14th straight red, the gamblers were heaping great amounts of money upon black acting upon the assumption that the wheel is "due" to come up black to "correct itself." But the law of large numbers operates more by "inundation" than by "compensation." This is such a famous event in the history of probability theory that this fallacy is often called the "Monte Carlo Fallacy."

It has been reported that in World War II soldiers left well-fortified fox holes to stay in bomb craters believing that the odds are against a shell landing in the same spot twice. Louise wins the lottery against great odds, so her husband decides that it is futile for him to continue playing the lottery since the odds are now against a person from the same family winning more than once. All these are cases of the gambler's fallacy. All rely on the tacit or implicit idea that essentially chance events have "memories." The probability of a flipped coin coming up heads is 1/2. The probability of the coin coming up heads on four straight flips is 1/16. If a coin has come up heads on four straight flips, the probability that it will come up heads on the fifth flip is still 1/2. The coin does not remember that it has come up heads four straight times, and so does not correct itself by compensating with a series of tails. Of course, over the very very long run the number of heads will approach 1/2, but there is no reason to think that this 1/2 figure will be reflected in every subset of a long sequence of flips of the coin. On a monthly lottery drawing, which is more improbable, that Ted Olds wins it twice, or that Fran Mee and Mike Zip, complete strangers, each wins it once? Of course, these are equally probable occurrences when calculated according to PRINCIPLE 2. Why then are we so surprised when Ted Olds wins twice? Why do we wonder about how improbable that must be? Because we tacitly assume that chance has a memory. Does lightning strike twice in the same spot?

One reason that people commit the gambler's fallacy seems to be that they confuse *frequencies* in some set of events with *specific sequences* of events. If you were asked which is a more probable result of a random selection from families with four children, a family of only girl children or one with a mix of sexes, you would correctly answer that the mix is more probable. One reason is that in sequences of four children there is only one way to get all girls, but many more ways to get mixed results. This could also be seen as a question about frequencies. Families with mixed sex children occur more frequently than those with all girl children. But if you were asked, which is more probable, family A or family B below,

	1st Child	2nd Child	3rd Child	4th Child
Family A:	girl	girl	girl	girl
Family B:	girl	boy	boy	girl

you may be tempted to answer that B is more probable since mixes are more probable than all-girl families. But this question was not about all-girl vs. mixed sex families in general, it was about the two *specific sequences* given above. The probability of each specific sequence must be calculated using the principles mentioned above. In this case, the probability of each family is:

$$1/2 \times 1/2 \times 1/2 \times 1/2 = 1/16$$

In the same manner, it is more probable for any two weeks that the lottery winners be from different families than that they be from the same family. This is a matter of general frequencies. But it remains true that the probability that first Jack and then Frank (who is unrelated to Jack) are winners is no different from the probability that first Jack and then Jack's mother Louise are winners. This is a case of two specific sequences.

We can remedy our tendency to commit the gambler's fallacy when calculating a probability by using the principles of the mathematics of probability rather than intuitive judgments about ideas of chance or randomness. More specifically, when thinking about the probability of sequences of events ask yourself whether the events are or are not independent, and whether the question is about general frequencies or specific sequences. Be aware that it is very common for people to have incorrect ideas about how chance operates.

Misperception of Equiprobability: We say correctly that the probability of a die coming up even is .5. This is because, first, it must come up either even or odd, and second, the number of ways for it to come up even is equal to the number of ways that it can come up odd. It is common for people to neglect the second of these reasons (Shaughnessy 1981; Dawes 1988). Thus, someone might argue that the probability that a thrown die will come up a three is .5, since it will either come up three or not. While it is true to say that a thrown die will either come up three or not, there is only one way for it to come up three and five ways for it to *not* come up three. One could argue that in baseball a batter either gets a hit or not, and so the probability of his getting a hit is 1/2. This means that baseball players would all bat .500 or more, an impossible feat, at least so far in the history of baseball. What is the probability that a family of three children will have children of all the same sex, assuming there is an equal probability of boys and girls? Someone might argue that you could have (a) all girls, or (b) all boys, or (c) two girls and a boy, or (d) two boys and a girl. Since two of these four are all the same sex, the probability is 2/4 = 1/2. What is wrong with this reasoning? The problem is that although it indeed must be either (a), or (b), or (c), or (d), the number of ways for it to be any of the above was ignored, and in fact (a), (b), (c), and (d) are not all equiprobable. Let's look at how many ways you can have three children.

There are eight equiprobable child outcomes, each with a probability of $1/2 \times 1/2 \times 1/2 = 1/8$. Two of the eight are all of the same sex, so the addition rule tells us that the probability of a same sex combination

	1st Child	2nd Child	3rd Child
1.	G	G	G
2.	G	G	B
3.	G	B	G
4.	G	B	B
5.	B	G	G
6.	B	G	B
7.	B	B	G
8.	B	B	B

is 1/8 + 1/8 = 2/8 = 1/4. Six of the eight are mixed-sex combinations, so the probability of a mixed-sex combination is 6/8 = 3/4.

The remedy for avoiding the fallacy of equiprobability is to be sure that the options you identify are, in fact, equiprobable when calculating probabilities. One check is to see if there are more ways to achieve one of the options than the other. If so, then they are not likely to be equiprobable.

Estimating Initial Probabilities

We have emphasized that in estimating the probability of some event's happening, the most reliable information upon which to base the estimate is knowledge of past frequencies. There are two very common rules of thumb or heuristics often used when estimating probabilities that it would be better to avoid. Since it would be better to avoid them, and since they are likely to lead us astray, we call them fallacies.

The Availability Fallacy: This is the assumption that when selecting the most probable occurrence from a list of possibilities, the occurrence that comes most easily to mind is the most probable. There is a "law of memory" that states that repetition increases memory strength. Kahneman and Tversky point out that the availability fallacy is the inverse of this law in that it assumes that memory strength is evidence for frequency (1973). The fact that people commit this fallacy has been shown in an interesting set of experiments by Amos Tversky and Daniel Kahneman (1973), and by Lichtenstein et al. (1978). Subjects were asked questions such as, "What is more likely—lung cancer or stomach cancer?," and "Is it more likely that an English word will begin with "r" or have an "r" as its third letter?" It was found that subjects overestimated the probabilities of events that they could more easily think up (e.g., words beginning with "r") as well as diseases that had recently received publicity, for example, lung cancer as opposed to cancer of the stomach (Wright 1984). Find a person who for some reason knows few people who are divorced. Find another whose friends seem all to have been divorced. Who is more likely to underestimate the frequency of divorce? What do you think is more likely, death by murder or death by suicide? Find someone who has just driven past a particularly gruesome traffic accident, and ask a question about the probability of traffic accidents. How do you think that the response will be different from a response to the same question had it been asked yesterday? The fact is that there are many factors that influence what most readily can be brought to mind. These factors would include frequency of occurrence, which is relevant to probability, but would also include how recent is the experience, the vividness of the experience, or our own preferences in the matter. None of these latter factors are relevant to the probability of the event. Therefore, when estimating initial probabilities, be suspicious of the first things that come to mind. Ask yourself, do I think this is more probable because it is easy to recall or has recently been discussed? If so, search for other possibilities and if you have time, research the statistics.

Scenario Thinking: Our claim is that the most basic sort of information used to estimate probabilities ought to be the past frequency of similar occurrences. If you were to ask someone to estimate the chance of having an auto accident driving from Los Angeles to San Francisco, how would he or she be likely to determine the value? A common error, known as *scenario thinking*, is to run mentally through a "scenario" of the trip, thinking of what could go wrong, and then arriving at some figure. A much more effective procedure would be to consult statistics on accidents during such trips. If you are an experienced auto mechanic asked to estimate the probability that you will finish a job before the day's end, you can either mentally review the scenario of the steps of the job, or consult another part of your mind remembering how many hours the same job had taken in the past (Tversky and Kahneman 1973). Scenario thinking may be necessary in cases where there are no past frequencies or, where the information is out of reach, but it must be recognized as being very open to distortion by emotional barriers such as bolstering. The next time you are at a wedding, ask the bride or groom what she or he thinks is the probability that the marriage will end in divorce.

Scenario thinking is itself subject to the fallacy of availability since the scenario is likely to reflect what we can easily call to mind. This is referred to by Tversky and Kahneman as the "bias of imaginability," which they treat as a type of availability. They state, "The risk involved in an adventurous expedition . . . is evaluated by imagining contingencies with which the expedition is not equipped to cope . . . [however] . . . the ease with which disasters are imagined need not reflect their actual likelihood" (Tversky and Kahneman 1985). When asked to estimate the probability of an occurrence, use frequency statistics rather than scenario thinking if statistics are available and within reach. If forced to use scenario thinking, be on guard against the availability fallacy and against bolstering.

Ignoring Base Rate Frequencies: When deciding whether it is more probable that something falls into one group or another, it is necessary to consider both the characteristics of the groups, and the relative size of each group. To ignore data concerning group size when deciding the probability that something is in one group or another is to ignore base rate frequencies. The percentage of Great Danes who have hip dysplasia is far greater than the percentage of retrievers with the disease. If a veterinarian told you that he had operated upon a dog with hip dysplasia, would you think it more probable that it was a retriever or a Great Dane? The answer should be retriever, since there are so many more of them than of Great Danes, there are many more retrievers with hip dysplasia than Great Danes.

Let's suppose that you knew that 30 engineers and 70 lawyers worked in a particular section of a company, and no one else. As you might expect, 70 percent of the engineers liked to do math puzzles in their spare time, while only 30 percent of the lawyers displayed this odd proclivity. Suppose that I randomly select someone from that section describing the person only as an inveterate math puzzle solver. Do you think it's more likely that it's an engineer or a lawyer? If you are anything like Tversky and Kahneman's subjects, you would guess that the puzzle solver is an engineer (1982). The tendency is to focus upon the description (inveterate math puzzle solver), associate that with the characteristics of engineers, and entirely ignore the base rate frequency of 70 lawyers and 30 engineers. If you think about it, there are exactly 30 percent of 70, i.e., 21 lawyers who like math puzzles, and exactly 70 percent of 30, i.e., 21 engineers who like math puzzles, so the probability is equal that either would be selected. When the base rates were reversed so that there were 70 engineers and 30 lawyers, the subjects did not change their estimates.

Base rate frequencies are important pieces of information when estimating initial probabilities. The evidence is that the only time that people utilize this information is when it is the only information available (Kahneman and Tversky 1982). Ignoring obvious base rate information is one of the reasons that we make errors because of stereotyping. Jean is a serious young woman who loves to read literature. Do you think that it is more likely that Jean is a librarian or a waitress? Most would say librarian, but since there are so many more waitresses than librarians, there are likely to be more serious waitresses who read literature than serious librarians who read literature (Taylor 1982). This is not necessarily to deny the accuracy of the stereotype of the librarian or of the waitress (whatever the latter may be), it is only to take into account the relative sizes of the two groups when estimating probabilities.

The answer to this is not to stop using stereotypical clusters in the estimation of probabilities. They are too useful to give up, especially when the clusters themselves are based upon frequency data, as when we know that the rate of hip dysplasia among Great Danes is very high. The remedy is to reserve the application of the stereotype at least until the base rate frequencies are considered.

The Fallacy of Raw Mean: It is often the case that we base probability estimates on data about averages or means. For example, if you find that the mean combined SAT score of students at Midwest University is 1050, and if your son's score was 1065, then you may conclude that it is most probable that he will find students at Midwest that are about at his level. Often, though, this is a mistake.

Frank decides to join Rotary rather than Lions or Elks because the average income of Rotarians is exactly his income, and he hates to socialize with those either more or less well off than he is. Jane is reassured to know that she is doing just as well as everyone else in her math class because her grade on the first test was just about the average grade. In both these cases there is either a confusion about what the term "average" means, or an improper inference from information about "averages," or perhaps both. Let's consider the ten members of Frank's Rotary chapter and their incomes, listed below.

What is the "average" income? If you ask someone to calculate an average they will generally calculate a "mean." That is, they will add all the incomes and divide by the number of incomes. The mean income above is $90,000 but Frank thought that by having an income that was exactly the average, most others would have incomes near his. He was thinking more about "mode." The mode is the figure that

	$		$
Smith	260,000	Livingston	28,000
Franklin	205,000	Adams	27,000
Martinelli	190,000	Lyle	27,000
Frank	90,000	Jennings	26,000
Gibbons	29,000	Habosh	18,000

occurs most often. In the strict sense, the mode of the above is $27,000 since there are two cases of that income, and only one case of every other. But more loosely, the mode is "about $29,000 to $26,000," since that is where most of the incomes congregate, and is a far cry from Frank's income. It is often useful to know the midpoint, that is, the point where half are greater and half are less. This is called the "median." In the case above, there is an even number of incomes, and so there is no one median point. We must take the mean of the two median points. There are four figures greater than Gibbons, and four figures less than Livingston. The mean of their two incomes is $28,500. That is the median income.

Frank wanted to be around people whose incomes were about like his. The average in the sense of "mean" did not give him the information he needed. It would have given him this information if the incomes had been more or less normally distributed, where the mode, mean, and median scores coincide. However this is rarely the case, and so in general we have to look not only at the "average," but also at the distribution. That is, we first have to determine the high and low figures. This will give us the "range" of values, that is, the difference between the highest and lowest values. We then have to determine how many figures are at various places along this range. That is the "distribution," telling you how much deviation from the mean that there is.

When seeking information about groups of numbers or statistics, beware of the ambiguous term "average." Determine if the report intends to stipulate mean, median, or mode. Be aware that it is almost always necessary to have information about range and distribution, in addition to "average," in order to infer probabilities from means.

Samples

We have emphasized that when estimating initial probabilities, try to base them upon frequencies that are known to exist. When talking about frequencies, you must identify (1) the parent population, (2) a subclass of the parent population defined as having some property, and (3) the percentage or fraction of the parent population that is the subclass. For example, out of the parent population of all children born in the United States, a subclass is all boys born in the United States defined by the property of being boys, and the percentage or fraction is approximately 50% or ½. Out of the parent population of all VCRs that roll off Sansui's assembly line, a subclass is all the defective VCRs from Sansui's assembly line, and the percentage is .4%. Thus, we can say that there is an .4% probability that a Sansui VCR will come off the line defective.

How do we determine what percentage a subclass is of the parent population? The most efficient way is to take a sample of the parent population, examine the sample to determine the percentage of the subclass in the sample, and then infer that the whole population will have the same characteristics as the sample. We could, of course, examine every member of the entire population that interests us. But there are many reasons why using a sample is preferred to examining the entire parent population. Samples are easier to work with than the entire population. They are significantly cheaper to examine since they are smaller, and for the same reason they take less time to examine. What is often overlooked is that in many cases your results will be more accurate if you work with samples, than if you try to examine the entire population. For example, if you have a fixed amount of time and/or money to spend trying to learn about some population, it is often much better to do a very thorough job of sampling than a sloppy job of trying to examine the entire population. This is true when there are classes of members of the population that will not be examined, that is, will be undercounted, or will be examined improperly. A good example of this last problem is the U.S. census. It attempts to collect information about the class of U.S. citizens by examining every household. In so doing, it undercounts the poor and the urban dweller due to the fact that they are more difficult to contact, their families are less easily identifiable, their homes are more difficult to reach, and some have no permanent residence at all. This affects the amount of federal aid going to cities, and the number of Congressional seats going to states with large urban and poor populations. In the 1980 U.S. census, the Census Bureau has good evidence that it undercounted black Americans by 5.9 percent. It was unable to add that undercounted group back into the population, however, since it had no way to determine the areas from which it came. Some statisticians believe that given the resources available to the Census Bureau, more accurate data would derive from well-designed sampling procedures.

So the procedure of sampling involves the attempt to learn about some characteristic(s) of a group or collection, which is called a "population." It could be the group of all the ball bearings produced by some particular company, the likely voters in a given Presidential election, the elm trees in New Jersey, or any other group. We proceed in the following steps:

1. Clearly identify the population that you want to collect information about.

2. Clearly identify the characteristic that you want to know about the population, making sure that the characteristic is observable or in some way detectable.

3. Develop some idea of how certain it is necessary for you to be about your final conclusion concerning the population. Are you looking just for some general guidance, or will it be a major disaster if your conclusions are wrong?

3. Select a sample or subgroup of the population.

4. Examine or otherwise test the sample for the presence of the relevant characteristic in the sample.

5. Infer that the population from which the sample was taken has the characteristic in the same proportion as the sample. From a technical standpoint, step 3 is often the most difficult since when basing information about a population on a sample, the sample must be truly representative of the population; that is, the characteristics of the sample must accurately reflect the characteristics that are of interest in the population. If this is not the case, then step 5 will not be justified. To assure that the sample accurately represents the population, there are three considerations of major importance: size, fairness, and validity of the sample test.

Sample Size

In the case of sample size the rule is that, all other things being equal, the larger the sample the more likely that the properties of the sample will reflect the properties of the parent population. More precisely, as the size of a properly selected sample approaches the size of the parent population, the greater will be the probability that the sample will reflect the parent population. This is a version of what is called "the law of large numbers." If you were asked which of the following sequences of coin tosses would be more likely to be near 50% heads: (1) ten tosses, (2) one thousand tosses, (3) one million tosses, (4) ten million tosses, you should have picked (4). If you were asked to rank the probabilities that the sequences were near 50% heads, you should rank them in the order that they are given, since in each case the samples are getting larger. This is an application of the law of large numbers.

Some studies have shown that people in general are sensitive to the fact that larger samples are more likely than smaller samples to be representative of some particular population, that is, people intuitively grasp the law of large numbers (Bar-Hillel 1982). However, the application of the law of large numbers is not always done correctly.

One classic problem was devised by Kahneman and Tversky (1972). They described to subjects a town in which there was a hospital where 15 children were born each day, and another hospital in which 45 children are born each day. As we know, 50% of children born are boys, but the exact percentage of boys varies from day to day; on some days it may be higher and on other days lower than 50%. For one year the hospital recorded the number of days on which the percentage of boys born was either greater or less than 60%. Which hospital recorded more such days? The law of large numbers tells us that the larger hospital should be closer to the mean of 50% boys, and so the smaller hospital should record more days of greater than 60% boys. As a consequence, the larger hospital should record more days of less than 60% boys than did the smaller hospital. The overwhelming majority of people concluded either the reverse of the correct answer or that the number of days was "about the same." However, as the 60% figure was raised to 70%, then to 80%, and finally to 100%, the percentage of people getting the correct answer increased (Bar-Hillel 1982).

While it is true that all things being equal a larger sample will better represent a population than a smaller one, it is not true to say that in sampling, the larger the sample the better. This is because it costs time and money to sample. So it is necessary to have samples that are large enough to give you the level of certainty you need without breaking the bank. If samples are properly selected, they can be small relative to the population and still give very accurate information. The sample used to predict presidential elections is typically between 900 and 1,200 persons, where the population of U.S. voters is close to 100,000,000. Similarly the ratings of the popularity of TV shows are based upon samples of 700 to 800 families.

Fallacy of Small Sample: This is the fallacy of basing a conclusion about a population upon a sample that is too small. This fallacy is a pervasive feature of media journalism. During a presidential election, a reporter roams the country to "take the pulse of America." Each night for a week he or she interviews four of five people from the area visited that day. This so called "person on the street interview" must inevitably commit this fallacy. Why should the views of one or two people walking on a particular street at a particular time be of any news interest if not because these views were meant to *represent* the views of others. Yet the sample is always too small to represent any group. R. E. Nisbet and L. Ross note that in the 1972 presidential e!ections, reporters were unable to give credence to scientific polls showing George McGovern losing badly, because of the enthusiasm of the crowds that greeted the candidate. This is a case where a small but "vivid" sample carries more weight in drawing conclusions about the population than a scientifically selected large sample (Nisbet and Ross 1980). One study presented subjects with a *New Yorker* article about a single welfare "stereotype," and with scientifically collected data about welfare use. The result was that the single case had more influence in the drawing of conclusions about welfare than did the data summaries. In another study, subjects were shown videotaped interviews with two separate actors posing as prison guards. One was well dressed, neat, well-spoken, and liberal in his attitudes about prisoners. The other was the opposite. The attitudes about "prison guards in general" were clearly influenced by which actor-guard the subjects viewed, indicating a willingness to generalize from a sample of one. Even when the subjects were told that the guard they were about to see was not typical, the video still had a strong impact upon attitudes (Nisbet and Ross 1980). The phenomenon of "vividness" indicates how important the reporter's choice of interviews to be shown on that evening's news really is. One vivid interview can offset in the viewer's mind whole reams of statistically accurate data. At the University of Michigan, students were given in-depth descriptions of possible courses that they could take. In addition, one group was given statistically formulated data summarizing the evaluations of each of the courses by all the students who had taken the course at the end of the previous term. The other group was presented with a small panel of upper-level students commenting upon and evaluating the courses. The results of the students' choices showed that they took the face-to-face panel discussion, despite its small sample size, far more seriously than the larger sample data (Nisbet et al., 1982). Of course, in this case the greater influence of the views of the few upper level students may have reflected an appropriate judgment based upon the superior credibility of the witnesses.

The Fallacy of the Law of Small Numbers: In probability theory, the law of large numbers implies that you can expect that very large samples will reflect the percentages and characteristics of some parent population to a greater extent than smaller samples. If you flip a coin one million times you can expect that the percentage of HEADS will be closer to .5 than it will be if you flip the coin fifty times. The fallacy of the small sample is the attempt to draw a conclusion about a parent population based upon a sample that is too small. The fallacy of the law of small numbers is the reverse. It is the attempt to draw a conclusion about the characteristics of a small sample based upon what you know about the parent population. Which is the more probable sequence of coin tosses—1, or 2, or 3?

	First Toss	Second Toss	Third Toss	Fourth Toss
1.	H	T	T	H
2.	H	H	H	H
3.	H	H	T	T
4.	T	H	H	?

The work of Tversky and Kahneman (1971) is again important here. Their research suggests that most people would consider #2 to be the least probable since the probability of H and of T are equal. In addition, many people would think that #1 was more likely than #3 since #3 is more "orderly" than #1, and chance is not "orderly." We know, of course, that each of the three sequences is equal in probability to the others, and that the probability of each is 1/16. But the research shows that even subjects who are very sophisticated about probability and statistics commit this error. No doubt each of us has committed it on numerous occasions.

It is true that the gambler's fallacy and the law of small numbers are closely related. They are, in fact, different reasoning processes that lead to similar mistaken conclusions. Suppose we look at #4 above and ask, which is more probable on the fourth toss–an H or a T? Some would reason that after two HEADS a TAILS is *due*. This is the gambler's fallacy since the assumption is that independent events affect each other's probability. Others would reason that since the probability of each is 1/2, then a sample of four should have 1/2 HEADS and 1/2 TAILS, so T is more probable. This is the fallacy of the law of small numbers, since it assumes that very small samples should have the same characteristics as their more general populations.

Sample Fairness

The intuitive idea of a fair sample is one that is similar to, or representative of, the population from which it was drawn, or at least similar enough to allow for inferences from the sample to the population. In actual practice, the fairness of a sample is defined by the *process* by which it was selected. The key to a fair selection process is a random selection process. A *random sample* of some parent population is defined as a sample in which every member of the population had an equal chance of being included in the sample.

If you wanted to know what percentage of adults in the United States consider themselves Democrats, you would not want to take your sample only from adults in Chicago, even if you sampled the entire city. This is because adults in Chicago are more likely to be Democrats than adults nation-wide. If you wanted to determine the percentage of defective Sansui VCR's, you would not want to take the sample only from the morning's production. It may be that this shift is particularly sloppy, or that workers are more efficient in the morning.

For a sample to be truly random does not mean that the sample is selected haphazardly. To the contrary, it is often quite difficult to assure that a sample has been selected randomly. We often watch TV reporters take a "random sample" of the opinions of "viewers" by standing on a corner and stopping passersby. This sample is anything but random. Think of all the built-in biases—the neighborhood could be predominantly rich or poor, black or white, union or nonunion, Republican or Democrat, male or female, families or singles, and so the list goes on.

Some parent populations are very homogeneous in the sense that there is not a wide range of divergence among its members, while other populations are very heterogeneous. Consider for example a women's Roman Catholic college of day, residential students. Compare that to an urban, nonsectarian, coed college, with day and evening divisions, of full and part time students of all ages. Clearly if you are interested in an opinion poll, one population is more homogeneous than the other; and just as clearly it is easier to sample a homogeneous population than one that is more heterogeneous. To sample the opinions of the students at the Catholic college, we could give each student a number, and then have a computer select a random sample from the collection of numbers. We could then give a questionnaire or interview to the sample members. This is a purely random selection process. In the case of the other college we would want to be sure that we got the opinions of commuters and residential students, the young recent high school graduates and the older students, the day and the evening students, and the men and the women. To assure this, we would need a very large sample to protect against some subgroup being underrepresented in the sample. We could also divide up the student population into relevant subgroups and randomly sample each subgroup. In this case, the size of each subgroup in the sample would vary depending upon the size of that subgroup in the population, although it is always necessary that the subgroup samples be large enough to be representative. This is called a stratified sampling procedure. It is this procedure that TV networks use to predict the outcomes of elections on election night. The more heterogeneous a population is, the greater the need for care in the sample selection process, and the larger the sample must be.

The Fallacy of Biased Sample: This is the fallacy of drawing a conclusion about a population based upon a sample that is biased, where the bias of the sample is the result of an improper selection procedure. Almost all "self-selected" samples will be biased unless they are treated very carefully by professionals. Thus, telephone polls where viewers call a 900 number to register an opinion or vote on some issue or candidate are invariably biased samples of the population. In politics, self-selected telephone polls are biased in favor of groups that watch a lot of TV, in favor of groups willing to pay the phone charge, in favor of groups with a strong commitment on an issue as opposed to a mild preference, etc. In cases where questionnaires are mailed to purchasers to determine attitudes toward some product they purchased, the returns are likely to be biased in favor of those who had bad experiences with the product. The point to remember is that it is a very complicated matter to get an unbiased sample of a population, and so we should be careful when generalizing about a population from a sample.

Sample Test Validity

In addition to the size and fairness of a sample, you must also be concerned with the validity of the test done on the sample. This concerns whether what was observed in the sample accurately reflects what interested you about the parent population. Suppose you are interested in percentage of defects in Sansui's VCRs, and that your sample is large and randomly selected. To save time, you assume that if the "ON" light activates when the "ON" button is pushed, the VCR is free of defects. This is hardly a valid measure of quality control. So if only 2% of "ON" lights failed to activate, you could not conclude that only 2 percent of Sansui VCRs come off the lines defective. Suppose you are interested in the attitudes of Sansui workers toward their managers. You select a perfectly constructed stratified sample and assign the manager of each subgroup to interview the workers in that group. This is not a valid test of the property under consideration. Since opinion polls are such a pervasive part of our lives, the question of validity in the construction of the test is tremendously important. If, shortly after a dangerous foreign policy incident, you happen to be asked by a pollster to evaluate the overall job of the U.S. president during his entire term in office, the chances are that your response is more a measure of your wish to be a good and supportive American than a true reflection of your opinion of the president's job. If we want to find out the percentage of "liberals" among U.S. voters, it is not sufficient to ask a well-chosen sample whether they are "liberal" or "conservative." From this question, we can only conclude that a certain percentage of people are willing to classify themselves as "liberals." Given that "liberal" is now a bad word in U.S. politics, that percentage of voters would be less than the percentage that would take liberal positions if asked issue by issue.

The *fallacy of invalid sample test* occurs when you draw a conclusion about a population on the basis of an examination of the sample that did not adequately test for the properties of the population that you want to learn about. This is most common in survey data where the questions are improperly posed.

Our interest in groups, and in how we learn about the characteristics of groups, stems from our interest in probabilities. Our contention is that frequencies of events or characteristics in groups are the best evidence for estimating probabilities. It is for this reason that we are interested in issues surrounding sampling. Recall too that our interest in probabilities stems from the fact that good decision-making relies on our ability to make accurate probability estimates.

Important Concepts

Random sample   Mean
Law of large numbers   Mode

Distribution	Median
Availability	Range
Base rate frequencies	Probability
Gambler's fallacy	Scenario thinking
Frequency in a sample	Raw mean
Sample	Specific sequence
Stratified sample	Population
Law of small numbers	Sample test validity

Problems for Analysis

Answer the following questions about probabilities, and explain the answers:

1. If the Jets have a 70 percent chance of beating the Patriots, what is the probability that they will not beat the Patriots?
2. If Harvard's drop-out rate between entering and graduating is 20 percent, and Sue has a 4 in 10 chance of being admitted, assuming Sue will accept if admitted, what is Sue's probability of graduating from Harvard?
3. If you flip a coin three times, what is the probability that it will NOT come up three straight heads?
4. If I buy that motel and if the new road goes through, I have a 40 percent chance of making it run in the black. Without the road, the chances are only 2 percent. My contacts give the new road a fifty-fifty chance. What is the probability that if I buy the motel, it will run in the black?
5. I select a card from a deck. What is the probability that it is a black three? Use Principle 2,c.
6. In country Z, there are 30 million children of which 50 percent are boys. If we were to inspect three sequences of six children each in the order of selection left to right, which selection sequence is the most probable? (Kahneman, Slovic, and Tversky 1985)

> A. BBGBGG
> B. GGGBBB
> C. GGGGGG
> D. None

7. In the country of Z mentioned above, all families of six children were surveyed. In 260 of the families, the exact order of births was

GBGBBG. What is your estimate of the number of families in which the exact order of births was BGBBBB?

> A. Much greater than 260
> B. About the same as 260
> C. Much less than 260
> D. None

8. It is early September, Wade Boggs of the Red Sox is batting .333 (that is, his season-long ratio of hits to hits-or-outs is 1 in 3), today he is 0 for 2 (no hits in two at bats), and is scheduled up to bat. Which is more probable:

> A. He gets a hit,
> B. He makes an out,
> C. Neither, they are equiprobable.

Identify the fallacies concerning probabilities and sampling in the following scenarios.

9. When Jack heard the tragic news of the accidental death of his young nephew, he experienced a secret sense of relief that now it won't happen to his own children. The odds against two such events in the same family would be incredibly large.

10. Mary was a clerical worker in the cardiac ward of the Children's Hospital. On Friday her son came home from his first day of high school football practice complaining of pains in his chest. Mary decided not to see their family doctor, going immediately to the very expensive cardiologist.

11. James was beginning a new job for which he was not sure he was qualified. The expert at the employment agency believed that he would be fired in a week. He just didn't have the experience. James was not dismayed, arguing that he had a fifty-fifty chance of success, since after all he was either going to succeed or fail.

12. Franklin had to drive to D.C. from New York. He has been afraid of driving ever since his accident. He could travel the Jersey Turnpike or Route 1. The morning he was to depart he heard of a terrible accident on the turnpike, so he decided to take that route since it's very unlikely that there would be two such accidents on the same day.

13. Jean bought a Pit Bull Terrier (Scrappy) for a pet, and to protect her and her three young children. Sam asked whether she wasn't

worried that the dog might injure one or more of the children. Jean thought about Scrappy, about how well he played with the little ones, about the time that her two-year-old stuck a pencil in its eye and laughed. She answered Sam that she couldn't conceive of Scrappy ever hurting the kids. It just would never happen.

14. Suppose that given your and your spouse's backgrounds, the probability that your child will have blue eyes is .09 and the probability that the child will have brown eyes is .61. What is the probability that it will have neither?

15. You enter a raffle in which there is only one winner among 350 players. You buy one ticket, as does your son. What is the probability that either you or your son will win the raffle prize?

16. Suppose that you and your son enter a lottery in which there are two winners. In this lottery there are 100 players. What is the probability that you win *and then* your son wins (the raffle tickets are replaced after each drawing)?

17. One thing that I learned from my week in Moscow was that the women of the Soviet Union are surprisingly fashionable. I just sat on benches along the main shopping streets for hours admiring thousands of beautifully dressed women going to and from work.

18. Ronald Reagan gets high marks for his dealings with the Soviet Union. A very large and well-selected sample was asked if they supported the President's goals of preventing war between the super powers and fully 80 percent answered in the positive.

19. My computer dating service here in Dallas has arranged a date for me with an attractive young woman who is well-dressed and well-educated. Everything seemed great until they told me that she speaks French fluently. I didn't say so, but I was really disappointed, because I had hoped for a good old American-born woman, and this one's probably French.

20. I have a medical practice that specializes in headaches. Not one patient of mine that I have treated with aspirin has ever experienced relief, and I can tell you that the number is in the tens of thousands. I think that it's time that the American public was told of the ineffectiveness of aspirin for headaches. There should be labelling to that effect.

21. "Well folks it's come down to this one field goal with four seconds left. If Kramer gets it the Lions win. It's fifty-fifty, he either gets it or he doesn't. A whole game coming down to the flip of a coin."

22. Some people say that American cars are not well made, but I'll tell you that I've had this here Bonneville for going on twelve years

now, and I fully expect to have her ten years from now. I don't know what they're complaining about.

23. American Presidents seem to always have wives that are stronger people than they. Look at Ronald Reagan and Gerry Ford.

24. Mimi works in the State Court building, which keeps records and statistics on marriage and divorce. She is about to be married, and a lawyer she works with suggests a pre-nuptual contract that would protect her assets in the event of a divorce. Mimi has nothing in principle against such an agreement, but thinks about how much in love she and Humberto are; about how they never fight; about how they agree on everything; about how placid Humberto seems to be; and so Mimi decides that such an agreement is unnecessary in their case.

25. Will has had two straights in a row in poker. He now has to decide either to go for a third straight or for a full house. He figures that he would never get three straights in a row, and for that reason decides to go for the full house.

26. In tests that were performed to determine how levels of aggression were influenced by violent TV, the aggression levels of the youngsters were measured by the number of times that a child would strike a life-sized stuffed doll of a man when told by a researcher to, "Punish that doll for hurting your friend."

27. Jake was trying to decide where to place his house on the large parcel of land he had bought. He noticed a tree that had been damaged by lightning. He put his house on that spot reasoning that at least here it would be safe from lightning.

28. Mary is a secretary at the department of health statistics in Washington, D.C. Her mother who is 53 has recently been very ill with heart disease, and Mary seems obsessed with the illness. Her husband has been constantly away on sales trips. Her son was doing a project for his ninth grade health class that was due in three weeks and asked her for information about heart disease. In answer to his question, Mary told him that it is her understanding that heart disease is the leading killer of women under sixty.

29. Lilco wanted to find out what the people of Long Island thought about the safety of nuclear power. From a very large and randomly selected number of Long Island homes, Lilco reassigned the duties of 24 day-shift linemen to do in-depth phone interviews during the times that they would normally be on the lines. Since 99.8 percent of all Long Island homes has a phone, Lilco was not concerned with a biased sample.

30. In a very large and well-chosen sample, Americans were asked whether they approved or disapproved of Colonel Oliver North. Sixty percent said that they approved. It is remarkable to me that sixy percent of Americans would believe that lying to the Congress of the United States is appropriate behavior.

31. When Jake saw the terrible accident along the highway on his way home he breathed a sigh of relief. At least it's not my turn today, he thought, and jammed the accelerator to the floor.

32. Jean knew that fully a third of the employees of United Electronics were women. She had been interviewed by two men so far. She relaxed after concluding that the next and last interview would most likely be with a woman.

34. "In an effort to find out in depth what the American people think of the latest scandal hearings in Congress, I'm here with the Phelps family in Waukegan, Ohio. There are three generations represented here, so let's see first whether the President still has the kind of credibility problem that polls have indicated he has."

35. *Jaws* III was in 3-D, and so was *Friday the Thirteenth* III. So every time they do the third version of a movie, they make it in 3-D.

36. A company sent out seven thousand questionnaires to the buyers of a new product to gauge customer satisfaction. One thousand people responded of whom 70% said they were dissatisfied. The company concluded that 70% of its customers are dissatisfied with the product.

37. Bob was astounded to discover that the average life expectancy in France in 1750 was 37 years, whereas today it is 70. He felt that he now understood why progress came so slowly in the past. As soon as someone discovered something, he died with very little opportunity to educate the next generation.

38. The average yearly income of the alumni attending the 25th reunion of Harkard University was $150,000 per year. You conclude that Harkard must be doing something right to produce alumni with such a high average income.

39. In a recent survey, the Arabs living in the West Bank and in Israel were interviewed by an Arab research team, and indicated that the great majority of them support the PLO over Jordan as representative of Palestinians. The interviews took place in the homes and workplaces of the interviewees, and the sample was large and well-chosen. The news media concluded that the Arabs of this region do support the PLO overwhelmingly.

40. Jack: Recent polls show that Catholic priests are not very supportive of the positions of the Pope on birth control and divorce.

Jake: Those polls are all wrong. My uncle is a priest and he supports Pope Paul 100%.

41. A recent poll found that people in the United States overwhelmingly consider themselves liberals. The poll had a very large and well-selected sample. Of the respondents, 67 percent chose (A) below, and only 33% chose (B).

(A) Do you favor the liberal idea of helping people in need, or,

(B) Do you favor the conservative idea that you should help yourself and forget about other people?

Should you conclude that conservative candidates ought to be alarmed by the results of this poll?

42. In order to test the frequency of police brutality in the nation, Hanna and Fallon, a social research firm, selected a large sample of police officers from around the country. The sample was selected according to the most rigorous statistical standards. Observers from Hanna and Fallon rode with the officers for 30 randomly selected work shifts. They found that police brutality in the United States is almost nonexistent.

43. If we ban violence on TV then the pattern of violence among our young will either increase, decrease, or stay the same. A one-third chance of decreasing youth violence seems to be something worth trying.

44. I didn't do so well in law school, but I'm either going to pass the bar exam or not. So my fifty/fifty chance is as good as anyone else's.

45. Briarmanor University advertises that the mean income of its graduates is $73,000 with surprisingly little deviation. It bases this figure on the returned responses of 30 percent of its graduates to a questionnaire mailed to every graduate. All agree that this was a surprisingly large response rate.

46. Larry Bird can win the game with a foul shot. Since he will either make it or not, the probability that the Celtics (his team) will win is 50-50.

47. Sally Jesse Noel's show this morning concerned the issue of who was more oppressed by the opposite sex—men or women. Sally thought that it would be interesting to conduct a nation-wide randomly selected telephone poll during the show from a huge sample of 8,000 respondents to the question, "Who do you think is more oppressed by the other sex—men or women." Sally explained, "I just want to know what the American people think about this issue." At the end of the

show it was reported that by a 66%–34% margin, Americans believed that women were more oppressed by men.

48. Dr. Stanley Blackburn has been a successful psychiatrist for 32 years. He is responding to the claim that in most cases people with personal problems can be helped over these problems by sympathetic, common-sense, advice and understanding from friends, families and other non-professionals. "I have seen over five thousand patients in my career, and in almost no cases did the attempted help of friends and families have any positive benefit. To the contrary, in most cases it made matters much worse. So this claim is absolutely false."

59. Carlo's daughter was accepted as a student at Kulane University, where in her last three years she would be required to live off campus, in the surrounding area. Carlo checked out the area, and thought of all the ways his daughter could be harmed, by muggings, rape, murder, or theft. He decided that it was too dangerous, and insisted that she reject the acceptance.

50. Since there had been complaints about Professor Sartorian's archaeology classes, the Dean arranged for a standardized teacher evaluation to be completed by all the students. On the day of the test, the Dean's secretary was ill, so the Dean asked Professor Sartorian if she would administer the test, which included fill-in sections and written comments. The Dean was surprised that, after all the complaints, the evaluations were quite positive.

51. "It's time we found out what Long Islanders think about the Shoreham Nuclear Power Plant issue, so I've come to the Smithaven Mall here in Lake Grove where we're reporting live. Here's someone now . . . Madam, excuse me but could you tell us your thoughts on whether the plant at Shoreham should open?" . . . etc, etc, "Well that completes our random sample of Long Islanders. Now back to you Peter."

Chapter 5

Reasoning About Causes

Because we live in an uncertain world we are forced to base our decisions on probability estimates. In particular, we need to have information that allows us to know what leads to what in the world, and what the probable consequences of various actions will be. We need, in short, to have a clear understanding of the causes of things. The more accurate our estimates of causation, the more will we be able to make sound and responsible decisions.

There is a difficulty here in that much of the information about causation comes from scientists working in technical areas in which we have no expertise. Therefore, we almost always get our scientific information second-hand, usually from journalists or other nontechnical writers. As a rule, scientists are usually very cautious about attributing causes. A scientist who learns that people who have heart disease also have had a diet rich in fats will report that discovery in a scientific journal, but will undoubtedly caution readers to be wary of jumping to conclusions. Since the scientist is intimately familiar with his own area, he knows that things are very complicated and that the statement "dietary fat causes heart disease" is, strictly speaking, untrue, because it is too simplistic. Yet, we are bombarded every day with statements in newspapers and on television that lead us to believe that some cause and effect relationships have been clearly proven when, at best, the evidence for such relationships is only suggestive.

The purpose of what follows is designed to make it easier for you to interpret what is meant by "cause" when used by scientists so that you can make more accurate probability estimates in your role as a decision-maker.

The *Because* of Inference and the *Because* of Causation

The first thing to note is that the word *because* in our language has two very distinct meanings, one of which has nothing to do with causes. In one case, what follows a "because" is a reason to believe in a claim, but is not the causal producer of the phenomenon. This is the *because* of inference.

I know he will win because he is ahead in the polls. (Being ahead in the polls is a reason for believing he will win, but is not the cause of his winning.)
   There must be fire somewhere because there is smoke. (The existence of the smoke is a reason to believe there is a fire, but is not the cause of the fire.)

On the other hand, the word *because* also is used to indicate that a cause will follow.

He is ahead in the polls because he is a good speaker. (His good speaking causes respondents to indicate they will vote for him.)
   There is smoke because there is fire. (Fire brings about smoke.)

In the case where the *because* is one of inference, the result is an *argument*, that is, an attempt to justify the truth of the claim that has been called into question. The following is an argument: "We should reform our prisons *because* they fail to rehabilitate, they are barbaric, and they create worse criminals." What follows the *because* in this argument are three reasons to believe prisons should be reformed.

When *because* is meant to indicate causation, the result is an *explanation*, that is, an attempt to describe what brought about a certain event or phenomenon. The following is an explanation: The earth remains in orbit around the sun because its inertial force moves it ahead, gravity pulls it toward the sun, and the two forces are in equilibrium." What follows the *because* in this case describes the factors that produce the phenomenon of the earth's orbit. In the following section, we will be interested in the *because* of causation, and how one decides when a statement about cause and effect deserves to be believed.

The Meaning of Causal Statements

Much of our knowledge of cause and effect comes to us in ordinary everyday experience. We drive more cautiously when there is snow on the ground, because we know from experience that snow makes it more difficult to stop and execute quick maneuvers. But despite the fact that we talk in causal terms and make causal judgments all the time, there is a good deal of confusion in this area, largely because we use the word *cause* in a wide variety of ways. In the above case, we could not reasonably argue that experience teaches that snow causes accidents or that speed causes accidents. Neither of those causal statements is true, as it stands. We would have to qualify such statements to make clear that we mean that snow and speed contribute in a causal way to accidents. It is almost never the case that one thing, by itself, leads to or causes some other event. Consider the following statements, all of which imply some sense of causation:

1. Jack's injury was caused by a fall from a ladder.
2. The increasing incidence of murder in the United States is the result of the availability of handguns.
3. Smoking causes cancer.
4. The plane came down because it lost all fuel due to a fuel-tank rupture.
5. This tree died because of insufficient water.
6. His death was caused by a massive hemorrhage.
7. He is a bachelor because he never married.
8. Smoking marijuana leads to heroin addiction.
9. Fertilization of the egg causes life to begin.
10. A college education will cause you to have a higher lifetime income.

Almost all statements of causal relations deal with phenomena that increase the probability of certain outcomes. We usually refer to such types of causes as contributing factors. "Smoking causes cancer" is a shorthand and inaccurate way of saying that smoking increases the probability of cancer. Some factors are said to be *necessary* in that, if they are not present, then the probability of an outcome is reduced to zero. Oxygen is a necessary factor for the presence of human life. Notice that oxygen is necessary, but not sufficient to guarantee human life. Are any of the above statements of this sort? Other factors are so powerful that they are *sufficient* by themselves to guarantee an outcome, i.e., their presence increases the probability of an outcome to 1.00. A certain alcoholic content will kill all of a certain type of bacteria. Notice that while the alcohol is enough, it is not the only thing that might be sufficient to do the job. Would any of the above meet this criterion? It is almost never the case that a factor is both necessary and sufficient, meaning that without it an outcome cannot occur and with it the outcome is certain. Many such instances turn out, upon inspection, to be merely definitions and not causal statements.

The most common errors we make when thinking about causation usually involve our imagining that a contributing factor is a necessary or a sufficient cause of some outcome that concerns us, or in overestimating or underestimating the relative strength of a contributing factor. Because things are so complicated, we often confuse minor contributing factors with important factors. Or we confuse contributing factors with sufficient ones.

People with college educations usually earn more money than those without such education, and therefore if we are interested in the earning power of our children, we should send them to college. Or should we? It depends on what sort of factor higher education is. It is unlikely to be solely sufficient. Is it necessary or contributory? If it is necessary, are other factors, such as ambition or aptitude, also important? Or is it possible that, despite the well-known relationship between college education and income, there is no cause and effect relation at all?

Causes and Correlation

A common source of difficulty in interpreting causal relations comes from our tendency to assume that things that occur together necessarily have some causal relationship to each other. The source of this error is plain enough. No causal relationship can be adduced between two things if they are not in some sort of conjunction; but many things are conjoined that bear no causal relation to each other. When things often occur together there is said to be a *correlation* between them, and while all causal statements involve things that are correlated, the obverse is not true. Things can be highly correlated and yet have no causal effect on each other. The correlation of two events suggests the possibility of causation, but is insufficient to sustain a claim of causation by itself.

Perhaps the most common error based on this mistaken inference is the fallacy *post hoc ergo propter hoc*. This is a Latin expression meaning ''after which therefore because of which'' and refers to the error of confusing sequence with cause. The tendency to commit the post hoc fallacy is what gives rise to superstitions. One day a baseball player notices that he has worn two different color socks. That same day he gets four hits, so he wears different color socks until he has a couple of bad days, and decides the effect no longer works. Mary gets the flu and drinks a lot of chicken soup. She is better within the week and is convinced the soup cured the flu. Frank becomes depressed after the death of his father. He sees a psychiatrist and after a year of treatment feels better, and concludes that psychiatry has the answer to depression. In all of these cases, the only evidence for the truth of the claim of cause and effect was that the particular effect followed the hypothesized cause. Correlation and temporal sequence are not sufficient to demonstrate a causal connection.

Temporal sequence is not the only sort of correlation that can be confused with a causal relation. Many things are often found together. Blue eyes and blond hair, high IQ and good grades, crime and drug abuse, are common examples.

Correlation and Class Membership

In general, things are said to correlate if they "hang together," are frequently found together. To be more precise:

A correlates with B if: The percentage of B in the class A is greater than the percentage of B in the class non-A (Giere 1979).

We know that crime (A) correlates with poverty (B). This means that the percentage of people who are poor (B) is higher among the class of people who are criminals (A) than among the class of noncriminals (non-A). It also means the reverse, that the percentage of people who are criminals (A) is higher among the class of people who are poor (B) than among those who are not poor (non-B). What a correlation does not imply is that the percentage of A in B is necessarily high. While it may be true that most people who commit crime are poor, it is certainly not true that most poor people commit crimes. In fact, the percentage of poor people who commit crimes is quite low. However the *percentage* is higher among them than among people who are well off.

As another example, suppose you believe there is a correlation between cars with rock music on the radio (A) and cars that get into accidents (B). This would mean you believe that the percentage of accidents (*B*) is higher in the class of cars playing rock (*A*) than in the class not playing rock (non-*A*). It is important to notice that even if this is true (and there is a correlation between *A* and *B*), it is certainly not true that all *A* are *B*, or even that most *A* are *B*. Not all cars playing rock music have accidents. In fact, very few cars playing rock have accidents. But it is true that people in cars playing rock have more accidents than people who do not play rock.

Notice also that the correlations above do not demonstrate causal relations. Does playing rock music cause accidents? Does having accidents drive one to rock music? Does criminal activity make people poor? Does poverty make people commit crimes?

The Correlation Coefficient

In the above cases, we talked about correlation in terms of qualitative classification, and can ask such questions as "Is the percentage of people who have heart attacks greater in the class labeled *males* than in the class labeled *nonmales* (females)?" One is either a member of the class male or the class female, and one is either in the class of people who have had heart attacks or in the class of people who have not. What about the relation between smoking and high blood pressure? Here we could talk about people who smoke versus people who do not, and attempt to determine whether the percentage of those with high blood pressure is greater in one class than the other. But such things admit of degrees, i.e. people can be light, moderate, or heavy smokers. And blood pressure can be normal, slightly elevated, or very high. In such cases, we can make more refined statements in which we relate the level of smoking (cigarettes per day) and the degree of high blood pressure. In this way we can show not only that smoking is correlated with high blood pressure, but, in addition, that the risk of high blood pressure rises with the level of smoking.

We can usually refine our understanding by moving from qualitative groupings to quantitative measures, and it is often possible to do so. We can relate poverty and crime in a qualitative way, but if we have enough data we can get a clearer picture by relating degree of poverty with degree of criminality, i.e., family income and average number of criminal convictions.

In measures that do admit of level, we describe the degree of relation by the *correlation coefficient* that falls between -1 and $+1$. Negative correlations occur when measures are inversely related, such as players' golf scores and their skill in the game. As they play better, their scores go down. The same is true of family income and crime. As income goes up, the number of criminal convictions, on average, goes down. Most of the time when we discuss correlations, we will be talking about positive correlations that range between 0 and +1. The higher the degree of relationship, the closer is the correlation coefficient to +1. Height and weight are correlated but not perfectly, and so the correlation between them would be greater than 0, but less than +1. IQ scores and height should not be correlated at all, and so the correlation between those things should be zero.

Notice that although the correlation between height and weight is fairly high, there is no sense in which one thing causes the other. You wouldn't advise someone to gain weight in order to grow taller. Probably other factors, such as genetic predisposition or diet, determine both.

Notice also that even where a causal relationship has been determined, such as between cigarette smoking and cancer, the correlation is far from perfect, i.e., is not +1. Many people get cancer who never smoke, and many people who smoke never get cancer. This means that smoking is a contributing factor, but is neither necessary nor sufficient, in itself, to produce cancer. Other things, such as diet or genetic predisposition, also play a role.

Generally speaking, a positive correlation between X and Y could be consistent with any of the following:

1. X causes or is a contributing factor in Y;
2. Y causes or is a contributing factor in X;
3. X and Y cause or contribute to each other;
4. X and Y are both caused by some third factor;
5. X and Y are only accidentally correlated.

In the example above, for instance, it is possible that poverty tends to produce criminals. It is also possible that criminal behavior tends to increase poverty. Perhaps they tend to reinforce each other. Poor people are more likely to commit crime due to their poverty, and once they become criminals is it harder for them to avoid poverty because of their criminal activity? Perhaps a third factor, poor education, produces both? Perhaps the finding is purely accidental? That might be the case in a correlation found on only one or a few occasions. Our superstitious baseball player made the error of confusing an accidental correlation with a real one. If the correlation is more widespread and found repeatedly, it is probably not accidental. The most important principle to remember in all of this is that:

CORRELATION DOES NOT PROVE CAUSATION.

Consider the following examples:

There was a medical report some years ago that levels of ear hair correlated with heart disease. This means (very loosely) that the people in the class "have a lot of ear hair" have a higher percentage of heart disease than people in the class "do not have a lot of ear hair." What does this mean? It probably means that some third factor, perhaps hormonal or genetic, produces both effects.

It has been reported that natives of a South Seas Island noticed a correlation between body lice and general health (Giere 1979). That is, the percentage of those who were healthy who had body lice was greater than the percentage of those who were ill who had body lice. They concluded that body lice are good for your health. In this case, they got the causation backwards. It was because the body was healthy that the lice were present. At certain temperatures the lice decide to abandon ship.

Unruly children often have parents who shout at them a lot. Does that mean that scolding children causes them to be unruly? If they were scolded less often, would they be better behaved?

A husband and wife visit a divorce counselor. The wife complains that the husband never compliments her cooking. The husband argues that his wife doesn't care enough to cook a decent meal. What seems to be causing what here?

Three Conditions of Causation

In order to demonstrate that a causative relation exists between two things, three conditions are essential. In order to conclude that X is a causal factor that produces Y, or that X is a contributory factor that increases the likelihood of Y, one must demonstrate:

Condition 1. That there is some degree of correlation between X and Y, and
Condition 2. That if X is changed, Y is changed, when

Condition 3. Everything else has remained the same, i.e. nothing else but
X has changed.

The last condition is known as the *ceteris paribus* condition and is absolutely essential. Without it how could we know that it was X that caused the change in Y and not the other things that changed?

Is there a correlation between having bits of tobacco in a man's shirt pocket and his likelihood of having a heart attack. The answer is clearly, yes. But is the relation causal? Could he reduce his likelihood of heart disease by not putting cigarettes in his shirt pocket, if everything else remained the same? No, not unless he gave up smoking, but that would violate ceteris paribus, and so no causal claim between dirty pockets and heart disease can be sustained.

Trying to satisfy all three of the above conditions is easier said than done. Finding things that correlate with some phenomenon of interest often requires painstaking detective work, since important factors are often not immediately apparent. It took years to establish the correlation between smoking and cancer. Today thousands of researchers around the world are attempting to discover what sorts of diet or lifestyles are correlated with various illnesses. Meterologists struggle to find the conditions that correlate with the formation of tornadoes. Social scientists are searching for those things that correlate with good grades, happy marriages, successful careers.

But having discovered correlations is not enough. The other two conditions must also be satisfied, and it is not easy to satisfy either. If a difference in Y is detected, is it meaningful? Could it be the result of faulty measurement or inaccurate instrumentation? Some will recall how in chemistry class they were admonished never to trust only one measurement, and if possible to have someone else confirm your estimate. How are we to assure ceteris paribus to assure that everything else is equal? Within the confines of a laboratory it may seem possible, but what about things that may impinge on the laboratory that we haven't thought about, such as radio waves or sunspots. How do we assure ceteris paribus where relations cannot be tested in laboratory settings, such as those between criminal activity and poverty? In truth we can never be *absolutely* sure that ceteris paribus has been satisfied, we can only be sure in varying degrees. For that reason we should translate, at least in our own mind, the statement "X causes Y" as "X probably causes Y" with the degree of probability depending on a host of factors. One of the most important factors in our degree of certainty is how tightly we have controlled things to satisfy the condition of ceteris paribus.

Experimental Control and the Ceteris Paribus Assumption

To show that a causal relationship exists, we must demonstrate that the change in X is correlated with a change in Y, and assure that everything else remains the same.

The most common way to do this is through controlled experimentation. In a controlled study, we hold everything constant except a suspected cause or experimental factor X. We then vary the level of that factor and measure any changes in Y. If we vary X and there is no change in Y then, of course, no causal relation can be inferred. If, on the other hand, we hold everything equal but the suspected cause and variations in it produce variations in the outcome Y, we can reasonably conclude that any difference must have been the result of the variation in the experimental factor or procedure. The paradigm for such a study in physics or chemistry is given below:

Experimental Condition

Substance A
  plus laboratory conditions
  plus experimental procedure (X)

                    . . . is followed by . . . substance Y.

Control Condition

Substance A
  plus laboratory conditions
  without experimental procedure (X)

                    . . . is followed by . . . substance A.

We think the logic of the above is clear. If the two substances (A) were identical and treated in identical fashion with the exception that one received the experimental treatment X (suppose for example, exposure to heat of a certain temperature) and the second did not, any resulting difference must be attributable to that procedure, as there is nothing else that could have caused the difference.

Nothing else, that is, unless there is a *confounding factor*, an undetected difference between the experimental condition and control condition. In that case, ceteris paribus was not met, and the logic of control was violated. Therefore, the conclusion that heat (in this example) is a causal factor may be erroneous, since something else may have caused the change. In the physics or the chemistry laboratory, it is not a simple matter to avoid confounding factors and thereby avoid violating the assumption of ceteris paribus. Such things as location in a laboratory, differential exposure to light, contamination of specimens, among others, can all lead to violation of ceteris paribus and can lead the scientist to attribute a finding to her experimental procedure when, in fact, it was produced by some uncontrolled variable. Careless handling of the specimen might contaminate the experimental or control substance such that the scientist attributes the outcome to the heat, whereas heat was a necessary factor but not a sufficient cause, and the contaminant was also necessary to produce the result. The only final defense against such errors is repeated testing in a wide variety of laboratories, because it is unlikely that the same contamination would result in each test.

Experimental Control in the Biological and Social Sciences

When attempting to develop experimental procedures for biological systems, the problems of assuring ceteris paribus are increased enormously. For one, it is almost impossible to obtain identical specimens for analysis, because different samples of biological systems vary much more than do samples of inorganic compounds. One can reasonably expect that a piece of platinum purified in the same test tube, when cut in half, will produce two identical samples. It is far more difficult to produce identical specimens of biological substances such as blood or tissue. Where can one find two identical organisms? Identical people? For example, without identical experimental subjects in a medical experiment, how is one to distinguish a necessary from a contributory factor in a cure that only works for some people some of the time. In other words, since organisms, and human beings in particular, are reactive in ways that inorganic compounds are not, a procedure may affect one individual differently from another, so that unless one can obtain identical individuals, one can never completely satisfy ceteris paribus, even with stringent controls.

Statistical Controls

As a means of approximating controlled experimentation, the biological and social sciences employ a variety of what are called "statistical controls." A simple example should illustrate the strategy. Suppose we are attempting to determine whether or not a new infant formula reduces the incidence of diaper rash. If we could find a pair of identical twins who were treated identically by their parents, then we might want to try the experiment on them. We would provide one child with the new formula and the second one with an identical formula without the new ingredient. We would instruct the mother to treat the children identically and then measure the extent of diaper rash on both after some reasonable time period. That sounds like the solution, but what if one twin happened to contract a virus while the other did not? How can we be sure they were treated *the same* by their parents? Such confounding factors cannot be ruled out. In practice, assuring "identity" in biological subjects is almost impossible, except under very special circumstances.

Random Samples

The use of statistical controls based on the theory of random sampling allows for a different strategy. Instead of obtaining identical subjects, we might attempt to obtain groups or samples of subjects that we believe differ in no important way. But how do we assure that our experimental group and our control group do not, in fact, differ in important ways?

From what we have learned about sampling, we know that a random sample of sufficient size will be representative of the population from which it is drawn. The larger the sample, the more it will be similar to the population. Therefore, if we take two random samples from a population, since they are both representative of the larger population, they should be similar to each other. Furthermore, the larger the sample size, the more similar to each other they are likely to be. In the limiting case, if our sample size were the same as the population size the samples (in this case the total population) would be the same and so, therefore, would any measurement made on them.

Practically speaking, we cannot perform an experiment on all the babies born in the United States. Therefore, we must limit ourselves to relatively modest samples. Following normal procedures, we would obtain two samples of babies. We would provide one sample with the new experimental formula and the other with a control formula, and measure any differences in diaper rash on a daily basis over a period of, say, three months. We would, of course, try to assure that other factors such as diet, bathing, etc., were not changed by the parents as a result of their being in the experiment.

The paradigm for such a statistically controlled experiment would look so:

Randomly sampled experimental group size = 25	Prescribed diet + with new ingredient	Number of days = with diaper rash in period
Randomly sampled control group size = 25	Same prescribed + diet without new ingredient	Number of days = with diaper rash in period

If there were any difference in the outcome (number of days with diaper rash in three month period), we could conclude that one of the following hypotheses is correct.

1. The difference was caused by some confounding factor such as a disease or different handling by the mothers, etc., produced by the experiment or from some bias in the original selection of the samples.
2. The difference merely reflects normal variation between the groups, which is to be expected when one samples less than the whole population.
3. The difference was caused by the new ingredient.
4. Some combination of the above.

But which hypothesis is correct? If we have chosen truly random samples and if we have tried to assure similar treatment, we can exclude #1 with some confidence. Why should one set of children be more prone to disease than the other, or more like to receive poor care? Remember, things like disease proneness and mothering-style are characteristics of the total population, and all random samples should approximate the incidence of such factors about equally since all are randomly drawn from and hence reflect the total population. We would, if we could, prefer to perform the study in a hospital where ceteris paribus is easier to assure.

If we are prepared to reject #1 as the causal factor, then the difference we found could only result from #2 or #3. If we can eliminate #2 as a reason, we can with confidence conclude that our new formula works, that it is a benefit to babies. Number 2 presents a problem because the two samples of babies will almost always differ to some degree, and that difference might be what caused the difference in outcome. While we cannot eliminate the possibility of such differences, we can, fortunately, get an idea of how large such differences are likely to be. We can obtain a more precise estimate of the range of differences that can be expected between two random samples taken from the same population.

Statistically Significant Differences

Imagine that you took a random sample of 25 people from the population of a large college and calculated the average height of the people in the sample, giving you a sample mean. Suppose you took another sample of 25 and did the same thing. Having done that, you then calculated the difference between the means of these two groups. Imagine doing the same thing a couple of hundred times and in each case calculating the difference between the two sample means you obtained. If you conscientiously did as you were told, you would have a long list of some several hundred numbers representing the differences between two sample means drawn from the same population.

If you studied the list, certain things would become obvious to you. The first would be that the average difference would be very close to zero, since sometimes the first sample will have a higher mean than the second, producing a positive difference, and sometimes the second will be higher, producing a negative difference, but overall the difference will cancel each other out. Furthermore, if you did the work all over again but this time took larger samples, you would find that the differences the second time would be smaller. This is so because as the sample size gets larger, the samples are more similar to the parent population, and hence the samples will be less different from each other. Very large samples will be almost identical.

In short, we can determine the relative likelihood of any difference between means that would result purely as a consequence of sampling, i.e., error (in estimating the population mean) due to sampling less than the whole population. *Sampling error* (McCall 1986, p. 181; Ferguson 1966, p. 135) here does not mean an error in something we have done. It rather refers to the fact that any estimate of the population mean will be only approximated by a measure made on some sample, and therefore the sample estimate is necessarily somewhat *in error*.

Returning to our diaper rash experiment, if there were no difference at all between the groups we would have to conclude that the new ingredient wasn't effective. However, what if the difference were such that on average the experimental group suffered 25 days of diaper rash, and the control group, on average, suffered on 30 days. What can we conclude about that? Can we conclude that our formula helped the babies? It depends, first, on the sample size, and, second, on the typical variation in such groups of children. If such a difference were most unusual, we could conclude that it probably resulted from the formula. Practically speaking, we would apply a statistical test (in this case we would use the t-test for differences between means) that would tell us whether this difference in days of discomfort is greater than would be expected from simple sampling variation alone. If it is, we can conclude that the difference between formulas is *statistically significant*.

Statisticians refer to possibility that a finding is the result of sampling error as the *null hypothesis*. It is the hypothesis that no experimental effect took place. In effect, a statistical test is one in which the null hypothesis is pitted against the hypothesis that the difference was produced by the experimental factor. If the scientist can reject the null hypothesis, *and if ceteris paribus has been assured*, he is left with the experimental hypothesis as the only option remaining.

One point is worth noting. Since almost any difference is at least theoretically possible, even very large differences could result from sampling error at least some of the time. In other words, some differences that are very unlikely are still possible. What the researcher has to do, therefore, is determine how unlikely a difference must be, if he is to conclude that it was not the result of sampling error, but rather the result of his ingredient or procedure. The probability he settles on is known as his confidence level, i.e. it determines how confident he is in concluding that a meaningful experimental effect was detected in his research. Theoretically he could choose any confidence level, but social and biological scientists generally choose confidence levels of 95% or 99%.

A scientist knows that some difference between his control group and the experimental group is inevitable. Thus, *before* he begins his study he must decide how often he will accept a finding as the result of his experimental factor when it really was just a product of random variation. For a scientist to choose a 95% confidence level means that he is taking a calculated risk that in 5 out of 100 cases he will make such a mistake. If he chooses the 99% level, he risks making that mistake only 1 in 100 times. An experimenter who finds a difference that could on average only occur 1 out of 100 times by chance variation alone has a choice, in effect, between concluding that in this particular experiment he has had the misfortune of producing that 1 in 100 chance event or that, rather, the difference he found was *real*, i.e., produced by his experimental variable. If he chooses the latter, he will, of course, be wrong in 1 out of 100 cases.

This last point is important and suggests that even tightly controlled experiments can occasionally provide inaccurate information. In general, we feel more confident that a result is reliable if it has been replicated in other experiments. This is because the likelihood of getting that 1 in 100 event, by sampling error alone, in repeated experiments is much less than in a one shot case. (Remember that the probability of getting two events in a row each with probability of .01 is .01 × .01 or .0001.)

You have probably seen reports of polls that state such things as: "55% of the population favors the death penalty with a margin of error of plus or minus 3%." The information given tells you that the polling organization took a sample large enough to assure that it would be within 3 percentage points of the actual percentage of the population as a whole. Another way of saying this is that the poll taker has chosen the 94% (probably the 95%) confidence level. And that he is sure, with that confidence level, that 95% of samples of that size would approximate the population by no more than plus or minus 2½%. Of course five out of a hundred samples will be wrong by more than that amount. The poll taker knows that, because he can calculate for any given sample size what sorts of deviations from the true population measure he is likely to get. As we discussed in Chapter IV, as the samples get larger they will more closely approximate the population. In a close election with polls showing the leader ahead by 1%, a 95% confidence level (with a margin of error of plus or minus 2½%) ought not to give a politician too much confidence.

The Detection Problem: False Negatives and False Positives

The problem for the decision-maker can also be formulated as a detection problem in that he has detected a difference, and he must decide whether the difference he has found is real in the above sense. If he sets his confidence level too high, he may fail to detect a real difference in the population and attribute the difference to sampling error. Such errors are known as *false negatives* in that the scientist falsely rejected the hypothesis that the difference was real. On the other hand, if he sets his confidence level too low, he may falsely conclude that the difference he found was the result of his experimental factor when, in fact, it was produced by chance variation. These types of errors are known as *false positives*.

For instance, if the decision-maker uses a lenient confidence level of .90, he is more likely to commit a false positive error and conclude that a finding is significant and therefore meaningful, than if he chose a stricter 99 percent level. But in choosing the higher level, he increases the likelihood of a false negative error, of failing to conclude that a difference was real, when in fact it was.

What type of error should you be more concerned with? It all depends on what you are trying to accomplish. If you are trying to determine whether a particular type of advertising campaign will be effective, and have decided to devote millions of dollars to the ad campaign if you think it is, you are probably well-advised to avoid false positives, since in that case your money will be thrown away. If, on the other hand, you are searching for drugs to improve the life expectancy of AIDS patients, you should probably be more concerned with avoiding false negatives. That would be a case where the drug really did work, but you set your confidence level so high you failed to detect it. If you made that error you might abandon a line of research which, had you continued with it, might have produced meaningful improvements for AIDS patients.

A similar problem arises when using tests for selection for job placement or for college admission, as well as for medical diagnosis. Since no test is perfect, every time a test is given it will produce a slightly different result. Each testing is, therefore, composed of two parts: one that reflects some underlying ability or condition in an individual, and a second part that is the result of normal variation in testing. If we decide that a cholesterol level above 200 is the cutoff mark for a "cholesterol problem," we will necessarily produce both false negatives and false positives. In other words, some people will be classified as requiring treatment when they really don't need it (false positives), while some who need treatment won't receive it because they will be erroneously classified as *normal* (false negatives). As in the statistical problem, trying to reduce one error increases the likelihood of the other error.

The normal variation in ability and aptitude testing means that institutions that rely on them will accept some people they shouldn't and deny admittance to some they should accept. Many colleges, aware of this problem, suggest that applicants take the exam twice to reduce this possibility. Note, however, that it is possible for a person to score above or below their *true* ability level on both occasions, even though the combination of both scores, since it is a larger sample, is likely to be closer to the truth. A very large sample of such testings is likely to provide an even closer approximation to the truth, but is, usually, impractical.

Statistically Significant vs. Important

The use of the word "significant" in statistics has caused much needless misunderstanding. All the word means in statistics is that a difference is unlikely to have been the result of chance, or normal sample variation. More precisely, it means that the probability that chance produced the difference is an acceptable risk to the researcher given his significance level. It means no more than that. Without knowing the confidence level chosen, we cannot even determine how unlikely the result was. What we do know is that if the typical variation in the population is small and the samples chosen are large, some exceedingly small differences will be determined to be "statistically significant."

It is important to understand that for a scientist working on a problem such as AIDS, any difference at all that is real, is important. It tells him he is on to something, that he is not barking up the wrong tree. The problem arises when his work is reported out of context. It is very important when evaluating a statistical finding that is significant, to take the following into consideration.

1. How large was the difference? If the difference is small, it may be practically unimportant in most cases, even though it was "significant."
2. What were the experimental circumstances in which the difference was found? Is it reasonable to generalize from the laboratory setting to the real life setting where we are going to apply the information?

Consider the following examples.

When the large New York City Westway project was being studied for its impact on Hudson River fish, the Army Corps of Engineers stated in their draft report that the project would have a "significant adverse impact" on fish life, "though not critical." In their revised final report, they said that the effect on fish life would be perceptible, but "difficult to discern from normal yearly fluctuations." The Court of Appeals, concerned about this apparent turnaround, demanded an explanation of how a significant adverse impact could become "barely perceptible." The Corps was unable to convince the justices that a "statistically significant effect" could be very unimportant, and the Westway proposal was aborted. According to representative Bill Green "The Court of Appeals . . . found the explanation to be Orwellian-like 'doublespeak' " (New York Times, Letters, Nov. 9, 1985).

Some psychologists (Bandura, Ross, and Ross 1963) have reported that boys who had been exposed to filmed violence were found to engage in significantly more violent acts than boys who were not exposed to such filmed activity. In one such study, the acts of violence consisted of punching a bobo doll. The problem here is to avoid jumping to the wrong conclusions. One should immediately ask. What sort of acts were measured? What was the precise difference? Was it a 50 percent increase or a 10 percent increase or a 2 percent increase? What was the nature of the film the boys saw and the setting in which they saw it. What are the implications of this finding to everyday life? If the study indicated a difference, let us imagine, of 10 percent between the boys who viewed violent TV and those who did not, does that mean eliminating violence from TV would, in fact, produce a 10 percent decrease in violence among the young in the world outside the laboratory. What types of boys were studied? It would make a difference if they were in a reformatory. Did the finding hold for all boys or only some? What might be some of the other consequences of such a move? Might it make TV-watching among boys, perhaps violent boys, less desirable, in which case they would spend more time simply "hanging out" and, as boys will be boys, engage in aggressive activities for want of something better to do with their time?

The problem illustrated by the second example is known as the *in vitro-in vivo* problem. This is the difference between the result obtained in the test tube (in vitro) versus what can be expected in life (in vivo). Has the scientist in his attempt to obtain adequate "control" created an experimental setting so different from any real life setting as to make generalization dubious or unreasonable. When a study can be generalized outside of the lab setting, it is said to have *external validity*. Many studies produce interesting findings that would be dangerous to rely upon since they lack external validity.

In short, a statistically significant finding is extremely important to scientists involved in teasing out the meaning of particular relationships. For the layman, a report of such a finding should produce a lot of questioning to determine the relevance of the finding to his own life or to his decisions in the public policy area. Too often such findings are bandied about to support a particular ideological or political position, and here, as always, a healthy skepticism is in order.

An Example

Suppose you are the principal of a high school and have been receiving requests from parents to introduce an after school prep course to aid students in preparing for the SAT. Since such an undertaking is expensive and you have a limited budget, you feel you need some evidence that such courses do, in fact, help people. In studying the literature, you find that by and large there is much controversy about this. The people who provide such courses claim they raise student scores. Critics contend that there has been insufficient evidence and lack of controlled experimentation.

Suppose you decided to go ahead and do your own experiment during the coming fall semester. How would you go about it? You might just introduce one section and test those students who sign up before and after they take the course. If the students did better after than before they took the course you might want to conclude that the course was a success. But how would you know that the improvement resulted only from the course, or that any of the improvement was the result of the course? Maybe students generally improve during the fall semester in any case. You have no way of knowing if the improvement you measured was really any better than such *natural* improvement. Since you have no control group to compare their performance with you cannot really conclude anything about the causal relationship between any improvement and the taking of the course. You would have committed the fallacy of *no control*.

Suppose you decided to include a control group in your study. If that group did nothing, you would be in danger that it was not the prep course *per se* that improved performance but something else about going to class after school. You would not have satisfied the ceteris paribus condition. Suppose you had as the control group students enrolled in another after school course, such as one on film appreciation. Suppose that students who took the prep course did better than the film students, and that difference was significant, i.e., greater than chance variation would predict. Can you conclude that the prep course did the trick? The answer is no, since the students in the two groups were probably different to start with. Perhaps only highly motivated, and highly qualified students enrolled in the prep course. Your control group and experimental group were not random samples of the population of interest. You would probably be on firmer ground if you randomly assigned half the students to the prep course and the other half to a similar course that was not designed to improve SAT scores, but was similar in all other ways. The difficulty of finding such a control condition, explains the paucity of the research in this area. The problem here is to avoid erroneous conclusions based on the fallacy of *inadequate control*.

To test the assertion that a course specifically designed to improve students' SAT performance will do better than no course and better than a similar classroom experience, would require that you do the following:

1. Randomly select a sample of students from the population of all those who will take the SAT.
2. Randomly select another group in the same way.
3. Randomly select a group of students who will receive no treatment at all.
3. Choose your confidence level.
4. Give one group the prep course and the other group a course with about the same amount of reading and mathematics in it, such as a course in decision-making, as an approximate control condition.
5. Test the two groups at the end of the semester. If the difference is greater than your significance level, you can conclude that the prep course is more effective in raising SAT scores than the alternative course. You would also want to compare both groups to the randomly selected group of students who did nothing at all, since maybe both courses made a difference.
6. Determine whether the difference produced by the course is important enough to expend the resources to make it available to all students. A difference of ten points might be statistically significant, but practically not worth the cost.

Even if you followed the above steps, there are certain dangers you should be aware of in evaluating the above experiment. All of the following are common confounding factors in experiments without controls, and are sometimes problems if controls are inadequate.

Placebo Effects

A common problem with research with human beings is known as the *placebo effect*. Placebo effects are common in medicine; they are the fairly frequent beneficial results obtained from medications or procedures that can be shown to result merely from the expectation of benefit. If people think a drug will help them, it very often will even if it is chemically inactive. Often, in such cases, the medical benefit is real and measurable, but even if there is no discernable medical improvement, patients often claim to feel better. How are we to control for the possibility that our students will do better on the SAT merely because they believe that taking a prep course will help them? Maybe their belief in the course will make them more confident and less nervous, and maybe they will do better for that reason and not because of the course content.

In medical research, this problem is overcome with *double blind* research in which identical looking medications are dispensed to experimental and control groups (subjects are blind to the effect) by nurses who do not know which is which (they are also blinded to the effect). But how do we get an adequate control in case of the prep course? We have tried to control for the prep course with another course in decision-making, and we may even suggest to the students that this is a good preparation for the SAT. But will the students be taken in? Probably not, unless we are very ingenious, and even then we will probably have to accept only "limited control."

Hawthorne Effects

A second closely related phenomenon is known as the *Hawthorne Effect*. Consider what happens when a new procedure is introduced into a school curriculum, a new method to teach math, for instance. There is usually a preparatory period, perhaps during the summer when the teachers are prepped. There are usually people spending a lot of time during the school year assessing, advising, admonishing. All this activity keeps the teachers on guard and to some extent on their toes, which is, of course, what is supposed to happen; everyone wants the new method to succeed. And if the students at the end of year have in, fact, performed better than controls using the old method, can we conclude the new method is better? Not yet. We must wait a year or two or three to see if the new method continues to excel. In any organization, the heightened interest and attention given to a group undergoing some change tends to enhance their performance. This is known as the *Hawthorne Effect*. It is extremely difficult to control for and generally a "wait and see" attitude is advised. Many a highly praised and "effective" reform in industry or education has turned out to be a clunker when the dust finally settled.

Experimental Mortality: The Case of Disappearing Subjects

Suppose a college were to claim that it can dramatically improve its students' reasoning ability. It claims to demonstrate this by showing that entering freshman had a mean IQ of 110, whereas graduating seniors had a mean IQ of 130. What they fail to mention is that the freshman class had 300 members, of whom only 100 graduated. Would you go to Mensa University to sharpen your mind?

This is a problem in any experiment or study that takes place over long periods of time and in which some effort is required of subjects— to travel to a laboratory, to keep a diary, to keep up with a rigorous diet or exercise program or program of study. If more subjects in the experimental group quit or drop out than do those in the control group, then the result could be almost totally the result of subject differences. Perhaps those who remained were more highly motivated, more willing to follow instructions, had more organized lives, etc. In our example, suppose the prep course were more rigorous and required more home work than the control course, so that more experimental subjects dropped out of it. If the students who remained were the *serious* ones, then of course one would expect them to do better whether they took the course or not.

In general, if *before and after* claims of improvement are made, check to see if there were adequate controls. If there were no controls and no figures on dropout rates, be very suspicious.

Regression to the Mean

Jill is a high school junior with excellent grades who has always done well on standardized tests. She took the SAT and got a disappointing combined score of 910. She was informed that practicing yoga before her next attempt was likely to help, and she followed that advice. Upon retaking the exam, her score rose to 1150, and she concluded that yoga did the trick. Do you think you could explain to Jill why her reasoning here is erroneous?

If we consider the idea of performances, we can say that people or processes have *expected* or *mean* levels of performance at any particular time. It may be a bowling average, a particular level of accomplishment in piano, distance from the bull's eye in archery, expected gross sales in a deli, or the average weight of an automobile coming off the production line. By definition, these mean levels are the levels that are most likely to be produced. Unless each performance is identical there will be variations from the average, but the probability that the average will come about is always higher than the probability of any other level of performance or outcome. Thus, if someone or some process produces an outcome very deviant from what is expected based on its true average, then the probability is high that the next outcome will be closer to the mean or expected value. If an automobile's average weight on a production run is 2,000 pounds, and one comes off the line at 2,050 pounds, which is very deviant, then we should expect the next car will be closer to the expected value of 2,000. If not, then there may be something wrong and probably the average is no longer 2,000 pounds.

The same is true with performance on, for example, a standardized test. If you perform much less well than you have reason to expect, it is more likely than not that your next performance will be closer to expectation, and you will probably do better. That is because standardized tests, as discussed earlier, even quite valid ones, are not perfect and cannot measure your real ability, but can only approximate your real ability. Any valid test score is thus a combination of your real ability and the normal variation that is to be expected. If you deviate a lot today, you will probably deviate less tomorrow.

Beware, however. We are not saying that the deviant performance in any way affects the next performance. That would be to commit the gambler's fallacy. The reason that the more expected performance usually follows a deviant one is because the more expected performance is *always* more expected. This tendency for more expected outcomes to follow less expected outcomes is known as *regression to the mean*.

Daniel Kahneman and Amos Tversky (1983) report that flight instructors they witnessed would criticize pilots whose landings were below expectations, and praise those who did better than expected. They found that especially good landings were followed by landings that were not as good, and really bad landings were followed by landings that were much better. The instructors concluded that criticism is a better motivator than praise. Were they right? Probably not, since regression to the mean appears to be a better explanation.

The only defense against this error is adequate controls. Imagine a remediation program to help slow math learners, which is instituted in a school district and targets the bottom 10 percent of third graders in math performance. Students included in that 10 percent probably have weak ability, but probably also had bad luck on the day they took the test and performed worse than even they should have. The next time such students take an exam, they may still lack ability, but since they will undoubtedly, as a group, have better luck, their scores will rise. The only adequate control would be another group of low scorers who did not take remediation. If you merely measured one group's improvement before and after remediation, they will appear to improve, but you will not know whether the improvement indicates that the remedial program worked or merely reflects regression to the mean.

This phenomenon is so pervasive that it has even given rise to a theory of stock market investing known as the *contrarian investment strategy*. In this strategy you look for stocks that have performed much worse than the market as a whole, and if one can find no obvious reason for the poor performance, buy them. The theory is that, barring good reasons, these stocks are performing worse than they should for reasons of normal chance variation, and should therefore do better in the future. They should, that is, regress to their mean performance. Of course, the same holds for performance that is better than expected. Many an investor has been disappointed by putting his money in the mutual fund that had the best track record during the past year. Was the outstanding performance based on sound management? How much was the performance the result of luck? If it were the latter, it is likely that the fund will return to its more expected performance and won't do as well the next go around.

Nonexperimental Survey Research

A great deal, perhaps most, of the everyday reporting of social science research in the popular media deals with survey data giving descriptive statistics such as unemployment rates, school drop out rates, etc. Very often, certain trends are noted, e.g., unemployment has risen during the last six months. Equally often, correlations are made and causes inferred. For instance, it is often reported that women on average earn about two-thirds what men earn. Some conclude that the reason for this is that women are being discriminated against and that something should be done about this discrimination. Now it may be true that women are treated unfairly in the marketplace, but there is hardly any evidence for that in the findings of differential earnings.

The propensity to jump to unwarranted conclusions is nowhere more apparent in the media than in the attempt to infer a cause from a simple correlation. But as we earlier warned, correlations by themselves do not justify inferring causal relations.

Ceteris Paribus in Survey Research

A common social science enterprise is to take interesting classes of people, such as men and women, or Jews and Protestants and Catholics, and attempt to determine if they, as classes, differ on any common measure, such as liberalism, income, or football watching. There is nothing inherently wrong in doing this, but it is dangerous if one jumps to unwarranted conclusions based on the correlations so obtained.

The reasons for this danger are rather straightforward. Since the process of breaking human beings into classes is rather arbitrary, one ends up with classes of people who differ in one way, such as religion, but may also differ in other important ways such as education, or average age of marriage, or culturally preferred occupations. In other words, since it is almost never the case that everything else is equal, we are more than usually troubled by violations of ceteris paribus.

For instance, what is one to make of a hypothetical finding that German Americans, as a class, have higher family incomes than Irish Americans, as a class? If we could be assured that the German Americans and the Irish Americans differed in no other way, then we could assert with some assurance that there is something about being a German American in itself that provides for higher income.

But of course, that is ridiculous. There must be something that German Americans do, or are, that accounts for the difference in family income. Could it be family size or the number of family members who work? Perhaps education plays a role. Perhaps German Americans prefer certain occupations that provide higher salaries. Perhaps they marry later and have fewer children. Maybe they are older as a group and so benefit from the advantages accruing to the older worker? Maybe they have been in America for more generations, and therefore find it easier to make their way in the American marketplace.

Clearly all of the above factors may be important, perhaps all are, in explaining a rather interesting if mystifying difference between two groups. The point here is that an interesting correlation such as that between group membership and family income is merely the jumping off point for an investigation to explain the correlation. The correlation, in and of itself, has no explanatory power.

The above point is often lost in political and ideological disputes where assigning blame seems more important than finding sound explanations. Thomas Sowell (1984), who has devoted a career to an attempt to unravel ethnic group differences, has been attacked for "blaming the victim," because he insists upon analyzing all possible explanations for group differences in family income, rather than accept the simplistic assertion that such differences are solely the result of prejudice and discrimination. He argues that while discrimination and prejudice no doubt exist, they can hardly be the only cause for such differences. The argument between Sowell and his critics need not detain us here. The issue is that given such correlations it is critically important to closely examine what factors are thrown into the bag labelled "black," or "German American," or "women." The need to understand the world, to understand what goes with what, and what causes what is too important for rational decision-making to adopt simplistic postures. In human affairs, very little is simple. There are probably a whole host of reasons why black Americans, for instance, score lower on the SAT tests than white Americans. To suggest that the difference is merely the result of discrimination is as silly as to assert that it is merely the result of differences in ability. A host of factors, such as family education, age of parents, number of parents at home, number of siblings, quality of schooling, peer experience, cultural traditions and values, job prospects, parental and community discipline, to name but a few possible factors, certainly play a role. Only when one has examined all the possible contributing factors can one begin to claim any understanding of the relationship.

Determining Cause by Statistical Decomposition

Remember, evidence for cause requires correlation and the ceteris paribus condition. In the case of gender and differential income, we would have to show that if the women in question had been men then there would be no difference in salary. This is, of course, impossible. Furthermore, it is just about impossible to set up an experiment in which everything else but gender would be equal. When the statistician attempts to understand why it is that females earn less than males, therefore, he generally attempts to break up or decompose the groups into smaller groups in which the ceteris paribus assumption more nearly applies. For instance the groups of men and women would be further broken down into groups that are similar on other important measures, such as:

a: Men,   aged X, occupation Y, years of service Z
b: Women, aged X, occupation Y, years of service Z

If men and women who are similar in ways X, Y, and Z still earn different amounts of money, he feels more confident that the difference is, in fact, attributable to gender, since these apparently important factors in income level have been taken into account. But there are other important factors besides age, occupation, and years of service. It is important to avoid attributing a cause falsely, we commit the *fallacy of inadequate decomposition* when we fail to thoroughly examine all the characteristics associated with the purported cause, and for that reason violate ceteris paribus. In the above instance, the scientist has not looked at education and marital status, both of which could have an impact. What if he were to break down the groups even further by factoring in education and marital status? If the income difference still remains, then he feels even more confident that gender is the culprit, since everything else appears to be equal. But here is the sticking point—what is it about gender that produced the difference? It is difficult to be certain that everything else is really equal. Maybe a difference is related to something subtle and difficult to assess, such as a difference in attitude toward work and family, ego involvement, or biological differences in temperament. Perhaps it is the result of prejudicial attitudes, or of outright discrimination. Perhaps it is some factor no one has yet thought about, all of which merely highlights the point that a correlation is only the first step in understanding. It tells us there is something that needs explaining, it doesn't do the explaining for us.

Many statisticians have claimed that they can do almost as well as the experimenter by using this sort of decomposition, by using "statistical controls." While such work is important and worthwhile, the conclusions generated are and must remain considerably more suspect than those produced in the laboratory. Jumping on the simplest or most plausible explanation may be satisfying, but it is rarely useful, except to forward ideological and political agendas. It is important to avoid the fallacy of inadequate decomposition.

The Problem of Limited Range

We have seen that we often attribute causes where only correlations exist. There is an opposite problem: we may fail to detect a causal relationship because there doesn't appear to be a correlation. That is often the case when we look at a group that is very homogeneous in some measure.

Consider Highbrow University, which only accepts students with combined SAT scores of 1300 or better. The admissions office has decided to discontinue the requirement that students submit SAT scores, because it has found no relation between a student's score on the test and a graduate's GPA. Is that a wise decision? The problem here is that the test may be quite good at predicting scores over the full range from 200 to 1600, but within any subrange it may be totally useless. If you only look at very capable students with extremely high college aptitudes then, of course, other factors, such as motivation, may be far more important.

Thomas Sowell (1984) has suggested that, by the same reasoning, the American Basketball Association might conclude that there is no relation between height and success in their sport, since clearly among people over six foot five other factors seem to be more important; or that age has no effect on sexual vigor, since a study of men in an old age home found no difference in sexual potency that in any way related to age. Octogenarian males seemed equally vigorous or as lacking in vigor as men in their seventies.

The point to remember is that if a group you are looking at happens to be very homogeneous with regard to some measure or characteristic, that characteristic is not likely to be important in explaining differences within the group. However, the same characteristic might be very important, as a causal factor for the population at large. This is especially important to keep in mind, since most of us operate within a relatively restricted range of people with whom we share similar incomes, education, or family composition. It is easy to assume that something that seems unimportant as a causal agent among the people we know is unimportant in general.

Demographic Factors

In general, we refer to characteristics of groups of people such as average age, average family composition, location, or typical occupation as *demographic factors*. Such factors often have important effects on outcome measures such as family income. To repeat our earlier point, whenever groups differ on one factor they almost always differ on many other factors. Similarly over time a group may undergo numerous changes, some of which may be the causes, others the results. Here also it is not always easy to determine which is cause and which effect. Consider the following examples.

A recent report indicated that while the economy was expanding and the employment rate increasing, paradoxically, per capita income was declining. What is one to make of that? What this suggests is that the new jobs must be low paying jobs. But why should that be so? Some have suggested that this is because the expansion of new jobs takes place in low paying service areas, such as in fast-food outlets. However, other statistics suggest that new jobs are increasing most rapidly in professional and managerial positions. What's up? Maybe nothing more than the demographic fact that in a rapidly expanding economy, new jobs are likely to open rapidly for people who have never worked before, such as young people fresh out of school; housewives who are tempted by higher wages to take jobs; or people with marginal skills who would not have been hired in a sluggish economy. In all these cases, the salaries of the new workers should be below the average for no other reason than lack of experience and seniority. New doctors earn less than experienced doctors, but no one would claim that medicine is a low wage occupation. In short, in any rapidly expanding economy that creates many new jobs, a majority of those jobs, in whatever field, will be paid less than the average, and hence per capita income may decline for that reason.

In the thirties, a study concluded that IQ declines with age. The researchers had measured the IQ of young people and of old people, and the young people had higher average IQs. But as everyone now knows, IQ is very much related to education and—you guessed it, in 1930 most older people had far less education than younger people. If you take one group of people and measure their IQs as they age, IQ does not, in fact, decline significantly until senility sets in.

Asians with Ph.D.'s earn more than Hispanics with Ph.D.'s. Why? For one reason, most Asians study in the sciences and other technical areas, whereas Hispanics, to a large degree, obtain training in areas such as education, social science, and similar fields that pay considerably less than fields requiring technical training (Sowell 1984).

Crime began to rise in the mid-'60s and did so until around 1980. Why? One factor is age. The postwar baby boom came of age in the 1960s and started to mature in the 1980s. A cursory glance at crime statistics will show that the age group 15 to 24 is a disproportionately crime-prone group. Any demographic trend that increases the proportion of 15 to 24 year olds in the population will almost always be accompanied by an increase in crime, illegitimacy, and other signs of social disruption, such as drug and alcohol abuse, suicide, and auto accidents, as well. Insurance companies charge young males more for auto insurance because young males are statistically shown to have more accidents.

Jews, as a group, earn a great deal more money than Puerto Ricans, as a group. There may, of course, be many reasons for this, but watch out for demographic factors. The average age of Jews is about forty, which is twice that of Puerto Ricans, whose average age is approximately twenty. Any group of forty-year-olds will earn a great deal more than any group of twenty-year-olds. For the same reason, all other things being equal, crime rates and illegitimacy rates should be higher among Puerto Ricans than among Jews. Forty-year-old women, by and large, give birth to fewer illegitimate offspring than do twenty-year-old women. When groups differ, check age differences (Sowell 1984).

Family income of Japanese is quite high. Why? One factor surely is that "family" income is very much dependent on the number of family members who have income. Japanese families, it so happens (Sowell 1984) have an average of almost three working members, while most other groups have two or fewer members who work. Two may be company, but, in general, a crowd of three will earn more, and it hardly matters, on average, what they work at.

Infant mortality among the poor is high compared to infant mortality among the middle classes. Why? Because poor mothers are often teenagers, whereas middle-class mothers are usually in their twenties. Children of teenage mothers have a higher rate of prenatal and postnatal difficulties.

Death from cancer and heart attacks has grown steadily during this century. Why? One reason is the dramatic decline of diseases of childhood and middle age. The result is that more people live long enough to die of heart disease and cancer.

Family income among Americans of African descent is much lower than family income among Americans of Asian descent. Is that because Asians work harder? Is that because African Americans are discriminated against? Maybe. But Black families, to a greater extent, are single-parent families, whereas Asian families are more often two-parent families. Two parents are likely to earn more than one parent, no matter what the source of income, and no matter how hard they work.

In general, if two groups differ on some factor of interest, consider such other possible differences as may contribute in a causal way to the noted difference, such as:

Average age;
Average family size;
Average level of education;
Quality of education;
Cultural traditions such as
   occupational preference and avoidance,
   age of marriage,
   inclination to save and invest,
   inclination to divorce,
   time of immigration to the United States;
Geographic location;
Etc.

Extrapolation Studies

Sometimes we have to make a decision to take some action or not, whose likely consequences are unknown. Should a school district undertake the task of building a new school? The answer depends on whether there will be more children entering school five or ten years from now. How do we know? We might ask people how many children they intend to have and use that information. But that doesn't take into account the rate at which people come to and leave the town. In such cases, about all the information we have is about what has already happened.

Suppose we have launched a public relations campaign for a political candidate, and have discovered that when we doubled the money spent on TV, his popularity rose 5 percent. Will he gain another 5 percent in the ratings if we double the expenditure again?

In cases like this, where we base our estimate of the overall relationship between two variables on the relationship between them over some limited range, we are engaging in *extrapolation*. Very often the information we get by extrapolating is worthwhile, but sometimes it is not. Extrapolation is a very tricky business.

Extrapolating Over Time

"If world population were to increase at the current rate, human beings would be standing shoulder to shoulder on every land mass by the year 2100." All of us have heard such talk and rarely take it seriously. It is good that we do not. The statement is patently nonsensical. Long before such an outcome would occur, world population would be halted for a variety of reasons, not least of which would be Malthus's three ugly horsemen; pestilence, famine, and war. There is nothing wrong with noting a trend and imagining what would happen if it were to continue for some particular length of time. It is often an amusing entertainment. Sometimes it can be very useful; sometimes it is dangerous for the rational decision-maker.

Once again "ceteris paribus" is the necessary ingredient. The usual extrapolation carries a hidden assumption, and such statements might better read, "If nothing else changes, and the current trend continues, then such and such will be the case." What is usually left out of the analysis is that as a trend continues, it almost always causes changes in other factors that make it more or less likely for the trend to continue. In this century, population projections have been almost always wrong, for that reason.

Consider the spread of AIDS. When it was first detected, the number of cases doubled almost every year. Some people alarmingly suggested that if the rate of increase were to continue, in a short time virtually everyone would be infected. However, once the ways in which the disease is spread became known, many people altered their behavior to avoid infection. Furthermore, when very few people are in the original pool of infected individuals, even a small increase in numbers will produce a very large percentage increase.

Once a disease begins to spread through a population, the number of people who are at risk and who have not yet contracted the disease necessarily declines. For that reason, most infectious diseases spread very rapidly in their early stage and then tend to level off and eventually decline when all individuals who do not have defenses against the disease are already infected. This is especially true for childhood diseases where most adults who survived the disease during their own childhood have an immunity to it. Such diseases tend to come in cycles, during which they spread rapidly among children and then die out for lack of uninfected children or adults who are not immune. They then reappear a few years later to attack the next cohort of not yet immune children. Such cycles can continue for years.

It is not at all unusual for biological and physical systems to operate in this self-limiting way. This makes extrapolation during the early stages of a process unreliable as predictors for later stages. The bacteria in grape juice, which convert the sugar to alcohol, are killed by the alcohol when it reaches approximately 12 percent. If you like to drink stronger beverages you will have to drink artificially distilled beverages, since they cannot be produced by natural fermentation, which is a self-limiting process.

Trying to predict a trend in time requires more than simple extrapolation. It requires a detailed analysis of all the factors producing a current trend, and an attempt to predict how they will operate in the future, while at the same time trying to determine if any new factors will be operating in that future. What is required is a fairly extensive simulation, which is costly, time consuming, and, in the final analysis, will often produce only an educated guess. It is a lot easier to simply assume that what is happening now will continue indefinitely. No wonder so many of us lose money in the stock market.

Extrapolating Over Dosage

Another sort of extrapolation, which is almost as tricky, involves trying to assess the effects of various dosages of drugs or various levels of poisons or radiation with which one has no experience by extrapolating from known dosages or exposures. If two aspirin take away minor pain, then maybe 100 aspirin would take away severe pain. But on the other hand, if 100 aspirin will kill you, then will two aspirin do you a little harm, i.e., go only a little way toward killing you? If a lot of knowledge is a good thing, why is a little knowledge dangerous?

You will, of course, recognize this as one of the more troubling and problematic issues of our time. If large doses of artificial sweetener cause cancer in rats, does that imply that small doses will do so in human beings? If exposure to large amounts of radiation is damaging, are small exposures? We have all heard the warning "there is no safe level of radiation." That may or may not be true for all sorts of reasons and would not interest us here were it not for a controversial type of extrapolation that is widely used in assessing the risk of various everyday products and potential environmental hazards.

The reasoning used is as follows: We know that cigarettes are dangerous, as it has been clearly established that those who smoke heavily and differ in no other important respect from those who do not smoke are far more likely to die of cancer. There is also independent, controlled laboratory experimentation to substantiate this finding. However, not all heavy smokers die of cancer. Clearly, cigarette smoking is a heavy contributor to, but not an absolute predictor of illness. Other factors must play a role in some as yet to be understood way. Nevertheless, if smoking two packs (40 cigarettes) a day increases your risk of cancer by a factor of 16, does it not follow that smoking one pack or 20 cigarettes a day will increase your risk by a factor of 8. It does, if one can assume straight-line extrapolation. Likewise, if you smoke 10 cigarettes a day, you increase your risk by 4, and if you smoke 5 cigarettes a day, you increase your risk by a factor of 2. While the above does not appear to be the case in the general population, there may be many reasons why the dangers of light cigarette smoking are not apparent. On the other hand, the assumption of a straight-line extrapolation may be wrong. Perhaps there is a threshold, and if you do not exceed it, no harm is done.

Let's look at the artificial sweetener controversy. Suppose rats fed the equivalent (to humans) of one hundred cans of artificially sweetened soft drink a day have a 50 percent chance of dying of cancer. Using straight line extrapolation, then rats who drink $\frac{1}{100}$ of that amount or 1 can a day should have $\frac{1}{100}$ as much risk as the heavy drinking rats, or $\frac{1}{2}$ of 1 percent chance of dying of cancer. Put another way, but using the same logic, if 100 out of 200 rats die from 100 cans of soft drink, then 1 out of 200 rats will die from drinking one can a day. If we assume that rats and human beings are similar, then we can also assume that 1 out of 200 humans who drink one can of soft drink a day will contract cancer. If we assume a population of 100 million drinkers of artificially sweetened soft drinks who drink one can a day, then we can assume that 50,000 Americans will eventually die because of their habit. The above may appear strange reasoning, but it is ·perfectly sound so long as one accepts the notion of a straight-line extrapolation of percentages as a function of dosage, and that humans and rats will be similarly affected. We also assume that there is no threshold for the effect, and that any dose, no matter how small, is dangerous. Similar reasoning is used to estimate the health risks of various forms of radiation. After the Chernobyl nuclear accident, there was a rash of estimates of the number of deaths, world-wide, that would eventually result from the environmental contamination produced by the accident. The above logic was used most often to arrive at estimates which, as one might expect, were quite varied in magnitude.

Of course, many people argue that such reasoning is utterly ridiculous, not because rats and humans differ, but rather because they believe there are, in fact, threshold effects for most potentially harmful chemicals. They argue, for instance, that the damage caused by radiation in small doses can be repaired by the body, and no lasting harm is done. Only when dosages are great and the body's defenses overcome does serious damage result. That certainly seems to be the case in the way our bodies deal with infectious bacteria.

We are in no position to resolve this argument here, and this is hardly the place to seriously discuss health risks. We have experts to consult for that purpose. The point is that risk assessment involving any sort of extrapolation is a risky business about which there is considerable controversy. In basing decisions on extrapolated data, it is important to fully understand the sort of extrapolation that was used to produce the estimates.

Unintended Consequences—Again

Since we are generally risk-averse, we are prone to take reports of risk seriously, as well we should. But as we discussed in Chapter 4, we are not always good at estimating the probability of risks, and we often overestimate them. While the dangers of underestimating risks are clear, the dangers of overestimating risks are often obscure. The danger is that in attempting to avoid one risk, which we have erroneously overestimated, we incur another risk, needlessly, which we may have underestimated. If, after a serious plane accident, we overestimate the risk of flying (due to the availability fallacy), and decide to drive rather than fly to California, we have put ourselves at the much greater risk of dying or being seriously injured in an auto accident.

Another problem is that since our state of knowledge is never perfect, we may trade off dangers we know about for dangers that are as yet undiscovered or about which we are unfamiliar. In earlier times, people accepted various medical treatments to deal with the potential threats of their illnesses, and died of the treatments about whose risks they were ignorant.

Sometimes we make such errors because we are unfamiliar with the risks we face in our everyday life. We have to be on guard for the *fallacy of isolated statistics*. This results when we act or decide on the basis of an isolated estimate and have no context in which to judge its meaning. "One third of the students drop out of the local college without graduating." Without knowledge as to average dropout rates, what is one to make of such a statement? Is the school's record good, bad, or average? Without comparative data, we simply do not know what the statement implies about the local college.

This fallacy is related to the fallacy of *no controls*, in that without some control group or frame of reference, we can seriously confuse what a finding means. When presented with such a statistic one should always ask: "Compared to what?" In the argument over the safety of nuclear power, many people were surprised to discover that the levels of radiation under discussion were often no greater than the increased exposure one might receive by moving to a high altitude city such as Denver, or of a few flights in an airplane.

An interesting example is provided by an incident involving the importation of Chilean fruit into the United States in 1989. Based on a telephone threat, government agents thoroughly examined large quantities of fruit and discovered two grapes tainted with three micrograms of cyanide. Based on that finding, the government temporarily banned all fruit imports from Chile, causing much economic hardship. Whether the government officials made the right decision in this case is difficult to determine without access to all the information they had. The public, however, might have looked at the grapes with three micrograms of cyanide in a different light were it widely known that according to Thomas Jukes (1989), Professor of Biophysics at Berkeley, "one domestic lima bean contains about a hundred micrograms of cyanide."

In a similar vein, some have advocated drinking organic apple juice to avoid Alar, a plant growth regulator in apples (present in some apples at .055 parts per million), which breaks down into a suspected carcinogen. "But organic 'apples' are often naturally moldy, and organic apple juice may contain up to 45 ppm [part per million] of patulin, a suspected carcinogen produced by the penicillium molds that grow on apples" (Jukes 1989).

The danger here of unintended consequences in the area of public policy is very real. If we overestimate the risks of nuclear power, for instance, we may incur the environmental costs and health dangers of coal burning, and in addition increase the risks inherent in transporting oil and liquid gas. And if our energy policy increases dependence on foreign oil, we may increase the risk of war to insure a steady flow of oil.

All such thought would be unnecessary if our experts could tell us how to avoid all risks so we could arrange our lives accordingly. But that is impossible and we must, of necessity, weigh risk against risk, as well as risks against benefits.

Conclusion

Perhaps you are now skeptical about ever being able to determine what causes what. GOOD! The plain fact is that it is extremely difficult to determine in the real world what the causes of things are, and how those causes actually work to have their effects. It is equally the case that most people have no idea how difficult a task it is to get things straight, and many go through life attributing causes to things on little or no basis. Of course, it is possible to know many of the causes of happenings in the world. But establishing such understanding is an extremely difficult and continuing process. The next time you hear someone say, "that's because . . . ," stop and ask yourself whether there really is any basis for the explanation offered.

Nevertheless, science has enormously enlarged our understanding of the world, and we would be foolish not to make use of good scientific information. We need not be experts to understand what scientists tell us. Nor need we be experts to detect the common misuse of scientific data for the rhetorical purpose of advancing particular arguments or causes. When provided with an assertion about some purported scientific finding, try to determine if ceteris paribus was satisfied. Were there controls? Were the controls adequate? Could the result have been due to placebo effects, or Hawthorne effects, or regression to the mean? Is a statistically significant result useful or meaningful in the circumstance at hand? When someone makes a claim about group differences, are the causal inferences justified or marred by the fallacy of inadequate decomposition? Have demographic factors been considered? If someone makes a projection, is it sound or based on improper extrapolation? What assumptions were made in doing the extrapolation? Be on the lookout for unintended consequences and isolated statistics.

In asking such questions, you are asking only that statements that others make about cause and effect meet the requirements of legitimate scientific inquiry. And while "truth" is elusive, you are more likely to approximate it with an open mind and concerted effort.

Important Concepts

Because in argument
Because in explanation
Necessary cause
Sufficient cause
Contributing factor
Post hoc ergo propter hoc
Correlation
Correlation coefficient
Null hypothesis
Ceteris paribus
Experimental control
Confounding factors
False negative
False positive
Fallacy of no controls
Fallacy of inadequate controls
External validity

Statistical significance
In vivo-in vitro problem
Placebo effect
Hawthorne effect
Experimental mortality
Regression to the mean
Double-blind research
Contrarian investment strategy
Survey research
Statistical control
Limited range
Demographic factors
Extrapolation over time
Extrapolation over dosage
Fallacy of inadequate
  decomposition
Fallacy of isolated statistics

Problems for Analysis

Identify the error(s) in each of the following, and explain where the reasoning went wrong in each case.

1. In her first year of teaching math, 20 percent of Mary's students failed the state exam, whereas system-wide the failure rate is only 15 percent. The principal recommended to the school board that she be fired. She appealed, claiming she had simply been very unlucky in the students assigned to her classes. How should the school board decide?

2. The principal selected the 10 students who obtained the lowest grades in a standardized reading test. He assigned them to a special reading instructor. When retested at the end of the year, the group showed marked improvement. He decided to make the position of

special reading instructor permanent. Was that decision warranted by the evidence?

3. Professor Beerswill came to believe that test anxiety, which troubled many of the students in his math class, could be alleviated by moderate amounts of alcohol. He explained his theory and called for volunteers and orally administered 4 ounces of alcohol to 15 students one hour before the midterm exam. Twelve of the 15 reported marked reduction in test anxiety. Based on his research, he has decided to serve two martinis before every exam to all who wish them. Is this a sound decision?

4. Professor Airhead discovered that over the past fifty years the hourly crime rate in New York City almost exactly mirrored the hourly temperature in Bangkok. Listed below is just part of his data.

	Number of Crimes in N.Y.C.	Temperature in Bangkok
11 P.M.	200	88
12 P.M.	300	90
1 A.M.	400	92
2 A.M.	500	94
3 A.M.	400	92

He wrote the FBI recommending that crime in the United States could be greatly reduced by foreign aid grants for air conditioning in Bangkok. He never got a response and was hurt. Should he have been?

5. Professor Esp believed some people had the ability to predict the future. He tested his theory by testing 5,000 students to see how many of them could guess 8 out of 10 coin tosses correctly. This is a fairly unlikely outcome to achieve through pure guessing. He found 200 students who had the ability. He tested them again and found 25 who got 8 or more right on the second trial. He tested this group again and found 5 who had retained the skill. Since the likelihood of guessing 24 or more out of 30 coin tosses correctly is exceedingly small, he concluded that while many people have the skill occasionally, some seem to retain the skill consistently over time. He formed an investment group with those five students and in 2 years they lost all their parents' money. Why? What went wrong?

6. While sipping a martini in her parent's country club, Alice noticed that many of the young women around her had been divorced and were now raising their children as single mothers, and those children seemed quite well-adjusted. Upon reflection, she decided that all those who

argued that single mothers had more trouble raising children were either misguided or sexist. What do you think?

7. The average income of the alumni attending the twenty-fifth reunion of the class of 1960 was $125,000. You conclude that your alma mater must be doing something right. Are they?

8. A recent report by the Association for the Preservation of Natural Childbirth indicated that on a test of self-esteem of 15-year-olds, those who had been breastfed scored significantly higher than those who had been bottle fed. John's wife thinks breastfeeding is simply a male chauvinistic way to keep women in their place. John, however, concerned about the future well-being of his newborn son, insisted that the child be breastfed, which he was. The boy is now 15 and is suffering from severe feelings of inferiority. What happened?

9. Mary Dogood discovered that in a surprisingly large number of serious auto accidents, the radio was found to be playing at full volume. She concluded that loud radios distract drivers. She immediately formed the Committee to Remove All Noise from Cars (CRANC) and proceeded to solicit funds to begin lobbying efforts in the state capital. Would you give CRANC any of your money?

10. Harold Cautious discovered while living in Arizona that rates for death by stroke are higher there than anywhere else in America. Wisely, he moved to Florida only to discover that there the death rate for heart attack is higher than any other state in America. Harold decided that warm sunny places are extremely deadly and moved to Anchorage where he died an untimely death from alcoholism. What was wrong with poor Harold's reasoning?

11. It was discovered that the mothers of autistic children often lacked a certain warmth when they dealt with their children. Paul Shrink proposed a psychological course in parenting for the mothers of autistic children. After ten years, the government cut off his funds because the children have shown no improvement. Where did Shrink err?

12. John did not do very well in high school. In truth, he is not a very good student. However, he was an excellent carpenter and was earning $10 an hour as an apprentice cabinet-maker shortly after graduating from high school. His mother however had read that those with a college education earn far higher salaries than those with a high school diploma. John, who always tried to please his mother, quit his job and enrolled in the local college. He is now living somewhere on Skid Row. Should he have been such a dutiful son?

13. Richard McKensie argued in a letter to the Wall Street Journal

(March 7, 1989) that increased expenditures on airline safety might increase deaths on highways. What do you think his reasoning was?

14. A study of hardened convicts serving life sentences in a state's institution for repeat offenders, concluded that, based on their records, severity of punishment was not a deterrent to crime. In order to reduce the deficit, the state legislature cut all sentences in half, feeling the reduction would have no effect on criminal activity. Did they do the sensible thing?

15. A senator, citing a significant difference between the crime rates of immigrants and the general population, argued that immigration should be drastically curtailed to keep out the "criminal element." What's wrong with his argument?

16. Many schools and colleges expanded greatly in the sixties and seventies. In the eighties, many of them went out of business because they couldn't meet their costs. Where did they go wrong?

17. One of the benefits of a college education is an increase in sophistication about the world. College administrators often point to the change from freshman to senior year on standard tests of intellectual sophistication and worldliness. Do you think they have a case?

18. Western University, interested in improving mathematics learning in its introductory sessions, decided to change to three 50-minute periods based on the following research. It chose four sections of Math I in the evening and gave them a semester of three classes per week. As a control, it used four sections of the identical course from the day schedule, which remained at two sessions per week. The students in the three-session-per-week courses did much better on an end-of-term exam. What do you think?

19. It has been found that executives who are more willing to take risks are wealthier and more successful than those who are risk-averse. It is for this reason that I am planning to open a clinic to help executives overcome risk-aversion. I hope to obtain significant corporate funding. Would you invest?

20. John had been running three miles every other day and has shown constant improvement since he began. To prepare for an upcoming 5-kilometer race, he started running 3 miles every day. By the day of the race, his performance had dramatically declined. Why?

Chapter 6

How to Think About Risk

Preliminaries

In this chapter, we will begin the process of introducing techniques for the analysis of *risky* decision problems. One of the most basic decision skills is the ability to recognize what kind of problem you are facing. There is a standard way of classifying decision problems, although the techniques for approaching each type will vary. In this chapter, we introduce the most basic techniques for the analysis of *decision-making under risk*. This is defined as a decision in which you cannot be certain what the exact outcomes of your choices will be. For example, if you choose to purchase stock in Ford Motor Company rather than GM, you cannot be certain whether the outcome of that choice will be to your benefit or not. This is because you cannot predict with certainty the changes in the market, and so the best you can do is to think of the probabilities that the stock will rise or fall, and by how much. In thinking about decisions under risk, then, we must always think about probabilities of some kind.

Structuring Decision Problems Under Risk

Our ultimate goal is to introduce certain decision rules that will help us select the optimal choice (or at least an acceptable choice) from among a set of plausible alternatives. However, these decision rules will work only if the problem is set up in a very specific way. This setting up of the problem is called, *decision structuring*, or *framing*. Specific structuring of a decision problem is similar to structuring the

dreaded "word problems" in beginning algebra. If Mary had three
times the money that James had, and James had one half the money of
Fred, and Fred had six dollars, how much money did Mary have? Here
we let x = Mary's money, $x/3$ = James's money, 6 = Fred's money.
James's money was one-half of Fred's, so:

$x/3$	=	6/2	
$2x$	=	18	
x	=	9	(Mary's money)

No doubt this type of problem could have been solved "in your
head" without going through this very specific structuring. But the
structuring is important nevertheless, because more complex problems
could not be solved "in your head," and the chances are that you
could solve this problem informally only because you at one time
learned the formal mathematical procedures. Those familiar with the
procedures of formal logic, or of writing computer programs, or of
studying micro-economics, or of motion problems in introductory
physics, or of following the directions to reconcile a checkbook, can
appreciate the need to structure a problem in a very specific way in
order to apply certain kinds of solutions. It is in this tradition that
decision theory imposes a specific, and very stylized format upon the
structuring of decision problems.

In the case of decision structuring, there are at least the following
reasons for following these strict procedures (von Winterfeldt and
Edwards 1986): (1) The preparation of the structure forces the decision-
maker to think through the cause/effect relations that might exist
between his or her choices and the consequences of those choices; (2)
Decision structuring indicates very clearly the types of information
that will be necessary to make the decision intelligently; (3) The
structuring of decisions forces the decision-maker to think through the
basic values that are being threatened by the challenge that is prompt-
ing the decision; (4) Decision framing assists in the invention of new
choices, new options for the solving of the problem; (5) The structuring
procedure aids in the invention of hedging options, that is, choices that
do well in all or most states of the world, (6) Decision structuring helps
in the resolution of disagreements in that it pinpoints exactly the areas
of values or facts that are the sources of controversy. In this way even
emotional issues of politics or personal disagreement can be transformed into problem solving endeavors; (7) Finally, decision framing

provides a very clear rationale for whatever choice is ultimately selected.

Since much of our decision-making is done as fiduciaries, it is very important to be able to give a rationale for our choices, especially when they turn out badly. We believe that with practice you will appreciate that problems that at first seem to be a "toss up" will turn out, after proper structuring, to have definite solutions. Let us look at a problem.

Svetlana is forty-two years old; lives in a remote area of the Ukraine in the Soviet Union; has a younger brother with Down's Syndrome as well as a child (her youngest) with the same disease. Following the birth of that child, it was necessary to hospitalize Svetlana for depression. She has two healthy children as well, and a good job as a physician in a local hospital. She is looking forward to becoming chief of medicine. Due to the fact that abortion is the preferred Soviet method of birth control, contraceptive measures are in short supply and of poor quality. As a result, all efforts at contraception have failed, and she is again pregnant. She has been refused permission to travel to Moscow (or anywhere else) for amniocentesis to determine if the child would have Down's were it born. The state favors the less costly procedure of abortion. In thinking of her options, the only one that is absolutely ruled out is to have the child with the intention of deciding at that time how to proceed. Svetlana calls you from her home to ask you to help her make the right choice.

It is immediately clear to you that the information presented above is insufficient. You agree to help Svetlana but need time to think. You promise to call her back, pour yourself a stiff drink, and begin to consider the issues. You decide first that your job is not to tell Svetlana what decision you would make if you were in her situation. This is so because you and Svetlana may have different views about such things as abortion, motherhood, adoption, the value of different kinds of life, the importance of a career, and so forth. Whatever advice you give must be within the framework of Svetlana's values, assuming they are not so wrong that you would want to convince her to change them. With this in mind, you begin to separate out some of the things that you do know from those that you do not know and that seem relevant. We must first begin with the process of *decomposition*, of breaking the problem down into its component parts. At the completion of this stage, the problem is *recomposed* in a manner that allows for effective decision-making.

Problem Decomposition

The first step in problem decomposition is to determine the goals that are threatened by the challenge to the present course. The best way to do this is to develop a *value tree* as described in Chapter 3. The first step in the value tree is to determine who the stakeholders of the decision ought to be. The value tree procedure provides a clear way of determining Svetlana's values, or *utilities*. As discussed earlier, the utility of something is the degree to which some decision-maker considers it good or bad, better or worse, based upon his or her relevant value commitments. Determining the goals that are threatened also involves knowing some facts concerning what is likely to happen if the present course is not changed. These are not value issues, but "empirical" issues. Recall that an empirical issue is a question of how things in the world are, were, or will be. In thinking about the nature of the challenge to the present course, about the value issues and the empirical issues, it is useful to distinguish what we do know from what we do not, but should, know.

We DO know:

1. She has been practicing birth control.
2. She is pregnant.
3. Her brother and one child have Down's Syndrome.
4. Abortion is available, and recommended by the state.
5. She insists upon making the decision now.
6. It is not possible to determine the health of the child now, a question that is clearly relevant in Svetlana's mind.
7. She has a family, a career, a medical history, a possible promotion.
8. She would prefer never to have gotten pregnant on this occasion.

We DO NOT, but should know:

9. Her values on abortion? If the child is healthy? Has Down's?
10. How likely is it that the child has Down's?
11. Her values on adoption? If the child is healthy? Has Down's?
12. Are there adoptive parents available?
13. Will she be able to take care of such a child?
14. Are there adequate abortion facilities available?
15. How does she feel about having another healthy child?
16. What was the cause of the Down's condition of her other child?

17. What are the views of her family members on #9, #11, #15.
18. Is it possible to change the mind of the state on her travel?
19. Does the fact that her brother has Down's affect the answer to #10.
20. How much weight does she give to the wants of her family members?

You could no doubt think of other relevant matters, but let's work with this list for the time being. Some of the knowns and unknowns in #1 through 20 involve empirical issues. Other issues concern what Svetlana believes that the world ought to be like. Some of the empirical issues are directly relevant, for example, the likelihood that the child has Down's. Others are relevant only for what they imply, for instance, the issue of the cause of the brother's illness matters because of what it implies for the question of the likelihood of Down's in the present pregnancy. Similarly, the value issue of #20 will have implications for the value issue of #9, since it determines the degree to which she will abide by her family's wishes.

Once we have some idea of the answers to the questions we have posed, we can then think of Svetlana's plausible choices. We say "plausible" because if we were to try to list all her options, the list would be endless and would result in a waste of time and other costs. In thinking about plausible choices, it is necessary to refer to the earlier discussion of the goals that are challenged in order to keep the choice selection relevant to the present problem. If "find a new job" were listed as an option, this would be rejected as irrelevant. We are interested only in choices that can help Svetlana achieve her goals under these circumstances. At this point, moral excluders should be introduced to eliminate any potential choices that would accomplish the decision-maker's goals but are ruled out for deontological (moral) reasons. In the type of case we are considering, the obvious option of abortion would be ruled out by many decision-makers as a violation of their moral codes. We will assume that this is not the case with Svetlana.

In this case, it is clear that Svetlana's pregnancy is a threat to things she values. It threatens her physical health, her emotional health, her career, her family life. It is also clear that the threat is much more severe due to the possibility of the child's having Down's. In thinking about a set of potential choices, it is necessary that the list be exclusive and (in practice) exhaustive. In light of this, Svetlana's choices seem to be:

Have an abortion,
Arrange for adoption,
Keep the born child.

Implausible choices such as emigration, suicide, etc., as well as irrelevant choices, have been eliminated in a previous rapid scanning of the situation.

It is now necessary to think of the factors that will affect in relevant ways the outcomes of these choices. Recall that the outcomes of a choice are the changes in the level of fulfillment of the decision-maker's goals that come about as a result of the choice. The description of the outcomes does not include how Svetlana evaluates these new situations. This is a separate matter having to do with the utility of the outcomes, which will be discussed later. Recall that this is a decision problem under risk, which means that the outcomes of the three choices listed above are not totally under Svetlana's control. Whether the child would be born with Down's, assuming that it was continued to term, is not under Svetlana's control, and yet will affect the outcome of her choices. For example, if she selects the "keep" choice and the child has Down's, the outcome is that she has added another Down's child to the family. If the child is healthy, the outcome is different. The factors that affect the outcomes of the choices and are not under the decision-maker's control are called *states of the world* (or "states"). To determine the proper states, you ask yourself what the outcomes of each choice will be. When, after some thought, you say "Well, that depends upon . . . ," then what follows the "depends upon" will be a state. In this case, the outcome of having and keeping the child "depends upon" whether or not the child has Down's. The relevant state is, then, whether or not the child has Down's.

Problem Recomposition

At this point we are going to introduce a technique for constructing a visual representation of decision problems under risk—the *decision-tree*. In general, the decision tree approach helps you in thinking through the structure of the problem by listing the plausible choices, the states of the world, the outcomes, the probability of states, and the utility or value of outcomes. The tree approach is sequential, that is, with the tree lying on its side the sequence in time is more or less represented from left (earlier) to right (later).

The Outcome Tree

The tree is lying on its side. At this level of representation, we will include on the tree only choices, states, and outcomes.

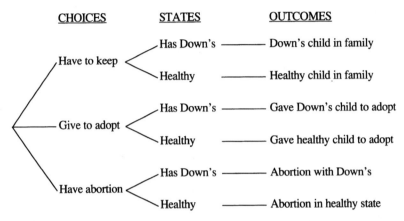

The decision tree for cases of decision-making under risk will always represent the choices and the states. In the example above, the outcomes are also represented. A complete description of each of the outcomes would have to include each of the goals that that decision is attempting to accomplish. As we will see, it is not always necessary to describe the outcomes on the tree, although it is always necessary to know what the outcomes will be, and it will always be necessary to specify on the decision tree the value of each of the outcomes. Since, in addition to choices and states what are represented are outcomes, the above could be called an outcome tree. We have abbreviated the descriptions of the outcomes. We repeat that it is very important in practice to describe the outcomes clearly, in terms of the effects of the choices on the goals of the decision-maker. To be able to formulate a decision problem under risk as an outcome tree is a very significant step in resolving the decision problem.

It may be useful at this stage to compare the bare structure of a decision under certainty discussed in Chapter 3 with that of the decision under risk. Recall the tree structure for a decision under certainty.

It is clear from the diagrams below that in the case of decisions under risk, the states intervene between the choices and the outcomes. The states are matters over which the decision-maker has no control,

DECISION UNDER CERTAINTY

<u>CHOICES</u>   <u>OUTCOMES</u>

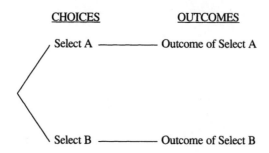

DECISION UNDER RISK

<u>CHOICES</u>   <u>STATES</u>   <u>OUTCOMES</u>

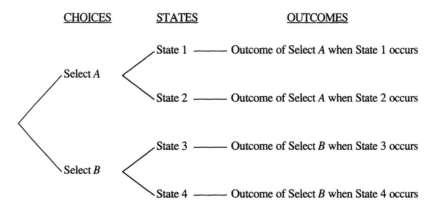

although he or she may have knowledge of the probabilities that one or the other state will occur. Recall that for any given choice, only one of the states will actually occur. Thus, the decision-maker is always uncertain what will result from his choices, and can at best predict with reliable probability estimates what will happen after his choices are made.

Let us try one more example.

I must decide today what I should do tomorrow for recreation. After a quick scan of options, I focus on making a tennis date with Terry to play at the park or asking Terry to come over to watch the U.S. Open Tennis Tournament on TV. In thinking about this problem my major concern is for the weather, which could turn out to be sunny, rainy, or overcast.

The outcome tree looks like the following.

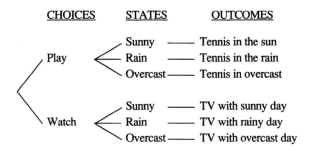

This does not seem like such a difficult business, but you will have guessed that the problems and decisions that we face in everyday life are more difficult to formulate than these examples. One of the difficult matters in setting up these decision problems under risk is the selection of the states. It is of course not easy to know what things will affect the outcomes of our choices. Beyond that, it is necessary to select states that are in practice *exhaustive*, that is, there are no other states that are likely to affect the outcomes of our choices in relevant ways. The selection of such states is a matter of practicality. There will always be possible situations that could count as states, but their probability is so low as to render them irrelevant. It is also necessary to select states that are *exclusive*, that is, that cannot occur together for any given choice. This requirement that the states be *exclusive* and *exhaustive* has the result that the probability that one and only one of the states will occur, given that a choice is selected, is effectively 100 percent, or 1. This may seem artificial; but it is necessary for the application of the techniques we will be introducing to handle decision problems under risk. Given this discussion of the meaning of "exclusive and exhaustive," it should be clear that your list of plausible choices should also have these characteristics for all practical purposes. Thus, if it is possible to simultaneously select more than one choice, then that should itself be a separate choice (exclusivity). If there are other plausible choices, then they should be listed (exhaustiveness).

Let us review the procedure so far described to set up problems of decision-making under risk.

1. Determine the specific goals that are threatened by whatever

situation has created the need for a decision. This is best done through the device of the value tree.
2. Separate out the knowns from the unknowns, and do your best to learn about the knowns.
3. Distinguish the choices, states of the world, and outcomes, by means of constructing an outcome tree.
4. Check that the choices are exclusive and exhaustive.
5. Check that the states are exclusive and exhaustive.
6. Check that the outcomes are described in terms of the goals that are threatened by the decision situation.

Multi-Stage Representation

Remember that we are not yet in a position to solve any decision problems involving risk, since this is still the stage of problem structuring. The problems that have so far been considered are single stage problems in the sense that there are no further states that depend upon which state actually comes about. Often however this is not the case. To show this, let us consider two similar problems: the first a single stage problem, and the second a multi-stage problem. The first problem is repeated from the Introduction.

Single Stage Problem

Frank has a tumor adjacent to a sensitive area of the spine. There is no way to tell if it is malignant except by removing it. Such a procedure is certain to be successful, but is very expensive. Frank has no medical insurance. His doctor tells Frank that there is a one-in-one-hundred chance that the tumor is malignant. If it is malignant Frank will certainly die, and if it is not, it will disappear on its own. Frank has enough money saved, but it was designated to pay for the Ivy League educations of his four very bright children.

Single Stage Outcome Tree

The tree below should seem familiar to you by now. If you don't feel comfortable with the single stage tree, then make up some simple decision problems and construct outcome trees for them with choices, states, and outcomes. Doing this is more difficult than you may think, and is very good practice. Let's complicate the medical problem by turning it into a multi-stage decision problem under risk.

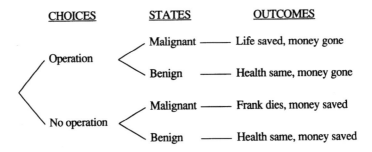

CHOICES   **STATES**   **OUTCOMES**

Operation
— Malignant ——— Life saved, money gone
— Benign ——— Health same, money gone

No operation
— Malignant ——— Frank dies, money saved
— Benign ——— Health same, money saved

Multi-Stage Problem

Frank's medical problem is exactly as described above except that his doctor adds that should the tumor be malignant, there is only a six in ten chance that the malignancy will be overcome by the procedure. If it is not malignant, the operation will have no significant effect upon Frank's health, only upon his savings. The cost of the procedure is not affected by whether the growth is malignant or benign.

Multi-Stage Outcome Tree

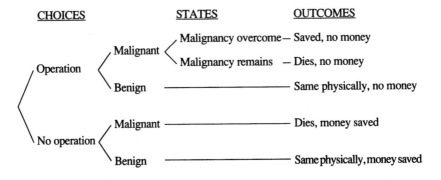

CHOICES   **STATES**   **OUTCOMES**

Operation
— Malignant
  — Malignancy overcome — Saved, no money
  — Malignancy remains — Dies, no money
— Benign ——— Same physically, no money

No operation
— Malignant ——— Dies, money saved
— Benign ——— Same physically, money saved

Note that on the multi-stage outcome tree the category STATES has a small tree under it. This is because there are different possible states depending upon whether (1) the operation takes place or not, and (2) the growth is malignant or not. If the operation takes place and the growth is malignant, then there is a possibility of success or failure by the surgeon. These possibilities are themselves states because they are not Frank's choices and yet they affect the outcomes of his choices.

The number of choices remains the same, but the number of states and what they are has changed. It is still possible that the tumor is malignant or benign, but there is a further possibility of the surgeon's success or failure. It is a situation like this in which the outcome tree can be of real help. Setting up the tree for the multi-stage problem was rather simple, since it is sequential.

This ends the discussion of how to formulate decision problems into representations of their choices, states of the world, and outcomes. Of course, we are not yet at the point where selections can be made from among the choices. This is because important elements of the problem are missing. These include the probabilities that the outcomes will follow the choices, the values or utilities that are placed by the decision-maker on the outcome, and some rule(s) to put these probabilities and utilities together to generate one or more optimal choices. When the decision tree is completed, it should look something like the following:

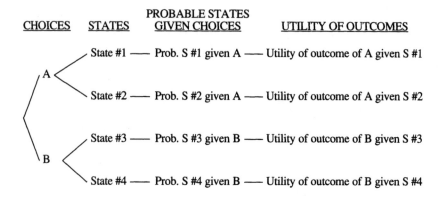

CHOICES	STATES	PROBABLE STATES GIVEN CHOICES	UTILITY OF OUTCOMES
A	State #1	Prob. S #1 given A	Utility of outcome of A given S #1
	State #2	Prob. S #2 given A	Utility of outcome of A given S #2
B	State #3	Prob. S #3 given B	Utility of outcome of B given S #3
	State #4	Prob. S #4 given B	Utility of outcome of B given S #4

Having set up the problem in this way, it is possible to apply some sort of decision rule to arrive at one or more rational choices. One of the points of decision structuring is to make possible the use of these decision rules.

Measures of Probability and Value

We have been discussing decision structuring. Recall that it is the purpose of decision structuring to put a decision problem in a form in which it can be solved. The solution to a decision problem requires the use of a rational process in the selection of one or more of the available choices. In the last section we carried the structuring to the point of constructing the outcome tree. At that point it is not, of course, possible to arrive at a solution as we have defined it. This is because there is no information concerning either the probabilities of the states or the utilities of the outcomes. Remember that by "utilities of the outcomes" we mean the degree to which the decision-maker values these outcomes relative to each other, based upon the value analysis. By "probabilities of states," we mean the degree of confidence the decision-maker ought to have that the various states will be realized, given the particular choices selected.

In the following sections we will extend the decision structuring to include a certain kind of information concerning probabilities and utilities. First, it is necessary to make a distinction between real probability numbers, and probability rankings. From the discussion on probability, we saw that real probability numbers occur on a scale from 0 to 1, or from 0 percent to 100 percent. A probability ranking simply says that one thing is more probable than another. In this regard, it is exactly like the utility ranking discussed in Chapter 3. Let's think of the probability of rain this week.

DAY	REAL PROBABLE NUMBERS	RANKING WORDS	RANKING NUMBERS
Monday	32%	Not too likely	1 (least)
Tuesday	98%	Almost certain	3 (most)
Wednesday	50%	A toss up	2 (middle)

The real probability numbers give us a good deal more information than the ranking numbers. For example, we know that the difference in probability of rain between Wednesday and Monday ($50\% - 32\% = 18\%$) is less than the difference in probability of rain between Tuesday and Wednesday ($98\% - 50\% = 48\%$). If we had only ranking information, this information would not be available to us. We are familiar with ranking numbers from concepts like class rank. The same is true of real utility numbers vs. utility rankings. Think of the way you would value the following cars. The real utility numbers are on a scale of 1 to 10 (least to most desirable).

Again, there is more information contained in real utility numbers than in mere ranking numbers. The real utility numbers give informa-

CAR	REAL UTILITY NUMBERS	RANKING WORDS	RANKING NUMBERS
Chevette	2	Better than nothing	1 (least)
Escort	4	Acceptable	2 (middle)
BMW	9	Great	3 (best)

tion about the distances between preferred items, as well as the order of the items. In the language of the appendix on measurement, they provide a "linear" or "interval" measure of utility.

Recall again from Chapter 3 what is meant by "ranking numbers" when applied to utilities. Ranking numbers tell you the *order of preference* of the outcomes, the most preferred being given the greatest number; the second most preferred being given the next smallest integer, and so forth; the greater the number, the more the preference. The numbers indicate that the items are equally spaced; that is, the ranking numbers used must be adjacent whole numbers. This is not realistic in most cases, but recall that we should look at ranking numbers as approximations to real utility numbers. Using ranking numbers has the advantage of simplicity.

Decision Rules

One of the purposes of decision structuring is to put the decision in the form of a solvable problem. The solution to a decision problem is defined as the selection of one or more rational choices. This selection is done by means of the application of a decision rule or rules to the structured problem. Since more than one possible decision rule can be applied to a decision problem, we need a way of deciding which rule to use. Choosing a decision rule could be called a "hyperchoice," a choice to decide how we will go about choosing (Clough 1984). The problem of hyperchoice is discussed in depth in Appendix B, but in general the decision of which decision rule to use is based upon the type of information that we have concerning the values of the outcomes and the probabilities of the states. Among the kinds of information that we could have are: value rankings, real utilities, probability rankings, real probabilities, no probability information, probability information categorized as greater or less than 50/50, or value information categorized as acceptable/unacceptable. The chart below lists some decision rules that would apply given certain combinations of value and probability information.

VALUE INFORMATION	PROBABILITY INFORMATION	DECISION RULE
Money values	Real probabilities	Expected value
Real utilities	Real probabilities	Expected utility
Utility rankings	Probability rankings	Weighted ranking
Acceptable/unacceptable	Greater than or less than 50%	Satisficing
Real utilities (one much better than others)	No information	Maximax
Real utilities (one much worse than others)	No information	Maximin

In the chart above, a reasonable decision rule, listed on the right hand side, corresponds to the type of probability and value information available.

The Dominance Rule

Perhaps the most fundamental rule of rational decision-making is the Dominance Rule. It functions in our decisions more as a choice eliminator than as a choice selector. That is, we use the dominance rule to eliminate potential choices that are in a fundamental way inferior to others available. Consider the following case.

PROBLEM: Jack can select game 1 or game 2. If he selects game 1 he will receive $400 if a coin toss turns up HEADS and $3 if it turns up TAILS. On game 2 he gets $350 if the coin turns up HEADS and $3 if it turns up TAILS.

You will immediately insist that he should play game 1. This is because the outcome of game 1 is better than game 2 if the "HEAD" state occurs, and the outcomes are equal if the "TAILS" state occurs. The tree looks like the following:

DOMINANCE RULE: Eliminate from consideration all Dominated Choices.

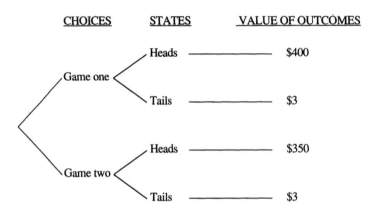

CHOICES	STATES	VALUE OF OUTCOMES

Game one — Heads ——————— $400

Game one — Tails ——————— $3

Game two — Heads ——————— $350

Game two — Tails ——————— $3

Choice 1 dominates choice 2 if the outcomes of choice 1 are at least as good as those of choice 2 no matter what the state, and there is at least one state in which the outcome of choice 1 is superior to that of choice 2.

In the above case, the choice of "game 1" dominates the choice of "game 2," so the latter is dominated by the former. It is easy to see that if a choice is dominated, then there is no state in which it is the superior choice, and there is always some state in which it is an inferior choice. So for the sake of the simplification of the problem, the dominated choice can be eliminated. The principle of dominance allows us to simplify problems by narrowing down alternatives before we structure problems.

Expected Value Rule

The earliest investigations into decision-making under risk occurred within the context of gambling problems. In a gambling problem, the value or utility is almost always measured in money. The probabilities are measured in the usual ways, by real probability numbers. Suppose that someone offered to sell you a chance. The chance is a wager:

PROBLEM: Throw one die. If it comes up either 2 or 3, then you get $60. If it comes up anything else then you get $9.

In this case, if someone offered you the wager for $2, you would be sure to take it. You couldn't lose. What is the maximum that you would pay in order to play the wager? On a tree, the problem of determining the values of the choice "Play" and the choice "No Play" looks like the following:

CHOICES	STATES	VALUE	PROB
Play — 2 or 3		$60	1/3 = ($20)
Play — 1,4,5, or 6		$9	2/3 = ($06)
		Expected Value	= $26
No Play — 2 or 3		$0	1/3 = ($00)
No Play — 1,4,5, or 6		$0	2/3 = ($00)
		Expected Value	= $00

In the tree above, the "EV" refers to "expected *monetary* value," which is called simply "expected value." The word "expected" is used to indicate that this is the average (mean) value that you could "expect" to receive per play if you were to play the gamble many times over. It is important to note that in the above case you would never receive $26 on any play of the gamble. You will always receive either $60 or $9. The $26 is the per play average that you could expect over the long haul. The more times that you play, the closer your per play average will come to $26. This is an application of the law of large numbers which was discussed earlier.

> *EXPECTED VALUE RULE*: Calculate the expected value of a choice by multiplying the monetary value of every one of its outcomes by the probability of that outcome's state, and sum all the products for that choice. Select the choice with the greatest expected value.

In the case above, your choices were to "Play" or "Not Play." The expected value of "Play" is $26, and the expected value of "Not Play" is $0. This means that you should be willing to pay up to $26 to play the wager. Recall that the $26 is what you have a right to expect to receive *on average per play* if you play the wager *many times*. It is not immediately obvious why this is a good reason that you should be willing to pay $26 to play the wager *only once*. The rationale that is usually given is that, although you will be playing this particular wager only once, you will in fact be wagering in general throughout your life. Your life will be a series of risky choices concerning, for instance, whether to have a particular surgery, whether to take a particular job, or whether to spend the money on a new ad campaign. And thus, the strategy is to be considered part of a long-term "life strategy" even though in this case you are only playing once.

There is a rather standard way of representing wagers, (or gambles, or uncertain prospects). In every case of a monetary wager, you will expect to get some money amount with a certain probability, and some other amount with the "remaining" probability. We say the "remaining" probability because the probabilities of the outcomes must sum to 1 (or to 100%) for each choice. In the above case, you are offered a wager that will give you $60 at p = 1/3 or $9 at p = 2/3. Note that 2/3 is just 1-p, where the original p is 1/3. Another way of representing this is:

$$(\$60/.33, \$9/.67)$$

This is read, "Sixty dollars at a probability of 33 percent or nine dollars at the remaining probability of 67 percent." More generally, we can represent any wager as:

$$(\$X/p, \$Y/ 1-p)$$

The expected value rule is extremely important because it has such a wide application in that one of the functions of money is to serve as a common denominator to compare the values of very different kinds of things. For example, the value to a surgeon of performing surgery may be the same ($10,000) as the value of that surgeon's swimming pool. For this reason, the expected value rule is relevant not only to the traditional gambling problems for which it was invented, but to any situation in which there is risk and in which what is at stake can be accurately measured in monetary terms. For example in business situations in which there is risk, the expected value rule is widely applicable. Consider the following problem.

PROBLEM: Lou has just inherited $15,000, and it is burning a hole in his pocket. He is considering the purchase of a piece of land for just that amount. He figures that if the town puts in water lines, the land will be worth $50,000 in ten years. Without the lines, the land will only hold its value. If he does not buy the property he will invest in Fairchild, a defense contractor. He figures that there is a 60% chance that the government will go ahead with "star wars." If it does, there is a 30% chance that it will be at full steam. In this case his stocks will triple in value. If it goes ahead less than full steam, the stocks will only double. If the government kills star wars, then the stocks will increase by $5,000. All the stock quotes are for ten years. His friends at the town tell him that there is a 40% chance for the water lines.

This is not too difficult a problem to structure. The choices, the states, and the outcomes are clearly described, the probabilities are given, and the goal is simply money. Look at the decision tree.

CHOICES	STATES	VALUE OF OUTCOME		PROBABILITY OF OUTCOME	
Land	Water lines	$50-$15=$35,000	x .40 =	($26,000)	
	No water lines	$15-$15=$0	x .60 =	($0)	
				EV =	$26,000
Stocks	Star Wars — Full	$45-$15=$30,000	x .18 =	($5,400)	
	Star Wars — Not full	$30-$15=$30,000	x .42 =	($12,600)	
	No Star Wars	$20-$15=$5,000	x .40 =	($2,000)	
				EV =	$20,000

Since the expected value of the "Land" choice is $26,000, which is greater than the "Expected value" of $20,000 of the "Stocks" choice, Lou should select the "Land" choice.

Let us look for a minute at how those probabilities were calculated. In a multi-stage decision tree, the final probabilities are calculated by *multiplying through the tree*. For example, check the tree below.

In the tree the probability of S-2 given choice A is stated as p = .8. The probability of S-1 given choice A is stated as p = .2. The probabil-

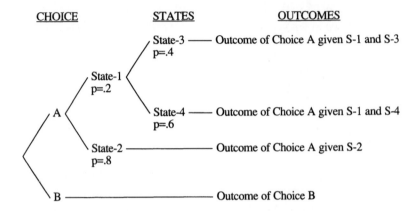

ity of S-3 given S-1 is stated as p = .4. It is necessary to calculate the probability of "S-1 *and* S-3" given choice A by multiplying through the tree, that is, multiplying p = .2 × p = .4 = p = .08. In like manner the probability of "S-1 *and* S-4" given choice A is p = .12. This is an application of Principle 2 (the multiplication rule) in the chapter on probabilities.

Limitations of Expected Value

There are some obvious limitations of the expected value rule. The first is that not all gains and losses can be measured in terms of money. The second is that the value of money, that is the utility of money, changes with changing circumstances. Five dollars is one half of ten dollars in denominations, but there are circumstances where five dollars would have greater utility than ten. If someone gives you five dollars when you are very poor, those dollars have added greater value to your money supply than if they had given you ten dollars when you are very wealthy. This is an instance of the diminishing marginal utility of money. As you add additional increments of money to your overall money supply, the utility of the additional increments begins to decline. But diminishing marginal utility of money is only one kind of case where the denominations of the money do not measure its real value or utility. Look at the following two wagers:

Wager A ($4,200/.40, $2,000/.60) EV = $2,880
Wager B ($9,800/.20, $800/.80)   EV = $2,600

The expected value rule is pretty clear at this point that you ought to select Wager A. But suppose that your child was being held for ransom of $8,000, and these wagers were your only sources of funds. In this case, you would clearly be irrational to choose Wager A. In fact, in this instance Wager A has little or no value, while Wager B could literally be a life saver. This is because there isn't anything like a smooth correspondence between the denominations of the money, and the utility of the money. The graph below depicts approximately the relationship in the case where the $8,000 is needed to save the child.

UTILITY

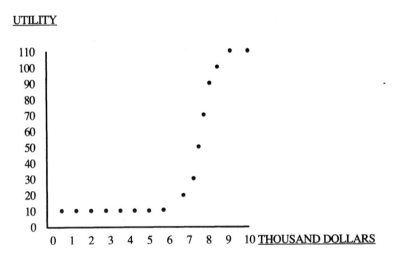

Notice the manner in which the utility of the money remains stable until the denominations approach the $8,000 level. Thus $4,000 has the same utility as $2,000. At $8,000 the utility increases sharply, and then begins to level off again. In this sort of case, and in cases far less dramatic, the expected value rule becomes seriously misleading. We can say then that the expected value rule is the rule of choice in circumstances where (1) the value of the outcomes can legitimately be measured in money, and (2) the utility of the money corresponds more or less smoothly with the denominations involved, that is, utility and money are linearly related.

Expected Utility

You will have no doubt guessed that in place of the expected value rule, we will substitute the expected utility rule. Expected utility is

calculated in exactly the same way that the expected value is calculated, except that utility values are substituted for monetary values.
Clearly this is the most sophisticated and important decision rule for
decision-making under risk. It is, in fact, the rule against which all
others are measured (Baron 1985). If we calculate the expected utility
of the two previous gambles using utility values taken from the graph,
the wagers would look like the following:

Wager A   (10/.40, 10/.60)   EU = 10
Wager B   (110/.20, 10/.80)   EU = 30

In this case, Wager B is the clear choice on the expected utility rule.
This is as it should be.

PROBLEM: Jane had dogs all throughout her childhood and now wants
her three-year-old Melinda to experience the joys of pet ownership,
preferably with a dog. Based on her family tree, and all other relevant
information she can find, there is a 40% chance that the child will be
allergic to either dogs or cats, a 20% chance of allergies to just dogs, and
a 40% chance of allergy to just cats. There is no chance of the child's
being allergic to both. Jane is convinced that dog ownership is the best by
far, cat is next, and anything else is worst, assuming the child is not
allergic. If the child is allergic to dogs, it can be kept outside. This is not
ideal, but the child still has a dog. If the wee one is allergic to cats, it (the
cat) will have to be disposed of.

The tree for the problem with utilities and probabilities is below.
The utility numbers in the matrix are based upon Jane's values of the
nine possible consequences. They are shown on the value line below.

THE EXPECTED UTILITY RULE: Calculate the expected utility of a
choice by multiplying the utility of each of its outcomes by the probability
of that outcome's state and sum all the products for that choice. Select
the choice with the greatest expected utility.

The expected utility rule is the most powerful of all the decision
rules. As such, the other decision rules will be judged by how close, or
how often, their decisions match the decisions of the expected utility
rule. Note that the expected utility rule is called for when we have real
probability numbers and real utility numbers. In fact, you can't get
any better than that. Because the expected utility rule is so important
as a decision rule, it has come under very close scrutiny by both

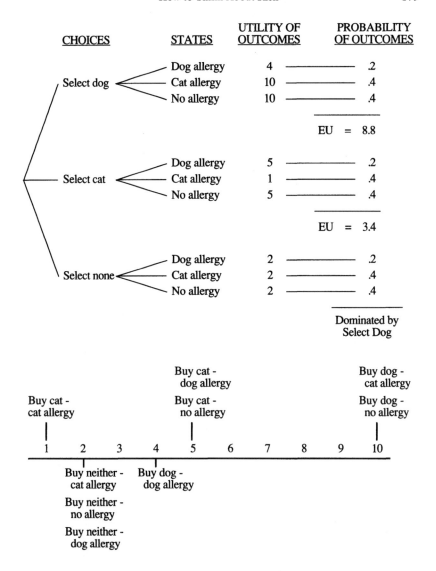

behavioral and normative researchers. Its drawback is that it demands that we have a way of measuring the value of things that is much more powerful than mere rankings. As with any procedure, a decision rule is subject to the "GIGO" problem, that is, "Garbage In Garbage Out." The fact that the utility numbers exist in a structured problem does not guarantee that they are accurate; if you put inaccurate numbers in, you will get a bad decision out. As we saw, the idea of measuring value, as one would measure weight or height, may seem strange. It really is not, but that topic is reserved for the appendix on measurement and utility. We should merely point out here that the ability to use the expected utility rule does assume that this measurement is possible. It also assumes that we have real probability numbers as measures of our degree of belief that the states will occur, given that specific choices are made. These and other assumptions have given rise to a great deal of very intricate theoretical and experimental research. Let us look at a different problem.

PROBLEM: Long before decision analysis was invented, the philosopher and mathematician Blaise Pascal gave a very practical argument to the effect that we should all practice a religious faith. He reasoned that even if you do not have proof that there is a God or not, there are other things to consider. What will happen if you practice and there is a God? If you practice and there is not? What will happen if you don't practice and there is? If you don't practice and there is not? Being unsure, Pascal assigned a .5 probability to the state that God exists.

Let us construct a tree diagram of the decision, measuring utilities on a scale ranging from $-1000 \ldots 0 \ldots +1000$.

CHOICES	STATES	OUTCOMES	UTILITIES	PROBABILITIES
Practice	God exists — Salvation		+1000	.5 = (500)
	No God — Lost Pleasures		–2	.5 = (–1)
				EU = 499
No Practice	God exists — Damnation		–1000	.5 = (–500)
	No God — Pleasures		+2	.5 = (1)
				EU = –499

Forgetting for a minute what bad theology this argument is, what should you conclude as to whether you should be a religious person?

Risky Decisions with Imperfect Information

One of the persistent criticisms of the expected utility model of rational choice, indeed of all of decision theory, is that it requires too much of the decision-maker. It requires that he or she have too much information about probabilities, too fine an analysis of values, and too sophisticated an approach to decision rules. It is certainly true that very often we are forced to make difficult decisions with limited information about probabilities. In circumstances such as these, there are some rational and effective approaches to the problems. Consider the following decision problem.

> PROBLEM: You are the director of public health for a retirement community in Florida (population, 50,000) and have received a warning from the National Center for Disease Control that a well-known strain of Asian flu has a chance of affecting your community. Unfortunately because of the unpredictable manner in which such diseases spread, the Center is unable to calculate the likelihood of your community's being affected. You are informed that past experience with the vaccine for this strain has been that 1 out of 10,000 people vaccinated will die from complications of the vaccine itself. Experience with the flu indicates a mortality rate for this age group at 18 per 10,000 among the unvaccinated, and 2 persons per 10,000 among the vaccinated (not including those who die of the vaccine itself). You know that upon your recommendation virtually the entire population will agree to be vaccinated. Should you recommend that all the citizens of your community be vaccinated?

We could construct the following decision tree for this problem.

In this case there is no probability information, although there is clear value information. One way to interpret the value information is to equate each death with one negative unit of utility. The utilities are provided on the decision tree below. It would certainly make sense in this context to try to avoid the possibility of the outcome that involves 90 deaths, even if to do so it would be necessary to cause up to five deaths. This kind of calculation is extremely distasteful, but it is a calculation that cannot be avoided by those involved in making social decisions. A decision rule that will more or less guarantee that the worst possible outcome will not occur is the *maximin rule*.

> *MAXIMIN RULE*: (1) Find the outcome with the minimum utility (the worst case outcome) for each choice, and (2) Select the choice that maximizes (has the greatest) minimum utility. Put in another way, select the choice with the most desirable worst-case outcome.

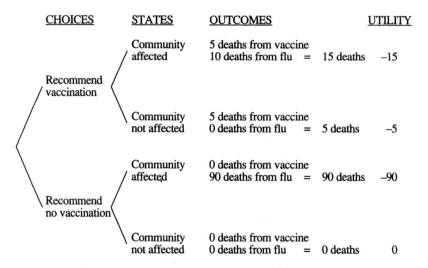

CHOICES	STATES	OUTCOMES			UTILITY
Recommend vaccination	Community affected	5 deaths from vaccine 10 deaths from flu	=	15 deaths	−15
	Community not affected	5 deaths from vaccine 0 deaths from flu	=	5 deaths	−5
Recommend no vaccination	Community affected	0 deaths from vaccine 90 deaths from flu	=	90 deaths	−90
	Community not affected	0 deaths from vaccine 0 deaths from flu	=	0 deaths	0

The maximin rule is sometimes said to be a pessimistic, or very conservative rule. This may be correct, but it is also a rule that is extremely reasonable under certain conditions for those whose expectations of disaster are run-of-the-mill. When a decision problem provides no probability information, and when one of the outcomes is clearly worse than others that are more or less alike, then it makes eminent sense to select the choice that gives you absolute protection against that worst possible outcome.

There is a tradition going back to the gambling origins of decision theory that recommends that when there is no probability information, you should assume that all states are equally probable. This idea, called the "Laplace criterion" or "the principle of indifference," may have something to recommend itself in areas where the states are determined according to the principles of pure chance, as in gambling. That is, there may be reasons in these cases of random distributions of probabilities to prefer an equiprobable distribution to some other distribution. But most decisions are not carried out in situations where the probabilities of states are determined randomly, and so the assumption of equiprobability surely makes less sense there. In addition, the Laplace criterion may have some rationale if we were forced to assume some probability distribution over the states, that is, if we had no other way to choose. But the maximin rule demonstrates that we do have alternatives to choice rules that employ probability information. To see how the addition of probability information changes the situation, consider the following alteration of the flu epidemic case.

PROBLEM: Having just made your decision as to whether the vaccination ought to be required based upon the information given, the Center for Disease Control calls with an urgent message that they have just succeeded, using the most advanced developments in probability theory, in calculating that there is a 5% chance that the flu will strike your community. The probability estimate is considered extremely accurate. What will the decision be now?

CHOICES	STATES	UTILITY	PROBABILITY
Recommend vaccination	Community affected	–15	.05
	Community not affected	–5	.95
			EU = –5.5
Recommend no vaccination	Community affected	–90	.05
	Community not affected	–0	.95
			EU = –4.5

With the probability of the flu epidemic now known to be a relatively low .05, the decision changes to recommend no vaccination program.

There is another circumstance in which the maximin rule should be considered. This is the circumstance in which there is probability information, but it is unreliable. It was reported in the February 2, 1989 issue of the *New York Times* that in the decade following 1977 the CIA had developed a large network of agents in Havana and in Cuban embassies throughout the world. The danger of "running" agents in this business is always that they are double agents, and that they will therefore become sources of damaging disinformation. This possibility was ruled out, according to the article, by the use of the polygraph test, a notoriously unreliable source of information. As it happens, the informers were double agents and had successfully fed false information from the KGB through the Cubans to the CIA for a decade.

It is probably possible to run an agent profitably, while being unsure of his or her allegiances, by always keeping in mind that the information on which that allegiance is based is unreliable. It is more likely though that, as a general rule, we should admit the following: Information known upon reception to be unreliable will probably be employed as if it were perfectly reliable, that is, will be indistinguishable in the manner in which it is used from reliable information. If this is true, then the following principle seems to make sense:

No probability information is better than unreliable probability information.

This would not be true if the lack of probability information was crippling to the decision-maker, but the example of maximin shows that this is not the case.

PROBLEM: General Andrews is faced with a serious battlefield decision. The enemy is advancing in superior numbers upon his men. He has been out of contact with them for some time and so does not know the extent of the losses of his men's superior fire power. He has only one report from a recent recruit to the effect that he thinks he saw a lot of supplies and equipment remaining. He thinks of the possibility of a strategic retreat as well as that of holding ground. The strategic retreat will somewhat threaten the rear lines, as will the failure of the groundholding strategy. The groundholding strategy will surely fail if the equipment has been seriously depleted. If the equipment is not seriously depleted, then the enemy will suffer serious casualties if the groundholding strategy is adopted. The general's other choice is tactical nuclear weapons to supplement the groundholding strategy. These will be certain to decimate the enemy's attacking forces. But just as certainly they will prompt the enemy to consider a similar response. General Andrews has only an out-of-date probability estimate of .05 of a tactical nuclear response by the enemy, but it was arrived at before hostilities began. But he is absolutely certain that if they so responded, there would be nuclear disaster for the region.

On a tree, the problem looks like the following. Here the reasonable thing would be to ignore the unreliable probability estimates. If the general were to estimate an 80% chance that the equipment was good and a .05% chance of nuclear response from the enemy, then the expected utilities would be:

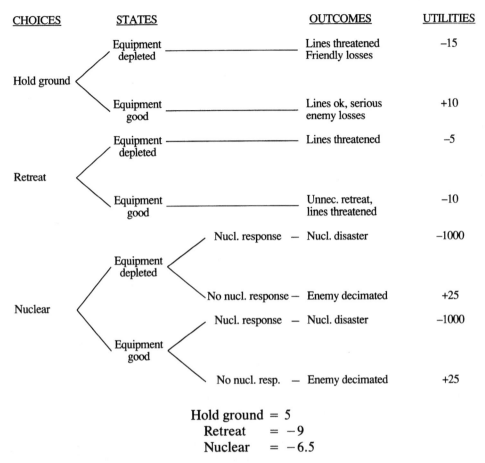

CHOICES	STATES	OUTCOMES	UTILITIES

Hold ground — Equipment depleted — Lines threatened Friendly losses — −15

Hold ground — Equipment good — Lines ok, serious enemy losses — +10

Retreat — Equipment depleted — Lines threatened — −5

Retreat — Equipment good — Unnec. retreat, lines threatened — −10

Nuclear — Equipment depleted — Nucl. response — Nucl. disaster — −1000

Nuclear — Equipment depleted — No nucl. response — Enemy decimated — +25

Nuclear — Equipment good — Nucl. response — Nucl. disaster — −1000

Nuclear — Equipment good — No nucl. resp. — Enemy decimated — +25

$$\text{Hold ground} = 5$$
$$\text{Retreat} = -9$$
$$\text{Nuclear} = -6.5$$

But with these potential losses, and the unreliability of the information, retreat is clearly superior to nuclear attack as a choice. The maximin rule in this case calls for retreat.

PROBLEM: Kurt is the agricultural minister for a developing country with a relatively arid geography. His nation is badly in need of lumber, and does not have the hard currency to continue to import it. He has to decide whether to engage in a massive program of reforestation, as was begun in Israel in this century. His major concern is whether there will be adequate rainfall over the next 40 to 50 years to sustain the trees and allow them to develop to full maturity. He, of course, consults records of past rainfalls, which are not encouraging. But he also knows that as the trees develop there will be atmospheric changes as a result of the trees, which could increase the probability of adequate rainfall over what it would have been had the trees not been planted. The plain truth is that he has no reliable probability information.

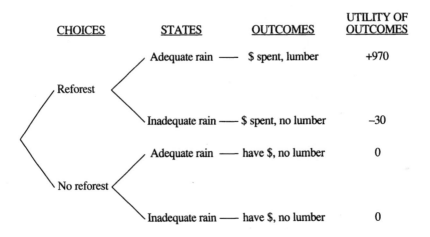

CHOICES	STATES	OUTCOMES	UTILITY OF OUTCOMES
Reforest	Adequate rain ——	$ spent, lumber	+970
	Inadequate rain ——	$ spent, no lumber	–30
No reforest	Adequate rain ——	have $, no lumber	0
	Inadequate rain ——	have $, no lumber	0

The utility numbers here represent a scale +1000 to −1000, where "0" represents the status quo of "no lumber," and a certain amount in the treasury. To have its own lumber is a tremendous gain, and to lose the money that would be needed to forest the land would be a minor loss. In this case, there is again utility information but no probability information. It should be further noted that the utilities are all more or less the same, except for one that is *significantly better*. We cannot use the expected value or the expected utility rule in this case because we have no probability numbers. As we have seen, there are decision rules that apply to situations in the absence of probability information. In this case the recommended rule is the *maximax rule*.

MAXIMAX RULE: (1) Find the outcome with the maximum utility (the best case outcome) for each choice. Each choice, then, will have a "maximum outcome." And (2) select the choice that maximizes (has the greatest) "maximum outcome." Put differently, select the choice with the most desirable best-case outcome.

This is sometimes said to be an optimistic rule. No doubt it is a rule that one would use if we assumed that the best will always happen. But it is not rational to assume that the best will always happen, especially when there is probability information to the contrary. That's just wishful thinking. The maximax rule does make sense when there is no reliable probability information, or when the states have, for all practical purposes, the same probabilities, and when the utilities are the same except for one that is *much better*. In these sorts of cases, there is little to lose and much to gain by selecting the choice with the greatest best case outcome. In the reforestation example, the maximax rule calls for the decision-maker to select the "Reforest" choice.

If you were to apply the maximax rule to solve the general's problem, the choice that would be selected would be "Nuclear." Yet with so little extra to gain, and so much more to lose, this hardly seems like the correct choice. This case does not fit the description of a situation for which maximax strategies are suited. True, there are real utilities and no probability information, but it is not the case that all outcomes are more or less the same in utility except for one that is much better. If fact, the reverse is true. All outcomes are more or less the same in utility, except that one is much *worse*. This situation calls for a rule that will guard against that *worst* outcome from occurring. The rule that most effectively guards against the worst is, as we have seen, the maximin rule.

PROBLEM: Mary is an avid sailor. She has recently moved to Long Island and plans to purchase a boat to sail on the Sound. She has narrowed her search to three different boats of very dissimilar design. One is a full-keel boat that draws five feet of water. Mary understands that this boat is very poor sailing in "light air," winds under eight knots, OK in winds of 8–12, good in 13–16, and pure joy over 16 kots. Her second option is a flat-bottom, centerboard boat that draws only 18 inches in the board-up position. It is a dream in light air, very good in 8–12, hard to handle in 13–16, and impossible in over 16 knots. The third option is a keel-centerboard that draws 2.5 feet with the board retracted. This boat is OK in light air, good in 8–12, OK in 13–16, and poor sailing in over 16. Mary will rarely be sailing in shallow water, and all boats are equal in her mind in all other respects. The probabilities of the various wind conditions are ranked as follows from most to least probable: 8–12 (4); 13–16 (3); under 8 (2); over 16 (1).

In this case, there are no real probability numbers for the states, but there are probability rankings. There are no real utility numbers for the outcomes, only rankings of utility based upon the verbal descriptions. The tree would look like the diagram on the next page.

The final RATING is the result of the *weighted ranking rule*.

WEIGHTED RANKING RULE: Multiply each utility ranking by its corresponding probability ranking and add all the products for each choice. Select the choice with the greatest rating (sum).

CHOICES	STATES	OUTCOME	OUTCOME RANK	PROB. RANKING	
Keel	Under 8	Very poor	—— 2	—— 2	
	8–12	OK	—— 5	—— 4	
	13–16	Good	—— 6	—— 3	
	Over 16	Joy	—— 8	—— 1	WR = 50 (Keel)
CB	Under 8	Dream	—— 9	—— 2	
	8–12	Very good	—— 7	—— 4	
	13–16	Hard	—— 4	—— 3	
	Over 16	Impossible	—— 1	—— 1	WR = 59 (CB)
K/CB	Under 8	OK	—— 5	—— 2	
	8–12	Good	—— 6	—— 4	
	13–16	OK	—— 5	—— 3	
	Over 16	Poor	—— 3	—— 1	WR = 52 (K/CB)

It is clear that the choice "CB" has the highest rating.

The Satisficing Principle

We have seen that a persistent criticism of the expected utility rule as a model of rational choice is that it requires the decision-maker to be too sophisticated about his or her knowledge, values, and approach to decision-making. We have handled some of this criticism by the introduction of rules, such as maximin, that require very limited information. But it remains true that all the rules we have so far adopted seek to identify *just one* choice as the *optimal* choice. Another approach would be to seek to identify one or more choices as *good enough*.

PROBLEM: Sam is trying to decide whether to purchase a show dog, a Lab, from Mary or Jean. Mary's dogs invariably turn out short and very muscular. Jean's dogs are always taller with a more athletic appearance. Sam wants a show winner but knows that fashion and fad among show judges is very changeable. Short and muscular Labs have for some time now been in fashion. He believes that in a year or so, when the dogs are ready to be shown, fashion has a better than fifty/fifty chance of changing. On the other hand Frank's Labs are tall and muscular, yet are yellow Labs unlike Jean's and Mary's. Sam has had yellows before and was sort of hoping for a black, though he was very happy with his yellow.

The Nobel Prize winning economist Herbert Simon pointed out many years ago that in certain situations it is asking too much for a decision-maker to select the *optimal* choice. It should be satisfactory to expect that the decision-maker select a choice that is *acceptable* (Simon 1957). If there is more than one acceptable choice, then it would be rational to select any of them, even if some were better than others on some more stringent standard. This idea he termed *satisficing*. To satisfice is to attempt to select an acceptable choice, rather than the optimal choice. When you are engaged in an optimizing strategy, each choice is compared to every other choice in order to select the best. When satisficing, the decision-maker establishes a standard of acceptability for a choice and compares candidate choices to this standard. When optimizing, it is necessary that every plausible potential choice be examined. When satisficing, the decision-maker need examine potential choices only until such time as one acceptable choice is found. The search can be terminated at that point.

You could define "acceptable choice" in numerous ways. One procedure in decisions with risk would be to label each outcome as "acceptable" or "unacceptable" based upon some value tree analysis, and select any choice that gives you a better than 50% chance of an acceptable outcome. If there is more than one choice that does this, then the satisficing rule does not distinguish among the choices. Simply select the first that comes to your attention.

With this criterion in mind we can inspect the following tree, which represents the problem of dog selection. It is clear that either "Buy Jean's dog" or "Buy Frank's dog" meets the satisficing criterion. Either choice is rational, and so, if Jean's dog had been considered first then the satisficing rule would have recommended that choice. In that case buying from Frank would not have been considered.

SATISFICING RULE: Label each outcome "acceptable" or "unacceptable" according to whether it meets some established aspiration level based upon a value analysis. Label each state as "p<.5" if the probability is less than 50%. Select *any* choice that provides a better than 50% chance of resulting in an "acceptable" outcome.

CHOICES	STATES	OUTCOMES	VALUE INFO	PROB INFO
Buy from Mary	Fashion remains	Win with M's dog	Acceptable	$p < .5$
	Fashion changes	Lose with M's dog	Unacceptable	$p > .5$
Buy from Jean	Fashion remains	Lose with J's dog	Unacceptable	$p < .5$
	Fashion changes	Win with J's dog	Acceptable	$p > .5$
Buy from Frank	Fashion remains	Lose with F's dog	Unacceptable	$p < .5$
	Fashion changes	Win with F's dog	Acceptable	$p > .5$

Note that this rule does not require real probability numbers, only that you be able to distinguish "greater than 50%" from the rest. Neither does this rule require utility numbers or even rankings, only that you be able to distinguish acceptable from unacceptable outcomes. In the problem above there are two choices that meet the satisficing rule and are thus rational choices. You may be tempted to recommend Jean's dog on the basis that it is black because that's what Sam preferred, but this would go beyond the intent of satisficing principle. The whole point of the satisficing principle is to simplify problems by requiring less information about values and probabilities. When we do that, we may not be able to narrow the rational choice down to just one. It should also be noted that you can add real probabilities to see if the chance of getting an "acceptable" outcome is greater than 50%. Note the following problem:

PROBLEM: In game A, a die is thrown. If it comes up 1 or 2, you get $3. If it comes up 3 or 4 you get $60. If it comes up 5 or 6, you get $65. In game B, a coin is flipped. If it comes up heads you get $55, and tails you get $45. In game C, a ball is drawn from a jar containing 20 reds, 20 whites, 55 blues, and 5 greens. If it is red or white you get $1000; if blue $50; if green, $500. As it happens you are desperate for a bus ticket to return home to visit a very sick parent. The bus ticket costs $57. Anything less than this is unacceptable. Below, (A) means "acceptable."

CHOICES	STATES	PROB. OF STATE	OUTCOME	
	1 or 2	p = .33	$3	
Game A	3 or 4	p = .33	$60	(A)
	5 or 6	p = .33	$65	(A)
Game B	Heads	p = .5	$55	
	Tails	p = .5	$45	
	Red or White	p = .4	$1000	(A)
Game C	Blue	p = .55	$50	
	Green	p = .05	$500	(A)

Checking the problem, we can determine that "$57 or more" is an acceptable outcome. Game A provides a (.33 + .33 =) .66 probability of an acceptable outcome. Game B provides a 0 probability of an acceptable outcome. And Game C provides a (.40 + .05 =) .45 probability of an acceptable outcome. Only Game A meets the satisficing criterion.

This ends the discussion of decision rules. There are of course other rules that have been formulated. Some are very complex, some very simple. The point to remember is that you should let the quality of the information determine which rule you will use. The quality of the information is not only a function of what has been given you in a real life situation; it is also a function of what you decide is *enough* given your circumstances. Sometimes you have imperfect information, but it would cost dearly in either time, money, or effort to get better information. You must decide if it is worth the effort. This in itself is a decision problem. These matters are taken up in the appendix on alternative decision rules.

Risk Seekers and Risk Averters

We have defined risk as the existence of states beyond the decision-maker's control that affect the outcomes of his or her choices. The degree of risk is a function of the size of the potential loss and the probability of that loss. That is, in every risky decision something is *at stake*. The greater the stake, the greater the risk. In addition, there is in every such decision some probability of loss. The greater that probability, the greater the risk. The term "loss" should be taken to mean becoming worse off than one is (actual loss), or becoming worse off than one could have been had one chosen differently (opportunity losses) (MacCrimmon and Wehrung 1986). Of course different people respond to risk in different ways. Some shy away at a cost, others seem to embrace it, and most fall somewhere in between. It is common in decision theory to distinguish between risk seekers and risk averters. One simple way to do this is by investigating a decision-maker's preferences for gambles. Suppose that you were offered the following choice:

CHOICES	STATES	OUTCOMES
A		$1000
B	Coin comes up Heads	$2000
	Coin comes up Tails	$0

You will note that the expected value of choice A is $1,000, and the expected value of choice B is also $1,000. The expected value rule tells you that you are to be *indifferent* between A and B. If we assume that utility is linearly related to money, that there is no increasing or decreasing marginal utility for dollars, the expected utility rule would also recommend that you be indifferent between A and B. If you were indifferent in this situation, you would be risk neutral. Assuming that money and utility are linearly related, if you preferred one choice over the other it would only be because of your attitude toward risk. Specifically, if you preferred the "sure thing" of $1,000 over the equally valuable gamble, it would indicate that you are a risk averter. This is because you would be preferring A only because it avoids risk, even in the face of the knowledge that it is equal in value to B. In similar fashion, if you preferred the gamble over the equally valuable sure thing, you would be a risk seeker. This procedure can be used not only to identify averters and seekers, but also to measure how much of an averter or seeker you are. For example, you can be shown the following decision tree.

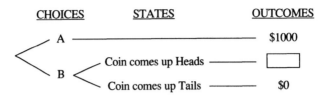

You are asked to put a dollar amount in the box that would make you *indifferent* between A and B. If you put in $2,000, then you would be neither a risk seeker nor a risk averter. If the number were greater than $2,000, then you are a risk averter. The greater the number that you would require, the greater is your aversion to risk. If the dollar amount was less than $2,000, you are a risk seeker. The smaller that it is, the greater is your risk-seeking propensity.

This procedure is clearly very limited. The fact is that very few people would not experience some increase or decrease in the marginal utility of money. For most, the dollar that brought them from $1,999 to $2,000 is not likely to be as valuable to them as the dollar that brought them from $999 to $1,000. If that were true, then the results of the test could reflect that fact rather than or in addition to any risk attitudes. This would not be a problem, though, if utility numbers were used in place of dollar values. There are other ways of measuring attitudes toward risk that avoid these types of problems (MacCrimmon and Wehrung 1986).

Why is it important to have some idea about your own attitudes toward risk? Extensive studies by MacCrimmon and Wehrung have shown that the whole approach toward decision-making is affected by whether one is a risk taker or risk averter. They describe the decision-maker's behavior in the risky situation by what they call the REACT Model, standing for Recognize-Evaluate-Adjust-Choose-Track. It is obvious that at the "Choose" phase, the risk seeker will take choices that involve greater potential loss and/or a higher probability of loss. It is also true however that at the earliest stage of problem recognition, the risk seeker perceives risks as being lower than that of the risk averter. At the evaluation stage when (among other things) you are assessing the reliability of the information available, risk seekers tend to take the information at face value, whereas risk averters tend to demand more information on probabilities, adopting worst-case scenarios. Risk averters would be more attentive to monitor or track the consequences of the decision than would risk seekers.

Is it better to be a risk averter or a risk seeker? In a very technical sense it is best to be neither, that is, it is best to be risk neutral. If you were gambling over the long run with an opponent who was risk neutral, and you were either risk seeking or risk averse, you would lose. There still may be some lingering beliefs that being a risk seeker is better, more "manly" perhaps, or more likely to lead to success. Unfortunately, the truisms of common sense are little help to us since we are told on the one hand "nothing ventured nothing gained," and on the other hand "all speed no control." The important study of the behavior of business executives by MacCrimmon and Wehrung is helpful here, since we often think of such managers as effective decision-makers. The authors used both artificial situations (questions such as those described above) and natural situations (for example, how someone's assets are distributed) to measure willingness to take risks. In both types of situations, business managers were significantly risk averse. Interestingly this fact was not consistent with their own evaluations of themselves. In measures of attitudes about their own risk propensities, executives consistently rated themselves as more risk seeking than they actually were. As MacCrimmon and Wehrung state, "The managers were more risk taking in their attitudes than in their behavior" (p.231). While we would think perhaps that people's willingness to take risks should be consistent, in fact they are not. For example, managers showed different risk propensities for personal decisions than for business decisions (MacCrimmon and Wehrung, p. 234).

> managers who are mortgaged to the hilt or who gamble on the golf course will not necessarily take risks at work . . . executives who hold all their personal wealth in secure assets or who purchase excessive life insurance may be their firm's greatest risk takers.

The study did show, however, a greater propensity to take risks in business decisions than in personal family decisions. Finally, the study showed that managers with higher incomes took more risks; chief executive officers took more risks; and more successful managers took more risks. None of this, however, justifies the conclusion that it was a greater willingness to take risks that led to greater income, responsibility, or success. It may be just the reverse, that higher income allows for greater risk, or that being a CEO makes risk taking more possible or desirable.

Risk Adjustment

The concept of risk adjustment can best be understood in the context of what we have called decision structuring. We have seen the steps leading to a properly structured decision:

1. Analysis of goals and objectives;
2. Formulation of choices;
3. Description of states;
4. Evaluation of probabilities of states given choices;
5. Description of outcomes in terms of goals and objectives;
6. Evaluation of utilities of outcomes;
7. Review for risk adjustment;
8. Selection of decision rule according to the type of available information;
9. Implementation of the decision;
10. Monitoring of progress of the decision.

The step immediately following the evaluation of utilities of outcomes, when the problem is almost completely structured, is the point at which the risk adjustment should take place. Naturally the point is almost always to lower the risk if at all possible. Given the components of risk, this means to lower the potential losses and/or to lower the probability of those losses. In one sense this step should be seen as a review of the structuring problem since if the risk can be lowered that action becomes one of the choices. But the step is not merely a general review, but one that focuses upon the lowering of risk. As such it is a very useful time to stop to think about the problem.

In thinking about risk adjustment, it is necessary to distinguish those methods that rely upon the self-deceptive techniques described, for example, by Janis and Mann, from rational and effective methods. Within the realm of effective methods, risk can be adjusted by simply avoiding, if possible, the risky situation, refusing to take the gamble. Or risk can reduced by being shared. This need not be "passing the buck." If you have a shipment of oil coming out of the Persian gulf, you can share the risk of financial loss by insuring the shipment. In that case some of the financial loss will belong to the insurance company. Risk can often be reduced by delaying the decision while more information is being collected. This would be the case in many decisions concerning medical treatment. A second opinion, or more extensive testing may reduce or even eliminate the risk. When your risk is the result of the possible behavior of another person, the risk can be reduced by negotiation with that person, or by increasing the risk to the other person. Increasing the risk to the other person does not necessarily mean "making him an offer he can't refuse." It may simply mean negotiating a valid contract, which if broken, subjects the other to legal liability. An example of this is a prenuptual agreement, which reduces the risk that one party in the marriage will lose assets upon divorce. If the other party attempts to take the assets upon divorce he or she will face legal action as a result of the contractual agreement.

MacCrimmon and Wehrung presented executives with descriptions of hypothetical risky situations to determine the degree to which they would attempt to adjust the risk rather than simply selecting one or another of the presented choices. The respondents consistently sought to adjust their risk prior to choosing. They used techniques of delaying choice, delegating choice, negotiating, and seeking further information.

The importance of focusing upon risk adjustment is, in the last analysis, to assure that the set of choices is exhaustive. If there exist significant steps that could reduce risk after the decision has been structured, then the decision was not adequately structured in the first place. Building risk adjustment into the structuring process increases the probability that the process of decision structuring will be effective.

Important Concepts

Decision-making under risk	Empirical issues
Outcomes	Choices
States of nature	Utilities of outcomes
Single stage problem	Multi-stage problem
Outcome tree	Outcome matrix
Exclusive	Exhaustive
Decision tree	Decision rule
Ranking numbers	Utility numbers
Risk seeker	Risk averter
Risk adjustment	Maximin rule
Maximax rule	Expected value
Expected utility	Dominance rule

Problems for Analysis

DIRECTIONS: The following are some problems that you can use to practice creating decision trees. Be sure to be very clear about the nature of the goals that the decision seeks to achieve. Recall that the type and amount of information available to you in the problem will determine how complete the tree is. The task is to structure the problem, determine the type of utility and probability information that is available to you, and select and apply the appropriate decision rule. In some instances, it will be necessary for you to provide utility and probability numbers based upon the information described in the problem. There is not necessarily only one decision tree for each of the problems, but you should have a good reason for structuring the situations as you do.

1. You are a medical doctor examining a patient complaining of pains in the area of the upper stomach and chest. You know the patient has a history of stomach disorders whose symptoms are similar to those of a heart attack, and that the patient is not wealthy and is uninsured. The tests necessary to rule out a heart attack are very expensive. You consider all these factors as well as the obvious possibility that the patient is experiencing a heart attack. You know from statistics that the overwhelming majority of patients presenting heart attack symptoms are, in fact, suffering from problems no more threatening than indigestion. Should you act on the assumption of heart attack or not?

2. Sandy and Fred work in the same firm and have been living together for some time. They are more or less engaged. Jim works in the firm also and has asked Sandy to the company benefit dinner, a night during which Fred is away on a trip. Sandy has "noticed" Jim in the past, and has wished that she had a chance to get to know him. On the other hand, if Fred found out that Sandy had dated Jim, it would be very painful for Sandy. She wonders if she should accept outright, reject outright, or suggest a more discreet meeting at Jim's place for dinner. (Hint: Use the expected utility rule or the weighted ranking rule.)

3. Lonny is thinking about going into medicine or the stock market. In the former case, he is certain of $200,000 per year whatever the economy does, due to the inelastic nature of the demand for medical services. In the stock market, his average yearly earnings will be $80,000 in a "bear" year (when the market is in a decline), and

$400,000 in a bull year (when the market advances). He estimates that the probability of bull years is 1 in 3.

4. Louise agrees with Lonny's analysis except that she is going into plastic surgery if she chooses medicine, a field of mostly upper-income patients. As a result, she calculates that she will make $250,000 in bull years in medicine when the upper-class cash is looking for a home, but only half that in bear years.

5. Linda needs one more class to graduate with a B.A. degree in mathematics, and needs a minimum of a B− grade on the course or she will not graduate. She has always wanted to take a course on the Bible, but has not been able to fit it into her tight schedule. The only two courses available to her at this time are "Introduction to the Bible as Literature," and the "History of Bolivia." Linda has never liked history, although she has done well when forced to study it. She discovers the history course to be a snap. The student evaluations published by the student association reports that 80% of all students receive a B− or better. The Bible course is taught by the college's most famous faculty member, who is also known as its best teacher. The same booklet reports that the probability of B− is 65%. (Hint: use the expected utility rule.)

6. Recall Fred and Sandy from the problem above. Fred has, in fact, been unhappy for some time in his relationship with Sandy. He would like it to end, but has problems when he thinks over his options. He has seen that Sandy is interested in her boss Jim with whom (unbeknownst to Sandy) Fred grew up. Fred believes that Jim would ask Sandy out if Fred encouraged him to do so, and that Sandy might leave Fred if Jim showed real interest. Fred has considered just breaking the relationship with Sandy, but in that event Sandy would get to keep the rent-controlled apartment. It was their written agreement when they began to live together that whoever left, the other would forfeit the apartment. Of course, Fred could do nothing but hope that Sandy ends the relationship, but he does not consider it likely that she would leave without some external motivation.

7. Sandy decides to sneak off to Jim's for dinner and has promised to bring the wine. She wants terribly to impress Jim, who is her boss. Sandy read in *Gourmet* magazine that white wine goes well with fish or chicken, and red wine should be served with beef. Rosé goes with either, but is considered déclassé in Sandy's circle, and so is ruled out. The red that complements the beef is rather delicate, whereas if Jim served turkey, Sandy knows she should provide a more full-bodied wine such as a red burgundy. If she were to bring the wrong red to a

meal that demanded a red, it would not be so bad as to bring a white to the wrong meal, or a red to a fish or chicken meal. Sandy would not consider bringing more than one bottle. It occurs to Sandy that Jim is one of those very devoted runners, and so probably avoids red meat. She also notes that the Thanksgiving holiday is only ten days away. Her choice is becoming clear to her. (Hint: weighted ranking rule?)

8. Jack is thinking about buying a motel, and has narrowed his choice down to three properties. Each is named after the route on which it is located, The Rt.2, The Rt.7, and The Rt.9. One of these routes is due to be expanded into a major highway, increasing motel traffic three-fold. Jack has learned that the governor of the state has a financial interest in the Pleasure Palace Motel and Video Room on Rt.2, and that a bitter enemy of the governor has a gas station on Rt.9. The governor's brother-in-law is the state highway commissioner. Route 7 and route 2 are very close to each other and so often receive each other's overflow. The purchase prices of the three are about the same, but the Rt.7 is 1.5 times as large as the Rt.2, which is the same size as the Rt.9. Jack ponders his options and decides to use the Expected Utility rule.

9. Jane wants very much to go to law school. Her mother, who is her hero, has a very successful law practice. Jane is a determined person and has always insisted that she be a career professional, as is her mother. She is considering whether or not to major in pre-law. This is a major that is highly concentrated in history, government, and literature. Statistics indicate that such a major would increase slightly her chances of being admitted to law school over what those chances would be in any other major. In the back of her mind Jane thinks that accounting would be her second choice if she could not be admitted to law school. She likes accounting, and did well in it in high school, but it is a poor second to law as a career choice. She knows that most accounting degree graduates have to enroll in CPA review courses upon graduation in order to have a chance to pass the CPA exams, and that's what she would do. Jane entered college with combined SAT scores of 920, and is now a B − student. You are Jane's adviser. Should she major in pre-law?

10. Helen is president of a small but successful electronics firm on Long Island. She is under pressure from her stockholders to expand drastically either to take advantage of the Reagan defense budgets, or of the recent increase in consumer spending due to the bull markets on Wall Street. Helen is cautious that an expansion into the military area runs the risk that Congress may cut back on the large military budgets.

She also worries that the market must eventually run its course, resulting in a contraction of consumer demand. Through her prudent management, Helen's firm is positioned to maintain its present levels of per year profit of $4 million even if the economy worsens or defense spending is cut. She feels that any contraction of demand would be a disaster if she expanded into either new field. Disaster to Helen means zero profit. Helen knows that due largely to their sloppy procurement practices the defense department would allow her a profit that would be double that of the consumer electronics field under consideration. Yet the latter would be likely to double her present profits. Her advisors tell her that there is a 4 in 10 chance that Congress will continue defense spending at'present levels rather than contract, and there is a 6 in 10 chance that the economy will not contract. What do you think?

11. Tom, an avid fisherman, is planning to spend his day off fishing on a small charter boat. Depending upon the sea conditions, the captain will go after blues, fluke, or blackfish. In heavy seas, which sometimes occur this time of year, he stays close and goes after blues; in the more common moderate seas he goes out for fluke; and in very calm seas he travels long distances for the more prized blackfish. This time of year he seldom goes after blackfish. Tom can pack only one kind of tackle. As it happens, bluefish tackle may catch some blackfish, but never fluke. Similarly, blackfish tackle may catch some fluke, but never blues, but Tom doesn't like blues very much. Fluke tackle catches only fluke. Each type of fish can only be caught in its own waters. Tom would always prefer catching more fish to fewer fish, no matter what kind. Which tackle should Tom bring?

12. Fran owns a struggling restaurant in a declining neighborhood. She makes a slight living from it, but one advantage of this is that she is able to live in an apartment over the business. She has been offered a fair price for the business, including the building that she would have to vacate. If she sold, she would return to her old job making pretty good money, most of which would be eaten up by housing costs. There have been persistent rumors that a large and exclusive condominium project is soon to be built in the neighborhood. She has no idea whether these rumors are true. Should she accept the offers?

13. The problem is exactly as in #8 above except that Jack has just heard that the governor is planning to use fire, health, and other codes to put The Rt.2 Motel out of business should Rt.2 be chosen as the highway to be expanded. This will clear away any competition for The Pleasure Palace Motel and Video Room. Upon investigation Jack

comes up with a best estimate that the chances are 6 in 10 that the governor will succeed in doing this should Rt.2 be chosen for expansion. He has also been able to determine that there is a .6 probability that Rt.2 will be expanded, and only a .05 probability that Rt.9 will be expanded. What does Jack's problem look like now?

14. Lucinda is considering a medical career, but is also drawn to Wall Street as a broker. She calculates her earnings in medicine as $250,000 per year, not being affected by the state of the stock market. When she thinks of the market over the next 40 years or so, she estimates that bull years will occur ⅓ of the time. In that case as a broker, she could expect to average about $400,000 per year. But she feels that there are also good and bad years during a bear market, the former (good years) occurring about 6 in 10 years. During these good bear years she feels she could expect to average $125,000, while during the bad bear years, it would be closer to $80,000. What is the structure of Lucy's problem?

15. Agamemnon must ask someone to the prom. Of course he would give his left arm to go with (yes, you guessed it) Helen, the most beautiful woman in all of Acropolis High School. But he has thought also of Helen's sister Clytemnaestra for whom he has the deepest respect, and whose company he enjoys in an intellectual sort of way. Helen seems to like him, but she has already been asked by Paris who is football captain at nearby Trojan High School. In addition, Helen is dating Menelaus, although she seems bored by him. Agamemnon is quite certain that Clytemnaestra will accept if he asks her first (there's at least an 80% chance), but if he asks her after having been refused by her sister, the odds are cut in half. To ask Helen on the rebound is out of the question, and he calculates his chances of Helen's accepting his first-time offer as 3 in 10. To not have a date for the prom is a disaster in the young man's life.

16. Larry is a friend of Lucinda with a similar problem. His options are stock brokerage or professional golf. He agrees that chances of a bull year are 1/3 and that in that case the $400,000 income figure is accurate. He also agrees that a clever broker will have good and bad bear years, and that $125,000 is correct for a good bear year, the probability of the latter being 2/3. But he believes that in a bad bear year there is only a 2/3 chance of the $80,000 that Lucy spoke of. In the other case, he calculates earnings losses of $30,000. Larry also feels that in a bull year his golf income could be expected to average $300,000, while otherwise it would be $125,000. What does Larry's problem look like?

17. Mary has applied to law schools. She prefers a Hofstra degree to the rest. She is also applying to Brooklyn Law (both day and evening schools with their three and four year programs), and NYU. She prefers Brooklyn Day to NYU. In fact, NYU is twice as far behind Brooklyn Day as the latter is behind Hofstra in her evaluation. Last is Brooklyn Evening, which is behind NYU to the same degree that Brooklyn Day is behind Hofstra. Her evaluations of the schools are based upon many different attributes, for example, location, future earnings power of graduates, legal specialization, rate of bar exam passage of graduates on the first try, etc. She arrived at the overall evaluations described above as a result of a multi-attribute utility analysis. The literature that Mary received from each school was a source of alarm to her. It described rates of successful completion of the law programs as follows: Hofstra (40%), NYU (40%), Brooklyn Day (60%), Brooklyn Evening (70%). Mary decides that flunking out of a school is bad in proportion that the school's degree is valued. She gets into all four programs. What does her choice look like? (Note: All above figures are hypothetical.)

18. You need money and a friend offers you a way to get some. You can pay him $20 to play a simple game. Throw a die. If it comes up a 1 or 2, you get $50. If it comes up anything else you get nothing. What does the Maximin recommend? What does the Maximax recommend? Are either appropriate decision rules? What does Expected Value recommend?

19. You have $100 and only that to apply to graduate schools in decision science. By far your first choice is the University of Chicago where the application fee is $100. Your other two choices are the University of Pennsylvania, and Stony Brook's Averell Harriman College. Each of those school's application fees is $50. You prefer the latter slightly. You have no idea as to which school is most likely to give you the financial support necessary to attend. If you cannot attend any school, you can work in your family's securities firm, an option that is as attractive as attending Stony Brook.

20. You are offered a choice between the following two wagers. (A) You will get $80 if you choose a clubs from a deck of cards, or $40 if you choose anything else. (B) You bet $120 if a die comes up a 3, or $15 if the die comes up anything else. Which wager should you select?

21. The odds that the Mets will defeat the Red Sox are 3 to 1. You are offered a wager for a price. The wager is: $120 if the Sox win, $40 if the Mets win. The price of the wager is $75. Should you play? (Hint: Here it is necessary to translate odds into probabilities. If the odds

that *A* will occur rather than *B* are *m* to *n*, then the probability that *A* will occur is $m/m + n$, and the probability that *B* will occur is $n/m + n$.)

22. Mary is the president of a flower shop. She is trying to decide whether or not to expand by renting the floor space of the shop next door. Her net income is now $75,000 per year. If she makes the move, her expenses will increase by $14,000 per year. She figures that there is a 20% chance that she can gross an additional $45,000 by expanding. In the event that this additional $45,000 does not occur, she will gross only an additional $4,000 per year. Put the decision on a tree and decide if Mary should make the move or not.

23. Gertrude is offered the following: She can take $1,200 and that's it. Or she can play the game. The game is to flip a coin twice. If it comes up heads both times she can throw a die. If the die comes up a 2 or 4, she gets $6,000. If it comes up anything else, she gets $600. If the coin does not come up heads both times then she can draw a card from a deck. If it comes up Clubs, she gets $3,200. If it does not, then she gets $480. What should she do?

24. The game is exactly as it is above in 23, except that you now know that Gertrude has no money, and needs $1,100 this week for life saving surgery for her child. (Hint: Check the concept of variations of marginal utility). Explain clearly the rule you are using and its rationale in this circumstance.

25. Ted is trying to decide if he should have an AIDS test. He is a heterosexual but has been fairly indiscriminate in his choices of sexual partners, including some whom he now knows to have been IV drug users, and even some prostitutes on occasion. He is in love with Betty and wants to marry her. So far he has used condoms on the two occasions when they have made love, but he knows that this will not be possible for long since Betty wants a child very soon. He does not trust the statistics that are available on the various percentages of the people of various kinds who have AIDS, nor does he trust the statistics on the chances of getting it from infected people. He just does not know. What should he do, and why? (Hint: Dominance rule?)

26. Arnie has a reasonably successful pharmacy in an expensive resort village. A salesman presents him with the possibility of carrying next season a new and extremely expensive cosmetic line. The initial outlay of cash to carry the line would be $52,000, nearly all of Arnie's cash reserves. The profit margin on the cosmetics is surprisingly small given how expensive they are, but there would be modest profits on the line (after expenses, including the initial investment), but only assuming that the coming ad campaign for the cosmetics is successful.

The campaign is being designed by an ad firm that is new and so has no track record as to its success. The line does not take up a great deal of room and so would not displace any other products, but there would be no possibility of return of unsold goods. Arnie knows that no other store in the village will be carrying the product line. (Hint: What do you do when you have no, or very unreliable, probability information?)

27. Sue Zemall stubbed her toe on your client Phil Theelucra's patio when she crashed his Fourth of July party. Her lawyer has filed suit for $100,000 for medical costs and pain and suffering. After consulting your partners, you have determined that there is a 20% chance that the jury will find in her favor, and if this happens, there is a ten percent chance that she will recover for pain and suffering and thus get her full $100,000. If they do find in her favor but do not grant the pain and suffering part, then she will receive her medical costs of $100. Sue has offered to settle out of court for $5,000. If your client accepts, his legal fees will be $1,000. If it goes to trial, they will be $6,000, with a 20% chance that, if the jury finds in Phil's favor, Sue will have to pay Phil's legal fees. Assuming that you have only your client's best interests in mind, what do you advise that he do?

28. Amber Lance-Chaser has been accepted to two Law Schools in Alaska where she wants to settle: Litigious College and Mouth Peace University. She is not a great student, and is only interested in practicing law, which means graduating and then passing the bar. Only 60% of Mouth Peace states graduate; but of those, 80% pass the bar. Litigious graduates 70% of its enrollees, but only 50% of these pass the bar. Where should Amber go to school?

29. Alex M. got a BB gun for his birthday. Two days later, while with a friend, he shot himself in the hand while trying to test the air pressure in the gun. He didn't know the gun was loaded. The BB lodged in his palm, and had to be removed by a surgeon in the emergency room of the hospital. The hospital had to notify the police since it was a gunshot wound, and the officer lectured Alex and his friend Robbie W. after they returned from the hospital. Alex's main worry was what to tell the kids in school about the bandages on his hand. If he told the truth he would be the object of ridicule. If he lied and said he fell, and he was found out it would be even worse. If he lied, he would not be found out unless his friend, who promised silence, blabbed. It does seem more likely that Robbie will tell than that he will not, but Alex doesn't have any idea how much more likely. He could of course be vague and avoid the questions, neither lying nor telling all. In this case, if they found out it would not be as bad as even

telling the truth. On the other hand this risks his being found out by seeming suspicious, and his being found out in this way seems more likely than if he lied, but he doesn't know how much. If they never found out, the outcomes would all be of equal value. What should he do? (Hint: weighted ranking?)

30. Fran is a history major in her senior year and is planning her courses for the last term. She is allowed to take one course on a pass/fail basis. She decides that it will be either Medieval French Literature or Calculus II. She estimates that each course is equally difficult and that she has a 40% chance of getting a "B" and a 30% chance of getting a "C," a 10 percent chance of getting an "A," and a 10% chance of getting a "D" or "F." Failing either course would be equally disastrous, and getting a "D" in French would be almost as bad since it's near her major. A "D" in calculus would be as about as bad as getting a "C" in French. Getting an "A" or "B" in calculus would be good, but not quite as good as an "A" or "B" in French. Clearly an "A" in French would be great. Which course would be more attractive to take on a graded basis?

31. Frank is running for mayor of Westfield, population 130,000. He has just gotten hold of some damaging information about the personal life of his opponent, Henrietta. He figures that if he makes it public and if it's true, he could gain about 50,000 votes, but only if the Westfield *Times* supports him in his charges. If it's true and the paper turns on him, he could lose up to 15,000 votes. He figures that there's a 60% chance that the information is true, and a 70% chance in that case that the paper will support his charges. If it's false and he has made it public, there's a 90% chance that the paper will turn on him, and he will then lose 30,000 votes. If the paper still supports him even though his charges turn out to be false, he figures he'll break even. Frank knows that Henrietta will be able to prove the charges false if they are false, and will thus assume they're true unless they're proven false. Neither side in the campaign at this point has any idea how the campaigns are going. Should Frank make the information public? (Hint: Assume that one vote equals one unit of utility.)

Chapter 7

Risky Decisions with Complex Outcomes

It is the purpose of this chapter to integrate Chapters 3 and 6, that is, to integrate the MAUT approach to the evaluation of complex outcomes with the discussion of problems under risk. In the section on multi-attribute analysis, we dealt only with decisions under certainty. The purpose of the multi-attribute analysis was to arrive at overall utility ratings for outcomes that were composed of multiple attributes. We then recommended that the decision-maker select the choice with the most valuable outcome. Since these were decisions under certainty, the outcomes were assured given that the choices were made. The basic point is, however, that multi-attribute analysis is a tool for the evaluation of complex outcomes. There is no reason to think that decisions under risk should not also have complex outcomes. Thus there is every reason to think that multi-attribute analysis can also be applied to the evaluation of the outcomes in decisions under risk.

Recall that the standard format for a decision problem under risk with complete information is the following:

<u>CHOICES</u>	<u>STATES</u>	<u>PROBABILITIES</u>	<u>OUTCOME UTILITIES</u>
Select A	State 1 ——	Prob (S1 given A) —	Util (Outcome of A given S1)
	State 2 ——	Prob (S2 given A) —	Util (Outcome of A given S2)
Select B	State 3 ——	Prob (S3 given B) —	Util (Outcome of B given S3)
	State 4 ——	Prob (S4 given B) —	Util (Outcome of B given S4)

In order to select the optimal choice using the expected utility rule, it would be necessary to have real utility numbers describing each of the four outcomes. In Chapter 6, these utility numbers were arrived at by techniques that dealt with the outcomes *as wholes*. It could be said that the utility numbers were attached by "eyeballing" the value of the outcomes. The motto of multi-attribute analysis is "divide and conquer," and there are very real advantages to this approach, as we have seen. In this chapter, we will develop a way to attach the utility numbers to the outcomes in decisions under risk through this divide and conquer approach.

Let's suppose that the decision-maker in the hypothetical decision above had three objectives, X, Y, Z, which he or she wanted to achieve in making the decision. This means that each of the outcomes above should be, in fact, a bundle or combination of levels of fulfillment of X, Y, and Z. The decision should be represented, then, as it is below:

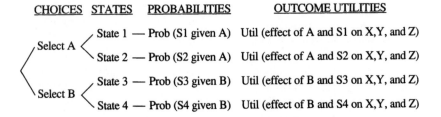

In the above schema we explicitly represent the fact that where the outcomes are complex, i.e., multi-attributed, the utility of those outcomes will be based upon some process that amalgamates the values of the components of the outcomes. In this case, for example, the selection of choice A with state 1 occurring will have an effect upon the level of fulfillment of objective X (that level having a specific value), of objective Y (that level having a specific value), and of objective Z (that level having a specific value). The utility of the outcome will be some function of those three values.

This is too abstract at this point, so let's look at a simple example to begin with.

PROBLEM: Nick is a bachelor from a very traditional family and is just beginning to plan his post-graduate years. He was very good in his finance courses and would definitely make excellent money were he to complete an MBA in finance. But troubles in mathematics give him only a sixty percent chance of success in the program. He could please his family and go directly into its dry cleaning business and make a respectable income with little advancement due to the family control, and its conservative business practices. On the other hand Nick was most interested in his psychology courses, and has thought about a Ph.D. in clinical psychology with emphasis upon alcohol and drug rehabilitation. While Nick wants money very much, and he wants to please his family (though not nearly as much as he wants money), his first priority (beating money slightly) is to work with people in need. On the other hand he could fail to achieve his psychology degree, and not be able to do that. He gives his chances of successfully attaining a Ph.D. at forty percent. If he fails in either program he would join the business, though with a loss of family respect. Both programs would drain his finances in the short run, and the psychology career would pay at about the same level as the dry cleaning business. Finally Nick is interested in job prestige, in which he ranks corporate finance ahead slightly of psychologist, with both significantly ahead of the family business.

The steps in dealing with this problem are as follows:

STEP 1: *Establish the value tree.* In this case the value tree would look something like the following.

GOAL	OBJECTIVES	ATTRIBUTES	FINAL ATTRIBUTE WEIGHTS
	Money (.4)	Long-term (.7)	.28
		Short-term (.3)	.12
Select best post-grad strategy	Service (.5)	Work in substance abuse (1)	.50
	Reputation (.1)	Family (.3)	.03
		Prestige (.7)	.07

STEP 2: *Establish a partial decision tree.* At this stage, the decision tree will include CHOICES, STATES, STATE PROBABILITIES, and a shorthand description of the OUTCOMES. The shorthand description of the outcomes reminds us that since we have established our value tree, the outcomes will be "bundles" of the five attributes on the value tree. The decision tree is not complete, of course, since no

outcome utilities are included. These will be supplied only after the value of each of the outcomes has been calculated using the MAUT approach. The partial decision tree for John's problem looks like the following:

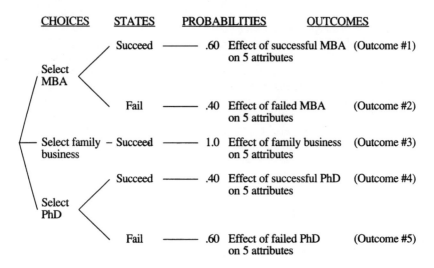

CHOICES	STATES	PROBABILITIES	OUTCOMES
Select MBA	Succeed	.60	Effect of successful MBA on 5 attributes (Outcome #1)
	Fail	.40	Effect of failed MBA on 5 attributes (Outcome #2)
Select family business	Succeed	1.0	Effect of family business on 5 attributes (Outcome #3)
Select PhD	Succeed	.40	Effect of successful PhD on 5 attributes (Outcome #4)
	Fail	.60	Effect of failed PhD on 5 attributes (Outcome #5)

STEP 3: *Evaluate each of the outcomes.* This involves constructing a matrix on which each of the four outcomes will be rated based upon the level to which they fulfill each of the five weighted attributes. A weighted sum will be calculated for each of the outcomes. This will be the *utility* of that outcome. The matrix will look like the following:

OUTCOMES	WEIGHTED ATTRIBUTES					WEIGHTED SUMS
	Money Short .12	Money Long .28	Psych Work .50	Family .03	Prestig .07	
Outcome #1	3/ .36	10/2.80	2/1.0	7/ .21	10/ .70	5.07
Outcome #2	3/ .36	5/1.40	1/ .5	2/ .06	3/ .21	2.52
Outcome #3	9/1.08	5/1,40	1/ .5	10/ .30	3/ .21	3.49
Outcome #4	2/ .24	6/1.68	10/5.0	6/ .18	10/ .70	7.80
Outcome #5	2/ .24	5/1.40	1/ .5	1/ .03	3/ .21	2.38

STEP 4: *Complete the decision tree.* This involves putting the utilities (weighted sums) into the decision tree and calculating the expected utility of each choice. Recall that the decision tree at STEP 2 did not have the utilities of the outcomes on it. This was because the outcomes were complex, consisting of such things as the effect of the choices on short-term money, long-term money, prestige, etc., and their utilities had not yet been evaluated. STEP 3 succeeded in evaluating the utilities of each of the five outcomes. We can now complete the decision tree by putting in the utility numbers, and applying the expected utility rule.

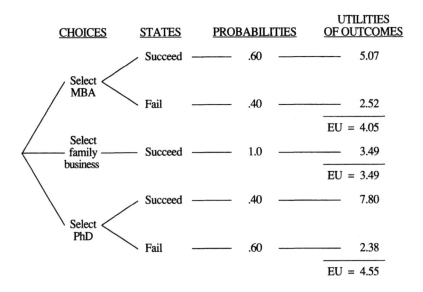

CHOICES	STATES	PROBABILITIES	UTILITIES OF OUTCOMES
Select MBA	Succeed	.60	5.07
	Fail	.40	2.52
			EU = 4.05
Select family business	Succeed	1.0	3.49
			EU = 3.49
Select PhD	Succeed	.40	7.80
	Fail	.60	2.38
			EU = 4.55

STEP 5: *Select the choice with the greatest expected utility.* The expected utility rule calls for the selection of Ph.D. in Psychology.

STEP 6: *Review and perform sensitivity analysis.* As with the multi-attribute problems under certainty, the results of the analysis may not conform to your initial preferences or intuitions. It is useful then to review the analysis to see if there is any way that it can *properly* be altered so that it does conform to the more holistic judgment. If this is not possible, then the analysis should prevail. One interesting question to ask is how much of a change in probability estimates, value weighting, or utility ratings it would take to change the decision resulting

resulting from the analysis. This is not an interesting question if the analysis agrees with initial judgments, or with others involved, but it is important if the two do not agree. It is also an important question if the results of the analysis do not agree with the views of others. Finally, it is important if there is some estimate of either probability or objective weight that you are not sure of. The sensitivity analysis of this type will tell you whether the alternatives that you are considering would affect the ultimate choice selection.

The question is, how sensitive is the result of the analysis (the choice of "Select Ph.D.") to changes in some of the variables? For example, if we were to alter the probability of success in the MBA program by changing it from .6 to .7, then the choice selected would be unchanged. If we were to change the probability of MBA success to .8, quite a significant alteration, the expected utilities of the MBA vs. the Ph.D. would be identical. On the other hand, we could alter the weights placed upon the objectives. If we were to reverse the weights given to "Money" and to "Service," again quite a significant change, the MBA would be preferable to the Ph.D. by a very slim 4.55 to 4.52. This indicates that it takes a very significant rethinking of either values or probability estimates to reverse the decision arrived at through this model. Knowing this increases one's confidence in the decision, and provides an added rationale should the decision be questioned. In more complex decisions, the kind of sensitivity analysis described here would best be done by using some standard spreadsheet software such as Lotus, or the like.

The Worry and Then Leap-in-the-Dark Approach

This procedure may seem long and cumbersome, but the fact is that in both time and energy it is most often far less demanding than the "worry and then leap-in-the-dark" approach that we very often use for important problems. Think of choices such as which home to buy, should I sell and move to Florida, should I recommend a new product line to the boss, should I file for divorce, which college should I attend, should I send my child to private school, should I run for school board, should I quit my job and go to law school, should I take an MBA degree at night, the list is endless. It is common in decisions such as these for us to spend great amounts of time worrying, randomly hashing over pros and cons in the middle of the night, and finally letting the press of deadlines force us to make a hasty, uninformed decision. This is the "worry and then leap-in-the-dark" approach, and it is accompanied by great amounts of stress with the ever-present temptations to bolster, rationalize, shirk, pass the buck, feast upon sour grapes, or otherwise lie and distort. Compared to the time and energy of that generally ineffective approach, to go through the steps listed above is far less demanding. It has the added advantage that while you are doing it you will continually be making progress toward the goal of making the decision, and so a great deal of the stress of decision making is relieved.

The following problem is a good deal more complicated than the problem we just completed. Ask yourself if this type of analysis might not have been helpful.

Selling Arms to Iran

In the following problem let us suppose that President Reagan had used the approach described above.

PROBLEM: President Reagan's advisers presented him with a proposal to sell arms to the government of Iran as a way to perhaps favorably incline the Iranian government toward the United States and also to win the release of American hostages being held in Lebanon. The President worried about public opinion, since he had campaigned on promises to be tough with terrorists. He also worried about the opinions of our allies, since we were at that very time attempting to pressure them not to sell any more arms to terrorists supporting nations such as Iran. He worried of course about American travelers who may be future victims of terrorist capture if it were thought that the United States would pay ransom for hostages. And of course he worried about the strategic position of the United States in regard to the USSR since the latter shared a common border with Iran. A pro-U.S. Iran had always been a cornerstone of the policy of containing Soviet expansionism, especially to the warm water ports of the Persian gulf. There are major uncertainties as to whether the hostages would be released even if the arms were sold, whether the public will find out about the deal, and whether Iran will become pro-U.S. even if the arms were sold. These are all matters that need to be considered in some systematic way.

STEP 1: *Establish the value tree.* An example of a value tree is below. The goal is to find the policy that best serves the interests of the U.S., its citizens, the hostages, the president, and his party. You may agree or disagree with these, and with the priorities.

GOAL	OBJECTIVES	ATTRIBUTES	FINAL WEIGHT
	(.2) Safety of citizens	(.2) Held now	.04
		(.8) Future travel	.16
Best policy	(.4) Strategic position — (1)	Pro-U.S. Iran	.40
	(.3) Relat. with allies — (1)	Trust U.S. word	.30
	(.1) Domestic support	(.6) Confid. in Pres.	.06
		(.4) Republicans strong	.04

STEP 2: *Establish the partial decision tree.* The decision tree below includes CHOICES, STATES, and PROBABILITIES. It does not include OUTCOME UTILITIES since these have not yet been calculated. The states that will most directly affect the outcomes of the choices are whether the hostages who are now in captivity are released or not. This was historically an extremely important issue for the decision-makers surrounding the president, as well as for the president himself. The second state concerned whether the arms sales became public, to both the U.S. public and to other future terrorists. This directly relates to the safety of future travelers, the relations with the allies, and to U.S. public opinion. The third set of states is whether the sales achieve a pro-U.S. government in Iran by placating moderate Iranian leaders. This was for some time the White House's official explanation for providing arms to a country that had expressed such hostility to the United States and its citizens. Probabilities are provided at each branching, and are then calculated. Note that the estimate is that selling arms would increase the probability of release only from .1 to .3, that it was under any circumstances likely that the deal would be made public, and that there was never very much chance that Iran would be induced to become an American ally by the deal. See if you agree with both the states and the probabilities.

STEP 3: *Evaluate each of the outcomes.* Since this is a relatively complicated case where each of the sixteen outcomes is a different bundle of the six attributes, it is useful to provide a verbal description of each of the outcomes before beginning the process of evaluation. This verbal description is as follows:

CHOICES	STATES	OUTCOMES	PROB.

```
                                                 ╱(.1)Pro-U.S. Iran    Outcome-1    .027
                          ╱(.9)U.S. actions public⟨
                         ╱                        ╲(.9)Not Pro-U.S.     Outcome-2    .243
                (.3)Released
                         ╲                        ╱(.1)Pro-U.S. Iran    Outcome-3    .003
                          ╲(.1)U.S. actions not public
                                                 ╲(.9)Not Pro-U.S.     Outcome-4    .027
      Sell arms⟨
                                                 ╱(.1)Pro-U.S. Iran    Outcome-5    .049
                          ╱(.7)U.S. actions public⟨
                         ╱                        ╲(.9)Not Pro-U.S.     Outcome-6    .441
                (.7)Not Releas.
                         ╲                        ╱(.1)Pro-U.S. Iran    Outcome-7    .021
                          ╲(.3)U.S. actions not public
                                                 ╲(.9)No Pro-U.S.      Outcome-8    .189


                                                 ╱(.05)Pro-U.S. Iran   Outcome-9    .0045
                          ╱(.9)U.S. actions public⟨
                         ╱                        ╲(.95)No Pro-U.S.     Outcome-10   .0855
                (.1)Released
                         ╲                        ╱(.05)Pro-U.S. Iran   Outcome-11   .0005
                          ╲(.1)U.S. actions not public
                                                 ╲(.95)No Pro-U.S.     Outcome-12   .0095
      Refuse to sell
                                                 ╱(.05)Pro-U.S. Iran   Outcome-13   .0405
                          ╱(.9)U.S. actions public⟨
                         ╱                        ╲(.95)No Pro-U.S.     Outcome-14   .7695
                (.9)Not Releas.
                         ╲                        ╱(.05)Pro-U.S. Iran   Outcome-15   .0045
                          ╲(.1)U.S. actions not public
                                                 ╲(.95)No Pro-U.S.     Outcome-16   .0865
```

SELL – OUTCOMES

OUTCOME–1: Four hostages released; future travelers endangered; Iran has pro-U.S. government; U.S. word perceived unreliable; President's credibility questioned; Republicans weakened.

OUTCOME–2: Four hostages released; future travelers threatened; Iran not pro-U.S.; U.S. word perceived unreliable; President's credibility questioned; Republicans weakened.

OUTCOME–3: Four hostages released; future travelers threatened; Iran has pro-U.S. government.

OUTCOME–4: Four hostages released; future travelers threatened; No pro-U.S. government in Iran.

OUTCOME–5: Four remain hostage; future travelers threatened; pro-U.S. government in Iran; U.S. word perceived unreliable; President's credibility questioned; Republicans weakened.

OUTCOME–6: Four remain hostage; future travelers threatened; no pro-U.S. government in Iran; U.S. word perceived as unreliable; President's credibility questioned; Republicans weakened.

OUTCOME–7: Hostages remain; future travelers threatened; pro-U.S. government in Iran.
OUTCOME–8: Hostages remain; future travelers threatened; no pro-U.S. government in Iran.

REFUSE TO SELL – OUTCOMES

OUTCOME–9: Hostages released; future travelers safer; pro-U.S. government in Iran; U.S. word strengthened; President's credibility stronger; Republicans stronger.
OUTCOME–10: Hostages released; future travelers safer; no pro-U.S. government in Iran; U.S. word strengthened; President's credibility stronger; Republicans stronger.
OUTCOME–11: Four hostages released; Pro-U.S. government in Iran; future travelers safety increased; U.S. word and President's credibility and Republican position the same.
OUTCOME–12: Four hostages released; no pro-U.S. government in Iran; future travelers safety increased; U.S. word and President's credibility and Republican strength the same.
OUTCOME–13: Hostages remain; pro-U.S. government in Iran; future travelers safer; U.S. word and President's credibility increased; Republicans stronger.
OUTCOME–14: Hostages remain; no pro-U.S. government in Iran; future travelers safer; U.S. word and President's credibility increased; Republicans stronger.
OUTCOME–15: Hostages remain; pro-U.S. government in Iran; future travelers safety unchanged; U.S. and President's word and credibility unchanged; Republican strength unchanged.
OUTCOME–16: Hostages remain; no pro-U.S. government in Iran; future travelers safety unchanged; U.S. and President's word and credibility unchanged; Republican strength the same.

When conducting the evaluation of the outcomes we can refer back to these verbal descriptions. The matrix summary of the evaluations of the sixteen outcomes is below. See if you agree with the utility rating numbers. The scale range is from − 100 to + 100.

STEP 4: *Complete the decision tree.* Put the outcome utilities (weighted sums) into the decision tree and calculate the expected utility of each choice. The complete decision tree with the utility numbers is on page 218.

OUTCOMES			WEIGHTED ATTRIBUTES					WEIGHTED SUM
	.04 Present Host.	.16 Future Travel.	.40 Pro-U.S. Iran	.30 Trust-U.S. Word	.06 Confid.in Pres.	.04 Repub. Strong		
O-1	100	−25	100	−25	50	25	=	35.5
O-2	100	−50	0	−50	−25	−25	=	−25.5
O-3	100	−25	100	0	50	25	=	40
O-4	100	−50	0	0	25	0	=	−2.5
O-5	−50	−25	100	−50	−25	−25	=	18.5
O-6	−100	−50	0	−100	−100	−75	=	−51
O-7	−50	−25	100	0	25	25	=	36.5
O-8	−100	−50	0	0	0	0	=	−12
O-9	100	100	100	100	100	100	=	100
O-10	100	50	0	75	75	75	=	41
O-11	100	100	100	25	25	25	=	70
O-12	100	50	0	10	0	0	=	15
O-13	−50	100	100	25	50	75	=	67.5
O-14	−100	50	0	10	25	50	=	10.5
O-15	−50	100	100	10	25	25	=	59.5
O-16	−100	50	0	10	0	0	=	7

STEP 5: *Select the choice with the greatest expected utility*. The expected utility rule calls for refusing to sell to Iran.

STEP 6: *Review and perform sensitivity analysis*. In the case of selling arms to Iran, sensitivity analysis would reveal that the priority placed upon the *actual* hostages (as opposed to future hostages for example) would have to be tremendously high in order for the decision to be reversed. This probably reflects the actual thinking of the president in going forward with the plan.

A Problem of Breast Cancer

PROBLEM: Susie has been married for eight years to Frank whom she adores. Their marriage has been troubled but very satisfying to Susie. Indeed, she has tried to envision what life would be like without Frank and found it very difficult to think how she would go on, or what she would do. The troubles in their marriage have centered around Frank's infidelities. Although Susie is intelligent, charming, and beautiful, Frank has in the past found it difficult to resist other beautiful women. He seems to have been on his good behavior for the last couple of years. But any

CHOICES	STATES			STATE PROBABILITIES		OUTCOME UTILITIES
Sell arms	(.3)Released	(.9)U.S. actions public	(.1)Pro-U.S. Iran	Outcome-1=.027	× 35.5 =	.96
			(.9)Not Pro-U.S.	Outcome-2=.243	× -25.5 =	-6.2
		(.1)U.S. actions not public	(.1)Pro-U.S. Iran	Outcome-3=.003	× 40 =	.12
			(.9)Not Pro-U.S.	Outcome-4=.027	× -2.5 =	-.07
	(.7)Not Releas.	(.7)U.S. actions public	(.1)Pro-U.S. Iran	Outcome-5=.049	× 18.5 =	.9
			(.9)Not Pro-U.S.	Outcome-6=.441	× -51 =	-22.5
		(.3)U.S. actions not public	(.1)Pro-U.S. Iran	Outcome-7=.021	× 36.5 =	.77
			(.9)Not Pro-U.S.	Outcome-8=.189	× -12 =	-2.27
					EU =	-28.3
Refuse to sell	(.1)Released	(.9)U.S. actions public	(.05)Pro-U.S. Iran	Outcome-9=.0045	× 100 =	.45
			(.95)Not Pro-U.S.	Outcome-10=.0855	× 41 =	3.5
		(.1)U.S. actions not public	(.05)Pro-U.S. Iran	Outcome-11=.0005	× 70 =	.04
			(.95)Not Pro-U.S.	Outcome-12=.0095	× 15 =	.14
	(.9)Not Releas.	(.9)U.S. actions public	(.05)Pro-U.S. Iran	Outcome-13=.0405	× 67.5 =	2.7
			(.95)Not Pro-U.S.	Outcome-14=.7695	× 10.5 =	8.07
		(.1)U.S. actions not public	(.05)Pro-U.S. Iran	Outcome-15=.0045	× 59.5 =	.27
			(.95)Not Pro-U.S.	Outcome-16=.0855	× 7 =	.60
					EU =	15.8

more unfaithfulness will definitely end the marriage. Another source of their marital troubles has been money. Frank has not been very successful in keeping well-paying jobs. Although Susie is an accomplished model who is in demand, she has not been able to work steadily since the birth of her daughter three years ago. She adores her daughter, who relies very much on her. Frank seems to take little interest in the child, and the child senses it. But Susie also needs the satisfaction of her career as a fashion model. Susie has just been found during a routine physical examination to have breast cancer. It is in early stages, but is considered serious. The physician outlined four possible courses of action, and strongly recommended the first (The probability numbers to follow are entirely hypothetical): Radical mastectomy, removing the breast and muscle tissue in the arm, with a five-year cure rate of 80%; partial mastectomy, removing the breast, with a five-year cure rate of 70%; removal of just the malignant tissue, not removing the breast, with a cure rate of 60%; and no surgery, using radiation and chemotherapy alone, with a cure rate of 40%. The first three procedures would also involve radiation and drugs. The first two procedures are extremely expensive due to prolonged hospital stays, the third is less expensive, and the last is the least. Frank's employment problems have left them temporarily without insurance, but Susie has just been offered a new job, which would provide insurance, but which she could not accept were she to choose any of the first three options. Susie is given three days to decide the course of action.

STEP 1: *Establish the value tree.* Susie's goal in life has been to live a satisfying and responsible life in the context of her family. What objectives is she interested in achieving? That is, how should her goal be subdivided into more specific elements? List objectives that do not overlap, that is, one is not a necessary condition or a way of achieving another. They may, of course conflict, and usually do.

    a. The long-term preservation of a good marriage with Frank.
    b. The well being of her daughter.
    c. Career as fashion model.

Susie's life, or Susie's personal happiness are not included as objectives since they are, respectively, a condition for and a function of the above, and thus to include them would be redundant and result in double counting.

On a scale of 1 to 10, the following is how she would measure the importance of these objectives relative to each other so that the three numbers sum to ten.

a. Her marriage   (.3)
b. Well-being of daughter   (.6)
c. Career as fashion model   (.1)

OBJECTIVES	ATTRIBUTES	RELATIVE WEIGHT	FINAL WEIGHT
a. Marriage (.3)	i. Appearance to Frank	(.8)	(.24)
	ii. Short-term cash flow	(.2)	(.06)
b. Daughter (.6)	i. No. of parents to care	(.8)	(.48)
	ii. Susie's earning power	(.2)	(.12)
c. Career (.1) —	i. Susie's modeling look	(1)	(.10)

STEP 2: *Establish the partial decision tree.*

CHOICES		STATES	OUTCOMES	PROBS
Radical	.8 Cure	.2 Frank faithful	O-1	.16
		.8 Frank unfaithful	O-2	.64
	.2 No cure		O-3	.20
Partial	.7 Cure	.2 Faithful	O-4	.14
		.8 Unfaithful	O-5	.56
	.3 No cure		O-6	.30
Rem.tiss.	.6 Cure	.4 Faithful	O-7	.24
		.6 Unfaithful	O-7	.36
	.4 No cure		O-9	.40
Rad.chem.	.4 Cure	.6 Faithful	O-10	.24
		.4 Unfaithful	O-11	.16
	.6 No cure		O-12	.60

The (very hypothetical) probabilities of cure are given in the cure rates. The probabilities of faithfulness are estimated on the basis of Frank's probable response to the various treatments in light of his past history.

STEP 3: *Evaluate each of the outcomes.*

VERBAL DESCRIPTIONS

0–1 Greatest appearance loss to Frank, most $ spent, both parents, no model career, other career for moderate income for child care.

0–2 Greatest appearance loss, most $ spent, child has mother only, no model career, other career for moderate income for child care.

0–3 Susie dies, most $ spent, child has father only, little long-term money for child care.

0–4 Serious appearance loss, much money spent, both parents, no model career, other career possible.

0–5 Serious appearance loss, much money spent, child has mother only, no model career, other career possible.

0–6 Susie dies, much money spent, child has father only, little long-term money for child care.

0–7 Appearance remains, maximum money spent, child has both parents, model career, very good income for child care.

0–8 Appearance remains, maximum money spent, child has mother only, model career, very good income for child care.

0–9 Susie dies, maximum money spent, child has father only, little long-term money for child care.

0–10 Appearance remains, little money spent, child has both parents, model career, very good income for child care.

0–11 Appearance remains, little money spent, child has mother only, model career, very good income for child care.

0–12 Susie dies, little spent, child has father only, little income for child care.

STEP 4: *Complete the decision tree.* In this case, we have used the matrix approach to represent the final decision problem. This approach is commonly used to represent decisions, though we believe that the decision tree is superior. The final decision matrix with the expected utilities calculated is shown on page 222.

STEP 5: *Select the choice with the greatest expected utility.* This calls for the removal of the malignant tissue.

STEP 6: *Review and perform sensitivity analysis.* In Appendix B, we discuss alternative decision rules, and the conditions under which rules other than expected utility should be used. As part of that discussion, we mention that the necessity to make certain decisions is unlikely to be repeated, because the events are unusual in one's lifetime and

Decision-Making: Its Logic and Practice

MATRIX

OUTCOMES		ATTRIBUTES				
	APPEAR (.24)	CASH (.06)	PARENTS (.48)	EARN.POW. (.12)	MOD.LK. (.10)	UTILITY
O-1	2 x .24 +	2 x .06 +	10 x .48 +	5 x .12 +	0	= 6.12
O-2	2 x .24 +	2 x .06 +	8 x .48 +	5 x .12 +	0	= 5.16
O-3	0 +	2 x .06 +	2 x .48 +	0 +	0	= 1.08
O-4	2 x .24 +	3 x .06 +	10 x .48 +	5 x .12 +	0	= 6.18
O-5	2 x .24 +	3 x .06 +	8 x .48 +	5 x .12 +	0	= 5.22
O-6	0 +	3 x .06 +	2 x .48 +	0 +	0	= 1.14
O-7	6 x .24 +	1 x .06 +	10 x .48 +	9 x .12 +	9 x .10	= 8.28
O-8	6 x .24 +	1 x .06 +	8 x .48 +	9 x .12 +	9 x .10	= 7.32
O-9	0 +	1 x .06 +	2 x .48 +	0 +	0	= 1.02
O-10	7 x .24 +	6 x .06 +	10 x .48 +	10 x .12 +	10 x .10	= 9.04
O-11	7 x .24 +	6 x .06 +	8 x .48 +	10 x .12 +	10 x .10	= 8.18
O-12	0 +	6 x .06 +	2 x .48 +	0 +	0	= 1.32

CHOICES	STATES			
	Cure/Faith	Cure/Unfaith	No Cure	EU
Radical	6.12 x .16 +	5.16 x .64 +	1.08 x .20	= 4.50
Partial	6.18 x .14 +	5.22 x .56 +	1.14 x .30	= 4.13
Remove tissue	8.28 x .24 +	7.32 x .36 +	1.02 x .40	= 5.03
Radiation/drug	9.04 x .24 +	8.18 x .16 +	1.32 x .60	= 4.27

because of the uncommon potential for great loss. This seems to be the situation of Susie and her family. In such a case, we want to think very carefully about whether or not a more conservative rule might be appropriate. One such rule could be simply to mark outcomes as acceptable only if they include a cure, and select the choice that gives the greatest probability of an acceptable outcome. Other possible rules are discussed in Appendix B. The point here is that although the expected utility rule is considered by most to be the standard of decision rules (Baron 1985), there are times when the most rational action may not accord with it. This point should not be taken as a recommendation to rely upon "instincts" or "intuitions," which are never adequate substitutes for thinking through a problem clearly, even with the aid of some specified procedure.

Two Complications

There are two complications, or further complexities, that we do not deal with in this text but feel it is necessary to mention. The first is that decision trees can be extended to be sequential in the sense that the decision-maker can plan further choices to follow specific states. For example, if I am choosing today to plan for either tennis or TV tomorrow, I will worry about whether or not it will rain. These are states. I can add to these states on the decision tree a further choice if I plan to play tennis and it rains. There are rather straightforward ways to evaluate the expected utilities of the choices in these types of sequential trees (Raiffa 1968).

The second complication lies in the fact that in combining the value tree from the MAUT analysis with the expected utility model it may be necessary to create different sets of weights on the value tree that correspond to different states on the decision tree. Suppose, for example, that you are trying to decide whether to purchase an expensive car or to save the money for a down payment on a house, but are unsure about whether or not you are going to receive a very large inheritance. Then the receipt of the inheritance or not would be states. The value tree that you would construct would put a different relative weighting upon, for instance, financial security if you had the inheritance than if you did not.

Problems for Analysis

DIRECTIONS: In the following two problems, we have provided a plausible, though somewhat oversimplified, structure. That is, we have provided a value tree and a decision tree. It is your job to fill in the relevant objective and attribute weights, the probabilities of the states, and the utility rating numbers in the matrix. You can then calculate the expected utilities.

President Truman's Problem

It is late in July, 1945. President Truman is meeting in Potsdam with the major allied leaders, Churchill and Stalin, to determine the shape of the post-war world. The status of Germany and parts of eastern Europe are still to be decided. The role of the USSR in the final victory over Japan is not yet clear. On July 16, the President received word that a successful test of the "fat boy," an atom bomb, had been made in Alamogordo, New Mexico. The information coming in suggested that the United States was now in possession of the most powerful weapon ever created. Truman informed Churchill, and a week later Stalin was told. It was agreed that the USSR would join the campaign to defeat the Japanese, though both Churchill and Truman worried about Soviet intentions in the Far East after Japan was defeated.

The defeat of Japan was, at this point, a foregone conclusion. The important issue had to do with the final cost of that Allied victory. The three-month battle for the tiny island of Okinawa, which ended on July 2nd, had cost the United States 75,000 casualties, including over 12,000 soldiers killed or missing. The island had been defended by 100,000 Japanese soldiers. The Americans lost 763 aircraft and 32 ships. An additional 368 ships were damaged, in large measure, by Kamikaze attacks.

Tentative approval had already been given to invade the mainland of Japan, and personnel and supplies were already being moved to that end. With a home army of one-and-a-half million soldiers, the invasion of the mainland would be uncommonly brutal. The Japanese had already demonstrated their tenacity and valor in the defense of the Pacific Islands. Most estimates of U.S. casualties from an invasion ran at about 500,000 soldiers; some were as high as 1,000,000. Japanese casualties, both military and civilian, would be many times that figure. Eventual victory would most likely require at least six months of fighting. Some were passionately questioning the need for "unconditional surrender" demanded at Potsdam. The United States is maintaining a naval blockade of the mainland but continues to sustain heavy losses from Kamikaze attacks. Daily bombing raids on Japanese cities were taking place with increasing ferocity. In March of 1945, waves of B-29s attacked Tokyo, creating a huge firestorm that claimed over 80,000 lives in one night. All in all, five square miles of the city have been reduced to rubble and ash. City after city continues to be attacked in like manner.

In this last week in July, the President must come to a decision. His options are to maintain the blockade and aerial bombardment; to give the final go-ahead for the invasion; to authorize the use of the two remaining atom bombs against Japanese cities to demonstrate the hopelessness of further resistance. Truman is very concerned about the prolongation of the war, not only because of the casualties involved, but also because of possible Soviet influence in the Far East, should they enter the war against Japan. He is also concerned about stemming Soviet expansion in parts of eastern Europe and feels that the continuation of the battle against Japan is weakening that effort. He is probably also considering the effect of a demonstration of the new bomb's power on Soviet expansionism.

What then should Truman do? The following provides a schema for the solution to Truman's problem. Complete that schema to determine the rational choice. If there are elements of the schema that you wish to reject, then create an alternative.

STEP 1: *Establish the value tree*. Fill in the priorities, using a range of 0 to 1.

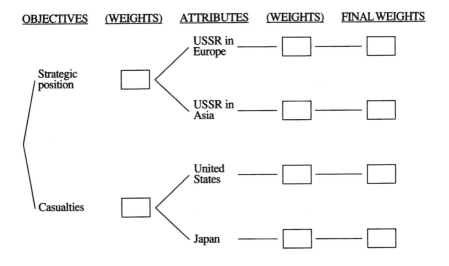

OBJECTIVES   (WEIGHTS)   ATTRIBUTES   (WEIGHTS)   FINAL WEIGHTS

Strategic position

USSR in Europe

USSR in Asia

Casualties

United States

Japan

STEP 2: *Construct the partial decision tree*. Fill in the probabilities, using a 0 to 1 range.

STEP 3: *Evaluate the outcomes*. Fill in the utility ratings on a 1 to 100 range. Put the final attribute weights from the value tree in their places. Calculate the weighted sum for each outcome.

STEP 4: *Complete the decision tree*. Transfer the outcome values (weighted sums) and probabilities into the tree below, and calculate the expected utility of each of the choices.

CHOICES	STATES	STATE PROBABILITIES	OUTCOMES

Blockade
- End 1 mo. — [ ] — 01
- End 6 mo. — [ ] — 02
- End 12 mo. — [ ] — 03

Invade
- End 1 mo. — [ ] — 04
- End 6 mo. — [ ] — 05
- End 12 mo. — [ ] — 06

Use bomb
- End 1 mo. — [ ] — 07
- End 6 mo. — [ ] — 08
- End 12 mo. — [ ] — 09

OUTCOMES   ATTRIBUTES

OUTCOMES	USSR in Europe	USSR in Asia	Casualties United States	Casualties Japan	Weighted Sums
	[ ]	[ ]	[ ]	[ ]	
Blockade End 1 mo. (01)					
Blockade End 6 mo. (02)					
Blockade End 12 mo. (03)					
Invade End 1 mo. (04)					
Invade End 6 mo. (05)					
Invade End 12 mo. (06)					
Atom Bomb End 1 mo. (07)					
Atom Bomb End 6 mo. (08)					
Atom Bomb End 12 mo. (09)					

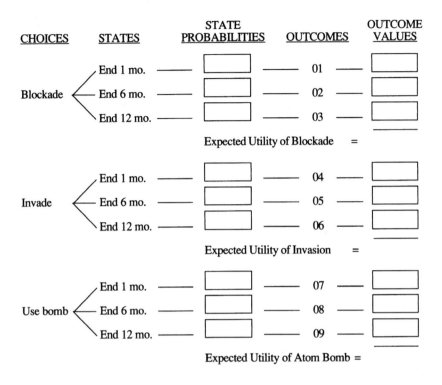

| | STATE | | OUTCOME |
| CHOICES | STATES | PROBABILITIES | OUTCOMES | VALUES |

Expected Utility of Blockade   =

Expected Utility of Invasion   =

Expected Utility of Atom Bomb =

STEP 5: *Select the choice with the greatest expected utility.*

STEP 6: *Review and perform sensitivity analysis.*

The Problem of the Contras in Nicaragua

PROBLEM: The problem here is to determine if the decision to support the Contras in Nicaragua is a rational one. You are the Secretary of State and must advise the President. You are worried about U.S. strategic positions in Latin America and in the world. You are also concerned about the political freedom and economic well-being of the Nicaraguans.

Step 1: *Establish the value tree.*

Step 2: *Establish the (partial) decision tree.*

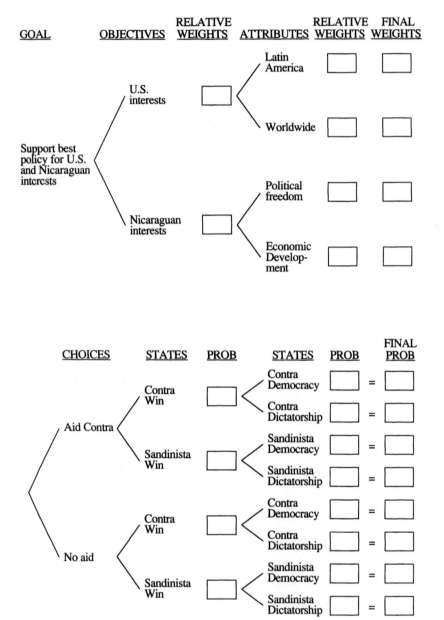

Step 3: *Evaluate the outcomes of the choices.*

ATTRIBUTES

OUTCOMES	U.S. in Lat. Am.	U.S. in World	Nicaragua Polit. Freedom	Nicaragua Economy Good	Weighted Sums
Aid Contras Con. win—dem					( )
Aid Contras Con. win—dict					( )
Aid Contras Sand. win—dem					( )
Aid Contras Sand. win—dict					( )
No aid Con. win—dem					( )
No aid Con. win—dict					( )
No aid Sand. win—dem					( )
No aid Sand. win—dict					( )

Step 4: *Apply the appropriate decision rule.*

Step 5: *Perform sensitivity analysis (see page 230).*

A Simple Car Purchase

John is working in Denver. He must buy a car immediately even though he knows that he will be transferred to Fairbanks, Alaska or Miami, Florida. His boss has informed him that he and two other employees will be transferred and whether they go to Alaska or Florida will be determined randomly by drawing from a hat. Two will go to Alaska and one to Florida. From a car buyer's guide John obtained the following information on the only two factors that concerned him. Car

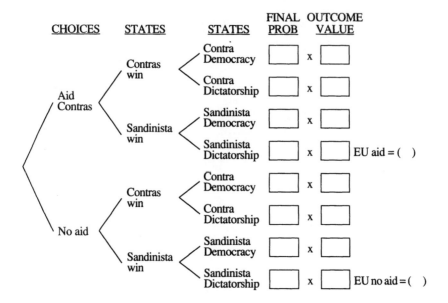

A got a 7 on dry or wet roads and a 6 on icy roads. Car B got an 8 on all conditions. Car A got a 5 on air conditioning, and a 7 on heating comfort. Car B got a 9 on air conditioning, and a 2 on heating comfort. John feels that handling should receive 60% of the weight, and temperature control the remainder. Within temperature control, staying cool and staying warm should receive equal priorities. Dry roads are 60% within handling, and wet and icy are 20% each. Which car should John buy?

The Shoreham, New York Nuclear Power Plant

Terry N. is an assistant to the Governor of New York and is faced with the decision of whether or not to recommend to the Governor that Lilco be given the final license to open the nuclear power plant at Shoreham, Long Island. Terry has been staying awake nights thinking about the problem. It seems that each morning Terry awakes to having made a different decision. For every rationale supporting one side, there seems to be another rationale supporting the other side. Sometimes Terry is tempted to flip a coin. Fran B. has been studying decision-making. Fran knows less about the nuclear power controversy than does Terry; but on the other hand Fran has learned some techniques that can be applied to decision problems that will, given a certain set of data and values, yield a specific result. Terry and Fran meet at a fund raising event, and it appears immediately to Terry that Fran can be of some assistance. Fran agrees (for a very steep fee) to spend a couple of days with Terry to help with the proper framing of the problem.

DIRECTIONS: You are to take the parts both of Terry and of Fran. Fran is to assist Terry in the rational formulation of the decision. Terry is to provide the data and the values. The initial part of your response should be in the form of a dialogue in which Fran elicits the necessary data and values to begin the analysis. In the end, there should be a clear decision, along with a clear rationale for why this decision ought to be preferred to the others. It is not expected that you, in taking Terry's place, have the kind of expert knowledge that Terry is likely to have concerning all the relevant factors. If and where you find it necessary to state probabilities, you are free to make very liberal estimates. You are also free to decide upon the values that Terry introduces into the decision. On the other hand, it is assumed that you have a general awareness of the issues involved, and thus it will be expected that you take into consideration the major factors that should go into the decision. You should make every effort to construct as realistic a case as possible.

Chapter 8

Decision-Making Among Rational Competitors

Consider the following problem situations. A quarterback is two points down, with the ball in the last minute of play. It is the fourth down, and his team is at the thirty-yard line. He must decide whether to try for a fieldgoal or to go for a touchdown. Suppose you are sitting in a poker game with a pair of kings. One of your opponents has just raised the ante by a sizable amount and you must fold or pay to stay in the game. Imagine that you are the regional head of marketing for a fast food company and have selected a potential site for a new outlet. You are aware that a number of your competitors are considering nearby locations. You want the location badly, but you know that you cannot sustain extended rivalry with the strongest of your competitors.

Think of the problems a security chief of a major airport has attempting to protect the facility against terrorist attacks. He wants to protect his patrons, but if his measures are too draconian he may seriously discourage use of his facility, resulting in financial loss. Consider the dilemma confronting a politician in a close election, who has come into possession of potentially damaging information about his competitor's personal life. Using the information may well win the election for him, but he has a few skeletons in his own closet that, if made public, would hardly do his prospects any good.

In all of the above cases, there is a need to make a decision. But what is the appropriate model? At first it may appear that some sort of expected utility model would apply, but there are problems with applying that model in each of the above cases. These examples differ in one very obvious and important way from the problems we have considered to this point in that the "states of the world" with which we must deal are dependent upon the choices of other people, who may be more or less rational. How are we to assign probabilities to the likelihood of their choices? If the other decision-makers who affect the outcome are irrational, it is almost impossible to hit on a satisfying set of probabilities. If they are rational, then they are clearly interested in forwarding their own goals and plans and, furthermore, are probably attempting to calculate what we are likely to do, just as we must attempt to assess their likely behavior.

One reasonable tactic we might take is to assume that they will approach the situation in the same way we would in their circumstances, i.e., as we assume any rational decision-maker would. But that requires that we have a set of guidelines for rational decision-making for situations whose outcomes depend on the decisions of others.

The Theory of Games

John von Neumann and Oscar Morgenstern, in their seminal work *The Theory of Games and Economic Behavior* (1947), describe decision-making tasks involving intelligent and intentioned competitors as games. They attempted to find sound solutions to problems whether or not the other participants are rational and cunning, or hapless fools. It is usually wiser to assume the other is rational.

A game is defined as a structured situation in which two or more individuals or actors (teams, firms, armies) have a conflict of interest, and in which each is trying to maximize his own return. The conflict of interest arises because it may not be possible for each to maximize his own return without damaging his competitor in some way.

Two broad distinctions between games should be made at the outset. Generally speaking, games between two players differ from games among more than two players, because in larger games the parties may form coalitions or alliances. The formation of alliances may be the most decisive factor for the participants in such cases. Therefore, a first important distinction is between games of two persons (2-person games) and games of more than two persons (*n*-person games).

A second important distinction exists between games in which there is an absolute conflict of interest between the parties (known as strictly competitive or zerosum games), and those in which there is less than absolute conflict of interest (where there exists some possibility of mutual gain). Games of this latter type are referred to as cooperative or nonzerosum games. Let us first examine the simplest case; the 2-person zerosum game.

Two-Person Zerosum Games: Games of Strict Competition

Most parlor games and athletic contests are strictly competitive in that there is no room for all parties to gain. While there may be great mutual gain for all parties in actually entering into a game (the entertainment value of many games and contests is, we think, obvious), once the game begins there will be winners and losers, and the winners will gain at the expense of the losers. Poker is a good example. Players put their money into a "pot," which, at the end of a hand, ends up in someone's lap. Money has been moved around the table, but it has been neither increased nor decreased by the play. The defining feature of zerosum games is that in them, utility (often in the form of money) is conserved. They are situations in which utility cannot be lost or gained, only redistributed. In such redistributions, if someone is to gain utility, someone must lose it. If one adds up the gains of the winners and subtracts from them the losses of the losers, the resultant sum would come to zero. Hence the term "zerosum."

Actually, zerosum contests are part of a broader class of games known as *constant-sum* games. In constant-sum situations, the sum of winnings and losses add to a constant value. Zerosum games are a special case where that constant sum is zero. Mathematically speaking, such situations are equivalent in that any constant-sum game can be converted to a zerosum game by subtracting out the constant value. Suppose two players each put $50 on the table, with the winner of a coin toss taking all. At the end of the game, one player will have all of the $100 that was on the table and the other will have $0, and the sum of their gains will be $100. But, of course, another way to look at that situation is that $0 was there at the start and one person won $50, and the other lost $50, and the sum of their gains is $0. However you look at it, though, whatever amount one party gained was gained at the expense of the other party. Because it has become common to refer to such situations as zerosum games, we will, for the most part, stick with this conventional designation.

In such games, the only room for mutual accommodation is an agreement not to play, to settle for zero payoff to each party at the outset, or to agree to return all winnings at the end of the game (which amounts to the same thing). It is hard to imagine why anyone would play a game under such circumstances unless they were using money as a means of keeping score and were playing for the sake of determining a winner. In that case clearly, winning has some positive utility and cannot be attained by all players. In other words, the game is still a zerosum game. Contrast such games with most economic enterprises. Consider a partnership between a famous chef and an entrepreneur with a failing restaurant in a prime location. In such a situation, both parties could win or lose a good deal. There is much room for mutual accommodation since in this case utility or money is not conserved. At the end of a year the partnership might have a good deal more or less money than it started with. In such *nonconstant-sum* or *nonzerosum* situations, the problem is not to "beat" the other fellow, but rather to cooperate with him to maximize joint profits. If competition is involved it concerns competing over the division of the profits. But more on that later.

When confronted by a zerosum game, the rational decision-maker has only one choice: to play or not to play. If he decides to play, then being rational, he must play to win. If he cannot avoid the game, then of course he has no option but to play to win. Further, unless there is some other consideration, he must play to win as much as possible. Any other strategy would be irrational. Since everything a player wins, he wins from his opponent, it follows, unfortunately, that in playing to win as much as possible, such a player is also aiming to inflict maximum damage on his opponent. It should be clear that this is not because he holds any animus toward the other, but only because he is solely concerned with his own interest. On the other hand, if a player has some interest in not fully exploiting a competitor, then he is not really in a zerosum conflict. If one allows a spouse a better than deserved showing in a tennis match, or if one fails to exploit a chess move so that a child can continue to enjoy the game, then one is not engaged in a zerosum contest. The essence of the zerosum game is that it is strictly and absolutely competitive. It is the strictly competitive nature of such games that serves as the basis for rational strategy in such situations.

If we know our opponent is rational, or merely assume he is, then it means that he is attempting to bring himself maximum benefit and at the same time cause us maximum harm. Therefore, we must attempt to defend ourselves against such maximum harm while attempting to maximize our own gains. That is why von Neumann and Morgenstern advise (in fact, require) the maximin strategy. Recall that the maximin choice is the one that protects against the worst that can happen. In games, it protects against the harm that an opponent is attempting to inflict in his rational attempt to maximize his own gain.

As an example, let us consider the problem of a football coach whose team is on the ten-yard line on the fourth down. It is early in the game with the score tied at zero. He has to decide whether to kick a fieldgoal or to pass for a touchdown. (For simplicity we exclude the running attack as a possibility.) The coach might begin by laying out the situation as a standard expected utility problem. Let us suppose that he has good statistics so that he can estimate the probability of a successful kick or a pass completion fairly well, given a conservative or normal defense by the other side. His preliminary analysis might look so:

SITUATION IF OTHER SIDE USES NORMAL DEFENSE

CHOICE	STATE	PROBABILITY	OUTCOME	EU
Kick	Fieldgoal	.9	3	2.7
	Failure	.1	0	
Pass	Touchdown	.2	6	1.2
	Failure	.8	0	

It seems clear from the above that kicking makes sense. However, this assumes a normal defense. What if the opposition decides to rush the kicker? Perhaps in this circumstance it would make more sense to pass. Here, our coach's statistics lead him to expect a slightly better likelihood of completing a pass, and a somewhat reduced probability of a fieldgoal, giving the following:

SITUATION IF OTHER SIDE RUSHES THE KICKER

CHOICE	STATE	PROBABILITY	OUTCOME	EU
Kick	Fieldgoal	.6	3	1.8
	Failure	.3	0	
Pass	Touchdown	.4	6	2.4
	Failure	.6	0	

In this case, the pass seems the better option. Let us attempt to represent this decision problem in familiar decision tree format as a sequential state problem. Let us assume, for purposes of illustration, that the coach guesses that the other team will use the normal defense 60% of the time and the rush 40%.

CHOICE	STATE	PROB	STATE	PROB	OUTCOME	EU
			Fieldgoal	.9	3	= 1.62
	Normal	.6	Failure	.1	0	= 0.00
Kick			Fieldgoal	.6	3	= 0.72
	Rush	.4	Failure	.3	0	= 0.00
						2.34
			Touchdown	.2	6	= 0.72
	Normal	.6	Failure	.8	0	= 0.00
Pass			Touchdown	.4	6	= 0.96
	Rush	.4	Failure	.6	0	= 0.00
						1.68

A small calculation reveals that the expected value (in points) of the kick at 2.46 makes it the better choice than the pass at 1.68. But there is a problem here in that such a choice is only better if we can rely on our probability estimates regarding our opponent's behavior. Up until now, when estimating the likelihood of states of the world or the likely behavior of others, we did not imagine that our estimates might, in fact, affect those probabilities. We may superstitiously imagine that if we are too confident of our belief that the sun will shine on our wedding, the weather will punish our hubris with rain. But such thinking is, of course, foolish, and we can confidently assume that whatever the likelihood of rain, our guessing will not influence it. Here, when confronting a reasoning opponent, our guessing may make a difference.

After all, if he can anticipate our reasoning and come to the conclusion that we will never pass in such a situation, then he can alter his own behavior to take advantage of us by rushing the kicker and in that way decrease our likelihood of success. Clearly the expected utility rule is inadequate in such cases (where our own estimates of probability can cause an intelligent opponent to change his behavior) and might cause us more harm than good.

Let us simplify our representation of the above problem slightly by merely giving the expected outcome and the points expected in the various circumstances. For instance, when we kick against a normal defense we have a 90% chance of success (gaining 3 points), and a 10% chance of failing (gaining 0 points), for an expected gain of 2.7 points. You will notice that we have intentionally left out any probability estimates for states (our opponent's actions) since any estimate we make will be, as we have seen, unreliable.

CHOICE	STATE	OUTCOME	EXPECTED PTS
Kick	Normal defense	90% chance of successful FG	2.7
	Rush the kicker	60% chance of successful FG	1.8
Pass	Normal defense	20% chance of successful TD	1.2
	Rush the kicker	40% chance of successful TD	2.4

As we cannot estimate probabilities reliably and we therefore cannot reasonably apply the expected utility rule, we will follow von Neumann and Morgenstern's advice and apply the maximin rule. Under the maximin rule, you look for the worst possible outcomes (the worst case) for each choice and make the choice containing the least damaging worst case. In this example, the worst outcome occurs when we attempt to pass against the normal defense, with little likelihood of success and with an EU of 1.2; therefore, using the maximin rule, we should avoid passing and attempt the fieldgoal. Or should we?

If our opponent is attempting to figure out what we are going to do, maybe he has second-guessed our decision and has decided we are going to kick, and therefore decides to rush so as to reduce our likelihood of success. But, if he has decided to rush the kicker, maybe we should second-guess him and pass. What to do?

The answer is what most football coaches know intuitively: that it is crucial to keep the other side guessing. Teams must mix things up for the very simple reason that if they become too predictable, the other side will know what to expect and take advantage of that knowledge. Von Neumann and Morgenstern call such an approach a *mixed strategy* and have developed a procedure that allows a player to determine the right mix in each case, here, for instance, how often to kick and how often to pass.

Before we go on, a few preliminaries are in order. The von Neumann and Morgenstern solution to this dilemma is simplified if we represent the above decision problem in matrix form. The matrix representation is given below, where EP = Expected Points.

OPPONENT'S CHOICES

		NORMAL DEFENSE	RUSH THE KICKER
OUR CHOICES	KICK	90% chance of successful FG EP = 2.7	60% chance of successful FG EP = 1.8
	PASS	20% chance of successful TD EP = 1.2	40% chance of successful TD EP = 2.4

In this depiction it is clear that how many points we are likely to get depends on our choices AND on the choices of our opponent. If we kick, we can assume an expected value of 2.7 points or 1.8 points depending on whether the other side defends conventionally or rushes the kicker. We have arranged our choices and the possible consequences of our choices in rows, and therefore we are the *rows player*. Likewise our opponent's choices and the outcomes are arrayed as columns, and hence he is the *columns player*. Generally, we simplify the matrix by including only the value or expected value of each outcome, producing the matrix below.

OPPONENT'S CHOICES

		NORMAL DEFENSE	RUSH THE KICKER	row minima
OUR CHOICES	KICK	2.7	<u>1.8</u>	1.8
	PASS	<u>1.2</u>	2.4	1.2

Notice that to simplify application of the maximin rule, we under-lined the worst outcome for each choice and have listed it in the margin under the heading "row minima." The maximin choice is the choice whose row minimum is the maximum of those row minima, which is the reason it is called "maximin."

One powerful advantage of the matrix representation is that it allows us to represent the choices and outcomes for each side simultaneously. In this case, we can see that our opponent has a decision problem as well. He must decide whether to apply a normal defense or rush the kicker, and his outcomes are also dependent on what we do. (We assume that he has the same statistics as we do to estimate the expected value of each outcome.) In this situation any gain we make, such as making a touchdown and moving ahead six points, is his loss, i.e., he moves behind six points. For that reason this is a zerosum game. His decision problem would look so:

OPPONENT'S CHOICE	OUR CHOICE	OUTCOME	EV OF OUTCOME
Normal defense	Kick	90% chance of failing to block FG	–2.7
	Pass	20% chance of failing to block TD	–1.2
Rush the kicker	Kick	60% chance of failing to block FG	–1.8
	Pass	40% chance of failing to block TD	–2.4

In the case of our opponent, the worst outcome is when we kick against the normal defense (he goes behind 2.7 points) and therefore, according to maximin, he ought to rush the kicker. But he has the same need to mix things up as do we in that if we know he is going to rush, then we will certainly be tempted to pass.

All of the above information is summarized in the matrix representa-tion given below. By convention, the columns players' (our oppo-nent's) winnings or losses are written to the right of the rows players' (our) winnings or losses. We have also enclosed them in parentheses. The column minima are underlined and given at the bottom of the matrix.

OPPONENT'S CHOICES

		NORMAL DEFENSE	RUSH THE KICKER	row minima
OUR CHOICES	KICK	2.7 (–2.7)	1.8 (–1.8)	1.8
	PASS	1.2 (–1.2)	2.4 (–2.4)	1.2
column minima		–2.7	–2.4	

Games with Saddlepoints

Before we attempt to determine the best strategy in the above case (we won't forget to do so), it will be easier if we start with a somewhat simpler problem. Let us modify the above situation slightly by assuming that our coach has reevaluated his statistics and changed his estimate of a successful TD pass under the rush condition. He originally assumed a 40% chance of success. Assume he has reduced that to 25%, which means that the expected points of the outcome when the other side rushes and we pass is now (.25 × 6 points) = 1.5, rather than 2.4. This gives the following revised matrix:

OPPONENT'S CHOICES

		NORMAL DEFENSE	RUSH THE KICKER	row minima
OUR CHOICES	KICK	2.7 (–2.7)	1.8 (–1.8)	1.8
	PASS	1.2 (–1.2)	1.5 (–1.5)	1.2
column minima		–2.7	–1.8	

This alteration changes things considerably, in that there is now no case in which passing is better than kicking. The choice of passing is a dominated choice or strategy. If you recall, one choice is said to *dominate* another if in every outcome it is either better (or equal to) the other. Kicking is clearly a dominating strategy in this revised setup. This means that no matter what the other side decides to do, we are better off kicking and therefore will choose to kick. If the opponent agrees with our reassessment, he will therefore rush the kicker, since that is his better choice once he has determined that we have ruled out passing. If you examine the matrix you will notice that even when we know the other team will rush, the best choice is to kick. For that reason, the outcome is said to be an *equilibrium outcome* and *stable*, since neither side has any reason to deviate from their original maximin choice, even knowing what the other side will do.

Situations such as this, where the outcome is, in essence, a foregone conclusion are said to be games with *saddlepoints*. The *solution* to this game is the outcome produced by our kicking and the other side rushing and providing the payoff of a 1.8 gain for us and 1.8 loss for the other side. Needless to say, not all games have saddlepoints. To determine if a game has a saddlepoint, use the following simple procedure:

1. Find the row minimum (the worst case) for each of Row's choices and underline it. Write these row minima in the margin of the matrix.
2. Identify the best of the marginal row minima and underline it. This is Row's maximin choice or strategy.
3. Repeat the process for the columns player.
4. Find the cell in the matrix that contains the outcomes for Row and Column when each makes his maximin choice. This is the maximin payoff cell.
5. The game has a saddlepoint if the maximin payoff cell contains both row and column values that are equal to the greater of the marginal minima, that is, that match the underlined marginal values. If that is the case then neither party can improve his position by switching his choice.

If there is a saddlepoint, neither side has any advantage in moving from his maximin choice, even if he knows for certain that the other side will always select his maximin choice. This is a reason for thinking of saddlepoint games as being stable or in equilibrium. The players will settle on their maximin choices and stay there, and the outcome so produced is therefore known as the *solution* to the game. In simple 2 × 2 games, such as the above, if one player has a dominating strategy then the game will have a saddlepoint. If games do not have saddlepoints then that means, practically, that the players have something to gain by hiding their intentions from the other side and had better mix things up, i.e., use a mixed strategy.

Mixed Strategies

Let us recall our earlier football problem, which is reproduced below.

OPPONENT'S CHOICES

		NORMAL DEFENSE	RUSH THE KICKER	row minima
OUR CHOICES	KICK	2.7 (−2.7)	1.8 (−1.8)	1.8
	PASS	1.2 (−1.2)	2.4 (−2.4)	1.2
column minima		−2.7	−2.4	

In this situation it is easy to determine that the maximin choice is still "kick" for Row and "rush" for Column. But the cell in the upper right, which results if both players use their maximin strategy, is not a saddlepoint since the payoff of − 1.8 to columns is not the same as the best of his marginal minima. This means that if the rows player knows that columns will take the maximin choice he can cause columns more harm by switching choices, and gain more for himself than he could by sticking with his maximin choice.

In other words, once we have determined that our opponent is going to rush, it makes sense for us to switch to "pass." But our opponent can also do such "what if" thinking. If he anticipates such a shift on our part, he can himself shift to his normal pass defense, and thereby reduce the likelihood that we will be successful. But if we can imagine that he will think this way, we can anticipate his switching and decide to kick. In effect, the worst thing that can happen to each player is for his choice to be discovered. For that reason there is no one choice on the part of either player that produces a stable outcome or equilibrium solution.

Maximin, which is designed as a safe strategy, will in all likelihood lead to serious loss in this case and hardly could be called a rational strategy. What to do?

Von Neumann and Morgenstern suggest that in situations such as this, where your opponent can anticipate your choices based on maximin and where that knowledge can lead to a better choice than maximin for him, you should resort to a *mixed strategy*. In a mixed strategy you randomize your choices according to a prearranged set of probabilities so that your opponent cannot determine what you are likely to do. The choices must be randomized, for if you follow any prearranged schedule, based on some principle, then your opponent will in time be able to determine that schedule and take advantage of you. Such games are often games of "pure intelligence" because if either side can determine what the other side will do, the more "intelligent" side will win. Only a strategy that keeps an opponent in the dark as to one's intentions can be considered a rational strategy.

The particular probabilities by which to randomize choices will depend on an attempt to minimize the damage the opponent can inflict. The particular mix is determined by a mathematical technique that need not concern us here. (See Appendix C for a rather simple algorithm to find mixed strategies for 2×2 matrix games such as this one.) For this particular game the appropriate mixed strategy requires that Rows kick 4 out of 7 times and pass 3 out of 7 times. The mixed strategy for Columns requires him to use a normal defense 2 out of 7 times, and rush 5 out of 7 times.

The *value* of the game is the amount that each player will obtain by using his appropriate mix of strategies, i.e., plays according to his *maximin mixed strategy*. In our example, if we kick and pass in a ratio of 4 to 3, and our opponent plays normal defense and rushes in the ratio of 2 to 5, we will on average get 2.06 points per play, and our opponent will lose that amount. If we use any other mix of strategies we may get less than this amount. By using the maximin mixed strategy, we can guarantee ourselves at least the value of the game (2.06).

The use of a mixed strategy has an intuitively obvious rationale in a game like football where such choices come up many times during a game or the course of a season. Since you have to mix things up to keep from being taken advantage of, you might just as well mix your strategies in the most advantageous proportions.

However, what is the rationale when a game is played only once, and how would you use it? Von Neumann and Morgenstern suggest that you find a way to choose the strategy randomly in the correct proportions. For instance, the rows player might put 7 slips in a box, 4 labeled kick and 3 labeled pass, and blindly pick a slip and then do what it says. If you follow the mixed strategy, then you can guarantee yourself some minimal *expected payoff*. In that regard it is like the expected utility rule. If you use the expected utility rule you cannot assure yourself the expected payoff on any particular occasion. Likewise, the maximin mixed strategy cannot, in any one game, assure any payoff. However, both allow you to arrive at expected values, and if you follow the logic of those rules you should, in the long run, do better than you would by following any other rules.

To summarize, the mixed strategy is necessary, on the one hand, to keep your opponent guessing. On the other hand, the mixed strategy requires the same justification as choice based on expected utility in a one-shot situation. In any one case, it may not produce a desirable outcome, but a lifetime of choosing in such a way should, theoretically, provide a higher return than any other set of principles.

Another Example

Consider a variant of the game SCISSORS-ROCK-PAPER in which SCISSORS cuts PAPER (and wins 4), ROCK breaks SCISSORS (and wins 6), and PAPER covers ROCK (and wins 2).

COLUMNS PLAYER'S STRATEGIES

		SCISSORS	ROCK	PAPER	row minima
P R L O A W Y S E R	SCISSORS	0, 0	$\underline{-6}$, 6	4, $\underline{-4}$	–6
	ROCK	6, $\underline{-6}$	0, 0	$\underline{-2}$, 2	$\underline{-2}$
	PAPER	$\underline{-4}$, 4	2, $\underline{-2}$	0, 0	–4
	column minima	–6	$\underline{-2}$	–4	

In this game, the maximin strategy requires that each side play ROCK, and the outcome of such play is 0 for both players. If they do, the outcome will be the middle cell with payoff of 0, 0. However, since these payoffs do not match the underlined minima for rows and columns, this game has no saddlepoint. This means that if a player assumes that his opponent is rational and therefore is going to follow the maximin rule and select ROCK, then it is to his advantage to play PAPER and win 2. But if the Columns player can anticipate Rows' move, which he can, then he is unlikely to accept a loss of 2 when he can shift to SCISSORS and gain 4. But if Rows thinks likewise, then he is likely to shift to ROCK, thereby winning 6. And so it goes. Maximin, when there is no saddlepoint, is simply not appropriate.

For this particular game, the appropriate mixed strategy requires that each player play SCISSORS ⅙ of time, ROCK ⅓ of the time, and PAPER ½ of the time. If both players use that particular mix of strategies, the outcome will be 0 for each player. Since the same moves are available to each participant and the payoffs are independent of which player moves, the game is symmetric and therefore the rational solution must be 0 to each party. Obviously not all games are symmetric, as we saw in our football example. In nonsymmetric games, all the maximin mixed strategy can assure is that losses for the weaker player will be minimized, which is what maximin is designed to do.

Eliminating Dominated Strategies

Most of the examples you will be encountering in this text will be simple games where there are only two strategies for each player. Such simple "2 × 2" matrix games can be extremely useful to highlight certain decision problems. Those who wish to do so can "solve" such simple games using the algorithm given in Appendix C. There will be times, however, when it will be useful to consider games with greater options, such as PAPER, SCISSORS, and ROCK. Unfortunately, the mathematical procedures to solve such games are beyond the scope of this text. If such games have a single saddlepoint, then the solution will be easy; the solution will be the saddlepoint. Furthermore, it is sometimes possible to reduce larger games to the simpler 2 × 2 matrix form to clarify the structure of the competitive situation.

Example

Suppose John were excused from his final exam in the Modern Novel course because he was out of town for a major ball game. He is now back and has the coming weekend to prepare for a make-up exam, which will totally determine his grade. As usual, John hasn't cracked a book all semester. He will be tested on *War and Peace, Lady Chatterley's Lover,* and *Catcher in the Rye.* The problem is that if he reads *War and Peace* he will never get to the other two, whereas if he reads the shorter books he will have to skip *War and Peace.* John's frat brother, who took the final on schedule, managed to sneak out with a copy of the test. He doubts the professor knows this. John has noticed that the professor seems preoccupied by the divorce he is going through. Perhaps the best choice is to memorize the answers to the stolen copy in the hope that the professor will simply give the same exam over again, given his marital problems and his reputation for laziness.

John's choices are:

1. Read and study *War and Peace*;
2. Read and study the two shorter books;
3. Memorize the stolen exam.

John, in trying to anticipate the testing strategy, figures the following: his professor may stress *War and Peace* because it is his favorite, and because he suspects many students don't read it; or, he can give a well-rounded exam with about 50% devoted to *War and Peace* and 25% devoted to each of the other books, which is what he did for the scheduled exam; or, he can use the exam he prepared earlier.

Suppose John has set up his decision or game matrix as follows, with his estimated grade in each cell.

PROFESSOR'S CHOICES

		MAINLY W & P	GENERAL EXAM	OLD EXAM	row minima
JOHN'S CHOICES	STUDY W & P	A	C	C	C
	STUDY OTHERS	D	C	C	D
	STUDY OLD EXAM	F	F	A	F
	column minima	A	C	A	

Let us assume for the sake of this example that the professor hates to give As and loves to give Fs (especially to *jocks* who cut his classes) and that his satisfaction is roughly inverse to John's, so that this can be characterized as a zerosum game. In other words, when John gets the outcome "A," which he values as +10 on his scale of utility, the professor's pain at giving the "A" causes him to rate the value of that outcome as −10 on his scale. He loves to give Fs, which he rates +10. Assume both rate Cs as 0. Clearly, such an inverse satisfaction assumes a perverse sort of professor. In any case, given these evaluations we can rewrite the matrix as follows:

PROFESSOR'S CHOICES

		MAINLY W & P	GENERAL EXAM	OLD EXAM	row minima
	STUDY W & P	+10 −10	0 0	0 0	0
YOUR CHOICES	STUDY OTHERS	+5 −5	0 0	0 0	+5
	STUDY OLD EXAM	−10 +10	−10 +10	+10 −10	−10
	column minima	−10	0	−10	

If you study the above matrix, you will see that the choice of studying the simpler books is dominated by the choice of studying *War and Peace*. The latter choice is better than, or equal to, studying the simpler books in all conditions. Furthermore, it is clear that the professor's choice of using a new general exam dominates using the old one. He much prefers to give John an "F" in the case where John studies the purloined test, and is indifferent in the other cases where John gets "Cs." Thus, we are left with the reduced matrix below:

PROFESSOR'S CHOICES

		MAINLY W & P	GENERAL EXAM	row minima
JOHN'S CHOICES	STUDY W & P	+5 −5	0 0	0
	STUDY OLD EX.	−10 +10	−10 +10	−10
	column minima	−5	0	

Clearly John's maximin strategy is to study *War and Peace*, and the professor's maximin strategy is to give a new general exam and the solution will be the outcome 0,0 in the upper right hand cell in which John gets a "C" for the course. Since the values in this cell are also the best of the marginal minima for both players, this is a saddlepoint and no mixed strategy is necessary.

Solving the Zerosum Game

Very few real-life circumstances fall into the category of zerosum games. Nevertheless, it is important to understand the maximin solution to the zerosum game since we will be using those solutions in important ways later.

1. Eliminate any dominated choices for each player. Remember that a choice dominates another if it is at least equal in every cell to the other and better in at least one cell.
2. When left with only undominated choices or strategies for each player, or with only two choices for each player, determine the maximin choice for each, and indicate the cell that will result if each player makes his maximin choice.
3. Determine if this cell is a saddlepoint. It will be a saddlepoint if the payoff to each player in that cell is equal to the best of the marginal minima for each player. If that condition is not met, then the game has no saddlepoint and a mixed strategy is required.

An Example: Guerrilla Tactics

Consider the options to the parties in the early stages of a guerilla war. The rebels excel at small scale *hit and run* tactics, such as ambushing government supply convoys in the countryside and terrorist attacks in the cities. These tactics, designed to undermine confidence in the government and so win support among the populace, are based on the assumption that the average person is anxious to avoid being identified with the losing side, and will tend to be sympathetic to whichever side appears to have the upper hand. The government, on the other hand, with its better organized and equipped army, is anxious to demonstrate its superior strength in large-scale confrontations with the guerillas. It much prefers to meet the enemy in the open areas it controls, since it is less effective in the countryside where conditions are difficult for armored and motorized equipment. The following matrix depicts this set of conditions.

The numbers are designed to reflect the concerns of both sides. Each wishes to avoid losing men and material. Furthermore, each side wishes to convince the general public that it has the upper hand. The value " − 10" in the matrix suggests a sizable loss of men, material,

GOVERNMENT

		DEFENSIVE STRATEGY	ACTIVE ENGAGEMENT	row minima
R E B E L S	CONFRONT GOV. TROOPS	$\underline{-10}$ $\quad\quad +10$	-5 $\quad\quad +5$	-10
	AMBUSH & TERROR	$\underline{+5}$ $\quad\quad \underline{-5}$	$+8$ $\quad\quad \underline{-8}$	$\underline{+5}$
	column minima	$\underline{-5}$	-8	

and public confidence. The following assumptions are built into the matrix: that a major confrontation by large formations on both sides will be costly to the guerillas (especially so if they attack fortified positions, the outcome in the upper left cell); that even if the government keeps most of its troops in fortified positions, some of their men will have to be exposed at least some of the time to rebel ambush. The outcome in the bottom left cell reflects the fact that, if the guerillas can ambush large convoys moving about the countryside, they will be able to inflict significant damage at limited cost to themselves.

To find the solution to this game, we need to determine the maximin strategies for each side. For the government, the worst outcome arises when they send large troop concentrations into the countryside on search and destroy missions, and are surprised on unfavorable terrain and sustain heavy losses without being able to do serious damage to the guerillas. Their best strategy is to remain in large, well-situated defensive positions, and accept occasional ambushes of their supply convoys by the guerillas. For the guerillas, the worst outcome occurs if they attempt full scale confrontation on government positions. Therefore, their maximin strategy is to attempt to "bleed" the government by harassing their convoys in the bush and by engaging in terrorist actions in cities. The outcome of these strategies is the intersecting cell on the bottom left. By inspection, we can see that this is also the saddlepoint and hence the solution to the game.

This is, indeed, the situation in the early stages of many modern insurrections. The government is forced to take constant but relatively small losses to the guerillas. Even though those losses begin to mount over time as the guerillas bring more of the countryside under their control, the government usually has such a large initial advantage that it often appears to have everything under control. This perception works to the disadvantage of the guerillas who, if they are to hope for success, must undercut the impression of government invincibility. They can only do that if they can obtain the arms and support for a successful frontal assault, which is unlikely in the early stages of an insurrection. A common strategy is to increase terrorist activities in cities. If such attacks are sufficiently audacious and deadly, they can so undermine confidence in the government that it may be forced to try to stop the attacks by destroying the guerilla bases in the country-side. In essence, the terrorist activity is an attempt to transform the game into the one depicted below:

GOVERNMENT

		DEFENSIVE STRATEGY	ACTIVE ENGAGEMENT	row minima
R E B E L S	CONFRONT GOV. TROOPS	−10 +10	−5 +5	−10
	AMBUSH & TERROR	+10 −10	+8 −8	+8
	column minima	−10	−8	

The only change is in the lower left cell where the stepped-up terror campaign makes the government's defensive strategy unjustifiable. Examination of the matrix will reveal that the saddlepoint has shifted to the lower right cell, and that this is the new solution to the game, where the guerillas can take advantage of their strength by ambushing the now more numerous government convoys moving through the countryside.

There the war will remain unless continued government losses earn the guerillas sufficient support, either from the populace or from friendly patrons, to mount successful large-scale assaults on government positions. The government will, of course, continue in its attempts to improve its ability to deal with the guerillas in the countryside so as to preclude that eventuality.

Examples

Let us consider another example, which, for sake of simplicity, we present without any attempt at a "scenario."

COLUMN PLAYER

		A		B		C	
P · L · A · Y · E · R	G	2	–2	9	–9	–7	7
ROWS	H	1	–1	3	–3	–9	9
	I	3	–3	6	–6	5	–5

Clearly the row player's H strategy is dominated by G and by I, and therefore should be eliminated to produce the following matrix:

COLUMN PLAYER

		A		B		C	
P · L · A · Y · E · R	G	2	–2	9	–9	–7	7
ROWS	I	3	–3	6	–6	5	–5

Just as clearly, column strategy B, dominated by A and C, should be eliminated, producing:

COLUMN PLAYER

		A		C		
ROWS	G	2	–2	–7	7	–7
	I	3	–3	5	–5	3
		–3		–5		

If each player uses maximin, the resulting outcome will be the cell A-I with payoff 3, – 3. Is this a saddlepoint? Since for the row player 3 is equal to the best of the row marginal minima, and – 3 is equal to the best of the column minima, it is a saddlepoint. This means that having settled on the maximin strategy, neither player can better his outcome by choosing some other strategy.

Consider another example:

COLUMN PLAYER

		A		C		
ROWS	G	2	-2	4	-4	2
	I	3	-3	1	-1	1
			-3		-4	

Here the cell produced by maximin choices by both players is A-G with payoff 2, – but in this case it is not a saddlepoint since for COLUMN, −2 does not equal the column marginal minima of −3, even though 2 does equal the row marginal minima of 2. Therefore, a mixed strategy is required. If ROW knows that COLUMN will play A, then he can do better by playing I, but since COLUMN can anticipate this, COLUMN could shift to C and lose only 1. And so it goes. A mixed strategy is necessary. The actual mix for this game is worked out in Appendix C. It turns out to be that ROW should randomize his choices in the ratio of 1 to 1, and COLUMN his choices in the ratio of 3 to 1. If either plays in this way, the outcome will be that ROW will win 1 and COLUMN will lose 1. If one player deviates from his maximin mixed strategy, then the other player may be able to adjust his strategy to take advantage of this deviation. The advantage of the mixed strategy, you will recall, is that if you use it, in the long run you can guarantee yourself some minimal expected payoff.

Nonzerosum or Potentially Cooperative Games

Nonzerosum games represent those cases in which there is some opportunity for mutual gain among the participants. The most widely explored of these games is the, by now famous, *prisoner's dilemma*. In this scenario, two individuals have been detained by the police and charged with robbing the local bank. Each is offered the chance to "cop a plea" by turning in the other and thereby improve his own circumstances. If both refuse to talk and the police have very little evidence on either, both can expect fairly light sentences. They might only be charged with illegal possession of handguns, which they had been carrying.

It is assumed that if one confesses and the other does not, then the one who confesses will go free and get the money to boot, while the other will languish in jail. Of course, if both talk, then no plea bargain is necessary and both go to jail, but with somewhat lighter sentences for having confessed and spared the state the expense of a trial. The reader is free to further embellish this scenario at his pleasure. The situation is typically depicted so:

PRISONER B

P R I S O N E R	A		MUM	TALK	row minima
		MUM	5 5	-8 8	-8
		TALK	8 -8	-5 -5	-5
		column minima	-8	-5	

Clearly this is not a zerosum game since the cells defined by TALK-TALK and MUM-MUM do not sum to zero. That is the defining characteristic of the nonzerosum case: there are some outcomes in which there is the potential for mutual benefit or mutual damage. The most sensible solution is to arrange the MUM-MUM payoff. This is often easier said than done. Not only must the participants agree upon strategy, they must also find some way to protect themselves against betrayal. If they are kept apart and so cannot talk, this is very difficult. Even if they could talk and come to agreement, how can they guarantee the agreement? This is a problem in the prisoner's dilemma, because the best joint outcome (MUM-MUM) is unstable since either player can do better by deviating from it and betraying the other. Such betrayal leads to the worst outcome to the one who is betrayed, while the best outcome goes to the betrayer. If both defect, they both lose. That is the dilemma.

At the least, the following conditions must be satisfied for the players to realize the potential benefit of cooperation in this situation.

1. Communication—The parties must be able to discuss their options and arrive at a mutually satisfying agreement.
2. Guarantees—They must in some way be able to guarantee that agreement. An agreement without a guarantee is, in such cases, tantamount to no agreement at all.

If these conditions cannot be met, the players are forced to fall back on a defensive strategy and protect themselves against the worst that can happen, i.e. to use the maximin strategy. In this case, if the prisoners believe each other capable of betrayal then each must "talk" to protect himself, with the result that they each end up with -5.

It is worth noting that in this game the TALK-TALK outcome is analogous to a saddlepoint in the zerosum game in that it is the outcome of joint maximin choices and represents a stable equilibrium. It is stable because for both players the maximin choice is dominating and, once they have settled in the outcome $(-5, -5)$, neither individual can do better by changing unless the other changes as well. Only a jointly agreed upon change can produce the better outcome. The cooperative MUM-MUM outcome lacks this stability because it is a dominated strategy. Once the players have settled on the outcome $(+5, +5)$, each can do better by defecting, so long as the other does not.

The outcome $(+5, +5)$ can be said to be *societally rational* in that it produces the highest payoff to the group or *society* composed of both players. But in order to achieve it, the two must cooperate and act as a single interest. If they cannot, they are forced to fall back on the principle of individual rationality embodied in the maximin rule.

Prisoner's Dilemma and Collusive Pricing

Consider an example from the economic sphere. Suppose two companies are the only manufacturers of disposable butane lighters, and suppose that each has a 50% share of the market of 10 million lighters a year at the wholesale price of $1.00. Assume a cost to them of fifty cents per lighter, netting·each $2.5 million in profit. A marketing study suggests that if one manufacturer drops his price to eighty-five cents then the price-cutting firm can capture 75% of the market. Furthermore, such action would increase the market to 12 million lighters. If both drop their price, the market will increase to 13 million lighters. Both manufacturers are confronted with the set of circumstances on page 257.

While this example omits a good deal, it illustrates a common problem in any market dominated by a few manufacturers. Given the following form, the problem is clearly a prisoner's dilemma in that if one cuts his price while the other does not, the price-cutter reaps a benefit at the expense of the price-holder. However, if both cut prices

FIRM B

		$1.00 PRICE	$.85 PRICE
	$1.00 PRICE	$.50 x 5 mil = $2.5 mil profit for Firm A $.50 x 5 mil = $2.5 mil profit for Firm B	$.50 x 4 mil = $2.0 mil profit for Firm A $.35 x 8 mil = $2.8 mil profit for Firm B
F I R M A	$.85 PRICE	$.35 x 8 mil = $2.80 mil profit for Firm A $.50 x 4 mil = $2.0 mil profit for Firm B	$.35 x 6.5 mil = $2.275 mil profit for Firm A $.35 x 6.5 mil = $2.275 mil profit for Firm B

they are both the poorer. It is obviously in their interest to engage in a collusive arrangement in which they guarantee the higher price. Without the guarantee they might find betrayal all too appealing. This is especially so if considerable time is needed to tool up to meet a competitor's supply and price. Laws barring such collusion are clearly designed to make such guarantees difficult to arrange. Just as clearly, firms can, through tacit understandings, refrain from price-cutting. Such tacit arrangements can go on for years and are not noticed until someone breaks rank and sets off a ruinous price war, sometimes forcing firms to sell below cost.

At this point it is important to note that not all nonzerosum games lend themselves so readily to compromise and mutual gain. The game of "chicken" should illustrate this point.

The Chicken Game

This game is seen in its simplest form among teenagers who have challenged each other to see who is chicken. They might both agree to drive cars at each other, straddling the dividing line, with the understanding that the first one who swerves and crosses the line is declared chicken and loses the contest. Of course, if neither side chickens, both suffer severe damage to their cars and, possibly, their persons. If both swerve at the same time, neither is chicken and the game is a draw. We can depict the game so:

		DRIVER B		
		SWERVE	STAY	row minima
DRIVER A	SWERVE	5 5	−15 10	−15
	STAY	10 −15	−50 −50	−50
		−15	−50	

We might justify the numbers we have assigned by the following rationale. If both chicken at the same time, both gain from having demonstrated their bravery, and little but time was lost. If one chickens before the other, he suffers the ignominy of having lost his nerve, of chickening out, and the other party gains from having demonstrated nerve and toughness. We are assuming in our evaluation of the outcome that the loss of chickening out is greater than the gain of winning, which is admittedly questionable without knowledge of individual goals. If neither party swerves, disaster results. We are assuming fairly prudent players, all buckled up with helmets, and reckon the loss as damage only to the cars. If the cars are of unequal value, then the losses would not be the same for both participants.

The most sensible solution for the players would be to agree to guarantee the jointly beneficial SWERVE-SWERVE outcome. Suppose they cannot agree and must operate as defensive individuals, i.e. play maximin. Examining the matrix will reveal that this produces the desired SWERVE-SWERVE outcome anyway. The problem is that the SWERVE strategy is not dominating, and this game lacks the equivalent of a saddlepoint. Once one player knows the other will, in self-defense, use the maximin strategy, then the other has a powerful incentive to move to the other strategy.

In fact, the outcome of the game is dependent almost entirely on the ability of the players to decipher each other's intentions. It is a game of bluff. If I know you are bluffing, I should not chicken out, whereas if I think you are serious I should. This is because the outcomes (−15, 10 and 10, −15) that result when one player swerves and the other stays are *both* stable equilibria (Rapoport 1969). Once one of those outcomes is settled upon, neither player has any incentive to change. The whole problem then, if one cannot negotiate a guaranteed solution, is to try to move to one of those outcomes. One way to benefit from the stability of those outcomes is to announce the intention to "stay" no matter what and to try to demonstrate to the other side that you are serious. If he believes you, then the only rational choice for him is to "swerve."

In most real life chicken situations, the parties will engage in various activities designed to signal their intentions to the other side, to convince the other side that they are serious and will not "chicken." It is generally agreed that the mobilization of forces prior to the start of World War I was undertaken to convince the enemy that one had every intention of calling the bluff. Similarly, the threats and posturing during the Cuban missile crisis can also be seen as a chicken game.

Consider the following possibility for our teenage daredevils. If one driver puts his car in the automatic drive mode, jumps in the back seat of the car and advertises his actions to the other driver (by, say, standing up in the back of a convertible), then he has clearly put the other driver in an untenable situation. (We assume here a very straight road and a car with extraordinary tracking capacities.) The other driver can stay the course and accept disaster, or swerve and accept the consequences of having chickened. The first driver has recognized an obvious fact about the chicken game; namely, that by taking an action that he cannot reverse, he has fundamentally transformed the game for the other party. It has become a simple decision problem in which the choice is to stay and lose 50, or swerve and lose 15; in that case, the only rational choice is to swerve.

Ranked Outcomes

As a way of gaining insight into the relation between the prisoner's dilemma game and the chicken game, it might be useful to depict the games using rankings instead of utilities. Looking at both games in this way gives the following:

PRISONER'S DILEMMA — PLAYER B

PLAYER A	MUM	TALK
MUM	3, 3	1, 4
TALK	4, 1	2, 2

CHICKEN — PLAYER B

	SWERVE	STAY
SWERVE	3, 3	2, 4
STAY	4, 2	1, 1

All prisoner's dilemma games and chicken games will take this form if the outcomes are ranked from best (4) to worst (1). Notice that they are the same except for the reversal in the two lowest ranks. In the prisoner's dilemma, the worst outcome results from being betrayed, whereas in chicken, the worst results if neither side "chickens." Rapoport, Guyer, and Gordon (1976) have, by the way, analyzed all *2 × 2 matrix games* in this way.

Notice that in the prisoner's dilemma, TALK clearly dominates MUM; it is better no matter what the other side does. In chicken, on the other hand, there is no dominating strategy; it is better to stay if the other person swerves, but better to swerve if the other party stays.

In both games it is societally rational to come to some mutually accommodating agreement and to avoid the mutually damaging outcome. In the prisoner's dilemma, failure to reach agreement guarantees the mutually undesirable outcome because it is the "safe" maximin choice for each player. In other words, the prisoner's dilemma has a fairly obvious noncooperative solution—the outcome where both talk—and is analogous to a saddlepoint in the zerosum case. A *noncooperative* solution is one that will arise as a product of individual choices and not out of mutually cooperative action. Remember, a solution to a zerosum game is some outcome with a definite payoff to each party that will result if both participants act in their individual best interests. In that sense, all solutions to zerosum games are *noncooperative*. No such obvious noncooperative solution is available in "chicken."

The Minimax Mixed Strategy and Noncooperative Equilibria

The problem for a player in this game is that there is no pure dominating strategy, and there is no safe mixed strategy he can use. In nonzerosum games, there does not always exist a satisfying mixed strategy solution as there is in zerosum games. The reason for this is that the maximin mixed strategy is defined for zerosum games without saddlepoints, in games that have no equilibrium solutions.

In chicken, however, the game has two equilibria, remembering that an equilibrium outcome is one from which, once it is settled upon, neither player has an incentive to deviate. The two equilibria are the two outcomes where one side stays and the other swerves. The problem for any one player is to attempt to achieve the equilibrium solution that is better for himself. But since there is no way he can guarantee an outcome in his favored equilibrium outcome, he risks maximum harm by an attempt. The only safe or guaranteed solution is the maximin choice of swerving, but if he acts on the basis of maximin and the other side knows he will, the swerving player exposes himself to almost certain exploitation.

There is something very unsatisfying to the maximin solution in this case. It seems to imply that it is somehow "rational" to always give in to those more willing to take risks. For this reason, game theorists have devoted considerable energy to trying to discover some alternative solution. From an intuitive perspective, it does seem that one would be better off if one occasionally stayed the course, called the bluff, as it were, if only to keep the other fellow guessing. After all, if the other is uncertain as to what you may do, he is less likely to take the risky option. Unfortunately, no generally accepted mixed strategy solution exists for this sort of situation.

In the zerosum game, a *maximin* strategy keeps your losses to a minimum since you maximize across your minima, as it were. Because of the zerosum condition this is equivalent to, in fact is identical to, a *minimax* strategy in which you keep your opponent's gains to a minimum. In the zerosum game, the minimax is the same as the maximin, since when you maximize across your minima, you are, at the same time, minimizing across your opponent's maxima. In other words, you receive the same payoff whether you play a maximin or a minimax strategy. This is not so in the nonzerosum game where maximin and minimax may produce different strategy recommendations.

One potential strategy in the chicken game might be to use the minimax strategy to keep your opponent in line by reducing his temptation to defect. One way to do this is to take the risky STAY choice. Another way would be to use STAY only some of the time, to use a mixed strategy of some sort. It turns out that in the nonzerosum game, one possibility is a mixed strategy based on minimax rather than maximin. In the zerosum game they would be exactly the same, but they will not be the same in nonzerosum contests. The maximin mixed strategy gives us a mix of choices that keeps *our loss at some minimal value,* no matter what the other side does. In the minimax strategy, on the other hand, we are given a mix of choices that keep *the other's gain at some minimal value,* no matter what the other side does. A mix of choices that will, in effect, provide a fixed payoff to the other that will be unaffected by what he does. In the maximin, remember, we sought a mix of strategies that would provide a fixed return *to ourselves* regardless of what the other did. Here, we fix the other side's return to some minimum.

When a chicken game is played repeatedly, such a strategy makes a certain intuitive sense. In the game played only once, it only makes sense if you can convince the other side that you will use such a strategy, and it is hard to see how it is any better than actually claiming that you will use the absolutely risky STAY strategy and go for broke. On the other hand, it might not be a bad idea to have a reputation of occasionally calling the bluff and of taking serious risks. Clearly, it is extremely important to choose wisely when taking a risk and to be sure it is compensated by the advantage of a reputation for risk taking.

The minimax mixed strategy solution to the nonzerosum game is unsatisfying as a decision rule in that, if we use it, we may, under some circumstances, receive less than we can guarantee by maximin. Nevertheless, it has some appeal as a device to use in attempting to convince the other to move to the cooperative choice. In essence it is a punitive strategy in which we say to the other, "Even if it costs me dearly, I will not let you profit greatly by bullying me."

The minimax, interestingly, does give rise to a kind of equilibrium if both sides use it (Rapoport 1969). Once I know you are using the minimax mixed strategy against me, I cannot change my winnings by changing my strategy, no matter what I have decided to do, and so I have no incentive to change from it. If for some strange reason I am using minimax also, then neither of us has any incentive to change. Remember, an equilibrium solution is one that, once settled upon, neither side is motivated to change. In effect, this means that the game of chicken has three equilibria. It has this one, where both use their minimax mixed strategy, and the other two that result when one swerves and the other stays.

As Rapoport (1969) suggests, this is only an equilibrium "of sorts," since it is hard to imagine why both players should adopt it in the first place, since it may provide less in return than a pure maximin strategy. However, this equilibrium "of sorts" will be of value when we discuss "evolutionary games" in a later section. For now it is enough to note that, at least technically, it allows for a third equilibrium in the chicken game.

Strategic Policy

One way to convince the other side in the chicken game that you will take the dangerous action and are not just bluffing is to claim that you view chickening out as worse than crashing. If one party can convince the other that he is "crazy" and will stay no matter what, or that the cost of being chicken is worse for him than the damage from a crash, then he has a clear advantage. Consider the problem from the perspective of Driver A if he assesses the outcomes in the following way:

DRIVER B

		SWERVE		STAY		row minima
D R I V E R	A SWERVE	5	5	-15	8	-15
	A STAY	8	-50	-50	-40	-50
	col minima		-50		-40	

The game is now no longer a simple chicken game. Rather it is similar to chicken for rows and similar to the prisoner's dilemma for columns. In this particular game, there is a maximin equilibrium solution, and it is the outcome in which rows swerves and columns stays.

Most readers will by now recognize that the nuclear arms race between the United States and the USSR can be seen either as a game of chicken, or a game of prisoner's dilemma, or some combination of the two. Both sides claim that they are playing prisoner's dilemma in that they claim that, for them, there are certain outcomes worse than a nuclear exchange. The United States, for instance, has claimed that loss of its interests in Europe could result in such an exchange. The strategy known as MAD (mutual assured destruction), which has been the policy of both sides for many years, creates the uneasy balance of terror in which each side claims that if nuclear attack is made on one side it will be immediately and automatically returned.

If this is the case, and the situation is, in reality, a prisoner's dilemma, then the only rational course is to negotiate the cooperative solution to avoid the grisly alternative of destroying the world. The point is that in the prisoner's dilemma there are only two rational outcomes: the mutually damaging maximin equilibrium outcome, and the far more rational negotiated solution.

However, should one party or both view the game as chicken then the problem is to get the jump on the other side. Some have argued that such a situation may have developed in the arms race because of improved missile delivery systems. As nuclear missiles become more accurate, they can be made less powerful but just as effective in destroying limited targets such as missile silos. One consequence is that it is now conceivable that Side A could wipe out the missiles of Side B without inflicting extraordinary civilian casualties. Side B could not respond with an attack on Side A's land-based missiles (since most are in the air) and could only respond by immediately releasing its missiles for a full scale MAD attack on Side A's civilian population. Such an attack following MAD would probably be met with a like response.

Consider the following scenario. The President of the United States has just been informed that the USSR has mounted a full scale missile assault, which is clearly designed to destroy the U.S. capacity to retaliate. He can order a full scale strike on civilian targets (following the MAD strategy of mutual assured destruction), or he can take the first strike without retaliation. If he retaliates, he can be sure that the USSR will also retaliate, producing *mutual assured destruction*. His dilemma can be depicted as follows:

USSR

	NO SECOND STRIKE	SECOND STRIKE
UNITED STATES NO RETALIATION	Loss of global power	Destruction of United States
RETALIATION	Maintain global power	End of the world

This is a most unsatisfying state of affairs, and it highlights the fears associated with the first strike capacity. It is one of the powerful arguments for arms limitations and is also an argument in support of some sort of strategic defense (SDI).

Evolutionary Games

One of the most interesting applications of game theory comes from the literature of evolutionary biology. Maynard Smith and Price (1973), in a ground-breaking paper, argued that much animal behavior could be understood as evolutionary solutions to nonzerosum games.

Since animals cannot talk, they cannot sit down and work out mutually desirable solutions to problems. They are likely, however, to evolve in the direction of solutions that foster their own survival and reproductive success. One should expect that over many generations those animals who have followed successful strategies, however blindly, will leave more offspring like themselves, i.e., those who follow the same strategies. Such strategies could be said to be genetically rational in that they are gene preserving.

Dawkins, in his influential book *The Selfish Gene* (1976), has amusingly suggested that an animal's "selfish" genes program themselves to behave in ways that best serves the genes' interests—to preserve and multiply themselves. In other words, successful genes that have spread through the environment can be said to have programmed their carriers "as if" they (the genes) were rational strategists.

Hawks and Doves

Animals are successful (in the above sense) if they survive and reproduce as well or better than other animals. For that reason, they are often in conflict over resources such as food and mates. Such conflict or fighting is often restrained, especially between members of the same species. Why should that be, since continual failure to win such fights almost guarantees evolutionary failure? Many have argued that this is due to the animals' altruistic tendencies that cause them to limit their fighting to the "good of the species." But such reasoning has been shown to be seriously flawed (Dawkins 1976). Maynard Smith and Price (1973) suggest, alternatively, that most such restraint in fighting may be self-serving rather than altruistic. They note the fact that fighting is dangerous, even for the stronger animal. The victor of a serious fight is often injured. Any wounds he receives may expose him to infection, at the least, and may be more permanently debilitating. In some cases, it may be better to back away from a fight, especially if the opponent seems stronger or if it is better to wait for a more propitious opportunity, especially the case for young animals who can expect their competition to weaken with age.

The following example, originally described by Maynard Smith (1976), is taken from Dawkins (1976).

The grid represents the choices of two animals confronting each other over some desirable resource, for example, an opportunity to mate, which is worth 50 "evolutionary success units." If they both act

ANIMAL B

		DOVE	HAWK	
A N I M A L	DOVE	+15, +15	0, +50	0
A	HAWK	+50, 0	−25 −25	−25
		0	−25	

like doves and do not engage in fighting, but rather attempt to wait each other out, then all other things being equal, each has a fifty-fifty chance of gaining the resource; but they will have wasted considerable time, which is valued at 10 units each. Therefore, the expected value, then, of the DOVE-DOVE outcome is $(.5 \times 50) - 10 = 15$.

If both immediately start to fight (act like hawks), the fight will be over fairly quickly, but each takes the chance of serious injury, which we value at -100. Assume the animals are equally matched so that each has a fifty-fifty chance of winning or sustaining serious harm. The expected value of the outcome when both fight is, therefore, $(.5 \times (50 - 100))$ or -25 units.

If, on the other hand, one animal starts to fight like a hawk, and the other is dovish and immediately withdraws, the total resource goes to the hawk $(+50)$, and the dove gets nothing.

The reader will notice that this is a variant of the game of chicken. As we have seen, there is no easy (mathematically determined) solution to that game, but rather a set of competing equilibrium outcomes.

Maynard Smith has discovered that there may be strategies that evolve over time and are stable within a particular animal population. Suppose in this population there are mainly doves who always run, and a few hawks who always fight. It would appear that over a couple of generations, there will be very few doves left in the population, which will be overrun by the offspring of the more successful hawks. However, as the number of doves declines, the potential danger of hawkish behavior increases, since the probability of damaging hawk-hawk encounters grows. If most animals were hawks, doves would be unlikely to win much (and then only in encounters with scarce doves), but they are also likely to escape serious injury. Long before all the doves were gone, the hawks would start killing each other off.

Maynard Smith discovered that in such cases one can find an optimum mix of types that will stay in equilibrium over time and is self-enforcing. The mix will involve what he called *evolutionary stable strategies*, or ESSs.

An evolutionary stable strategy is one which, played against itself, is better or equal to any other strategy played against itself, and is also better or equal when played against any other strategy. For example, if all members of the population were hawks and playing hawk against other hawks produced a higher payoff than any other strategy, then hawk would be as ESS. Practically, it would mean that a mutant type who used another strategy could not thrive and would eventually die off.

If, however, the behavioral tendencies of a mutant type produced outcomes that were equal to the dominant type, then it would have the opportunity to establish itself and the population might then contain two ESSs in equilibrium. In a population consisting only of hawks and doves, there is such an equilibrium and it is reached when the proportion of hawks to doves is in the ratio of 7 to 5.

Maynard Smith notes that such an equilibrium need not consist of hawk types and dove types, but could consist of animals predisposed to a mixed strategy of playing hawk and dove in the ratio of 7 to 5, i.e., play hawk $7/12$ of the time and dove $5/12$ of the time. If a mutant subgroup arose in such a mixed strategy population and was predisposed to be dovish, let us say, $3/4$ of the time, they would not do as well in interaction with each other as those who were less dovish, and played dove $5/12$ of the time. Likewise, any subgroup of mutant types who played hawk more than $7/12$ of the time would not do as well as those who acted "normally." The consequence is that over time any deviation from the equilibrium ratio should evolve in the direction of that ratio. That is why it is said to be a *self-enforcing* ratio.

In the case of the HAWK-DOVE game where the ratio of 7 to 5 represents an animal population whose members use a mixed strategy, it turns out that these ratios are the same as those prescribed by the *minimax mixed strategy*. An interesting property of the minimax strategy, as discussed earlier, is that if both players use it, "it represents an equilibrium of sorts" (Rapoport 1969, p. 139). If both players use the mixed strategy in the HAWK-DOVE game, both would receive a fixed sum and a player's own behavior would not affect the payoff he receives. That is because the minimax strategy keeps the other players payoff at a fixed value, and he gets that value no matter what he does.

For that reason, then, the resulting outcome would be in equilibrium, since neither could better his outcome by changing. Quoting Rapoport (1969, p. 140):

The equilibrium strategy . . . depends on the assumption that the other is like me. So the only reason for him to choose the mixture is the assumption that I shall play it and moreover shall expect him to play it. The mixture is the only "prominent" one among the three equilibria. But its prominence is due only to its mathematical symmetry, not to any advantage it confers on the players.

We agree with Rapoport and find it hard to imagine why one player should assume that the other will play just as he does, *except in the special case where the players are programmed to act similarly, as are many animals*.

In the Hawk-Dove game that outcome provides a payoff of 6.25 to each animal, which is better than the maximin outcome of 0, but not as good as the negotiated *good of the group* outcome of (15, 15). Unfortunately, animals cannot negotiate and guarantee the *good of the group* outcome. But, in the case of animals, there is good reason to suppose that the others will use the same strategy since their actions are determined not by a rational calculation of their interests in the individual case, but rather by their programmed tendencies to respond in ways in which their successful, and often common, ancestors responded.

Suppose you are a member of a group of mutant types in the above animal society and instead of being "normal" and abiding by everybody else's inherited tendency, you and your type tended to play hawk much more frequently. Because of the nature of the minimax strategy, you would gain neither more nor less than every one else when dealing with normals, and hence your gene for hawkishness has no advantage among normals, and would not spread in the population. Moreover, when confronting your own type, your mutant strategy, since it is not stable, would tend to drift into actions producing worse outcomes, and hence your type would start to decline. The same holds for subgroups of dovish mutants.

If, on the other hand, the population for some arbitrary reason were to drift away from the minimax ratio to 3 to 1, hawk to dove, then mutants who were more hawkish would do less well, whereas mutant who were more dovish would do better. And, as more dovish types did better, their dovish gene would spread and the population would gradually move back to the equilibrium 7 to 5 strategy mix. Likewise, if the population were to become more dovish for some arbitrary reason, then more hawkish types would have an advantage, and in time the population would return to the equilibrium 7 to 5 ratio.

To this point we have arbitrarily limited ourselves to only two strategy choices, namely hawk and dove. In any animal population, additional strategies may become available through mutation, and they may be better or worse than the two we have considered above. In general, if a new strategy becomes available and it does less well than the existing strategies, it will die out. If it is better, it will spread and drive out the original types. Smith and Price (1973) found that the alternative strategy "retaliator" is evolutionarily stable. Retaliators act like doves unless confronted by hawks, in which case they act like hawks. A population consisting of hawks, doves, and retaliators will eventually evolve into a population of retaliators (Smith 1976). Perhaps the biblical injunction to take an eye for an eye and a tooth for a tooth is grounded on some fairly basic evolutionary realities. In other words, even though taking the other's eye doesn't get your eye back, it does tend to level the playing field, at least between the offender and his victim.

In light of the above, it is interesting that in experiments in which the prisoner's dilemma is played repeatedly by subjects, a common strategy is to play "tit for tat", i.e., play cooperatively unless betrayed and if betrayed, retaliate. A computer program, proposed by Anatol Rapoport, following the *tit-for-tat* strategy, was more successful than any other in a computer contest of such repeated or iterated playing of the prisoner's dilemma (Hofstadter 1983). Maynard Smith found that, if the probability of continued repetition is high, the *tit-for-tat* strategy is, in fact, an ESS.

Stop Signs, Laws, and ESSs

Four-way stop signs are chicken games of sorts. Suppose that going first is the best outcome and is valued as worth 4, going second is second best worth 2. Sitting in your car and waiting is third best and worth -2. Going at the same time as the other is worst and worth -10, since it may result in an accident. This can be depicted so:

COLUMNS

		WAIT	GO
R O W S	WAIT	-2, -2	2, 4
	GO	4, 2	-10, -10

The rules governing who goes first are man-made ESSs. Rules such as "car on the right goes first" or "first to arrive goes first," are simple, orderly rules that benefit those who abide by them. They allow for selecting one of the two desirable outcomes in a way that over the long run, benefits all drivers equally. There is no advantage to deviation, since such deviation almost always produces the undesirable GO-GO outcome.

Such situations, often called *games of coordination*, are interesting in that they are very common and the rule settled upon is fairly arbitrary. The rule—"those on left go first"—is neither better nor worse than the rule that gives the go-ahead to those on the right. The major problem arises if some do not know the rule or do not abide by it, and they are likely to disappear fairly quickly, though they will undoubtedly take some law abiders with them.

Dawkins (1976) points out that because the critical thing in such cases is coordination, it is possible for counter-intuitive rules or ESSs to develop. The example he uses is the well-known advantage that most animals have on their own territory. Many animals seem to be affected by a rule that suggests that they should act like hawks on their own territory and doves on others'. Acting in the opposite way by retreating from one's own territory and acting tough on one's neighbor's, which appears counter-intuitive, could develop into an ESS, but almost never does. Why is such a rule so uncommon? Would a rule that gave the right of way to the car that entered *last* be effective for purposes of coordination? Why wouldn't people like it?

Solutions like the one "first to arrive has the right of way" are so easy to understand, they seem almost natural. They are also inherently fair in that they are symmetric. There is no reason for anyone to suppose that they will, in the long run, suffer any disadvantage from the rule. Such obviously useful and symmetric rules are sometimes referred to as *natural solutions,* in that even if the rules didn't exist one expects that they would naturally evolve within a population. As we will see, such natural solutions play an important part in negotiations.

Battle of the Sexes

Dawkins (1976) describes another hypothetical animal game, which is given below. It assumes a population of females who are either coy or fast, and a population of males who are either faithful or philandering.

MALE ANIMAL

			FAITHFUL	PHILANDERER	row minima
F A					
E N	FAST		+5, +5	<u>−5</u>, +15	−5
M I					
A M	COY		+2, <u>+2</u>	<u>0</u>, 0	<u>0</u>
L A					
E L	col minima		<u>+2</u>	0	

The values are arrived at in the following way. We assign each offspring a value of 15 units, and we assume that value is the same for males and females. Time wasted in courtship is valued at 3 units, and the cost of caring for the offspring is rated as 20 units.

The top left cell results when a fast female is paired with a faithful male. They each benefit by +15 by their offspring, from which we must subtract −10, which is their share of the cost of caring for their offspring. The outcome is, therefore, 15 − 10 = +5.

The payoff in the bottom left cell is the same, except they must subtract 3 for the time wasted in courtship. Therefore, their payoff is 15 − 10 − 3 = +2.

The top right cell is the outcome where a fast female mates with a philanderer who, true to form, deserts her. They both gain 15 by virtue of gaining an offspring, but since the male neither lost time nor energy in courtship or child care, he keeps all 15 units. The female, on the other hand, must singlehandedly invest the 20 units required for childrearing and hence is left with 15 − 20 = −5.

The bottom right cell occurs when a philanderer tries to induce a coy female to mate with him. Since she is coy and demands a lengthy courtship, he loses interest. Not much is gained or lost by either in such unproductive encounters.

From the matrix we can see that there is no clear dominating strategy for either side. If the world is full of faithful males, fast females do better against their coy counterparts, but not if there are philanderers lurking in the woodwork. Likewise for males, if all females are coy it does not pay to philander, but if some are fast, then it might.

It turns out that these are evolutionary stable strategies and will reach equilibrium if females play fast and coy in the ratio 1 to 6, and if the males are faithful and philandering in the ratio 5 to 3.

Suppose we introduce modifications in the above. Let us say, for example, that all females are vengeful and inflict bodily damage on males who betray them. Let us say that they are 50% successful in inflicting such harm at a cost of -40 to the male, with no cost to themselves. In that case the payoff to a philandering male with a fast female is now $15 - \frac{1}{2}(40) = -5$. The modified game would look so:

MALE ANIMAL

		FAITHFUL	PHILANDERER	row minima
F A E N M I	FAST & JEALOUS	+5, +5	–5, –5	–5
A M L A	COY	+2, +2	0, 0	0
E L	col minima	+2	–5	

In this new game the male player has a dominating strategy, and that is for males to be faithful. Females can then safely be fast, resulting in the equilibrium outcome of $(+5, +5)$. Such an outcome arises infrequently among animals, perhaps because the female is usually smaller and is unlikely to inflict much harm. Human females, of course, often have fathers who are capable of carrying out the vengeful desires of their daughters and often have a selfish interest in doing so. And shotguns to boot. Such an arrangement is becoming less common among humans for reasons that need not concern us here.

Summary

The zerosum game in being strictly competitive imposes the protective, maximin solution on rational participants. In the nonzerosum or potentially cooperative game, the maximin is a strategy of last resort, which is used because the cooperative, mutually beneficial outcome cannot be arranged. One unequivocal conclusion we can draw from the literature on the nonzerosum game is that individualistic, defensive strategies are almost always less rewarding than cooperative strategies. Gains that could have been achieved are lost because of the need to protect oneself. Animals, lacking the capacity to guarantee cooperative outcomes, are forced to sacrifice potential gains. Humans, on the other hand, are not so hobbled. For a decision-maker entering a potentially cooperative decision problem, the most important task is to elucidate the potential for mutual gain and the means to achieve it. The second most important task is to educate the other participant to the wisdom, over the long run, of striving for the mutually beneficial outcome. That is a major concern of the business known as bargaining and negotiation and is the subject of the next chapter.

Important Concepts

Zerosum game	Chicken game
Nonzerosum game	Cooperative solution
2-person game	Noncooperative solution
n-person game	Minimax strategy
Row and column players	Minimax mixed strategy
Maximin strategy	MAD strategy
Saddlepoint	Evolutionary stable strategy
Maximin mixed strategy	Hawks and doves
Equilibrium solution	Battle of the sexes
Dominated strategies	Games of coordination
Value of the game	Natural solutions
Prisoner's dilemma	

Problems for Analysis

1. Consider the game of matching pennies. Suppose you win $1.00 if two coins match, and lose $1.00 if they differ. Depict this as a matrix game. Does it have a saddlepoint? Is a mixed strategy required? If so, what do you think it is?

2. Using the original battle of the sexes matrix, show how punishing fast females by a penalty of 10 units would create a new set of strategies. Assume the attempt to punish the fast female is successful 50% of the time.

3. Suppose you were the member of a criminal organization that had a rule that stool pigeons were always eliminated. Suppose you and another member of the organization found yourselves in an actual prisoner's dilemma in an actual jail. Assume both of you estimate the loss of your life at -50. Depict your situation. Does the game as you have depicted it have a unique equilibrium solution, i.e., a saddlepoint? What is it? How does this depiction differ from the normal prisoner's dilemma?

4. Consider two people who come to a door that opens toward them. Why is the rule that the person who opens the door goes second "natural?" Think through the actual movements required in this case. Why should the man open the door if a woman is present? Why is this natural? What is the rule for men and women when the door opens in? What would be most natural, especially if the door is heavy?

5. Albert wants to see the latest "Dirty Harry" movie, which on his scale rates a +10. Mary dislikes "shoot 'em ups" but she likes going to the movies with Albert and rates this outcome a 5. She would prefer the ballet, which she rates a +10. Albert hates ballet, but he wants to go out with Mary and rates this outcome +5. They both agree that staying home watching the tube is a loser, and both rate it a 0. Depict this situation as a game. Is there an equilibrium saddlepoint? What sort of game is it? What are the equilibrium outcomes? What would playing tough in this situation entail? How might they resolve the game amicably?

6. It was late in the term and you, during a moral lapse, plagiarized a paper for your philosophy class. It appears that many students have done likewise. You are currently receiving a C in the course and could probably write a C paper if you took the time. You think that the plagiarized paper would get you a B, provided it isn't discovered.

At the last class before the final exam, the teacher announces that he knows many students have plagiarized. He makes the following proposal. Those who admit to plagiarizing can rewrite their papers and hand them in by the final. They will not be penalized for their cheating. He promises to spend the rest of the weekend trying to find the plagiarizing and will give a failing grade in the course to any students who have plagiarized and didn't admit it. He announces that in the past he has been able to prove plagiarism in 100% of the cases when he was suspicious and took the trouble to find out. Since the college doesn't discipline students for plagiarizing, he says he will not report the reason for the failing grade, unless a student contests it.

Getting a C in this course (which you expect if you rewrite your paper) is worth + 5 to you. This, however, will probably hurt in your physics course where you had hoped for a B. You will probably only get a C in physics if you spend time writing the paper. This you count as worth − 10 to you as you are an engineering major. This amounts to a − 5 for owning up. Failing a philosophy course you rate as − 25. On the other hand if you can get away with cheating, you get the + 10 for the B in philosophy and + 10 for a B in physics for a total of + 20.

The professor says that his pain in seeing you get away with cheating is worth − 10 to him. He really enjoys catching and failing cheaters, which is worth + 20, but he doesn't like to waste a weekend, which he counts a − 10, so that overall catching cheaters is worth 10. Giving normal grades to students who deserve them he rates at + 5.

Depict this as a game. What should you do? Does the game have a saddlepoint?

Chapter 9

Bargaining and Negotiations

Introduction

Bargaining and negotiation are particularly human phenomena. Because we can imagine alternative futures for ourselves and others and because we can communicate, we often engage in discussions with others over how best to achieve a future state of affairs better than the one that currently exists. Negotiations are decision problems and warrant the same sort of thoughtful analysis we have applied to other such problems, plagued as they are by the sorts of difficulties with which we have, by now, become familiar.

But there is a social dimension to bargaining that makes it at once more rewarding and more perilous than other sorts of decision-making. Human beings in cooperation can often create advantages that singly would be impossible. All the riches of civilization would disappear in a flash if we were forced to live the life of solitary individuals, a life, according to Thomas Hobbes, that would be "nasty, brutish, and short." Therefore, we are wise to actively search for ways in which we can, in cooperation with others, improve our lot.

The perils of negotiations arise because we are, by and large, exquisitely sensitive to our own needs and interests and are attuned to resist attempts at our own exploitation. In other words, we demand fairness in others' relations with us. Sibling rivalry is the most primitive manifestation of just how fundamental this sense of fairness is. The problem is that, being individuals with personal histories, tastes and idiosyncratic perceptions, we may have very different ideas as to what is, in any situation, fair. The danger is that, in attempting to obtain a fair share in some arrangement, one person may so offend the other's sense of fairness that a mutually rewarding possibility can deteriorate into a bitter battleground of recrimination and retaliation.

In the following pages, we will introduce a way of thinking about negotiations and about fairness that should make it easier to maintain an objective perspective. Such a perspective, because it is objective, can be readily adopted by all participants and may therefore make a mutually gratifying accommodation more likely.

All negotiations have two aspects; cooperative group decision-making, and division of gains. In the first aspect, some change from the present course is proposed by one party to another and then discussions are held to determine if such a change can be mutually beneficial. Various alternatives will be discussed and their costs and benefits scrutinized. In this part of negotiations, the parties are in effect coming together as a group or team and are acting as fiduciary decision-makers attempting to maximize the *team's* gain. The team consists of all parties to the negotiations.

The second aspect of negotiations requires deciding upon the best way to parcel out among the team members the expected rewards of their common effort. Here, individual interest will be paramount. Each participant, rightly, expects a reasonable or a fair share of the rewards, and given the *self-serving bias*, is likely to expect more, perhaps, than the others think he is entitled to. The key for each member is to get a fair share but not demand so much that the team effort is aborted.

It is extremely important to keep these two aspects, group decision-making and division of gains, separate. As a simple example, if two people have decided to play a game of golf, they must decide, as a team, where to play, and each might prefer a different golf course. The point here is perhaps too obvious, but if they cannot agree on a course, they lose the pleasure of the game. The problem is that the course they choose is partly a pure decision problem and partly a division of gain problem, and it is easy to confuse the two. The obvious, and the rational, solution is to choose some course for that day's play and, having done that, compensate the one whose preferred course was not chosen by some *side payment* to maintain fairness. In practice, this is usually an agreement to use the other's preferred course on the next occasion.

In serious and complex negotiations, it is not always so easy to keep the two aspects separate, but failure to do so almost always causes difficulties, because rather than seeking the best choice for the team, members seek advantages for themselves in the choice. The legislator who insists that a particular facility be located in his state or district is an obvious example of the distortion of the decision process that occurs when the division aspect is allowed to take priority.

By and large, if these two aspects can be kept separate, negotiations can proceed in a cooperative spirit of mutual gain. Finding the best decision for the team is difficult enough without confusing it with the equally difficult task of deciding on an equitable distribution of the gains of cooperation. It will shortly become clear that there is no hard and fast rule as to what is a fair division. We think it is wise, nevertheless, for any person engaged in negotiations to make clear that he expects to treat the other fairly and expects such treatment in return. It is well to keep in mind that a joint enterprise, whether it be a business, or a sports team, or a friendship, or a marriage, cannot operate at its maximum potential if some members feel slighted and put upon. Even negotiations that produce no ongoing activity, as in the sale of an item, can have an impact on the reputations of those engaged and follow them into other negotiations. A reputation for excessive greed, as a reputation for excessive timidity, is unlikely to do one much good. A reputation for fair and honest dealing is not something to be taken lightly; it may, in many cases, be the strongest card a negotiator holds.

In the following discussions we will devote much of our interest to the division aspect of negotiation. This is not because it is more important than the group decision-making component; it is usually less important for reasons we have already discussed. The power of decision-making techniques to help resolve disputes as to the best course of action for a group comes into sharpest focus in negotiations where the ability to call on objective standards, such as the expected utility rule, will be richly rewarded. Sometimes it will be necessary to educate the other parties about these rules and their legitimacy, and such efforts will, in general, be richly rewarded as well.

Bargaining with Minimal Threat Potential

The simplest cases of negotiation are those where people can gain something by cooperation, and risk little if they fail to come to agreement. Since all nonzerosum games are occasions where mutual accommodation can benefit both parties, they have been used by decision theorists as models for fair division in bargaining and negotiations. Consider the following variation of our old friend the prisoner's dilemma:

PLAYER B

		COOPERATE	DEFECT
P L A Y E R A COOPERATE		5, 5	–8, 8
DEFECT		8, –8	0, 0

You will notice that we have relabeled the prisoners "players." The MUM strategy is now called COOPERATE and the TALK strategy is called DEFECT. This is the conventional practice in the "generic" prisoner's dilemma. Also the mutual defection outcome is set at 0, 0 in this example.

The Characteristic Function Form

Players in this game really have only two practical options. They can, on the one hand, find some way to arrange the joint cooperative outcome of 5, 5, and guarantee it. If they are unable to do so, then they must resort to the secure maximin choice of defection, which produces the outcome 0, 0. The outcomes resulting from betrayal, -8, $+8$ and $+8$, -8, should never occur among rational participants and therefore can be ruled out of consideration. Such betrayals can be viewed in bargaining as attempts to take unfair advantage of the other. As we have seen, such betrayals generally invite counterbetrayal and can degenerate into unproductive tit-for-tat exercises. In any case, a rational agent would not accept an agreement that lacks guarantees against such betrayal.

Put another way, in any nonzerosum game the players can act individually, or they can act as a team. If they act as a team, they will choose the outcome that provides *the team* with the maximum return. The team will, in effect, act as a single rational decision-maker. The situation is transformed, as it were, by the guaranteed agreement, from a competitive situation into a straightforward decision problem.

To reflect this transformation, game theorists often depict such situations in what they call "characteristic function form." The characteristic function form is an abstract depiction that lists the amount that each participant can get on his own by adopting a defensive strategy, i.e., his maximin value, and the mutual gain to be realized if the participants act as a team, i.e., the maximum joint outcome. This is given below for the above situation:

$$v(A) = 0 \qquad\qquad v(B) = 0$$
$$v(A \text{ and } B) = 10$$

The above is read to mean that the value of the game to Player A, v(A), using his maximin strategy is 0, which is also the value of game to Player B, v(b), using his maximin. These values can be referred to as the "security levels" for the players, since each can be assured of those amounts without any cooperation from the other. However, if they cooperate, they can realize a *joint* gain of 10. In other words, there is a potential profit of 10 units to be achieved if they can find a way to guarantee the cooperative outcome.

Up to this point we have not dealt specifically with how they should share the joint reward available to them, but have assumed that each will receive the amount officially given in the payoff matrix. In a symmetrical game, such as the one given previously, the equal split of 5 each seems most reasonable.

The Fundamental Bargaining Problem

While the fifty-fifty split is, in one sense, the most satisfying solution and is, in a way, the most *natural*, it is not a necessary solution. As we shall see there is no generally agreed upon method to determine the most rational division of winnings. This has led to a number of attempts to define a fair *division*. The problem with these is that, in general, they can only work if both parties agree on what is fair and are perfectly honest with each other. While such is sometimes the case, as when a married couple is anxious to resolve a marital dispute, it is not always the case. Even if the parties agree on what is fair, they may have different assessments as to how that definition of fairness should apply in the particular case. And as we shall see, it is not generally in the interest of the parties to be perfectly honest with each other. These problems will be taken up in later sections. For now we will examine the limits of game theory in its prescriptions to decision-makers attempting to resolve a bargaining dispute.

What if one of the parties, Player B, argued that he was somehow entitled to more than 5 in the cooperative outcome? He might base that claim on any number of arguments, such as a claim that he *needs* the gain more than does the other. What if he were to argue that unless he gets 7 of the 10 points available he will not cooperate. He might, in effect, be demanding a "side-payment" of 2 for his cooperation, resulting in the outcome of 3, 7.

If you were Player A, what would you do? You could, of course, argue that B's claim is ridiculous. On similar grounds you could make a demand for the 7, 3 split, which benefits yourself. On second thought, why not go all the way and by similar reasoning demand 9 of the 10 for a split of 9, 1.

Suppose, for a second, that the other player made such a demand and refused to budge, taking the attitude that if you do not accept his proposal of 7, 3 he would just as soon accept the noncooperative 0, 0 outcome. Suppose you really believed that the other side were serious. You would then be left with the choice of accepting 3 or getting 0. As a rational decision-maker, you are required to choose the outcome providing the higher payoff, and would therefore be advised to take the 3 and go home.

That is true only if you decided the other person wasn't bluffing. You could, instead, refuse the offer and continue to demand the 50-50 split. But on what basis? You might argue that it is fairer, but what if the other person claimed he didn't care about fairness, or that in his mind his division was fairer, and gave all sorts of reasons why.

Graphical Representation (Optional)

It is sometimes useful to depict the above in geometric form. If this sort of presentation troubles you, be assured it is not necessary to look at the problem in this way.

The *x* and *y* axes on the graph represent the amount each player would get playing his maximin choice. In this case they are the same as the *security levels* for each player, that is, the amount they can get without any cooperation from the other person. As such, they are secure or guaranteed payoffs. As you move up the graph, the columns player's payoff increases; as you move to the right, the rows player's payoff increases. The origin, 0, 0, represents the outcome where both get 0 if both make the maximin choice. The point 5, 5 is the outcome when they cooperate and split the payoff equally. The movement northwest on the graph from, 0, 0 to 5, 5, is in effect a movement that benefits both players at the same time.

The point 7, 3 is the outcome where the players cooperate and share

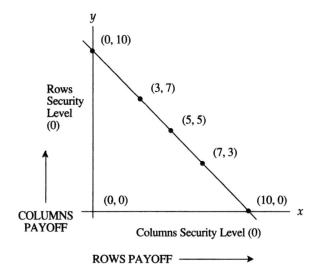

the winning with Rows getting 7 and Columns getting 3. The point 3, 7 represents the division were Rows gets 3 and Columns 7.

The line running from northwest to southeast through the point 5, 5 is the bargaining line for this problem. The bargaining line represents the mix of payoffs, all of which are rational as solutions to this nonzerosum game. It is bounded by the maximin value or security level for each player. Any point on the line is rational in the sense that it is the best outcome for the team or partnership, and, in addition, no individual is expected to take less than he could get on his own (by choosing according to maximin).

The problem for the bargaining agents is to find some mutually agreeable point on the line. Failure to do so will result in a zero gain for each of them if they are forced to resort to their maximin strategy. The most obvious solution is the midpoint on the line 5, 5, but as we have seen it is not a necessary solution.

Solutions to the Bargaining Problem

Von Neumann and Morgenstern, when discussing this problem, came to the conclusion that there was no purely rational basis on which to divide the mutual gain. They argued that the issue could only be resolved on the basis of psychological factors or what they called "bargaining ability, etc." for instance, a person's ability to convince the other side of his willingness to accept damage or the validity of a claim to a larger share of the winnings.

The von Neumann and Morgenstern "solution" to a game in characteristic function form is really a set or range of paired payoffs. Any pair of payoffs is said to be a rational solution so long as each player gets at least what he could get on his own, and the team as a whole gets the maximum that is available. It would be irrational for the team to take an action that produces less than it could obtain, and it would be irrational for any member of the team to take less than he could get on his own.

Such a solution is also said to be "Pareto optimal," after Vilfredo Pareto, the Italian economist, who argued that a "societally rational" choice for a group or society was one that produced an outcome in which some members of the society do better and no one does worse than in any other available outcome.

Consider the payoff 9, 1, in our example. Certainly that cannot be acceptable? But if confronted with a certainty of gaining 0 or gaining 1, then of course a rational person should prefer 1, although he is unlikely to be happy with that amount. What about the outcome where one player takes all the gain and the other receives nothing. Even this outcome is, formally at least, a solution in that the player who receives nothing should be indifferent between cooperating and defecting. In practice, however, it is very unlikely that anyone would cooperate in such circumstances. This extreme example clearly illustrates the main point of the von Neumann/Morgenstern solution in that the actual payoff division requires the decision of two individuals; no individual on his own is in a position to enforce a demand other than his maximin value, which in any case he can get without the help of the other. The division of the winnings, within the cooperative outcome, therefore depends on psychological factors (bargaining ability, for instance) and not purely rational ones.

The problem also neatly illustrates the *framing* effect that operates in bargaining. If you were asked if you would rather have $2 or $0, you would undoubtedly answer "$2," but if asked if you would accept a split of $8, $2 in a situation similar to the above you might well, out of pique, choose $0 rather than accept such a lopsided division. While this would be irrational in a once-in-a-lifetime case, it might not be as a general overall policy, especially if other things such as reputation or self-esteem are considered along with monetary value. But more on that later.

Example—A Fair Price

The simplest bargaining problem we encounter in our everyday affairs is the purchase or sale of something that has no fixed or established price. Suppose you have decided to buy a new car and wish to dispose of your old one. You have been advised that you can do much better by selling your car to a private party rather than to a dealer. You do not wish to simply trade in the old car, since then it will be difficult to know whether the price you are given for your used car merely reduces the discount you can probably negotiate on the new one.

You have decided to put an ad in the paper. What should be your asking price? What is the worst offer you should accept? Obviously you would not advertise your least acceptable offer, but will give a somewhat higher price, since you wish to get more than your worst price. How would you go about establishing the asking price? If you are like most people, you will scan the ads in your local paper and check the *book price* for your car.

How would you determine the lowest offer you would accept, your bottom line as it were? A reasonable way would be to find a price of which you can be assured. You might visit two or three local dealers and see what they are willing to offer. Your least acceptable offer will, in other words, be an amount you can guarantee without actually dealing with another private party. It is in a sense a "secure price," or your "bottom line," and is referred to as your *security level*. Note that this is totally independent of what you think you deserve or what you paid, but is totally dependent on the market, what other people are willing to pay. Dealers will generally pay less than private parties because they do not want the car *per se* but wish to sell it at a profit after deducting the costs of advertising, insurance, and storage. For that reason, the car is likely to be worth less to a dealer than to an independent buyer. Suppose you have settled on $4,000 as your least acceptable offer, since you already have three firm offers from dealers at that price.

What is a "fair" price. Suppose you decide that a fair price would be one in which you and the buyer *split the difference*. But in order to do that you need to determine your buyer's least desirable price, his security level. How would you determine that? You must put yourself in the position of a buyer. He will undoubtedly *shop around* and will have determined the lowest price at which he is sure he can buy the car from a dealer. Clearly, factors such as mileage, condition, and

options, will be taken into account. Suppose after shopping around
you conclude that a car such as yours in similar condition is being
offered in dealerships for $6,000, and you conclude that that will
undoubtedly be the maximum offer for any private buyer. Of course,
if there are many private individuals offering to sell cars like yours,
then the determination of maximum offer would be based on their
prices. For the sake of the example, let us suppose you are the lone
private seller.

BUYER

		BUY	DON'T BUY
SELLER	SELL	Price minus $4,000 $6,000 minus Price 0	0 0

	DON'T
	SELL
		0
		      0
			0
			      0

The above matrix assumes that if buyer and seller cannot agree to a
price, they will be forced to go to a dealer and accept his price, i.e.,
their bottom line. The 0s in the matrix represent the fact that neither
party gains anything above his bottom line if they fail to come to some
agreement. If the final price is $5,500, then the seller will have gotten
$1,500 more than he could have gotten from a dealer, or $5,500 −
$4,000 = $1,500. The buyer will have gotten a car that would have cost
him $6,000 at a dealer for only $5,500, for a saving of $500, or $6,000
− $5,500 = $500. In other words, the sale represents an arrangement
where they have agreed to split the joint gain of $2,000 in the division
$1,500, $500. (Note—there are other ways to depict this situation as a
nonzerosum game. This depiction is a normalized version, which we
will learn more about later.)
    The above matrix can be represented in characteristic function form
so:

$$v(\text{Seller}) = 0 \qquad v(\text{Buyer}) = 0$$
$$v(\text{Seller} + \text{Buyer}) = (\$2,000)$$

If there are many buyers and sellers, the problem will be more
complicated. Bottom lines in that case will have to be determined from
what offers have already been taken. The "dealer price" is used as the

security level in this example because it represents a secure standing offer, a clearly defined fallback position. If there is a firm offer from a private buyer then, of course, this would constitute the security level for the seller. Likewise, if the buyer has a standing offer from a seller, then that represents his security level. In such cases, security levels can change fairly quickly, which is why markets are so tricky.

Graphical Representation (Optional)

The above is given graphically so:

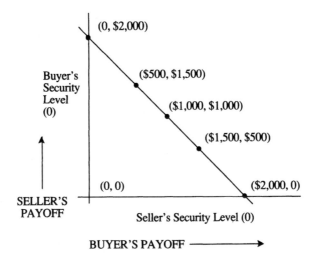

From the matrix, it is clear that the buyer and seller will have to find some point on the bargaining line that is satisfying to both.

The Value of Objective Standards

In this simple case, what will the bargaining involve? Suppose buyer and seller could agree about the above numbers and on a simple "split the difference" agreement. In that case the participants would save a lot of time and effort by a transaction in which the car changed hands at $5,000. But things are not usually that simple and mechanical.

Certainly it makes sense to start with such preliminary agreement, and most sales usually do. Fisher and Ury, in their influential book

Getting to Yes (1981) advise that it is wise to bargain over objective standards, and on this we agree. Both participants will usually know what cars like the one under discussion are "going for" and will, in general, have realistic bottom lines or security levels. The nitty-gritty of negotiations will involve the application of that knowledge in the particular case. How good does the car look? How well has it been maintained? Is the mileage too high or too low for the model year? Does it have desirable options? Objective standards usually exist or can be found: for example, independent mechanics can be brought in; standard mileage is usually known; books list the value of various options. In general, these objective standards simplify the negotiating process by narrowing the range of reasonable prices considered.

But, alas, there are other factors that are difficult to objectify, and this is where *bargaining ability, etc.* comes into play. For instance, the worth of a particular color to a buyer is one such factor; or the personal value to a buyer of a particular option. It is in bargaining over these subjective factors that individuals can attempt to gain an advantage. If a seller really believes a potential buyer may walk away because he has his heart set on a red car or leather seats, then it might be worth reducing the price to make the sale.

But how is one to know whether such concerns are serious. What if a buyer can convince you that he agrees that $5,000 is a fair price, but he has only $4,700 to spend. How are we to know if he is bluffing? We can refuse the offer as a test, but if the potential buyer is serious we will have killed the sale. This is why, in such circumstances, it is wise to exchange phone numbers and get back to each other if no better offer comes along.

In general, it is good policy to come to agreement over those things that can be quantified. In doing so, you effectively narrow the bargaining range as much as possible so that there is less to bargain about. But after that has been done, each participant is very much on his own, and will have to assess threats and bluffs, pretty much by the seat of his pants. Of course, if you have taken the time and energy to find and apply objective criteria so as to narrow the price range, the amount that is left to threaten and bluff with should be relatively small.

Bargaining Costs and Time

In face to face negotiations such as the above, bargaining costs are generally small, and the time frame generally short. However, when negotiating a major purchase, such as a home, there are legal fees, interest payments, and other financial considerations that tend to mount over time. These expenses are a positive inducement to reduce bargaining time and concommitant costs.

Even in our example, time may entail certain costs. For the seller, there are advertising costs, and delay in his ability to purchase a new car. Conditions may change, making it harder to sell the car. For the buyer, who presumably needs a car, not concluding a deal means he must remain without one for a longer time, all of which suggests that bargaining is rarely cost free. In general, a deal made today is better for both parties than the same deal made tomorrow because of these costs. In a sense, delay reduces the overall value to be gained by the negotiators. As such it may be wise to close a deal that is "reasonably" attractive, rather than haggle to save a small amount that would be wiped out by bargaining costs. This is all the more true when you must pay for professional negotiating services, interest charges, and other expenses.

Fairness in Nonsymmetric Cases: Differential Contributions

Negotiating a sale price is usually easier when most of the attributes can be objectified (such as with automobile options or mileage) than with subjective utilities (such as the desirability of a car's color). Consider the following, somewhat more complicated example.

Suppose Jackie is an aspiring young writer, who has begun discussions with her high school friend, Anna Green, a famous TV personality, to write a book about Anna's career. Given Anna's popularity, everyone expects that the book will sell well and earn a good deal of money, probably in the millions of dollars. Of course, nothing is certain and the book could flop, especially if Anna's TV show falls in popularity and is taken off the air. Jackie and Anna have contacted a publisher who has offered to pay them 25% of the book's future earnings. Jackie is currently teaching school, earning $25,000 a year, and can take a year's leave of absence to write the book without sacrificing her seniority and pension benefits. Anna is earning $500,000 on her TV show and personal appearances. She is happy to be able to work with her friend and has offered her $50,000 as a salary (which she would have to pay to any writer) and, in addition, 10% of their joint earnings.

Jackie is offended by this offer and thinks that since she is doing most of the work, she should get at least half the earnings. Anna says that this is out of the question. Nobody would buy the book without her stardom, and besides there are plenty of young writers who would jump at the chance for instant fame. Anna and Jackie have come to you to help them resolve their dispute and arrive at a fair division.

Before you agree to *arbitrate* their dispute, you might first ask them if they really want to arrive at a fair division, and second, if they are prepared to be perfectly honest with you. Suppose both agreed to those conditions.

You then ask them both to estimate as objectively as possible the book's future earnings, and after consultations with various experts they have come up with a figure of $2,000,000 of which their 25% would net them, as a team, $500,000. At least this is their best guess. Also, since Jackie's salary is a cost to the partnership of $50,000, the estimated payoff to be divided would be $450,000.

As another consideration you would want to determine if there is anything else, beside money, to be gained in the partnership. Both agree that it would be fun to work with the other, and Anna would certainly be gratified to help her old friend. Jackie also agrees that a successful book would launch her career as a writer and that is worth a great deal to her. But how are they to value such things?

Before trying to place a utility on these nonmonetary gains, let us try to represent this in characteristic function form. This will be easier if we first create a *joint outcome table* as follows:

JOINT OUTCOME TABLE FOR ANNA AND JACKIE

	No cooperation	Cooperation
	Some other writer writes book on Anna	Jackie writes book on Anna
Payoff to Anna	Share of $450,000, No special feeling about stranger	Share of $450,000, Good feeling from working with Jackie
Payoff to Jackie	No money for book, $25,000 from teaching unpublished writer	Share of $450,000, $50,000 salary published writer

Suppose for present purposes of illustration we allow that each values money equally, and we assign 1 utility unit to each $10,000, so that the total of 50 utility units is represented by the $500,000 in expected earnings. The writer's earnings after the salary comes to $450,000 or 45 units, given the fact that $50,000 represents a realistic salary to an "unknown" for writing such a book.

After much hemming and hawing, Anna agrees that working with her old friend would probably be easier and more rewarding than working with a stranger and agrees that 10 utility points is certainly a reasonable valuation for Jackie's cooperation. Jackie thinks about how much being a *published* author is worth, and decides that she probably would be willing to sacrifice $200,000 or 20 utility units to achieve that desirable goal.

Since we are trying to decide what share of the money Jackie should get, let us call Jackie's share X and Anna's share will necessarily be $45 - X$.

Suppose either party objected to your request that she put a value on such things as friendship and argued that comparing money and friendship is like trying to compare apples and oranges. You might respond that anything can be compared to anything else and explain how in multi-attribute analysis all attributes are translated into utilities. That is what utility is for—to act as a common currency for the valuation of disparate things. Remember that if you cannot compare the value of the things at stake, you can have no basis for rational choice.

We can now put the utilities arrived at above into our outcome table, so:

	NO COOPERATION	COOPERATION
	Some other writer writes book on Anna	Jackie writes book on Anna
Payoff to Anna	All of $450,000, No special feeling about stranger $45 + 0$ $= 45$	Share of $450,000, Good feeling from working with Jackie $45 - X + 10$ $= 55 - X$
Payoff to Jackie	No money for book, $25,000 from teaching unpublished writer $0 + 2.5 + 0$ $= 2.5$	Share of $450,000, $50,000 salary published writer $X + 5 + 20$ $= 25 = X$
Joint Gain to Anna & Jackie		$55 - x + 25 + X$ $= 80$

We can see that if they work together they share \$450,000 (45 units). Anna works with her preferred writer (10 units). Jackie gets a nice salary (5 units) and fame (20 units). This adds up to 80 units to be gained by cooperation. We can now represent this in characteristic function form so:

$$v(\text{Anna}) = 45 \qquad v(\text{Jackie}) = 2.5$$
$$v(\text{Anna and Jackie}) = 80$$

What is immediately obvious here is that Jackie appears to have a lot more to gain in cooperation, since Anna is going to get her book published no matter what. In other words, Anna adds more value to the partnership than does Jackie. Without Anna's fame there is no book. All that Jackie can add is her work, which can be gotten elsewhere, and her friendship, which cannot. In addition, much of the joint value comes from the value Jackie placed on being published, which is worth 20 units to her, but nothing to Anna. What we really want is an estimate of the "net gain" from cooperation, what each gains *over and above* what they could get on their own. To compute net gain, we have to "normalize" the characteristic function. Let us first find the net gain in an abbreviated outcome table (Remember Jackie's share is X and Anna's share is $45 - X$):

JOINT PAYOFF TABLE

	NO DEAL	COOPERATION	
	STRANGER WRITES BOOK	JACKIE WRITES BOOK	NET GAIN FROM COOPERATION
PAYOFF TO ANNA	45	$45 - X + 10$ $= 55 - X$	$55 - X - 45$ $= 10 - X$
PAYOFF TO JACKIE	2.5	$X + 5 + 20$ $= X + 25$	$X + 25 - 2.5$ $X + 22.5$
JOINT PAYOFF	47.5	$55 - X + X - 25$ $= 80$	$10 - X + X + 22.5$ $= 32.5$

Notice that Anna and Jackie, if they do not get together, will obtain 47.5, so that the 80 they obtain through cooperation represents a net gain of 32.5 over their maximin amounts.

The Normalized Characteristic Function

The normalized characteristic function tells us the *net gain* to be achieved in the cooperative outcome. By setting the value for each player acting alone at 0 and then setting the value of the joint outcome at the net gain, we produce the following normalized characteristic function for Anna and Jackie:

$$v(\text{Anna}) = 0 \qquad v(\text{Jackie}) = 0$$
$$v(\text{Anna and Jackie}) = 32.5$$

In other words, if they work together they realize a net gain of 32.5 over what each would get not working together. For future reference, you can always normalize a characteristic function by subtracting the value of each player's maximin value from his own value and from the value of the joint outcome. This is equivalent to putting each player's payoff through a linear transformation as we did when discussing the distinction between zerosum and constant sum games. This is done below for this example:

$$v(\text{Anna}) = 45 - 45 = 0 \qquad v(\text{Jackie}) = 2.5 - 2.5 = 0$$
$$v(\text{Anna and Jackie}) = 80 - 45 - 2.5 = 32.5$$

Fair Division Schemes

Remember, you were asked to recommend a fair division of the gains. But should we divide the total gain or the net gain? A fifty-fifty split of the total gain would give each partner half of 80 utility units. It would not consider Jackie's work nor would it take into account Anna's fame. In other words, it would treat each partner as if she contributed equally to the outcome. Therefore, each would get 25 units of monetary value (the split of $500,000).

The division of the nonmonetary gains is somewhat more complicated. They cannot actually split these up, but they can compensate each other. Jackie gains 20 units from publishing and Anna 10 units for Jackie's help, or 30 units in all. Each would get 15 of these nonmonetary units in an equal division. But since Jackie cannot give Anna part of the 20 units she receives for being published, she should compensate Anna in some way to be fair. This could be achieved if Jackie transferred 5 units in money to Anna, compensating Anna for the extra nonmonetary gain she received. If they did that, the final outcome would result when Anna got $250,000 + $50,000 = $300,000 in cash and, in addition, Jackie's help. Jackie would receive $250,000 − $50,000 = $200,000 plus the gain of becoming a published writer. We might call such a division the *naive egalitarian division scheme*.

Such a division looks only at the payoff in the cooperative outcome and ignores what each contributed to the outcome. Jackie's work is not taken into account, and neither is the fact of Anna's fame. But, after all, shouldn't Jackie's work be compensated in some way, and shouldn't Anna's fame play a role. It hardly seems fair to ignore the fact that without Anna's well-known name there would be nothing to gain in the first place. If we take these things into account, we might adopt what we call a *value-added division scheme*. This is found by splitting the *net gain* as given in the normalized characteristic function. In this example, that would be ½ of 32.5 or 16.25 to each partner.

In practice, this involves splitting the "net gain" from cooperation among the partners who then get, in total, one half of the net gain plus whatever they would have gotten anyway without the partnership.

In our example, Anna gets 16.25, which we add to the 45 she can get on her own, for 61.25 in total. Jackie gets 16.25 plus the 2.5 she can get by herself for a total of 18.75. Notice that if you add these two totals together you will get 80, which is, of course, the total gain from cooperation.

There is a problem here, especially for Jackie, since she gets so much more out of the partnership than does Anna. Jackie is getting $50,000 for her work (5 units) and 20 units for her chance to be published, or 25 units in all, above and beyond any share of the royalties. This is more than she is entitled to in the value-added division scheme, 6.25 units more to be precise. If she agrees to the value-added scheme, she should, by rights, compensate Anna by 6.25 units, or $62,250. This means she should contribute her writing, which is worth $50,000, without a salary and in addition pay $12,250 to Anna for the privilege of doing so.

While that may appear strange, it does, in fact, make a good deal of sense in light of how important becoming *published* is to Jackie. If it really is important, then this is a golden opportunity and well worth paying a price to obtain. After all, many struggling artists work for nothing and pay agents and teachers in the hopes of being recognized. Anna is offering Jackie instant fame in one fell swoop. The division makes sense given what each adds to the deal. Jackie adds almost nothing that Anna cannot obtain elsewhere. Anna on the other hand "makes the deal" with her fame.

What should you advise the partnership? In all fairness you would have to explain the difference between the pure egalitarian and the value-added division scheme. They would then have to negotiate what they would use, *before you have worked out the numbers.* In other words, they would have to agree on an objective criterion of "fairness" before actually seeing how it would come out in their particular case. If they did this and agreed on the value-added scheme, they would come to the conclusion that Anna's original offer was generous to a fault.

What if Anna said that she wished to give as much to Jackie as she could and still be doing the "rational" thing. Clearly the most extreme division, 45, 35, would fit that bill. If Anna wished to give more than 35, she would have to take less than what she could get on her own. The practical consequence of this division would be for Jackie to get the $50,000 salary (5 units), be published (20 units), and receive the remaining 10 units in money or $100,000. That would leave Anna with 45, which is equal to her security level. She cannot rationally accept less than that. Jackie could reasonably ask for that much, though she is unlikely to get it. She cannot ask for more and expect to be taken seriously by a rational negotiator.

Graphical Representation (Optional)

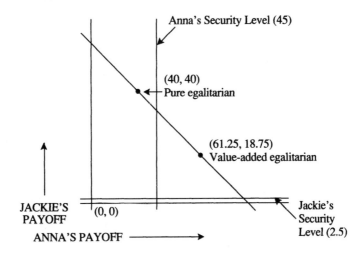

Jackie's problem is that Anna's security level is so high (so far to the right) that it truncates the bargaining line. Since a Pareto optimal solution must fall within the security level of both players, the set of solutions that are rational include only those on the line bounded by the lines defining each player's security level. In effect, it creates a new bargaining line. Clearly, the pure egalitarian split, which is defined as midpoint of the line bounded by the x and Y axes, lies outside the set of rational solutions. The value-added solution, on the other hand, lies at the midpoint of the new bargaining line, and is therefore clearly acceptable for von Neumann and Morgenstern.

The limits of the bargaining line are the payoffs of 45, 35, in which Anna is very generous and 77.5, 2.5 where Anna demands an enormous payment from Jackie just for the privilege of becoming famous through writing Anna's book. Since being published is worth 20 points to Jackie, she would have, in this division, to fork over 17.5 utility units, or an equivalent in cash, i.e. $175,000.

The Cost of Honesty in Bargaining

The above illustrates why, at least in bargaining, honesty may not be the best policy. If Jackie denied that she placed a high value on becoming a published author, and if Anna believed her, she would have done much better. Suppose she claimed no desire at all to be "published." This would reduce the total gain to 60 and the characteristic function would look so:

$$v(\text{Anna}) = 45 \qquad v(\text{Jackie}) = 2.5$$
$$v(\text{Anna and Jackie}) = 60,$$

which when normalized looks so:

$$v(\text{Anna}) = 0 \qquad v(\text{Jackie}) = 0$$
$$v(\text{Anna and Jackie}) = 12.5$$

The value-added division scheme would provide 6.25 plus their noncooperative value to each partner, or 8.75 to Jackie and 51.25 to Anna. This would suggest that Jackie is entitled to $82,750 or $32,750 in addition to her salary of $50,000. But she could only make such a claim because she misrepresented the value of the venture to her bargaining partner. This generally is the case. In such cases a primary tool is to undervalue the outcome *vis à vis* some important factor and so effect an outcome, which appears equitable but is, in fact, advantageous to yourself. Since this is true for both parties, negotiations often come down to an attempt to *smoke out* the other side's true values and attempt to use them to your own advantage. Here, as usual, it is often helpful if one can find objective ways to assess the values individuals place on things. Sometimes, when many factors are involved, it is possible to gain some insight by suggesting trade-offs. Obviously there is great room here for deception, and no ready rule is likely to suffice.

An interesting arbitration scheme is designed to overcome each side's tendency to distort the values placed on things and to overestimate what is acceptable. In this scheme, the arbitrator requires each side to submit its *last best offer*. The arbitrator then chooses the one last offer that he considers closest to a reasonable division. It is important to note, in this scheme, that the arbitrator must choose one or the other offer, and cannot propose a compromise such as a split-the-difference solution. The virtue of this scheme is that it forces each side to move away from their extreme position and closer to her own security level, since failure to move far enough could result in the other side's proposal being more acceptable.

The Advantages of Honesty About Interests

Let us suppose that Jackie and Anna, in the above example, are truly anxious to come to a fair and equitable solution that allows each of them to gain the maximum the situation allows. Would it really pay for them to attempt to deceive each other about the value of a partnership? After all, if Anna really believed that Jackie didn't care about being published, she might conclude, for that reason, that she might just as well attempt to strike a better deal with a stranger. If Jackie seems to want too much, she might begin to question whether she can risk her autobiography on an untried talent; for the amount Jackie is demanding, Anna might conclude she can get a more seasoned writer to do the job.

Perhaps it is best for Jackie to be honest, at least with herself, about her goals and her opportunities. If she really does wish to start a writing career, Anna's offer *is* a golden opportunity. Perhaps she should admit that to Anna and ask for a salary no greater than what any other writer would get. If she does write the book and it is successful, she will be in a position to strike a hard bargain in the future, since she will have much more to bargain with—her proven talent.

The point is for Jackie to keep clear in her mind her long-run goals and objectives, and to remember that the bargaining is a means of achieving those goals and is not an end in itself. We often forget this in the heat of negotiations and become so concerned with driving a hard bargain and "winning" that we lose what really matters to us. Fisher and Ury (1981) make a similar point when they stress the importance of negotiating interests rather than "positions." Too often, we take a stand, or a position, that may, by some reasoning, be justified, but does not actually accord with our fundamental interests. If Jackie were to argue that only a fifty-fifty split of royalties is "fair" and holds fast to that position, she will undoubtedly lose her opportunity.

By shifting the emphasis to interests, Jackie would be in a much better position to convince Anna that she is the best writer for the job and is entitled to just compensation. She could point out that the value of the deal to herself, however large, really doesn't affect what Anna has to pay to get her book written. She will have to pay some amount, and she might just as well pay that to Anna who, as an old friend can aid her in refreshing her memory, tracing down old friends, etc. Of course, such honesty is unlikely to be fruitful if Jackie really has nothing to offer beyond her skill as a writer. If she really is weak, she will have to accept that fact and strike the best deal she can. If she can downplay the value of being published, this may help, but not if it ends up killing the deal.

The point is that in most negotiating situations it is not easy to determine just how honest you should be. Further, you are unlikely to know how honest the other party is. In the final analysis, your own personal judgment is critical. In any case, we agree with Fisher and Ury that it is almost always to one's advantage to clearly define interests and to bargain over them. Posturing over positions is sometimes necessary when dealing with others who are themselves using that tactic, but since doing so is often counterproductive, it is usually worth the time and effort to educate the other side and to encourage the abandonment of such posturing.

Recapitulating to This Point

Bargaining and negotiation involve the attempt of parties to realize the potential benefit provided by some set of circumstances. They must agree on a joint strategy to achieve their ends, a team effort as it were, as well as find some way to guarantee cooperation in their joint strategy. In addition they must agree to some division of the joint gain.

These considerations give rise to the characteristic function representation, which looks so:

$$v(A) = \text{Maximin value for } A \quad v(B) = \text{Maximin value for } B$$
$$V(A + B) = \text{Joint gain in cooperative outcome}$$

According to von Neumann and Morgenstern, a solution is one where the joint gain is obtained, and each party gets at least what he could get alone, in his maximin choice. This represents an almost infinite number of possible division schemes. We have discussed two that can be defined as *fair*; the naive and the value-add egalitarian schemes. The former is the same as the latter if each player contributes equally and adds equal value.

In the naive egalitarian scheme, we divide the joint payoff equally and ignore the maximin values of the players. In the value-added scheme, we take into account the maximin values of each player by normalizing the characteristic function that gives the net gain achieved in the cooperative outcome. We divide that net gain equally, and then give each participant his share of the net gain and, in addition, his maximin value. In the case of Jackie and Anna, Anna got more in the value-added scheme because she contributed more to the joint outcome.

For a variety of reasons, most people would feel more comfortable with the value-added division scheme, not least because it is consistent with the principles associated with free-market economies. This scheme produces the same result as does the *Shapley Value* (see Shubik 1975, p. 131), which was designed for use in *n*-person games, i.e. games of more than two players.

The advantages of such *arbitration schemes* is that they help individuals who wish to arrive at a fair division define what, in a practical sense, fairness might be. The problem with such schemes is that they are open to the abuse of dishonesty where nonobjective values are involved. There is a real inducement for people to misrepresent their bottom lines and thus inflate their contributions to the joint outcome. In most negotiations, such fair division schemes depend on mutual acceptance of them. If either party chooses to ignore them, then any outcome that is rational, according to von Neumann and Morgenstern, is possible.

On the other hand, if most or all members of society agree on the virtues of some definition of fairness, then that definition may come to define a *standard of behavior* (von Neumann and Morgenstern's phrase) expected by members of society. As such, those who fail to abide by it may find themselves socially undesirable. In any one negotiation, there may be a real benefit to those who ignore the expected standard. In the long run, however, they may find themselves excluded from desirable joint enterprises. After all, there are many individuals with whom one can join if one needs a partner. Why should one choose as a partner someone who does not share your conception of fairness? Some people, because of great wealth or power, may be in a position to offer great rewards to others even in grossly unfair social arrangements. But, it is just as true, at least within modern societies, that people do not long admire those who abuse their wealth and power, and are often punished by those who believe them guilty of such abuse. For that reason, we believe it is sensible to strive to define fair division in most cases and to attempt to resolve disputes fairly. We further believe that doing so can probably be defended as rational, at least from the perspective of the long run.

Damage and Threat Potential

All of the bargaining situations we have discussed to this point lacked a feature common to many negotiations, namely the potential for serious loss. In the previous examples the worst that could happen was that a potential gain would be lost. Economists call such losses "opportunity costs"—the lost opportunities that one incurs by taking any particular course of action. For instance, any purchase imposes such an opportunity cost in that the money used to make the purchase cannot now be used to earn interest or to make an alternative purchase.

Consider our original formulation of the prisoner's dilemma where there was the potential for actual losses:

PLAYER B

		COOP		DEFECT	
COOP		5	5	–8	8
DEFECT		8	–8	–5	–5

PLAYER A

This can be summarized in a joint outcome table so:

	Maximin Strategy	Cooperative Strategy	Net Gain
Player A	−5	5	10
Player B	−5	5	10
Group (A & B)	−10	10	20

which gives the following characteristic function:

$$v(A) = -5 \qquad v(B) = -5$$
$$v(A + B) = 10$$

Normalized this is:

$$v(A) = -5 - (-5) = 0 \qquad v(B) = -5 - (-5) = 0$$
$$v(A + B) = 10 - (-5) - (-5) = 20$$

In normalizing a situation such as this where the maximin values of the players are negative, subtracting those negative values is the same as adding those values to the value of the individual player and to the joint outcome, which gives the above. This normalized version is given below:

$$v(A) = 0 \qquad v(B) = 0$$
$$v(A + B) = 20$$

Here, since the situation is symmetric, the egalitarian and the value-added egalitarian division schemes provide the same resolution, i.e., 5 to each player. Notice, however, that the potential for loss has considerably expanded the range of outcomes considered rational according to von Neumann and Morgenstern.

By agreeing to cooperate, the players have generated a joint gain of 20. In the egalitarian division scheme, each prisoner has avoided going to jail and therefore has gained 5, and each will gain 5 from the cooperative choice, for a net gain of 10 each over the −5 each would have obtained in the competitive outcome. In essence, their agreement allows them to exploit a mutual net gain of 20 points above what they could obtain from competitive play. How they divide that 20 points will determine the final solution to the game. Their only real tool in such negotiations is their threat to resort to maximin and the credibility of that threat.

Suppose B demanded all 10 points available in the cooperative outcome for himself. If effected he would realize a gain of 10, but in addition he gains from avoiding the loss of -5 in his maximin, for a total net gain of $+15$. A in that case would be left with saving the loss of -5 for a net gain of $+5$. While he is unlikely to accept such a lopsided arrangement, he is better in it than he would be in the competitive outcome, where he loses 5.

What if B demanded an additional payment of 1 unit so that he obtains 11 points (or a net gain of 16). This would result in -1 (or a net gain of $+4$) for A. Once again A is unlikely to accept, but he would still be better off with -1 than he would with -5. By similar reasoning it can be shown that any division up to 15 (or a net gain of 20) for one player and -5 (or a net gain of 0) for the other would fit the von Neumann and Morgenstern definition of rationality in that such a solution would provide for both players at least what they could get without cooperation.

In our earlier (no loss) version, the most extreme outcome that was acceptable was 10, 0 or 0, 10. Here, the most extreme acceptable outcomes are -5, 15 and 15, -5, for the reasons given. Put another way, the possibility of loss opens us up to greater exploitation; or, more simply, more is at stake and therefore more can be gained.

A wide variety of criminal activity involves raising the stakes by threatening serious losses. The mugger, the hostage-taker, and the blackmailer all demand ''compensation'' for refraining from inflicting bodily harm, harm to loved ones, or harm to our reputation, respectively. One minute before being confronted by a mugger, we are on equal terms with him, but in an instant, his threat enlarges the stakes and we find ourselves happy to pay him to get away with our lives. If we can invoke an equal counterthreat, we are in a much better position. Unfortunately, as we will see in later sections, we are not always in a position to effectively invoke such counterthreats, and sometimes counterthreats can be more damaging than giving into the extortionate demands.

Given that many people are risk-averse, they tend to use a different bargaining approach where serious damage is possible than they would when only opportunity costs are at stake. From a purely rational or economic point of view, the presence of potential losses should not really make any difference. Ideally, players should normalize the characteristic function not only on paper, but in their minds. If they do so, then bargaining is always over potential gains, even though some of those gains are really losses that can be avoided. Nevertheless, the potential for serious losses would seem to make a qualitative difference in the way many of us approach bargaining.

One possible reason is the threat to the status quo represented by potential losses. Also, such situations are more stressful than those where only opportunity costs are at stake. Since most of us are risk-averse, a gain foregone seems less threatening than an actual loss. Also, if no losses are at stake, our present situation, i.e., the present course, is not disturbed. We can all think of opportunities we have missed, but somehow they do not affect us as much as losses we have actually sustained. How many people commit suicide because they didn't invest in the stock market when, if they had, they could have made a fortune?

Graphical Representation (Optional)

The above characteristic function can be represented graphically and is given below. You will notice immediately that in this case, where losses are involved, the bargaining line is extended rather than truncated as when maximin values are positive. The horizontal line running through -5, -5 and 15, -5 represents the columns player's concession level and is, as it should be, below the x axis. It represents the amount (-5 in this case) that he can guarantee by himself. Any amount above that is a gain from cooperation, and he should prefer any amount to his concession level of -5. The same is true for the rows player whose concession level is indicated by the vertical line running through -5, -5 and -5, 15. It is clearly to the left of the y axis. In short, any division that adds up to 10 is acceptable as a solution, including the division where one player ends up with -5 or a net gain of zero, for himself.

Differential Damage and Threat Potential

In the above example of the prisoner's dilemma, we assumed the loss would be the same for both parties. This is not a necessary assumption and may be, in many cases, unrealistic. Suppose one party

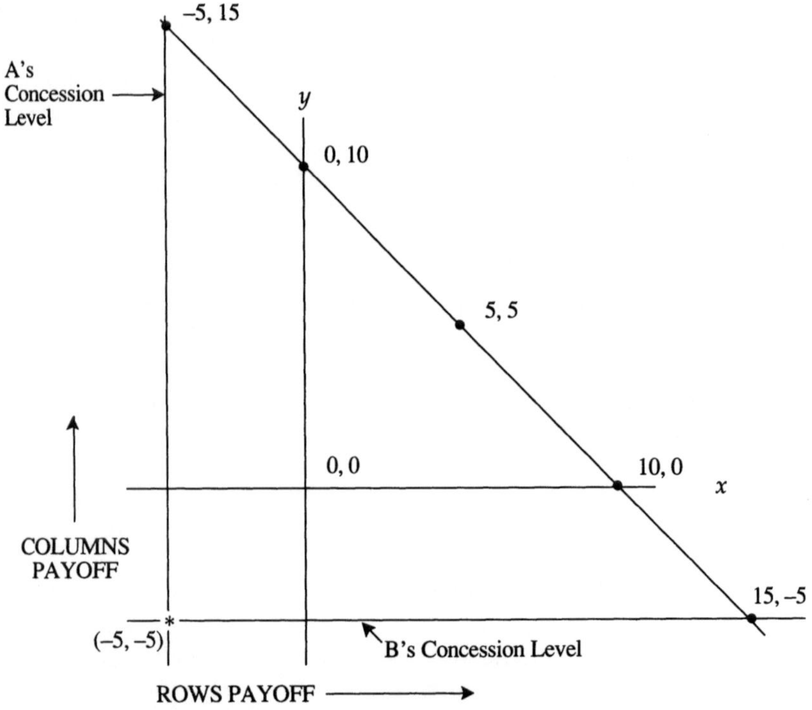

in the prisoner's dilemma is much more distressed about going to jail than the other; there is no need to assume that both parties value the pain of jail equally. Let us suppose that Prisoner B is much more unhappy about the prospects of prison life than Prisoner A, or that one prisoner has a record and so would serve more time, giving the following matrix:

PRISONER B

PRISONER A	MUM	TALK
MUM	5 5	–8 8
TALK	8 –16	–5 –10

The preceding matrix was obtained by doubling the value of the loss to Prisoner B of going to jail; Prisoner A's values have remained unchanged. There is still the joint gain of 10 obtained by cooperation, but now a mutual loss of 15, most of which is borne by Prisoner B. Another way of looking at this is to suggest that Prisoner B has much more to gain by avoiding jail than does Prisoner A. If they should arrive at a cooperative outcome and split the 10 points equally, A gains 15 since he avoids jail and gains the 5 points that result from coopera-tive outcome. B only gains 10 by that reckoning, since he only saves 5 by avoiding jail. The joint outcome table for this version of the game looks so:

	Maximin Strategy	Cooperative Strategy	Net Gain
Player A	–5	5	10
Player B	–10	5	15
Group (A & B)	–15	10	25

The characteristic function of the game is:

$$v(A) = -5 \qquad v(B) = -10$$
$$v(A \text{ and } B \text{ in cooperation}) = 10$$

which when normalized becomes:

$$v(A) = 0 \qquad v(B) = 0$$
$$v(A \text{ and } B \text{ in cooperation}) = 25$$

If we assume the parties can agree to the mutually cooperative outcome, what is a rational division in this case? What is a fair division? Suppose they agree on the fifty-fifty split. Should they use the naive or the value-added division scheme?

The naive egalitarian scheme, you will recall, divides the payoff equally and treats each individual as if he came to the outcome as an equal. In this case, that would require ignoring the differential potential for loss and both would get half of the gain of 10, or 5 each.

On the other hand, if both players choose to take potential losses into account and use the value-added division scheme, under that scheme they would divide the total net gain of 25, and each would obtain 12.5, and then add that amount to their maximin value. Adding 12.5 to A's maximin of −5 gives 7.5. Adding 12.5 to B's maximin value of −10 gives B 2.5. This makes sense because part of B's 12.5 gain is the 10 he gets for avoiding jail, whereas A's gain includes the smaller avoidance of −5 and his payoff reflects this. Under the naive egalitarian scheme, where each gets 5, the transaction nets B a net gain of 15 above his maximin level, and A a gain of 10 above his.

Remember that according to von Neumann and Morgenstern any payoff that provides at least −5 to A and −10 to B is rational. It is pretty clear in this case that A is in the better bargaining position since he loses so much less than B if he resorts to his threat and refuses to cooperate. Imagine how much stronger his position would be if he had nothing at all to lose, i.e., he didn't really mind going to jail.

Given the above, it is clear that the worst thing that could happen to B is his honest disclosure of his fear of jail. If he could hide that from A, he would be in a much better bargaining position, although he might wish to grant some concession to A, since he (B) really doesn't like the prospect of jail. But in granting any concession in this particular situation, he may expose his weakness. In this case, as in the problem of Jackie and Anna, honesty has a price, and as in the earlier example, the attempt to deny the truth in this case also has its cost. If A suspects the truth and B fails to grant a concession, then a deal might be killed and B put in jail.

One further point: the additional value given to A in the value-added division scheme for this game doesn't come so much because he has added more value, but rather because he gains less through cooperation than B and therefore can claim that, in fairness, he should be compensated by getting a larger share of the joint gain. In effect, he can say to B, "You should be happy with a small actual return, since you gain so much simply by avoiding jail." Looked at in another way, however, he does in fact add more to the joint net payoff of +25 than does B when both refrain from their maximin choice.

Graphical Representation (Optional)

The graphical representation of the above version of the prisoner's dilemma is given below. It is clear from the above figure that the potential for losses moves the concession level for each player off the *x* and *y* axis. But since A loses less in his maximin choice, his concession level is not as far to the right of the *y* axis as B's concession level is below the *x* axis.

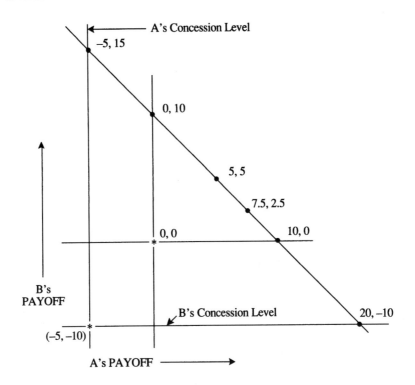

Any outcome in which each gets at least his security level is considered rational, according to von Neumann and Morgenstern, including the outcome in which A takes all 10 of the joint gain and demands a side payment of an additional 10 from B, resulting in the payoff of 20, − 10. At the other extreme is the payoff of − 5, 15, which reflects the fact that since A has less to lose by defection, he is less exploitable. On this new bargaining line, the value-added egalitarian division of 7.5, 2.5 is at the midpoint and is clearly more advantageous to A than the 5, 5 division at the midpoint of the line defined by the *x* and *y* axes.

Threats and Arbitration Schemes

In all the above examples, we assumed that each player would calculate his security level based on his maximin strategy. There may be cases, however, where deviating from the maximin can cause little harm to one player relative to his maximin and at the same time considerable harm to the other. This would be equivalent to one side contemplating using a *minimax* strategy so as to damage an opponent even if it is costly to himself. Remember, in the maximin strategy you operate to minimize the other's gains, rather than minimize your own loses as in the maximin strategy. In such cases the value-added arbitration scheme may not make sense, in that it depends on each side's maximin values. Rapoport (1969) suggests that in such cases an alternative arbitration scheme proposed by John F. Nash (1953) may be more appropriate, in that it takes into account such considerations. We bring this up here only to warn the reader that in such cases his bottom line may be the worst outcome that can be imposed by the other side, and not, as in maximin, the worst outcome that the other side can *rationally* impose. The terrorist who threatens to blow up an airplane may be invoking such a threat. His maximin strategy might allow him to get away with his life, but he may be willing to lose his life to carry out a threat that, to the other side, is so costly as to be unthinkable. In much of what follows, however, we will ignore such special cases. Needless to say, we do not doubt that such circumstances can and do arise.

Example

Consider the following example. Albert, who is in his mid-forties, has put his life savings of $100,000 into a small electronics business. In addition, to secure the necessary capital he took on as an equity partner a venture capital firm which invested $200,000 and owns 40% of the operation. The equity partner is a well-financed firm with a broadly diversified investment portfolio.

During the past year, the cost of microchips, which are important components in all of Albert's products, has skyrocketed for reasons he could not have foreseen. The consequence is that his company has been losing money and lacks the capital to buy critical supplies. He believes the current shortage of microchips will abate within the year, and has gone to his equity partner for additional funds of $25,000 and, in return, is prepared to grant them an additional 5% share of the company's stock. The venture capital firm agrees with his assessment of the microchip situation and is willing to put up the additional funds, but they want an additional 11% of the company's stock, which will give them a 51% controlling interest. Is this a reasonable offer? What should Albert do?

In trying to assess this problem, we have to find some way to value the company's shares. Let us suppose that by independent evaluation all agree that the firm, as long as it remains in business, is fairly valued at (has net asset of value of) $500,000, which means that each 1% share is worth $5,000. This is why Albert offered 5% for the $25,000 he needs. In effect Albert and his partners are trying to arrive on how many shares each should have in the company. Let us designate the proportion of shares that Albert receives in these negotiations as x, and the proportion of shares his partners receive $(1 - x)$.

Let us avoid the game matrix in this case and go directly to the joint outcome table, which might look so:

	NON-COOPERATIVE OUTCOME	COOPERATIVE OUTCOME
ALBERT	Loss of savings Loss of job	x percentage of healthy firm
EQUITY PARTNER	Write-off of Investment	$1 - x$ percentage of healthy firm

Clearly Albert is in a bind. He cannot expect to survive without the additional funds, and he has no one else to turn to for those funds except his current partners. There is simply not enough time to find a new investor.

Let us now attempt to establish reasonable estimates of each side's maximin or security level in the event that cooperation cannot be arranged. If the firm folds, the venture capitalists will have to write off their original $200,000 investment, but since their other investments are doing quite well, the actual loss would be considerably less since they could use that loss to offset tax liabilities on their other gains. They calculate, therefore a net loss of approximately $100,000, should the firm go bankrupt.

In purely economic terms, Albert would lose his investment of $100,000. In addition, he will lose his current position, and while it is true that he can get another job, that will take some time. He will also suffer a $50,000 after-tax loss of income in the interim, even with the tax advantage conferred by the $100,000 loss.

As discussed before, a deal will involve a transfer of shares, with the percentage of the company's shares going to Albert being x. His partners, in turn, will be left with $1 - x$ percentage of the shares, and in addition will be out the $25,000 to keep the company afloat. But that additional money will increase the value of the firm to $525,000. For simplicity, all dollar amounts are given in thousands of dollars. Plugging these into the outcome table gives the following:

	NON-COOPERATIVE OUTCOME	COOPERATIVE OUTCOME
ALBERT	Loss of savings Loss of job $= -\$150$	x shares in healthy firm $= (x)\$525$
EQUITY PARTNER	Write off of Investment $= -\$100$	$(1 - x)$ shares of healthy firm $= (1-x)\$525 - \$25$
ALBERT & PARTNERS		$x(\$525) + 1 - x(\$525) - \$25$ $= \$525 - \$25 = \$500$

which gives us the following characteristic function:

$$v(\text{ALBERT}) = -\$150 \qquad v(\text{PARTNER}) = -\$100$$
$$v(\text{ALBERT AND PARTNER}) = \$500$$

which when normalized produces:

$$v(\text{ALBERT}) = 0 \qquad v(\text{PARTNER}) = 0$$
$$v(\text{ALBERT AND PARTNER}) = \$750$$

If we apply the value-added egalitarian scheme, each should get $375 above his maximin level, or $225 for Albert and $275 for the partners. This means that Albert would end up with 45% of the firm and his partners with 55%. Of course, any outcome in which Albert lost less than $150,000 and his partners lost less than $100,000 and both shared in the $500,000 the company is worth, would be "rational" according to von Neumann and Morgenstern. In Albert's case this means that an outcome that gave him as little as 30% of the company should prove acceptable, since that would represent a loss equal to $150,000. By similar reckoning the venture capital firm could reasonably accept an offer in which they ended up with as little as a 20% share, since that is equal to a loss of $100,000.

In this example, our analysis suggests that the venture capital firm is in a better bargaining position than is Albert. It should be clear upon reflection, however, that this analysis grossly underestimates the power of the firm *viv à vis* Albert. This is so because our analysis ignored three fundamental problems, to which we now turn.

The first problem is one we have managed to avoid so far—that people differ in the utility they assign to such things as money. It is simply not reasonable to assume that Albert places the same value on money as do his partners. The loss of $100,000 to an investment firm with millions of dollars of assets cannot realistically be equated with the loss of a person's total assets. This is related to our earlier discussion of the diminishing marginal utility of money.

Second, the only thing at stake for the venture capital firm is the economic value they attach to the various outcomes, and these represent a small percentage of their total operation. For Albert such is not the case. For him, the bankruptcy of the firm would be devastating, especially at this point in his career. He would be wiped out. No doubt he could find employment and get back on his feet, but it would be years until he could recoup his losses. The psychological costs to himself, his loss of self-esteem, and the difficulty of finding an adequate position are not considered in our analysis. Neither are the psychological and social costs to his family and employees. Clearly the above figures are woefully inadequate to represent the situation in which Albert finds himself.

A third consideration is the fact that the marginal utility of each share is not equal. The shares that give one side or the other the controlling interest are clearly more valuable than those that merely increase the degree of ownership. Clearly, the venture capital firm wants control, and just as clearly Albert does not wish to give it up. If Albert loses control of the firm, he must give up the sort of independence he had sought in going into his own business in the first place. He could at any time be removed as president and be reduced to a mere shareholder. The above figures do not reflect this reality.

The last two problems can be dealt with by the careful assignment of utility to each outcome for each player. The first problem dealing with comparisons of utility is an extremely vexing problem in utility theory, and cannot always be readily solved. It is possible, however, to approximate its effects in many cases.

Suppose we estimate that Albert's utility for money is twice that of the venture capital firm. Let us examine the characteristic functions again in this light. For simplicity, let A = Albert and P = his partners.

CHARACTERISTIC FUNCTION   NORMALIZED
$v(A) = -\$150 \quad v(P) = -\$100$ $v(A) = 0 \quad v(P) = 0$
$v(A + P) = \$500$ $v(A + P) = \$750$

Suppose we wish to divide the net gain of $750 equally between them according to the value-added scheme but wish to do so in terms of utility rather than money. Such a division would require that the venture capital firm get twice as much money as Albert, since they value it half as much as he does. If the amount Albert got were x, then the partners would have to get $2x$ if they were both to get equal utility. In other words, the same dollar represents 1 unit of utility to Albert and ½ unit of utility to his partners. Also, Albert's share and his partners' share must equal the total of $750,000. Algebraically, $x + 2x$ = $750,000 and x (Albert's share of the net gain) must be $250,000 and his partners' share $500,000. If we add these values to each side's maximin value, we get $100,000 for Albert and $400,000 for his partners. A *fair* return here gives Albert a 20% share of the firm, and his partners a controlling 80%.

We didn't take into account the potential psychological loss that Albert will suffer in his maximin outcome. Had we done so, he probably would have received even less in a fair division. On the other hand, we did not figure in the value of *control per se,* the value of which would give Albert a greater share to compensate him for his loss of control. That would depend in large measure on the relative worth of control to Albert and to his partners. However we look at the problem, it is clear that Albert is in a weak position and will probably lose control of his company. How much he gets in compensation will depend on its relative worth and his bargaining ability.

One advantage of analyzing the problem in this way is that it clearly highlights major sticking points. In this case, Albert values his current position as CEO very much and views losing control with as much fear and distaste as going bankrupt. If both parties are honest in assessing their interests, then some middle ground may emerge that serves the interest of both parties. If the venture capital firm is not unhappy with Albert's management performance, they could reassure him by agreeing to a long-term, a 5-year contract for instance, guaranteeing his continuation as CEO. By *sweetening* the deal in this way, they gain what is paramount for them—control of a potentially profitable enterprise at relatively modest cost. In attempting to exploit Albert to the maximum, they might drive him, either out of despair or pique, to prefer bankruptcy.

The fact that it is difficult to come to clear-cut solutions in such bargaining problems need not discourage us. It is important to remember that the most important step in negotiations is getting a clear understanding of what interests are at stake for each party and the relative costs and benefits of various bargaining outcomes. This our modeling surely allows us to do. The fact that we cannot get a precise, mathematically determined outcome is inherent in the nature of such situations and is why von Neumann and Morgenstern were eventually forced to rely on *bargaining ability, etc.*

A final note related to the issue of the comparison of utilities is in order. Consider the comments of Luce and Raiffa (1957) on the problem:

> We should point out (again) that one of the basic assumptions of game theory, and of the bargaining model in particular, is extremely doubtful, namely: that each player knows the true tastes—the utility functions—of the others. . . . In most situations, a player's preferences are only partially known to an adversary and falsification of one's true feelings is an inherent and important bargaining strategy. An arbiter, to be successful, must skillfully ferret out at least part of the truth. This reality is seriously idealized in game theory, and thereby the theory is severely restricted.

While we agree with Luce and Raiffa here, we also believe it is possible to exaggerate the difficulty. In cases where you are bargaining with someone with similar resources and social standing, reasonable estimates of his valuations can be made by putting yourself in his shoes, so to speak. When the individuals have resources or backgrounds that produce profound differences in bargaining power, valuations can often be estimated by consulting with others so that necessary adjustments can be made. Generally, the past choices of others give us some guide to their preferences, as can knowledge of institutional needs when negotiators represent such institutions, such as unions or firms.

Complex Multiple Issue Negotiations

In many negotiations, such as those involving divorce, labor-management relations, business acquisitions, or international treaties, there will be a number of different issues, the potential to invoke a variety of threats and counterthreats, and the potential for various sorts of gains.

Consider labor-management bargaining. There usually are a number of issues that have been identified as "negotiable": wages, vacation time, health benefits and retirement contributions, absenteeism, job security, management prerogatives to evaluate and fire undesirable workers, and work schedules, to name but a few.

In such bargaining, each side will have to perform a multi-attribute analysis to determine its minimal agreement value for each issue and attempt to ascertain the minimal agreement value of the other side. Each side will overstate its own bottom line or security level, and will assume, correctly so, that the other side is overstating its bottom line. But here another problem arises, and that has to do with the relative weights that each side places on the various issues in its multi-attribute analysis, and these can differ significantly. Management may consider its right to regulate and fire workers to be more important than all the other issues combined. Labor may agree on the importance of management's ability to fire, for different reasons, but may weigh wages as far more important than work rules. The problem here has two aspects. First one must determine minimal acceptable levels. Second, one must discover the appropriate trade-off formulas between, for example, changes in work rules for increases in salary. Since one does not generally know the other side's absolute minima nor the weights for them, the problems are enormously complicated. In such cases, it is important to keep relative value weights and minimal acceptable levels secret. If, for example, labor does not know that management has placed absenteeism high on its list of desired things, it might give that away too "cheaply."

But there is a danger in failing to indicate the significance of an item. If labor underestimates the importance of some change in work rules, the union might find itself on strike because of management's unreasonableness, i.e., its failure to compromise on what it thought were *trivial* issues. The problem here is trying to determine just how honest about issues one should be. One can hardly bargain over true interests without being fairly open about them, but if one is too open, one is likely to be taken advantage of.

Consider a labor-management negotiation in which the total package is worth one million dollars. Let us assume that labor and management have estimated that their corporation will realize an additional $1,000,000 in the coming year. (We assume that they have come to similar estimates, which is an unlikely and, in most cases, an unnecessary assumption).

Trying to determine the absolute minimal value for each item or issue is extremely troublesome. What is the minimum concession level for labor on wages? For any worker, it could be the salary obtainable in another job available to him if a long strike forces the closing of a plant. This value may seem unreasonably low to most workers whose current salary may be much higher than that. And in many cases in the past where strikes could be used as job actions designed to inflict pain but not mortal wounds, perhaps such estimates would have been too low.

On the other hand, if management threatens a totally hostile posture as it has, recently, in the airline industry and as the government did in the case of the air traffic controllers in 1980, it may seem reasonable indeed. In those cases, labor took the position that management was bluffing (without, it should be noted, particularly powerful reasons for thinking so) and failed to make prudent adjustments in their bottom line. The consequence was that they failed to make an offer acceptable to management and unfortunately called management on its "bluff." Since labor lacked the ability to prevent hiring nonunion labor, they lost.

This is hardly the place to attempt a full discussion of the manner in which each side should assess its minimal agreement values and appropriate trade-offs. It is enough to suggest that these considerations are among the most important aspects of rational negotiations. Once one has estimated within reasonable grounds the range of rationally acceptable payoffs, the actual bargaining will involve an attempt to find grounds of mutual overlap with the other side, while attempting to move the solution to a point most favorable to one's own side. There is always the danger that one will press too hard and drive for a bargain that is unreasonable for the other side. There is much room here for educating the other side as to what is reasonable for them to accept. One final point. Almost all negotiations involve the actual bargaining between the parties "at the table" and negotiations between the negotiators and their clients. It is sometimes more important for one's own side to have a clear and justifiable understanding of the situation—meaning clear definition of bargaining lines, minimal acceptable positions, threat potential, and possible threat damage—than it is for the other side. The client must, after all, accept the deal if there is to be a deal.

For much the same reason it is important to avoid gloating. If you think you did especially well in negotiations, tell your side, but none too loudly; the other side may be listening. All too often the parties to negotiations lose sight of the fact that the whole purpose of the exercise is to come to some mutually beneficial arrangement, and rarely is it appropriate to think of winning in such discussions. Winning and losing are appropriate goals in zerosum contests; they rarely are in nonzero-sum cases.

Example

Suppose a small, failing airline, Ace Air, has just been bought by someone known to take losing operations and turn them into money-makers. Suppose, further, that the contract between Ace Air and its union is due to expire on June 1.

Ace is currently losing $1,000,000 a year. In management's view, this is because its operating expenses, which include $5,000,000 in salary and benefits, are simply out of line with earnings given the current competition in the field.

Management's opening proposal to the union is based on their plan to turn Ace Air around. They estimate that under their plan the airline could stay alive and earn a profit of $1,500,000 a year, which would represent a reasonable return on their owners' investment. In addition, the plan calls for an across-the-board cut of 10% in salaries and benefits, and new work rules that would increase the average work week by 10%. Included in management's proposal are miscellaneous demands that seem to have been made merely to confuse the issue, such as a demand that workers be disciplined for failure to show proper respect for patrons and managers.

The union leadership agrees with management's estimate of earning potential but believes those earnings can be achieved without any changes in work rules if management would clean up its act. The union argues that if managers gave up their three-martini lunches and got the new computer system on line, the airline could easily turn the nice profit estimated. It argues that management, in addition, could save a great deal by establishing its own repair operations rather than con-tracting them out at exorbitant prices, as is now done. It furthermore believes that $500,000 is more than enough to satisfy the investors and that the other $1,000,000 in expected earnings should be distributed among its 100 members to provide an additional $10,000 per worker in salary increases and benefits. They also have listed a number of demands they feel are terribly important for their workers' sense of well-being and self-respect, such as refurbished dressing rooms and redesigned uniforms, which would greatly improve worker morale at minimal cost to Ace.

Both sides agree that a strike would damage the company and, if it went on beyond a few days, could result in the company going out of business.

We can represent this relatively simple negotiation (by industry standards) in the joint outcome table below.

JOINT OUTCOME TABLE

	NO AGREEMENT COMPANY FOLDS	NEGOTIATED AGREEMENT
MANAGEMENT	Loss of investment	Share of $1.5 mil
UNION	Loss of jobs	Share of $1.5 mil

Generally speaking, it is necessary for each side to adopt a bottom line, or minimal concession level beyond which they will not budge and to do so for all the items under negotiation. Once that is established they need to develop reasonable trade-off formulas: i.e. how many extra hours, if any, they are prepared to give for how many dollars of salary; how much change in the medical plan for hours worked; and so on.

The need for each side to determine the appropriate bottom line is difficult to do with any precision; but some estimate must be made. Perhaps the union can estimate what workers can get in jobs they can reasonably hope to obtain. They could use that figure, and it might be an expected value, taking into account the probability that workers will actually be able to get those jobs. Let us suppose, in this case, that the union feels confident that all of their members will eventually find replacement jobs. They further assume that the new jobs on average will provide salaries of approximately 90% of what they are currently getting at Ace, including comparable fringe benefits. They expect, however, that the average worker will require about 7 weeks to find new employment.

Using these estimates they might conclude that, even if the company folds, their members on average will end up in salaries only 10% less then they are currently getting. Therefore, it would not make sense to accept a settlement below that, and it represents a sort of maximin or bottom line for them. But how should they figure in the loss of 7 weeks salary, which represents about 15% of current salaries? Suppose that they expect a three-year contract. In that case, it would make sense to spread this loss over three years, which means that their bottom line for salaries ought to be reduced by one-third of 15%, or 5% per year. This reduces their bottom line to 85% of current salaries. They could, in other words, take up to a 15% salary reduction and their members, on average, would be better off than if Ace Air were to go bankrupt. The union would, of course, inflate these estimates when explaining its position to Ace management. The union leadership also feels that minor work rule changes can be made to sweeten the deal for management, but only so long as extra work time is not involved. If management wants longer hours they will have to pay for them.

The bottom line for management might be determined in the following way. They could estimate what they could obtain for the assets of the corporation put on the block after it closed its doors. That figure might come to more than the airline is worth now with an operating deficit and a costly union contract. Management would then estimate as realistically as possible the dollar amount that such a figure could realize in some equally risky investment. Suppose they estimate that they could liquidate the airline and come away with $10,000,000, which is about what they paid for Ace. They estimate that in another enterprise, or in the stock market, they could realize a return of approximately 10%, netting them $1,000,000 on their investment. That would be their bottom line, assuming similar tax liabilities, etc. In other words, they should not agree to any settlement with the union that provides them with less than $1,000,000 a year in profits. They would, in turn, claim that alternative uses of their money would be much more profitable than the uses proposed by the union negotiators. In addition, the management team agrees that there is some merit to union demands that they increase managerial efficiency, but this has already been figured into their estimate of $1.5 mil profit for the coming year. Let us call management's negotiated share of this profit x and the unions share $1.5 - x$. If we place these values in the joint outcome table we get the breakdown shown on page 319.

This produces the following characteristic function:

$$v(\text{Union}) = -\$750,000 \qquad v(\text{Ace Air}) = \$1,000,000$$
$$v(\text{Union} + \text{Ace Air}) = \$1,500,000$$

JOINT OUTCOME TABLE

	NO AGREEMENT COMPANY FOLDS	NEGOTIATED AGREEMENT
MANAGEMENT	Alternative investment = $1,000,000	Share of $1.5 mil = X
UNION	Alternative jobs = −.15 * $5,000,000 = − $750,000	Share of $1.5 mil = $1.5 − X

Which if normalized is:

$$v(\text{Union}) = 0 \qquad v(\text{Ace Air}) = 0$$
$$v(\text{Union} + \text{Ace Air}) = \$1,250,000$$

The normalized joint value was found by adding together the two values of "no agreement" ($1,000,000 + −$750,000 = $250,000) and determining what is gained by moving from that value ($250,000) to the joint value of mutual cooperation ($1,500,000). The gain is $1,250,000.

From this we can see that Ace Air's original proposal for a 10% cut in salaries and a reduction in total of salaries of $500,000 was within the range of rational (von Neumann and Morgenstern) solutions. The union's demand of a 10% increase was also within that range, since that would have given them $500,000 of the gain of $1,500,000, leaving management with $1,000,000, which does not go below management's security level.

If we apply the value-added division scheme, each side would receive $625,000 above its bottom line, which would give $1,625,000 to Ace Air. In that scheme, the union would get $625,000 above −$750,000 or −$125,000, which would amount to a 2.5% cut in salaries. For the average worker that would amount to a salary reduction of $1,250.

Suppose the union agreed with the above analysis and proposed the alternative solution where they would accept a salary freeze and let management take all the new profits. That would produce a division of the normalized gain of $1,250,000 in which management got $500,000 above its alternative investment, and the union $750,000 above its bottom line. One would not be surprised were this to be the actual outcome in such a situation. Even though the split is not equal according to the value-added scheme, it is relatively close and does not require anybody to be worse off than he is right now.

Negotiation as Subgame

One often overlooked possibility in any negotiation is that one or both sides may see this particular game as merely a "move" in a much larger game. A union may "play tough" in one negotiation to demonstrate its willingness to call the bluff and thereby improve its bargaining in future negotiations. In the previous example, management may have decided to take over this company *because* it was falling and *because* it had to shortly negotiate a contract. They might have been willing to take a temporary loss, force the workers to concede, or close the company. Management's reasoning might be that if the workers concede, then they have a bargain in Ace Air. If, on the other hand, the union plays tough, they can sell the assets, buy another airline, and do the same thing again. In this new venture, however, they are very likely to find the union more conciliatory since, by then, the word would be out that they are "crazy," in that they make unreasonable demands and then go for broke. At the least, they can expect future union negotiators to act more prudently at the table.

Threat Actions with Escalating Damage

Strikes and lockouts are among the most extreme threats available to labor and management. When such actions are understood to be part of negotiations and no mortal wounds are intended, i.e., management has no intention of breaking the union or cannot do so, there are still significant costs to such actions. In particular one runs into the problem of bargaining costs—with a vengeance—since the costs tend to escalate over time.

Consider a labor-management negotiation such as the one previous in which the total package is thought to be worth 1.5 million dollars.

The bargaining essentially concerns how much of those profits should be maintained as profit by the company and how much will be provided in a "package" of benefits for workers. Let us further suppose that a strike or lockout will cost the company and the workers $100,000 a day, jointly, for every day it is in effect. The invocation of the threat in this case, by either side, has the result of diminishing the amount to be divided by $100,000 a day, so that after fifteen days they will no longer be negotiating over a share of the expected gain, but over the distribution of the expected loss. In general, long strikes are more costly to management, especially in industries that cannot find replacement workers. This is so is because only a minimal amount can be obtained from labor. In a long strike, labor can lose wages and benefits, but it generally cannot realistically be assessed a full share of the costs of a long strike. There is some minimal amount beyond which they cannot be expected to go, since they can generally get alternative employment. This is less true during times of high unemployment.

Therefore, management has to absorb these cost or go bankrupt. Often, going bankrupt results in substantial losses to the owners, and is therefore not a practical alternative. Therefore, management often has to accept a higher share of such losses, which are usually translated into higher prices and potential long-run loss of market share. In recent years, aggressive management has attempted to reverse this situation by threatening the permanent loss of jobs, and has, at times, made that a creditable threat by invoking it. In such cases, highly paid workers with much seniority may find the costs associated with strikes as costly as management.

It is also important to avoid the fallacy of *sunk costs*. Just because we already invested heavily and committed ourselves emotionally to some course of action, such as a strike, does not mean that we should continue *because* of what is already invested. Remember each decision should be made in terms of what may and may not happen, not on what is past.

A game illustrating this problem, the *dollar auction game* (Shubik 1971), is one in which "an auctioneer auctions off a dollar to the highest bidder, with the condition that both the highest bidder and the second highest bidder will pay" (Shubik 1975, p. 303). Imagine that in such a game you have already bid $.50, and someone else bids $.55. What should you do? If you stop now you have lost $.50, but if you go on you may find yourself still bidding against an opponent who offers $.95, because that bid, if winning, would still earn him $.05, but you would lose $.90. Should you then bid $1.00 to cut your loss to zero? Should you bid $1.50 against $1.45 to cut your loss to $.50 from $1.45?

Clearly, as soon as you became aware of the nature of such a game, you should drop out, and write off the sunk costs to experience. Unfortunately in many struggles, the parties will continue to throw good money or lives after bad in an attempt to recoup their losses. They forget the need to ignore sunk costs, or the negotiators may fear the retribution of their constituents for having lead them down the primrose path, however innocently. It would appear better in such cases to "own up" than to continue a costly escalation.

As a general rule, threats should only be made when creditable and when you are prepared to take action on them. You should only be prepared to take action if the costs of doing so are compensated by either short- or long-run gains. If you can do equally well without threats you are wise to do so, since you may underestimate the damage of your threatened action and you may also underestimate the threat potential of your opponent and the damage to the existing relationship.

Your opponent may also have long-run goals (such as reputation in future dealings) that require him to call a threat and take the damage, even if severe. He may also believe you are bluffing and invoke the threat when attempting to call a bluff. On the other hand, failing to use creditable threats to influence negotiations would be foolish, especially where the other side has invoked its own creditable threats. The important point in all of this is that in using a threat, you are almost certainly reducing the size of the joint gain available through coopera- tion. If, and when, a deal is finally struck, there will, necessarily, be less to divide.

One important problem arises if the parties are using professional negotiators, such as lawyers or labor union leaders, to represent them. In such a case, the interests of the professionals may not be completely aligned with those of the affected parties. Theoretically and sometimes even legally, they should be, but rarely are. Professional negotiators may value a reputation for toughness more than the parties they represent. They may, therefore, be more willing to take risks and make threats than the parties they represent. This is a real problem that should be confronted honestly by all involved. Professional negotiators may be more ready to see the logic of the expected value model than are their clients. In other words, lawyers may take the attitude "win some and lose some", but most individuals who go to court either win or lose and rarely make it up "in the long run" in other court appearances, and may have little to gain in the long term from a reputation for toughness.

Negotiations and Threats with Uncertain Outcomes

In many negotiations, the use of threats is complicated because their consequences may be uncertain. This is certainly the case in wars between equally matched opponents. Sometimes it is also the case in bargaining among lawyers, where the ultimate threat is going to trial. It is well known that lawyers consider going to trial risky business, even when they think they have a very strong case. The problem for the negotiator is to estimate the probability that the desired outcome will, in fact, be produced. Here the expected value model can be used, but it is especially important for the client to participate not necessarily in determining estimates of probable success, but in assessing and evaluating the possible outcomes. This is sometimes a problem because clients may consider an out-of-court settlement of $200,000, for example, more attractive than a 50-50 chance of obtaining $400,000 from a trial even having to deduct court costs. The possibilities here for conflicts of interest and of differing perceptions are obvious. In the movie "The Trial," Paul Newman played a lawyer desperate to win a major malpractice case for a young, not particularly well-off, couple. He rejected a substantial offer from the hospital being sued, without consulting his clients, based on his belief that he could do better in court. Newman won the case and did get a better decision for his clients, but by any reasonable standard of fiduciary responsibility, he should have been disbarred.

Common Hindrances to Effective Negotiations

When parties sit down at the negotiating table it is inevitable that they bring various kinds of preconceptions and biases that may interfere with a mutually desirable resolution of the issues. We have already stressed that negotiations can be fruitful only if both parties see the possibility of gain. If either side believes that nothing can be gained, then bargaining is either a waste of time, or a charade to buy time for some other action. For this reason, it is important for a negotiator to assure that the person on the other side of the table believes that negotiations are likely to be to his or her benefit. Put in another way, it is important that both sides seek to maintain an attitude or spirit of cooperation and a belief that each is bargaining in good faith. There are a number of common problems that often undercut such a spirit. We enumerate those that are most damaging and provide some suggestions to limit their damage.

The Desire to Win

Professional negotiators often are acting as fiduciaries for others and have been hired or elected because of their perceived abilities as bargaining agents, so it is usually in their interest to perform well. One problem occurs if it is difficult for the client to evaluate negotiation strategies because he thinks in terms of winning or losing. The client usually has a general idea of what would be a good settlement. Any better agreement will be interpreted as "winning," anything worse as "losing." Very often, the negotiator has been hired or elected on a claim that he could achieve an outcome more desirable than other potential candidates. Sometimes, as in the case of law firms, this is merely inferred by the negotiator's reputation. Preliminary discussions are usually held in an attempt to arrive at a reasonable negotiating target.

The problem here is that any target or group of targets set before the negotiations begin are merely uninformed estimates. Once set, however, such targets can easily become fixed in the mind of the negotiator, forcing him to demand unreasonable concessions from the other side. The negotiator finds himself torn between the unfolding reality at the negotiating table and the powerful and unrealistic expectations of his constituency. Under the stress of the negotiations, he may forego real benefits in areas of strength because the original estimates of strength were too low, in a vain attempt to achieve a target that was originally set too high. Or worse, he can find himself engaged in arranging agreements that "look good" because they satisfy the original criteria at the cost of real benefits.

Define Interests Rather Than Positions

In their influential book, *Getting To Yes,* Roger Fisher and William Ury (1981) of The Harvard Negotiation Project, outline their theory of principled negotiations, the most important principle of which is to avoid bargaining over positions in favor of bargaining over interests. At a practical level, this means determining what interests your party has in the negotiations and avoiding premature targets or "positions" as a means to satisfy those interests. This is the same problem encountered earlier in the discussion of determining goals and objectives and avoiding confusing means with ends. It is important here to recall the importance of sound decision structuring.

Determining interests, especially in democratic groups such as unions, is no easy matter. It is made more difficult if members espouse the belief that bottom lines must be defined in terms of positions (a certain dollar amount in salary, specific health benefits, specific holidays, or work rules). Often the first and most important task of the negotiator is to educate his client or constituents. He must first attempt to ascertain what is in the best interest of his constituents, what their beliefs are as to reasonable positions, and the means to satisfy those interests. Then, the negotiator must stress the difference between means and interests and attempt to convince the constituent to maintain flexible positions. He must, in short, educate his constituent as to just what negotiations are all about. If he fails in this, he must enter negotiations hobbled by preconceived notions as to what is possible and desirable. Under those circumstances, it is unlikely that the negotiator will achieve a satisfactory outcome.

Anticipate Dangers and Costs

The negotiator must set clear priorities before negotiations begin, and know which objectives can and cannot be compromised. He must anticipate in advance the difficulties he is likely to encounter, and make reasonable estimates of the costs of negotiating. He should remind himself of the *sunk costs trap,* and not be seduced by the notion that since he has put so much time and energy into a negotiation, its outcome had better look good. It may not *look* good, in light of his efforts or his constituent's desires, but it may well be all that can reasonably be attained under the circumstances. Many a good law, or good deal, or peaceful settlement has been lost in the vain effort to achieve an imagined ideal. One must not forget that in negotiations, an outcome that is good for your side may be bad for the other side. In negotiating, it is sometimes wiser, especially when the costs of failure are great, to adopt a satisficing as opposed to an optimizing orientation.

The negotiator must, as we discussed under the topic *binding the will,* anticipate situations in which he is likely to blunder. All-night negotiating sessions often produce agreements that negotiators later regret. In marathon negotiations, the desire to be done with the whole business may serve as a barrier to sound reasoning. The negotiator must prepare himself for serious threats and the sort of stress such threats can induce; he must decide ahead of time, and in full consultation with his constituents, the risks he is prepared to take, and determine what risks are unacceptable. The negotiator has an obligation to protect his client's interests and prepare himself for situations or conditions where he is likely to betray those interests due to weakness, stress, or fear.

If the negotiation is a group effort as most are and, in our opinion, should be, it is important to avoid the dangers of *groupthink*. Under pressure, the team has to maintain an open attitude toward dissent. Group solidarity is critical in many negotiating situations, especially to avoid giving the impression of weakness or indecisiveness. But the need for such solidarity must never be allowed to cloud the judgment of those who must sit at the table and, in the final analysis, act for the group. For instance, if many in a union are in disagreement with the majority, there is no virtue in failing to acknowledge that reality when assessing strategy. Attempting to achieve solidarity artificially by denying dissent is unlikely to be successful. Group solidarity is more likely to be obtained by giving dissenting voices a fair hearing and trying to find means to accommodate their concerns. Group action is not likely to be effective if supported by a slim majority who impose their will on a disaffected minority.

Group Conflict and Decision Rules

One of the advantages of the various decision rules that have been discussed in earlier chapters is their use as objective criteria to resolve disputes over what action a group should take. If members of a group can agree to act on the basis of the expected utility rule, for instance, they can devote their energies to determining probabilities, goal weights, and utilities. Such values, in turn, can often be determined by objective criteria. As such, a problem is transformed from one of clashing personalities and interests to one of discovering reasonable valuations. Whatever is decided, it more likely to be accepted as fair to the extent that the procedures producing the decision are themselves seen as fair and impartial.

Educating the Other Side

It is our belief that determining one's own interests and fostering the attitude of satisfying interests rather than "winning" is the most critical phase in the whole negotiating process. It is almost as important that the other side has the same degree of understanding of the goals of the negotiation. If they do not, then it is absolutely critical that they be educated. One advantage of using professionally trained negotiators is that they usually do not require such education. In general, however, such an attitude cannot be assumed and must be determined. Here the use of impartial decision-making techniques can be useful for arriving at mutually desirable outcomes.

Negotiating Interests

Given that both parties have a clear idea of their interests and view negotiations as a means to satisfy those interests, the actual work of negotiating over means or "positions" can begin. Creative, or what Fisher and Ury (1981) refer to as *principled negotiations*, involve finding means or positions that serve the interests of both parties. This is often easier to achieve than might, at first sight, have been anticipated. For example, workers usually have an interest in increasing their financial well-being. Management usually has an interest in increasing profits. Taking positions as to some specific salary level is more often than not counterproductive. If, on the other hand, both sides recognize the legitimate interests of the other, they can work to find solutions that increase profits and the financial well-being of the workers. Sometimes, of course, such solutions may not exist, but often they do. Furthermore, if such a solution is, in fact, impossible, it is far more likely that the fundamental reasons will be clarified. Any outcome agreed upon will take into account those reasons, and perhaps attempt to address them in cooperative ways (such as exploring means by which management and labor might modify practices so as to increase competitiveness).

The Place for Toughness

It is important to emphasize that taking a cooperative attitude in negotiations should not be confused with weakness or naiveté. Nor should the admonition to define and negotiate interests be interpreted to mean that one should be completely open about those interests; deception about a minimal level of acceptance, in particular, is usually necessary in even the most cooperative bargaining. Nevertheless, it is generally harmless to be honest about interests, since they are usually already understood by both sides. Management knows workers want higher incomes and better working conditions. They may not be aware of the extent to which workers desire greater opportunities for pride in work, but divulging that interest is hardly likely to hurt labor's interest. Labor usually knows that management wants greater flexibility in using its labor force; little is lost for management to be forthright in asserting this interest or its fundamental interest in profits. A negotiator can be unyielding, or "tough," when it comes to holding to interests, without being thought unreasonable. Obviously, it is necessary for the negotiator to forward the interests of his clients; he would be negligent to act otherwise. On the other hand, being tough on some apparently arbitrary position, which is not clearly in the client's interest, is neither reasonable nor responsible. As a general rule, then, we advise the client to be open and forthright about his interests while keeping the bottom line under wraps.

Bad Faith Negotiations

When one side or the other has no intention of modifying its initial demands and positions, it has entered into negotiations in bad faith. The negotiations are, in effect, a charade to buy time for some action or to present a facade of reasonableness. The negotiations between Hitler and various European ministers represent this point. Hitler had his plans settled, but appeared undecided while engaging in negotiations. Sometimes, arms limitation negotiations are entered into for obvious public relations reasons. Under such circumstances, the best strategy is to call the bluff and ask for a halt in negotiations until real bargaining is desired. To continue when the other side is in bad faith merely allows the ploy to work. A word of caution is in order. The side operating in bad faith may wish the other side to pull out of negotiations so that it can take action, such as attack, or call a strike or lockout, on the pretense that such action was precipitated by the other side. It is important, therefore, for the party pulling out to carefully evaluate the last offer and compare it to its own bottom line.

Under some circumstances it may be wise to accept the offer, especially if it is clear that the other side will not move and the offer is considerably better than the bottom line that will result if there is no agreement. This may be difficult if the last offer is designed to be demeaning or humiliating. Prudence may dictate that one accept a temporary and perhaps humiliating setback with a view to building one's resources in preparation for a different fight on more favorable grounds. If one's position is weak and the other side appears to want a showdown to exploit that weakness, it would be irresponsible and unwise to take on a losing fight to avoid humiliation. One will be humiliated in any case.

If, on the other hand, one is not weak, then a tough refusal to continue a charade is clearly in order.

Keep Personalities and Reputation in the Background

One straightforward virtue of bargaining over interests is that the negotiators can take the position of disinterested fiduciaries. As such, they can approach their task as a complex problem to be solved to the advantage of their constituents. To the extent that they take such a position, there is absolutely no place for competitive posturing, or egotistical one-up-man-ship. In truth, activities designed to aggrandize a negotiator's private concerns are not only counterproductive but also a corruption of the negotiating process.

Conclusion

In the final analysis, negotiations are a uniquely human activity. Much that is good about the world comes about through concerted group effort arrived at by serious negotiators honestly representing their own or their constituent's interests. Much of what is bad about the world comes about because negotiators fail to find ways to arrive at mutual accommodation. Negotiating anything is a sometimes treacherous, but potentially highly rewarding enterprise. It is more likely to be rewarding if it is taken seriously. It is essential to be aware of the sorts of deception that you are likely to encounter, and the times when you may need to practice deception yourself. It is important to understand threats—their uses and their costs—including those unanticipated. One must beware of the sunk costs trap, the risks of using threats, and the runaway escalations that can result from their invocation.

As in any decision problem, risks must be assessed, values defined and measured, and outcomes thoughtfully evaluated. The more you think about such things and understand them, and are honest with yourself, the more likely are negotiations, as are all decision problems, to be seen as an opportunities for creative and productive endeavor, rather than as threats to personal well-being and social harmony.

Important Concepts

Bottom line, security level, or
   minimal concession level

Bargaining range or line

Differential threat potential

Naive egalitarian division

Value-added division

Bargaining costs

Threats with escalating damage

Negotiation as subgame

Educating clients and constituents

Negotiating interests vs. positions

The place for honesty and
   deception

The value of objective criteria

Independent mediation

Bad faith negotiations

Fiduciary

Problems for Analysis

1. Suppose Alex and Erica have decided to take advantage of the upcoming Labor Day parade in their town by setting up a lemonade stand to earn some extra money. They figure that they should be able to sell 200 cups of lemonade at $.50 a cup for a total of $100. They will need at least $20 for supplies such as lemonade mix, cups, materials for a sign, etc. Unfortunately, Alex has frittered away all his summer earnings and cannot ask for an advance on his allowance from his father, who is extremely annoyed with his free spending ways. Erica has the $20, which she has agreed to "invest" in their joint venture. However, she has to give a piano recital in the "young talent show," a major part of the day's festivities. For that reason she must be away for 4 of the 8 hours that the stand would be in operation. Both children could also work for the town on clean-up duty and earn $3/hour. Alex could work the full 8-hour shift, but Erica could put in only 4 hours on clean-up work.

    Draw up a joint outcome table showing the payoff to Alex and Erica if they cooperate on the lemonade stand and if they don't, and if they work for the town. Assume their estimate of $100 in earnings is correct. How should they divide it? Use the naive egalitarian and added-value division scheme. Which makes more sense? Why? What is the range of acceptable payoffs according to von Neumann and Morgenstern? Should Erica be compensated for her risk? How should they divide the money if Alex's marginal utility for money, since he doesn't have any, is twice what Erica's utility for money is?

2. Frank of Northside Pizza is calculating his advertising and pricing strategy for the upcoming Memorial Day weekend. He estimates that his normal prices will net him $3000 over the weekend. If he cuts prices 30% and his competition fails to do so he will net $4,500, but if

he fails to cut prices and his competition does cut by 30%, then his business will net only $1,500 over the weekend. If he and his competition both cut prices, he will net only $2,500.

Ralph of Ralph's Pizza is doing similar thinking. He expects to net $5,000 at his normal price. A price cut in the absence of a cut from Northside will net $6,000, but if Northside puts pizza on sale at a 30% reduction and he doesn't, he will net only $2,500. If both cut prices then he will net $3,000 for the weekend's business.

Suppose they have met accidentally at a local tavern after work. Ralph points out how their constant price wars resemble the prisoner's dilemma. Suppose they agree that they should act collusively in restraint of trade. How should they divide the fruits of their nefarious action?

3. Raoul and Canarsie have been in the printing business for ten years and now can't get along with each other. When they began the business, they decided that if it was ever sold, Raoul would get 40% and Canarsie the rest. It is now worth $800,000, but Raoul doesn't agree with the arrangement since he believes he has put more than 40% into the business over the last ten years. He thinks he is entitled to half. He threatens to get a very tough lawyer, his uncle, to bring suit. His uncle assures Raoul that he can certainly get half by going to court, but it will cost $40,000 in lawyer's fees and court costs. Assume Raoul's uncle is correct. That would leave Canarsie with $400,000 from a court case and $60,000 in court costs. Canarsie has no uncles who are lawyers.

Draw up the joint outcome table for this problem. What are the range of acceptable outcomes, taking into account the threat potential of both sides? What would be the value-added egalitarian solution taking into account threat potential? What do you think Canarsie should do?

4. Charles and Rhoda work in Gina's law office. They have become essential to Gina's practice, but of late have gotten into constant bickering with each other. It is becoming tiresome and is beginning to affect Gina's reputation. Gina has offered to arrange 5 sessions of one hour each in a program of interpersonal counseling. In order to induce them to take the program, Gina has offered to give them each 2 days off from work for each session they attend. Rhoda loves to spend time with her grandchildren more than anything else. On a scale of -10 to $+10$ she would rate a day off at $+10$. She really dislikes the idea of counseling and thinks that the whole process would be demeaning, especially with that nasty Charles. She rates each hour of counseling

as −4, on her scale. She is not that disturbed with the status quo and rates it 0 on her scale.

Charles finds the whole thing amusing, since he enjoys teasing the women at work, who, with the exception of thin-skinned Rhoda, don't seem to mind. He has nothing much to do after work except watch TV, but days off are pleasant enough. On his scale of utility, he assigns a day off as worth +3. He doesn't think much about the counseling either way, but rates it a −1. Charles, also, is not unhappy with the status quo and rates it 0 on his scale.

Gina will allow them to divide up the days off any way they want, so long as they use whole days. If they agree to attend the program, but can't agree how to divide the days, she will simply give each ten free days off. They must attend all five sessions or the deal is off.

How do you think they should divide the days off if they agree to the counseling? Should they each get the same number? How many should each get? Give the reasoning which led to your settlement.

5. Renée and Charles are negotiating their divorce. Together they own a house worth $175,000; a Jeep worth $15,000; a Toyota worth $10,000, and a parcel of land in East Hampton worth $160,000. In addition, Renée owns an apartment in Sacramento, California, which she got in a previous marriage, worth $300,000, but Charles in a prenuptial agreement has agreed not to make any claim on it in case of divorce.

On the other hand, Renée had promised to work full time as a designer during their marriage so long as there were no children. They have had no children, but Renée never worked a day during their four years of marriage. She could have earned $50,000 a year after taxes, and Charles feels they would have been at least $200,000 richer if she hadn't been so incredibly lazy. Charles therefore believes he is entitled to some part of the California apartment, and has threatened to sue to get a fair share. Renée is anxious to get out of the marriage and has agreed to give Charles $50,000 in compensation for her failure to work, from a mortgage she will take on the California property, and half of everything else. In a court suit that Renée is certain to contest, Charles believes he can get half of their joint property and at least $100,000 from the apartment as compensation for Renée's failure to work. He figures his legal fees will be $30,000, whereas Renée has a friend who he knows will represent her for half that or $15,000.

Suppose Charles is right about what he can obtain in court. Find the concession or security level for each party. What is the range of acceptable divisions? What would be the added-value division? Should Charles take Renée's offer or go to court?

Appendix A

Measurement and Utility

The purpose of this appendix is two-fold. First, it will discuss the nature of measurement in general. That is, it will ask and answer the question, "What is it that we are doing when we 'measure' something? What are the different kinds of measurements? And why is it necessary to measure things?" Having done this, we will apply that discussion to the question of the measurement of value, that is, utility. It is our experience that the idea of measuring value or utility is met with some skepticism. How is it possible to use numbers to measure one's "inner feelings"? For example, how can you compare the value that someone places on an automobile with the value that is placed on a cherished family heirloom?

The first answer to these types of concerns is that skepticism ought to be nourished and encouraged. Much of what passes for "objective," or "scientifically" measured phenomena belongs in the dust heap. The fact that something is presented or represented with numbers proves absolutely nothing about its credibility. Something is neither more nor less worthy of our belief because it is measured, or presented numerically. Everything depends upon how the numbers were arrived at.

On the other hand, the idea that "inner feelings" cannot be measured because they are "hidden" or "private" betrays a misunderstanding about the nature of measurement. The fact is that science has, from its very beginnings, engaged in the practice of measuring "hidden" phenomena, phenomena that cannot be directly observed with one or more of the five senses, for example the measurement of elasticity of demand, a widely used and basic concept in economics. The question then is not whether such measurement can be done, but (1) what does it mean to measure utility or anything else?, and (2) how

333

can utility be properly measured? It is useful in understanding measurement to think of the numbers resulting from a process of measurement as being similar to a model, as in a "scale model." In fact, the term "mathematical model" has become a common one, especially in the social sciences. Let's spend a brief time, then, thinking about models of a physical type.

Models

During a civil suit for damages brought because of an auto accident, one party brings a "model" of the accident to the court. Meticulously constructed to scale, it depicts an intersection with overhanging traffic lights, and a car going north on a green light being struck on its right side in the middle of the intersection by a truck going west through a red light.

The following points about such a model seem correct (Black 1962).

1. A model is always a model "of" something to which it points—the original.
2. The model is designed to say something only about that on which it is modeled. Thus we are allowed to "read off" features of the model and attribute them to the original. These attributions are called "legitimate inferences" from the model to the original.
3. Some features of the model are irrelevant, that is, they are not intended to be attributed to the original. To attribute an irrelevant feature to the original is an "illegitimate inference" from the model to the original.
4. The statement of which inferences are legitimate and which are illegitimate constitutes an "interpretation" of the model.

We can now apply the previous discussion to our auto accident.

1. The model represents an event that has occurred in the past.
2. It is designed to allow the legitimate inferences that the struck vehicle had the green light, the striking vehicle had a red light, the vehicles were a car and truck respectively, the car was headed north, etc. This helps the jury visualize the scene, and discover who was at fault.
3. The model is not intended to allow the inference that the original vehicles in the accident were made of wood, that they were each

under one pound in weight, that the road was green in color (as it is in the model), etc., even though these are all features of the model.

4. The interpretation in this type of case is probably not explicitly stated, but it is none-the-less real. There is a joke to the effect that Pablo Picasso once found an American sailor laughing at one of Picasso's paintings. "They say this is supposed to be a woman," said the sailor. "Look how big one of her breasts is, and look here! Her head is a triangle!" "Can you show me a picture of your girlfriend?" asked Picasso. The sailor does as he is asked. "And is it a good likeness?" "Excellent, that's just what she looks like," replies the sailor. "She's quite short isn't she," suggests Picasso facetiously.

In some cases very elaborate interpretations of models or pictures are necessary, as when an art critic interprets a Picasso painting. In other cases the interpretations are so familiar that we forget that they are there at all, as when the sailor forgot that the photo had to be interpreted. Because the photo of his girl was only two inches high, we cannot infer that the actual girl was only two inches high.

Mathematics

What is mathematics about? Suppose the football coach draws a formation such as the one below on his chalkboard to prepare his team for the coming game.

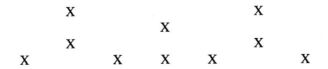

It is clear to his team that his represents, refers to, or is about, the opponent's primary defensive formation. This is a model of some phenomena that the coach wants to talk about. And when he takes his chalk, circles one of the Xs, and draws an arrow, it is clear that this represents an expected physical movement on the part of some real player in this position.

On the other hand, think of a Monopoly board with its pieces, in the middle of a game. What does that represent, or refer to? When a player purchases a railroad, what is that saying about some real railroad in the real world? The answers seem to be that the board with its pieces does not represent anything, and the purchase of a railroad in the game does not refer to any real purchase anywhere.

In both the case of the coach's formation on the board and the Monopoly game, there are correct and incorrect moves. But they become incorrect in different ways. If the coach's diagram indicates that the defensive linemen will follow a split end as he goes out for a pass, it is incorrect. It is incorrect because *in the actual world* beyond the chalkboard this will not happen. If a player in Monopoly simply picks an opponent's piece from the board and puts it aside, he does something incorrect. But it is incorrect only because it breaks the rules of the game, and not because of what the world beyond the Monopoly board is like. The Monopoly board and all its pieces is not a model, and so does not say anything, does not refer to anything beyond itself. In the language of logical theory, the chalkboard has a *semantics*— something beyond itself to which it points, and some rules stating how to "read off" from the board to the world. The Monopoly game has no semantics. It does, though, have a *syntax*—a set of rules that distinguish what moves are allowed and what moves are not allowed. In fact, the chalkboard has both a semantics and a syntax, where the Monopoly game has only a syntax.

Now let us look at the following three "things":

(a) $aPb \cdot bPc \to aPc$
(b) $y = mx + b$
(c) $40 + 40 = 80$

What is a referring to? What does it mean? The only answer is, perhaps nothing and perhaps something. It depends upon whether anyone, any person, has decided that it should refer to something, and how that referring should be accomplished. That is, a does refer to something if it has a semantics, and it does not if it has none. It only gets a semantics by being given one by some person.

What about b? Exactly the same should be said. Perhaps you recognize that b is a "linear" equation. What that means is that if you apply certain very precise rules to b, and carry out those rules on graph paper, you will come up with a straight line on the graph paper. That is, "$y = mx + b$", when numbers are inserted for the letters, represents a straight line on a piece of paper, given the semantics of analytic geometry. Take away that semantics, and every other semantics, and "$y = mx + b$" represents nothing, and means nothing. But even when "$y = mx + b$" represents nothing, there is still a syntax, which tells you that certain things can be done and certain other things cannot be done to it. For example, if I accept that "$y = mx + b$", the syntax *forbids* me to then write, "$y + b = mx$". And that same syntax *allows* me to write, "$y - b = mx$". The syntax that I am referring to is called, "algebra." Algebra is nothing more than a set of rules that say how I can, and how I cannot, move around the "pieces" in equations. To write down what the syntax says that I am not allowed to write, is to break the rules that govern how I can move my "pieces" in algebra.

What then is mathematics about? By itself it is about nothing. Mathematicians can fill their chalkboards, yellow pads, and their computers with formulae until their faces are blue, without having said anything about anything. When they are engaged in "pure" mathematics, it is no different than an extended chess match in which new tactics, defenses, and moves are being continually discovered. The chess match may be brilliant, creative, and interesting, but it is *about* nothing. Like chess, mathematics has no built-in semantics.

Perhaps you agree with this when it concerns "pure" mathematics, but not when it concerns simple arithmetic, as in "$40 + 40 = 80$". It seems that this equation is correct not because of the rules of arithmetic, but because of the actual world. After all, when you put 40 of something together with 40 of something, you get 80 of something. This is just how the world is. The figure on the left in the next diagram represents two rooms, each occupied by 40 people, with the rooms separated by a dividing wall. To the right is a figure representing the two rooms having been joined into one room by the removal of the dividing wall. Having joined the two rooms, there are now 80 people in the new larger room.

| 40 | + | 40 | | = | | 80 |

This is a clear instance, so it seems, of the fact that the sentence "$40 + 40 = 80$" is true, and not only in this case, but in every case. What the description of the people in the rooms did was to give "40 + 40 = 80" a semantics. Can you think of a case, a semantics, in which the sentence "40 + 40 = 80" is not true? Look back at the figures above. Now assume that the numbers represent degrees of temperature Fahrenheit. Each of the two separated rooms has the temperature of 40° F. When the rooms are joined by the removal of the dividing wall, will the resulting room have a temperature of 80° F? Obviously not. This seems to be a case where "40 + 40 = 80" is false.

In fact, what we need to do is make a clear distinction between the statement "40 + 40 = 80" as a statement of arithmetic, and the statement, "If you add 40 people to 40 people by removing a divider wall then you will have one room with 80 people." The statement of arithmetic is true. All this means is that the rules of arithmetic do not prohibit it. The statement about people is not any longer arithmetic. It is true because that's how the world happens to be. The statement about the people is an empirical statement, not a purely arithmetic statement. Like any empirical statement it is either true or false, but never necessarily true or necessarily false.

Let us agree, then, that mathematics is a very large collections of squiggles, of pieces of a game, with a very complicated set of rules about how these squiggles can be moved around. These squiggles can be given a semantics, an interpretation, in which case they cease to be examples of mathematics and become empirical statements about the world. This way of looking at mathematics is not universally accepted. It is referred to as a formalist view of the nature of mathematics, and stands opposed to platonist, logicist, intuitionist, and other philosophies of mathematics. It is not our claim that this view is the winner, or even the leading candidate, in the very technical philosophical discussions about this matter. But it is a very legitimate option and is very useful for our purposes (Ellis 1968).

Measurement

What is measurement? Measurement is the attachment or association of numbers to things or quantities in order to accomplish some purpose (Stevens 1946). This famous definition by Stevens serves as the inspiration for a more formal definition:

Where P is some set of physical objects or events, A is some function, and B is some mathematical system, by measurement A on P we mean a function which assigns to each element p_i of P an element $b_i = A(p_i)$ in some mathematical system B (Coombs, Raiffa, and Thrall 1950).

While the more formal definition seems needlessly abstract, it does indicate the elements that make up a case of measurement. In every instance of measurement there are at least the following:

That which is measured: What gets measured is a thing or event in the world, or more commonly, a quantitative property of a thing or event in the world. A quantitative property of a thing is some property about which it makes sense to speak of more, less, or equal amounts. Quantitative properties may be very concrete and easily observable— such as the height of a person, the length of a boat, or the volume of a container. Quantitative properties can sometimes be abstract and only indirectly observable, as in the cases of *IQ,* time, wind/chill factor, and the atomic weight of an element.

There is nothing mysterious about the existence of quantitative properties. There are as many such properties as people need in order to understand what they need to know about the world. In fact, you can make up new quantities as you need them. When it was noticed that the weather person's forecast of the temperature for the coming day did not satisfactorily predict how cold the day would *feel,* a new quantity was invented. The "wind chill factor" is a quantity that is a function of temperature and wind velocity. If you owned a men's store, you might want to price slacks by the size. Rather than using just waist, or just inseam, you could make up the quantity "waistseam," which is the sum of waist and inseam measured in inches. You could then sell the slacks at one dollar per unit of waistseam. Waistseam is a quantitative property that is a function of one or more other quantitative properties. The measurement of such a "derived" property is sometimes called "derived" measurement. When something is measured directly, without having first to measure something else, it is called fundamental measurement.

A set or system of numbers: Measurement involves the use of numbers. If there were no numbers, there would be no measurement. In fact, it's likely that numbers were created in order to have measurement. The set of numbers used in measurement creates a model of the quantity that is being measured. This set of numbers is called a "scale." A scale is any set of numbers used as a model of a quantitative property.

You might wonder how it is that a set of numbers can be a model for something in the real world. It is one thing to be a physical scale model of an auto accident, and quite another to be a set of numbers. But we must recall the earlier discussion of the nature of models. The model need only have some characteristics in common with the original. Can you think of any characteristics that the positive integers, 1,2, 3, . . . have in common with the height of pianos? Here is just one. If 30 is a smaller number than 32, and 32 is smaller than 34, then it follows that 30 must be a smaller number than 34. The same is true of pianos. If piano A is not as tall as B, and if piano B is not as tall as C, then piano A will not be as tall as piano C. So there is at least one property that the size of numbers and the height of pianos have in common. In fact, there are many such similarities between the properties of numbers and the properties of quantities. Because of these similarities, it is possible to use numbers to model the quantitative properties of things. The similarities you focus upon between the numbers and the things measured determine the type of scale that your measurement produces.

Why bother to use numbers as models rather than just dealing with the things themselves? The answer to this is the same as the answer to why we use scale models. Think how much easier it was to bring the scale of the accident into the court rather than bringing in the actual intersection (or bringing the court to the intersection). So it is a good deal easier to carry around the numbers that model the intelligence of your workers in deciding who should do which jobs, rather than trying out each worker at each job. And it is a good deal easier to carry to the rug store the numbers that model the square footage of your living room, rather than bringing in the living room itself.

A rule for assigning the numbers to the quantities: In every case of measurement, there must be a procedure for assigning the numbers to the quantitative properties. In the case of very concrete observable properties such as weight, this procedure can be simple. It could be: place the object on a beam balance and read off the number of units of weights that must be put on the other end in order to balance the beam. Associate with the weighed item the number indicating the number of units of weights. In the case of more abstract quantities such as waistseam, the procedure will be more complex. In the case of even more complex properties such as IQ, the procedure becomes extremely complex, and subject to many possible errors.

Scale Types

We have already defined a scale as a set of numbers used to model some quantity. A scale is a (numerical) model of some quantitative property. As a model it has all the features that we originally ascribed to the model of the traffic accident. Let's list them again:

(1) A scale is always a model "of" something to which it points, some quantitative property of a set of items.

(2) A scale is created for some purpose, to say some things about the quantity, and not to say other things. Thus we are allowed to "read off" from the scale certain features of the numbers, and attribute these to the quantities. What we are allowed to read off from the scale and attribute to the quantities are called "legitimate inferences" from the scale to the quantity.

(3) Some feature of the numbers that make up the scale are irrelevant, and are not intended to be attributed to the quantity. To attribute these irrelevant features to the quantity being measured is to make an "illegitimate inference" from the scale to the quantity.

(4) The statement of what features of the numbers making up the scale are relevant, and what features are not relevant defines the scale type, and is an interpretation of the scale. So, the type of scale that we are dealing with will depend upon the amount of information that the scale contains about the quantity being measured. We will discuss four of the most important scale types.

Nominal Scales

On occasion all that we want to accomplish by attaching numbers to things is to use the numbers for identification and classification. That is, we want to be able to distinguish one thing from another. This is true of the social security number, of the numbers on the uniforms of basketball players, and of license plate numbers. It may seem odd to think of such numbers as constituting a scale, but they do fit our definition. Suppose then that during a basketball game one shot is made by number 16, and a later shot is made by number 32. Suppose that you read this in the next morning's newspaper. Here are some inferences that you could draw. See which ones you think are legitimate.

1 The first shot was made by someone half the age of the second.
2. The two shots were made by different people.

3. The player making the second shot was heavier than the player making the first shot.

You will probably guess that only #2 is a legitimate inference. The numbers representing the players provide information only about who is the same and who is different. In fact, any set of player numbers will be equally satisfactory, will provide the identical information, just as long as each different player has a different number. We could then think of a "rule of assignment" such as the following: If (a) and (b) are things to be measured by a nominal scale, and if $f(a)$ and $f(b)$ are the numbers assigned to (a) and (b) respectively, and "iff" means "if and only if," then the scale will be adequate when:

1. $f(a) = f(b)$ iff (a) is the same item as (b),

and

2. $f(a) \neq f(b)$ iff (a) is not the same item as (b).

This leads to the idea of a "permissible transformation" of a scale. Recall that a scale is just a set of numbers that is a model of some things or quantities. A permissible transformation of a scale is anything that can be done to the numbers that make up the scale that does not in any way alter the information that the scale contains. In the case of a nominal scale almost anything can be done to the numbers, and they will still serve their purpose. If for example we added 10, or multiplied by 2, or subtracted 9, or multiplied by 3 then added 5, to the players' numbers, the numbers would still all be different for different players. What would happen to the scale if we multiplied each number by 0? Is that a permissible transformation?

Ordinal Scales

Perhaps the reason that you found the idea of a nominal scale to be odd was that, normally, we think of measurement as indicating something about more or less of some quantity. Sometimes a set of numbers is constructed that supplies information only concerning the "order" or "ranking" of some quantity. The numbers indicate only which quantity is bigger than another, while saying nothing about *how much* bigger. For example, suppose you constructed a class rank for a class of fifteen students based upon their grade point averages. The rank is below.

NAME	AVERAGE	RANK	TRANSFORMATION #1	TRANSFORMATION #2
Jane	99	1	2	3
Frank	95	2	4	6
Jim	95	2	4	6
Sue	92	3	6	9
Belinda	90	4	8	2
Jake	87	5	10	5
Joy	86	6	12	8
Larry	86	6	12	8
Henry	86	6	12	8
Kim	84	7	14	1
Laura	81	8	16	4
Jack	80	9	18	7
Celia	80	9	18	7
Annette	78	10	20	0
Ronald	42	11	22	3

The ordinal scale is made up of the set of numbers under "RANK." Note what the numbers under the "RANK" column indicate, and what they do not indicate. In other words, let's be clear as to the legitimate and the illegitimate inferences. Put simply, if two people have the same ranking number (ordinal number, to be precise), then they have the same average. If one has a larger number than another, then he or she has a lower average. And if one has a smaller number than another, then he or she has a higher average. We can put this rule for assigning the numbers as follows:

1. $f(a) = f(b)$ iff (a) is equal to (b) in the relevant quantity
2. $f(a) > f(b)$ iff (a) is less than (b) in the relevant quantity
3. $f(a) < f(b)$ iff (a) is greater than (b) in the relevant quantity.

In reading the above, recall that $f(a)$, $f(b)$, are the *ordinal numbers* associated with the items (a), (b). Note also that ">" and "<" mean "is greater than" and "is less than," respectively. Finally, ordinal numbers usually go from greater to lesser as the items go greater to lesser. In this case, however, the ordinal numbers go lesser to greater as the items go greater to lesser. That is, in the case of class rank, the lesser the ordinal number the greater the average. This is why conditions 2 and 3 are the way they are.

Suppose that you had only the class rank numbers, that is, only the ordinal scale. Which of the following are legitimate inferences from the scale to the averages?

1. Belinda's average is ½ Frank's since her rank is twice his.
2. The difference is ranking numbers between Belinda and Celia is 5, so Celia's average is 5 points less than Frank's.
3. Since Frank and Jim have the same rank, they must have the same average.
4. Joy has a smaller ranking number than Jack, so she must have a higher average.
5. The difference is ranking numbers between Annette and Ronald is only 1. Thus the averages of Annette and Ronald must be closer than those of Belinda and Celia.

Of the above, only 3 and 4 are legitimate inferences from the ordinal scale. An ordinal scale gives no information concerning the size of the differences between averages. An ordinal scale gives information only about rank order of the items according to the relevant quantity. A permissible transformation of the scale is any operation performed on the numbers that preserves the order, including identity, of the original scale. Such a transformation is sometimes referred to as a "monotone" or "ordinal" transformation. Above, there are two transformations of the original ordinal scale. In transformation #1, the rule was to multiply the original scale numbers by 2. In transformation #2, the rule was to multiply the original by 3, and subtract by 10 when the result was between 10 and 19, by 20 when between 20 and 29, etc. Is either of these transformation rules a permissible transformation of the original scale?

Interval Scales

Perhaps the greatest defect of the ordinal scale is that it gives no information about the size of the differences or intervals between the quantities that it models. For example, Ronald and Annette are only 1 point apart on the ordinal scale and 36 points apart in actual average. On the other hand Jake and Joy are only 1 point apart on the ordinal scale and only 1 point apart in average. It would be much more informative if the scale could provide information about the intervals (the size of the differences between items) as well as just the order. This is what an "interval scale" provides. Let's look at a week's temperatures in both Fahrenheit and Celsius, and some transformations of these scales.

DAY	FAHRENHEIT	CELSIUS	TRANSFORM. #1	TRANSFORM.#2
Mon.	32	0	0	0
Tues.	50	10	30	0
Wed.	59	15	45	5
Thurs.	77	25	75	5
Fri.	86	30	90	0
Sat.	89.6	32	96	2
Sun.	51.8	11	33	1

In the above chart, all of the numbers are transformations of the Celsius temperatures. Let's look first at just the Celsius and the Fahrenheit numbers. Note first that the order of warmth is the same on the two different scales. Sunday is hotter than Tuesday on both, Monday is the coolest day on both, etc. Not only this, but the order of the intervals is the same. The difference in temperature between Tuesday and Wednesday (5° C, 9° F) is greater than the difference in temperature between Friday and Saturday (2° C, 3.6° F). Thus we can infer from this scale that it warmed up more from Tuesday to Wednesday than it did from Friday to Saturday. This would not be a legitimate inference from an ordinal scale. So interval scales provide all the information that an ordinal scale provides, plus information about the order of the intervals between items.

What the interval scale does NOT provide is information concerning the ratios between the items measured. For example, the Celsius temperature for Friday (30° C) is three times greater than the Celsius temperature for Tuesday (10° C). This does not mean that Friday was three times hotter than Tuesday. These ratios between the scale numbers are irrelevant features of the numbers, and cannot be read off from the numbers to the original. We can see that Friday was not three times hotter by checking with the Fahrenheit scale. This provides all the information of the Celsius scale, and no more. On the Fahrenheit scale the ratio of three to one between Friday and Tuesday has NOT been preserved. The number 86 is not three times the number 50.

The rule for constructing an interval scale is more complicated than that for the ordinal scale because the information that you want the scale to contain his greater. Let's say that (*a*), (*b*), (*c*), and (*d*) are items to be measured on an interval scale. And $f(a)$, $f(b)$, $f(c)$, $f(d)$, are the numbers which make up the interval scale which models (*a*), (*b*), (*c*), and (*d*). And let's say that "(*a,b*) IG (*c,d*)" means that the interval or difference between (*a*) and (*b*) is greater than that between (*c*) and (*d*) on some quantity. And let's say that (*a,b*) IE (*c,d*) means that the interval is equal. Then any numbers $f(a), f(b), f(c), f(d)$, which satisfy the following conditions will be an adequate interval scale. The following are, then, the rules for assigning the numbers.

1. $f(a) > f(b)$ iff (*a*) is greater than (*b*) in the relevant quantity.
2. $f(a) = f(b)$ iff (*a*) is equal to (*b*) in the relevant quantity.
3. $(f(a) - f(b)) > (f(c) - f(d))$ iff (*a,b*) IG (*c,d*).
4. $(f(a) - f(b)) = (f(c) - f(d))$ iff (*a,b*) IE (*c,d*).

Strictly speaking these four conditions are redundant since conditions 1 and 2 are implied by the two that follow them. Do you think that transformations #1 and #2 in the table above are both permissible? In fact, if you have a set of numbers $x_1, x_2, x_3, \ldots$ which make up an interval scale, you can always get another set of numbers $y_1, y_2, y_3, \ldots$ with exactly the same information by performing the following operation on the *x*'s:

$$y = mx + b \qquad \text{where } m > 0$$

This is called a "linear transformation" (Ellis 1968). Interval scales are sometimes called "linear scales" because their information is preserved by a linear transformation. And so interval scales are sometimes said to be "unique up to a linear transformation," which means "contains the same information (unique) in spite of (up to) being altered by a linear transformation." Note that you can get the Fahrenheit scale (the *y*'s) from the Celsius scale (the *x*'s) by the following operation:

$$F = 9/5C + 32 \qquad \text{Here: } m = 9/5, b = 32.$$

Ratio Scales

We will not go into ratio scales to any degree. The point of a ratio scale is that the numbers contain all the information of an interval scale, plus ratio information about the items mentioned. Thus to the four rules above for the interval scale, we would add the following:

5. $f(a) = m(f(b))$ iff (a) is m times greater than (b) in the relevant quantity.

Thus if 32 inches is the height of table (b), and 64 inches is the height of table (a), then from the fact that $64 = 2 \times 32$ we are allowed to infer that table (a) is twice as high as table (b). That is, for example, we could infer that by placing one table (b) on top of another table (b), the result would equal the height of table (a). Ratio scales are unique up to ratio (multiplicative) transformations. If you perform a linear transformation $(y = mx + b)$ on the numbers making up a ratio scale, you destroy some of the information contained in the original (assuming that $b > 0$). The scale of 0 to 1, or 0 to 100% that measures probabilities is a ratio scale. Another feature often mentioned about ratio scales is that they have a "natural 0," that is, the absence of what is measured. This is true in the case of absolute temperature where "0" is the absence of molecular motion, but not of the normal Fahrenheit temperature where "0" is not the absence of anything.

The Measurement of Utility

Recall what utility is. It is the value that some decision-maker places on something. Alternatively, the utility of an outcome is the degree to which the decision-maker believes that the outcome will fulfill his or her goals. Can utility be measured? The answer is, "of course it can." Anything about which it makes sense to say that there is more or less, can be measured. Can love itself be measured? Suppose that we ask Mary whom she loves the most: her son Eddie, her neighbor's daughter Joy, or her husband Jake. She replies that she loves Jake and Eddie equally, and both more than Joy. In this case, we can measure Mary's love for the three as follows:

Item	Scale
Eddie	1
Joy	2
Jake	1

On what kind of scale have we measured Mary's love? You no doubt identified it as an ordinal scale. So, any quantity can be measured just as long as there is some way in which we can determine when there is more, less, or equal amounts of it. In the case of Mary's love, we took her word for it. The question that interests us then is not "Can it be measured?," but rather, "Can it be measured on a scale that contains the kind of information that we need?" Before we answer this last question, we have to determine what kind of information our scale must contain to do its job.

Scales of Utility

We have already seen that we can accomplish a great deal in decision theory using only ranking numbers, that is, using only an ordinal scale of utility with the added stipulation that the scale numbers always be adjacent. The use of the weighted ranking rule was an example of a very useful decision rule that requires only an ordinal scale of adjacent numbers. What we actually did when we used the weighted ranking rule was to treat the adjacent ordinal numbers as if they were equal interval numbers. We were thus pretending that the items measured were all equally distant from the items that were immediately greater and less. While this was a simplification that we knew was not true, it was acceptable whenever the cost of greater realism in the scale outweighed the benefit of achieving that realism.

It is also true that in economic theory where the concept of utility was first developed, there is a great deal that can be accomplished using just an ordinal scale of utility. This is true in what is called ordinal demand theory. This theory is primarily concerned with deriving (proving) the law of demand, which states that the number of units of a commodity demanded increases with a fall in price, and diminishes with a rise in price (Hicks 1956). Using what is called "indifference curve analysis," economists are able to justify this principle while assuming only that consumers are able to rank their preferences on an ordinal scale. It is also possible to accomplish a great deal in welfare economics, the theory of fair and rational social distributions of goods, while employing an ordinal measure of utility only.

But in fact, economists have always preferred to be able to employ an interval measure of utility, assuming that it could be shown that such a measure could be developed. The reason for this rests with their desire to employ the principle of diminishing marginal utility.

This is the idea that if you have one car and you add a second, you add a certain amount of value or utility to your "collection" of cars. If you have eight cars and add a ninth you have also added a certain amount of utility to your collection of cars. But the ninth car added less utility to the collection of eight cars than the second car added to the collection of just one car. Another way of saying this is that if you took the second car from the collection of two, you would subtract more utility than if you took the ninth car from the collection of nine. Suppose that $u(1)$, $u(2)$, $u(8)$ and $u(9)$ are the numbers that model the utilities of the *collections* of one, two, eight, and nine cars, respectively. In order to represent the fact of the diminishing marginal utility of the additional cars, these numbers must be such that:

$$[u(2) - u(1)] > [u(9) - u(8)]$$

Going from one car to two cars makes a greater difference than going from eight cars to nine cars.

Remember that ordinal scales do not allow us to infer from the scale numbers any information about the sizes of the differences between the quantities in the world. So an ordinal scale of utility will not allow us to use the principle of diminishing marginal utility. Only some form of an interval scale will accomplish this.

In decision theory, the principle of diminishing (or otherwise fluctuating) marginal utility is important as well. We have already seen that one of the drawbacks of the expected value rule is that it does not account for the fluctuating marginal utility of money. We have also seen that what we ultimately want to do is to replace the expected (monetary) value rule with an expected utility rule. For this, we definitely need a measure of utility that is interval, or linear. So, our question is not, "Can we measure utility?," but rather, "Is there a procedure that will result in an interval measure of utility?"

Below, two such procedures are provided, both of which give rise to interval scales. There are, however, two important differences between them. The first procedure does not require that the subject whose utility is being measured make choices or have preferences between gambles, while the second procedure does. And the first procedure requires that the subject be able to make judgments about how large the *differences* in preferences between items are, and the second procedure does not. So we have a riskless procedure that requires judgments of preference differences, and a risky or gamble-based procedure that does not require such judgments.

From the time that the gamble-based procedure was introduced by von Neumann and Morgenstern in 1947, economists and early decision theorists have placed great emphasis upon these two differences. Following the operationalist idea that two different measurement procedures would define two different concepts, they have generally refused to consider the quantity that the riskless procedure measures to be the same quantity as what the gamble procedure measures. The first quantity they preferred to call "value," while the second they continued to call "utility" (Ellsberg 1968; Shoemaker 1982). Almost to a person, these economists and early decision theorists preferred the gamble-based procedure. Let's look at the two approaches before discussing the reasons for this preference.

The Jevonsian Experiment

The possibility of the following riskless procedure was envisioned in the nineteenth century by the English economist William Stanley Jevons (Jevons 1957, Weldon 1950). Assume that it is the ability of quart bottles of liquor that is being measured.

Scotch (s)	Vodka (v)
Bourbon (b)	Irish Whiskey (i)

Step 1: The person is asked to rank the items except (v) in preference. She answers that (b) is preferred to (i), and (i) to (s). If $u(b)$, $u(i)$, and $u(s)$ are the numbers of the scale that measures the utility of the items, then:

$$\text{Condition 1: } u(b) > u(i) > u(s)$$

Step 2: The person is asked to rank the size of the difference in preference between the three items. She answers that the difference between (b) and (i) is greater than the difference between (i) and (s). That is, Irish Whiskey and Scotch are closer together in value that Bourbon and Irish Whiskey. So, our scale numbers must also satisfy:

$$\text{Condition 2: } [u(b) - u(i)] > [u(i) - u(s)]$$

For example, the scale below will do:

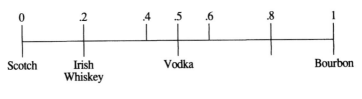

Since: Condition 1: $1 > .2 > 0$

           Condition 2: $(1 - .2) > (.2 - 0)$

     or $.8 > .2$

Placing Irish at .2 rather than .4 is arbitrary at this point, in the sense that .4 would have done just as well. In fact, any positive number less than .5 would have been satisfactory. But as more items (liquors) are placed on the scale by asking similar sorts of questions, Irish will find its "true location."

Step 3: The person is now asked to find a new item such that the difference between it and Bourbon is equal to the difference between it and Scotch. That is, it is half way between Bourbon and Scotch. She answers, Vodka, and places it at .5 on the scale as above. This satisfies:

Condition 3: $[u(b) - u(v)] = [u(v) - u(s)]$

Any set of numbers that satisfy Conditions 1, 2, and 3 will be sufficient for an interval scale of utility, and so will be sufficient for our purposes. Any transformation of the above numbers by a linear equation will produce numbers that represent equally well the person's utilities for the various sorts of liquors (Ellis 1968). What we have called (after Weldon 1950) the Jevonsian experiment is very close to what Von Winterfeldt and Edwards (1986) call the direct rating technique. They also describe various sorts of consistency checks that can be performed with the subjects to test the reliability of the numbers.

The Ramsey-von Neumann-Morgenstern Method

This approach was suggested in *The Theory of Games and Economic Behavior* (1947), a work that we have already mentioned. To be historically accurate, the gamble-based method was first proposed by the philosopher Frank Plumpton Ramsey in 1926 in an article "Truth and Probability," but due to his very early death at age 26, Ramsey's work remained unknown until the early 1950s (Ramsey 1931). The Ramsey-von Neumann-Morgenstern method asks the person to choose between options, where in every case the option will be a wager (gamble, uncertain prospect). Thus in theory, the scale is based upon observations of the subject's choices (choice behavior), rather than upon answers to questions about his or her preferences or degrees of preference difference. Recall from earlier chapters that we represent wagers as follows:

$$[x/p, \ y/(1-p)]$$

This is the wager in which you will get x with a probability "p", or y with a probability "$1-p$". Note that you will never get both x and y on the same occasion of the wager. For example:

$$[\$100/.2, \ \$20/.8]$$

Here the expected value of the gamble is:

$$(\$100 \times .2) + (\$20 \times .8) = \$36$$

The Ramsey-von Neumann-Morgenstern procedure is as follows:

Step 1: Ask the subject to order the liquors in order of preference. Suppose that the response is that Bourbon is preferred to Vodka, and Vodka is preferred to Irish Whiskey, and Irish Whiskey is preferred to Scotch.

Step 2: Since Bourbon is the most preferred and Scotch is the least preferred, assign numbers $u(b)$ and $u(s)$ to Bourbon and Scotch respectively so that $u(b) > u(s)$. To make it simple, assign a "1" to Bourbon and a "0" to Scotch, so that $u(b) = 1$ and $u(s) = 0$. We can now determine a number for Vodka, and another for Irish Whiskey. These numbers will be between 1 and 0, since both are less preferred than Bourbon and more preferred than Scotch.

Step 3: Offer the person a choice between (1) Vodka for certain or (2) the gamble [Bourbon/p, Scotch/$(1-p)$] and ask the person to state the probability (the value of p) at which he will be *indifferent* between the sure thing and the gamble. Suppose that he will be indifferent between the two when $p = .5$. Then we can calculate the number that measures the utility of Vodka by setting it equal to the gamble.

$$u(v) = [(u(b) \times p) + (u(s) \times (1-p))]$$
$$u(v) = \quad (1 \times .5) + (0 \times .5)$$
$$u(v) = .5$$

So the value of Vodka is half way between Bourbon and Scotch, as below.

Step 4: Ask the value at which he or she will be indifferent between Irish Whiskey for certain, and the wager Bourbon at p and Scotch at $(1-p)$. Suppose the answer is .2. Then:

$$u(i) = [(u(b) \times p) + (u(s) \times (1-p))]$$
$$u(i) = \quad (1 \times .2) + (0 \times .8)$$
$$u(i) = .2$$

Thus we have the scale:

And so it turns out that once the "1" and "0" have been assigned to the greatest and least preferred items, whatever the probability value is that the subject chooses in the indifference question becomes the utility value of the sure-thing item.

One of the great accomplishments of von Neumann and Morgenstern was to list a small set of conditions (the von Neumann-Morgenstern axioms) which, if fulfilled by the subject, would guarantee that:

1. An interval scale of utility exists,

and that

2. The person will use the expected utility rule to determine the value of gambles.

The authors were also able to show that if the person used the expected utility rule, then he or she must be following these conditions. Thus the axioms were logically necessary and sufficient conditions for being an expected utility maximizer. This provided a·very convenient way of testing whether people's choices are according to the EU rule, since if they violated any of the conditions it followed that they were not using the EU rule. There are different ways of formulating the von Neumann-Morgenstern axioms, one of which is as follows. For any three items (*a*), (*b*), and (*c*):

1. Either (*a*) is preferred to (*b*), or (*b*) is preferred to (*a*), or (*a*) is indifferent to (*b*).
2. If (*a*) is preferred to (*b*), and (*b*) is preferred to (*c*), then (*a*) is preferred to (*c*). If (*a*) is preferred to (*b*) then (*b*) is not preferred to (*a*). And (*a*) is never preferred to (*a*).
   If (*a*) is indifferent to (*b*), and (*b*) is indifferent to (*c*) then (*a*) is indifferent to (*c*). If (*a*) is indifferent to (*b*) then (*b*) is indifferent to (*a*). And (*a*) is always indifferent to itself.
3. If (*a*) is preferred to (*b*) and (*b*) is preferred to (*c*), then there is a PROB $= p$ $(1 > p > 0)$ such that the person is INDIFFERENT between (*b*) and $[(a)/p, (c)/1-p]$.
4. If the person is indifferent between (*a*) and (*b*), then for any other item (*c*), the person will be indifferent between $[(a)/p, (c)/1-p]$ and $[(b)/p, (c)/1-p]$.
5. If (*a*) is preferred to (*b*), then the person will prefer: (*a*) to $[(a)/p, (b)/1-p]$ where $(1 > p > 0)$.
6. Reduction of compound bets—omit.

There has been a tremendous amount of work done in an effort to test both the behavioral and the normative adequacy of these axioms (Shoemaker 1982).

Conclusions

It is not entirely clear why both economists and early decision theorists have so unanimously preferred the gamble-based approach of Ramsey-von Neumann-Morgenstern to the riskless method. One objection was that the Jevonsian procedure relied upon the person's "introspection" of his or her preferences and preference differences. The use of introspective data has been suspect in the social sciences since the advent of operationism in economics and its cousin, behaviorism in psychology. In contrast, the gamble-based approach was said to be based upon "choice behavior." However, the gamble-based approach was based upon judgments of indifference, and it was never clear what behavior (other than "verbal behavior") was indicative or indifference.

There are some other objections that are considered and rejected by Von Winterfeldt and Edwards (1986). Their candidate for the "real reason" for the traditional preference for the gamble-based approach is a commitment to "minimalism." The Ramsey-von Neumann-Morgenstern method requires only judgments of preference and indifference; whereas the Jevonsian approach requires these, plus judgments of degrees of preference difference. Von Winterfeldt and Edwards note that the Jevonsian approach is a great deal easier to apply and so appeals to "engineering-type minds" (such as themselves, presumably), while the preference for minimalism is characteristic of the "formalists" who have dominated the field. It should also be mentioned that the gamble-based approach makes little sense unless we assume a reasonably sophisticated sensitivity to the workings of probability upon the part of the subject. This works against the "minimalist" nature of this option. Finally, it has been suggested that since the utility measure will be used to predict choices in risky decision environments, it ought to be constructed from risky choices (Shoemaker 1982). This is not a strong argument. In fact, it is the other side of an argument in favor of the riskless approach. Relying as it does upon choices involving gambles, the gamble-based approach does not allow the disentangling of preferences for outcomes from attitudes towards risk. Thus a person may, using the gamble-based approach, give Irish whiskey an identical utility value of .2 on two separate occasions while having a relatively stronger desire for Irish whiskey on the second occasion. They would have this equal rating on the two occasions despite the stronger desire if, on the second occasion, the person was more risk-averse than on the first. The Ramsey-von Neumann-Morgenstern method does not allow us to discover this difference, whereas the Jevonsian method does. When all the arguments are given, the issue will eventually be decided on empirical and pragmatic grounds. Empirically, Von Winterfeldt and Edwards argue that there is reason to believe that the riskless approach is both more valid and more reliable than the other. Pragmatically, it is very much more simple to apply the riskless method, and Edwards reports that attempts to use the gamble-based method *in vivo* to develop utility functions of managers have been met with strong resistance.

Important Concepts

Models	Interpretation
Semantics	Scale types
Syntax	Permissable transformation
Jevonsian experiment	Ordinal numbers
Ramsey-von Neumann- Morgenstern	Measurement

A Measurement Problem

This summer you attend a local college close to home to pick up three extra credits. You enroll in one of those exotic communications courses, which turns out to be largely films and random discussion with the final exam as the only grade. The final exam consisted of one question, "What was the meaning of this course for you?," so you have no idea what your grade will be. You visit the instructor who makes an offer: "I'll give you a "C" for sure, or you can choose a wager in which you have a 95% chance of an "A" and the remaining 5% chance of a "D−". I never give an "F". When you jump at the chance, she recants, changing the 95% to 80% and thus the 5% chance of a "D−" to 20%. When you still want the wager, she again recants, making it a 70% chance of an "A" and 30% chance of a "D−". As this recanting continues, and as she continues to decrease the probability of an "A" while proportionally increasing the probability of the "D−", there will come a point at which you are *indifferent* between the sure thing "C" and the wager with its chance of an "A". The wager she is offering looks like the following: "A" at $x\%$, "D−" at $100 - x\%$.

The following is a list of nine options. In each case it is a choice between the certainty of a particular grade, and a wager in which you get an "A" with some probability and a "D−" with the remaining probability. You are to state the probability (of getting the "A" in the wager) at which you will be *indifferent* between the "sure thing" grade and the wager. State the probability of getting the "A" in % chance, e.g., 30% chance, 90% chance, etc. Of course, the remaining probability in % chance of getting the "D – " will be 100 minus the probability in % chance of getting the "A". Remember, there are no correct or incorrect answers. You should try to think of each of the nine options separately.

INDIFFERENT BETWEEN

Sure Thing   Wager

1. C for sure   or   _____% chance of an "A" with _____% chance of a "D–".

2. B for sure   or   _____% chance of an "A" with _____% chance of a "D–".

3. D for sure   or   _____% chance of an "A" with _____% chance of a "D–".

4. B+ for sure   or   _____% chance of an "A" with _____% chance of a "D–".

5. C– for sure   or   _____% chance of an "A" with _____% chance of a "D–".

6. A– for sure   or   _____% chance of an "A" with _____% chance of a "D–".

7. C+ for sure   or   _____% chance of an "A" with _____% chance of a "D–".

8. D+ for sure   or   _____% chance of an "A" with _____% chance of a "D–".

9. B– for sure   or   _____% chance of an "A" with _____% chance of a "D–".

We can now calculate the utility that you give to each of these sure-thing grades. We know from our discussion of expected utility theory that the value of a wager (or gamble, uncertain prospect, etc.) is calculated by multiplying the value of the items in the gamble by their probabilities and adding the results. So the value of $(x/p, y/1-p)$ is calculated as: $(x \times p) + (y \times (1-p))$. We will measure the values of your grades on a scale of 0 to 100, giving the "D – " a 0 and the "A" a 100. Once we do this, then the value of any of the "for sure" grades in the nine above cases comes out to be exactly the % that you gave to the "A" in the wager. Let's see how this works. Suppose for the "A – " in number six above, that you were indifferent between getting it for sure, or getting the wager with a 95% chance of an "A". Since you were indifferent between the sure thing and the wager, they must have equal value. We set them equal to each other, so that the first line below just says that the utility of one is equal to the utility of another. From there we calculate:

$u(A-) = u(A \text{ at } 95\% \text{ with a } D- \text{ at } 5\%)$
so $u(A-) = (100 \times .95 + 0 \times .05)$
so $u(A-) = 95$

So the utility of each of the "sure things" on the left is exactly equal to the probability number that you filled in as "___% chance of an "A"." To get a picture of how you value each of the grades relative to each other, fill out the graph below by finding the point for each grade, and drawing a straight line between each point.

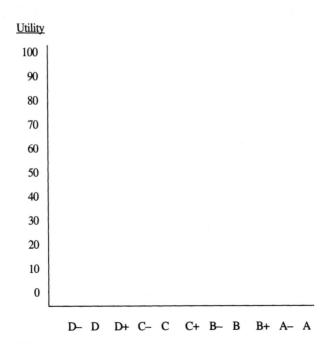

We would expect that the curve that you have produced will climb very slowly from left to right until you get to about "B−" or "B" at which time it climbs more quickly, leveling off between "B+" and "A".

You will recognize the procedure above as the Ramsey-von Neumann-Morgenstern procedure for measuring ability. Your next problem is to measure the utility of these grades using the Jevonsian experiment. Do not refer back to the above results when doing this. Compare the utility numbers later.

Appendix B

Alternative Decision Rules

Why Alternative Decision Rules?

This appendix introduces some alternative decision rules for decision-making under risk. The term "alternative" in this context refers to decision rules that are different in various ways from the expected utility rule. Jonathan Baron distinguishes between normative and prescriptive models of decision-making (1985). A normative model is one that describes the decision-making of a flawless decision-maker, a perfectly rational being. A prescriptive model provides a set of rules for the rest of us, riddled as we are by imperfections, to guide us as closely as possible to the normative model. Thus a normative model serves as the yardstick for the evaluation of the prescriptive rules. In this context, the expected utility rule provides the normative standard for the evaluation of the other decision rules.

There are a number of reasons why the investigation of such rules is interesting. First, the information necessary to employ the expected utility rule is not always at hand. Particularly in regard to probability information, we have already mentioned that it is often desirable to act on the assumption that there is no probability information rather than trying to use unreliable data while keeping in mind that it is unreliable. Second, the implementation of the expected utility rule takes time, and the stakes are often not high enough to justify the use of such time. Third, several of the alternative rules allow us to ignore probability information altogether. Since there is a good deal of data to the effect that people do not handle probability information very well, these could be useful additions to someone's decision-making tool box (Kahneman and Tversky 1972). Fourth, the structure of a decision

359

problem often allows us to deviate from the expected utility rule with a reasonable chance of impunity. For example, in a decision problem with risk, if all the probabilities are more or less the same it may be possible to simply disregard the probability information.

If there are alternative rules to the expected utility approach, how should we decide when to use one or the other of these various alternatives? D. J. Clough refers to this issue as the question of *hyperchoice,* that is, the decision as to which decision rule to adopt. His view is that the choice of a decision rule is a matter of "subjective personal preference. . . . You cannot get away from it, except by agreeing to adopt a standard approach that has been sanctioned by someone else, usually some peer group" (Clough 1984). We think, to the contrary, that it is possible to develop at least a set of reasonable rules of thumb as to when to adopt specific alternative decision rules. It is probably possible to develop a rigorous set of "metarules," a "theory of hyperchoice" for rational choice behavior. Such a theory would be based upon both the empirical results of choice simulations concerning the circumstances under which each rule approximates the expected utility rule, and upon *a priori* reasoning concerning the nature of rational action. While such a question is a normative one, no normative issue can escape purely empirical and practical issues in its resolution (Mullen 1979). This appendix will not develop such a theory of hyperchoice in any systematic way, but will make some suggestions toward that end. The simulation approach to the problem of hyperchoice has been developed recently by decision theorists (Thorngate 1980; Payne 1982; Bordley 1985), while the rational evaluation of decision rules has been a topic among economists and others for forty years (Luce and Raiffa 1957).

In this appendix we will introduce a decision problem with varying types of probability and utility information, and then arrive at a rational choice using some interesting alternative decision rules. We will then discuss some work that has been done in the evaluation of these rules. The problem for analysis is as follows.

> PROBLEM: Mary is an avid sailor. She has recently moved to Long Island and plans to purchase a boat to sail on the Sound. She has narrowed her search to three different boats of very dissimilar design. One is a full-keel boat that draws five feet of water. Mary understands that this boat is very poor sailing in "light air" (winds under eight knots), OK in winds of 8–12, good in 13–16, and pure joy over 16 knots. Her second option is a flat bottom, centerboard boat that draws only 18 inches in the board-up position. It is a dream in light air, very good in 8–12, hard

to handle in 13–16, and impossible in over 16 knots. The third option is a keel-centerboard that draws 2.5 feet with the board retracted. This boat is OK in light air, good in 8–12, OK in 13–16, and poor sailing in over 16. Mary will rarely be sailing in shallow water, and all boats are equal in her mind in all other respects. The probabilities of the various wind conditions are as follows from most to least probable: 8–12 (.35); 13–16 (.28); under 8 (.25); over 16 (.12).

If we were to solve this decision problem using the expected utility rule, we would do it as follows. The range of utility numbers is $-10...0...+10$.

CHOICES	STATES	PROB	OUTCOME	OUTCOME UTILITY	
	Under 8	.25	Very poor	–5	
Keel	8–12	.35	OK	2	
	13–16	.28	Good	4	EU of Keel = 1.65
	Over 16	.12	Joy	9	
	Under 8	.25	Dream	10	
CB	8–12	.35	Very good	6	
	13–16	.28	Hard	–2	EU of CB = 2.87
	Over 16	.12	Impossible	–10	
	Under 8	.25	OK	2	
K/CB	8–12	.35	Good	4	
	13–16	.28	OK	2	EU of K/CB = 2.34
	Over 16	.12	Poor	–1	

Figure 1

RESULT: Select choice (CB).

Rules That Use No Probabilities

We have already noted that one of the more interesting alternatives to the expected utility approach is to eliminate probability information in the selection of the rational choice. In that case, the decision tree would look like that on page 363. The terms "max for Keel," "min for Keel," etc., and "average utility" are explained below.

Some of the decision rules that might be investigated in this circumstance are as follows.

Maximin Rule

(1) Find the minimum outcome utility for each choice. (2) Select the choice with the maximum minimum utility. This rule is generally attributed to von Neumann and Morgenstern (1947).
RESULT: Select choice (K/CB).

Maximax Rule

(1) Find the maximum outcome utility for each choice. (2) Select the choice with the greatest (maximum) maximum utility.
RESULT: Select choice (CB).

Greatest Average Utility Rule

(1) Calculate the average (mean) of the outcome utility numbers for each choice. (2) Select the choice with the greatest mean utility number.
RESULT: Select choice (Keel = CB − Keel and CB are equal).

This rule is also referred to as the "equiprobable rule." If we knew that one of the probabilities was far greater or smaller than the others, even if we did not know what that probability was, we would never use the average utility rule. In a sense then this rule makes the assumption that the probabilities of the states are more or less equal, and so has the name "equiprobable rule." A tradition established by mathematician Pierre Laplace recommends that, in the absence of probability information, we should assume that the probabilities of the states are equal. While this *Laplace Criterion* has a certain rationale when dealing with events that we know to be purely random, based upon the concept of entropy (Clough 1984), when dealing with other types of events, it has little to recommend it.

CHOICES	STATES	PROB	OUTCOME	OUTCOME UTILITY	
Keel	Under 8	—	Very poor	5	(min for Keel)
	8–12	—	OK	2	Ave. utility for Keel = 2.5
	13–16	—	Good	4	
	Over 16	—	Joy	9	(max for Keel)
CB	Under 8	—	Dream	10	(max for CB)
	8–12	—	Very good	6	Ave. utility for CB = 1.0
	13–16	—	Hard	–2	
	Over 16	—	Impossible	–10	(min for CB)
K/CB	Under 8	—	OK	2	
	8–12	—	Good	4	(max for K/CB)
	13–16	—	OK	2	Ave. utility for K/CB = 1.75
	Over 16	—	Poor	–1	(min for K/CB)

Figure 2

Minimax Regret Rule

(1) Identify the maximum utility for each *state* (not for each choice). (2) Subtract each state's utility numbers from that maximum to arrive at what you would have lost had you selected a particular choice and that maximum state had occurred. These are your "regret" numbers. (3) Identify the maximum regret number for each choice. (4) Select the choice with the minimum (smallest) maximum regret number. The minimax regret rule is generally attributed to the statistician Leonard Savage (1951). See Figure 3 on page 365.
RESULT: Select choice (K/CB).

The psychology behind the minimax regret rule is that you judge the effectiveness of your choices on the basis of the opportunity losses that these choices create. Thus once the decision is made and the state, that which you do not affect, occurs, you ask yourself, "How much have I lost by not having selected the choice with the maximum outcome given the state that did in fact occur?" The regret rule attempts to avoid the maximum loss based upon the anticipatory regret or opportunity loss concepts of losses. The conditions for the use of the minimax regret rule are the same as those for the maximin rule.

Approval Voting Rule

(1) Find the average utility for each *state* (not for each choice). (2) Mark an outcome "Acceptable" if its utility is greater than the average for that state. (3) Select the choice with the greatest number of acceptable outcomes. Brahms and Fishburn (1978) formulated this rule that is similar to the satisficing rule except that in the latter the choices are evaluated sequentially with the first acceptable choice being selected (Simon 1957). In the approval voting case, each choice is evaluated against every other choice. See Figure 4.
RESULT: Select choice (Keel = CB).

The manner of defining "acceptable" is relatively arbitrary. In actual circumstances there is likely to be a natural set of external criteria based upon a value analysis that would define an acceptable outcome. In that case you would use that set of criteria and then follow the rule accordingly. For example, in the case we are using we could define an acceptable outcome as "OK or better." Then Keel and K/CB would tie with three acceptable outcomes each.

CHOICES	STATES	PROB	OUTCOME	UTILITY	REGRET NUMBER
Keel	Under 8		Very poor	−5	15 (max regret for Keel)
	8–12		OK	2	4
	13–16		Good	4 (state max)	0
	Over 16		Joy	9 (state max)	0
CB	Under 8		Dream	10 (state max)	0
	8–12		Very good	6 (state max)	0
	13–16		Hard	−2	6
	Over 16		Impossible	−10	19 (max regret for CB)
K/CB	Under 8		OK	2	8
	8–12		Good	4	2
	13–16		OK	2	2
	Over 16		Poor	−1	10 (max regret for K/CB)

Figure 3

CHOICES	STATES	PROB	OUTCOME	UTILITY	
Keel	Under 8	——	Very poor	−5 (ave. = 2.3)	
	8–12	——	OK	2 (ave. = 4.0)	
	13–16	——	Good	4 (ave. = 1.3)	Acceptable
	Over 16	——	Joy	9 (ave. = −.66)	Acceptable
CB	Under 8	——	Dream	10 (ave. = 2.3)	Acceptable
	8–12	——	Very good	6 (ave. = 4.0)	Acceptable
	13–16	——	Hard	−2 (ave. = 1.3)	
	Over 16	——	Impossible	−10 (ave. = −.66)	
K/CB	Under 8	——	OK	2 (ave. = 2.3)	
	8–12	——	Good	4 (ave. = 4.0)	
	13–16	——	OK	−1 (ave. = 1.3)	
	Over 16	——	Poor	3 (ave. = −.66)	Acceptable

Figure 4

Ranking Rule

(1) Rank each outcome 1,2,3, . . . from least to most desirable. (2) Find the average of the ranking points for each choice. (3) Select the choice with the greatest average ranking points. See Figure 5.
RESULT: Select choice (Keel = CB).

Rules That Use Probability Rankings

The Weighted Ranking Rule

(1) Rank each state 1,2,3, . . . from least to most according to how probable they are. (2) Rank the value of each outcome in the same manner. (3) Multiply the value ranking by its corresponding probability ranking and sum the products for each choice to arrive at a weighted ranking number for each choice. (4) Select the choice with the greatest weighted ranking. See Figure 6.
RESULT: Select choice (CB).

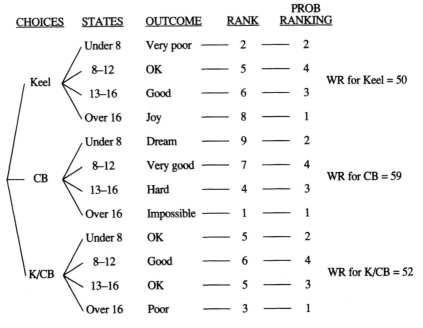

CHOICES	STATES	PROB	OUTCOME	OUTCOME RANK	
Keel	Under 8	——	Very poor	—— 2	
	8–12	——	OK	—— 5	
	13–16	——	Good	—— 6	Ave. rank for Keel = 5.25
	Over 16	——	Joy	—— 8	
CB	Under 8	——	Dream	—— 9	
	8–12	——	Very good	—— 7	
	13–16	——	Hard	—— 4	Ave. rank for CB = 5.25
	Over 16	——	Impossible	—— 1	
K/CB	Under 8	——	OK	—— 5	
	8–12	——	Good	—— 6	
	13–16	——	OK	—— 5	Ave. rank for K/CB = 4.75
	Over 16	——	Poor	—— 3	

Figure 5

CHOICES	STATES	OUTCOME	RANK	PROB RANKING	
Keel	Under 8	Very poor	—— 2	—— 2	
	8–12	OK	—— 5	—— 4	
	13–16	Good	—— 6	—— 3	WR for Keel = 50
	Over 16	Joy	—— 8	—— 1	
CB	Under 8	Dream	—— 9	—— 2	
	8–12	Very good	—— 7	—— 4	
	13–16	Hard	—— 4	—— 3	WR for CB = 59
	Over 16	Impossible	—— 1	—— 1	
K/CB	Under 8	OK	—— 5	—— 2	
	8–12	Good	—— 6	—— 4	
	13–16	OK	—— 5	—— 3	WR for K/CB = 52
	Over 16	Poor	—— 3	—— 1	

Figure 6

The Weighted Approval Voting Rule

(1) Rank the states according to probability. (2) Determine which outcomes are Acceptable either by the method used in approval voting or by an external value analysis. (3) For each choice, find the sum of the probability rankings corresponding to the acceptable outcomes. (4) Select the choice with the greatest ranking sum. See Figure 7.
RESULT: Select choice (CB).

The Weighted Elimination By Aspect Rule

(1) Rank the states according to probability. (2) Determine which outcomes are Acceptable either by the method used in approval voting or by some external value analysis. (3) Beginning with the most probable state, eliminate any choice with an unacceptable outcome on that state. Continue if necessary to the next most probable state until there is only one choice remaining. Amos Tversky (1972) formulated this rule.
RESULT: Select choice (CB)—see decision tree in Figure 7.
            Select choice (K/CB)—when acceptable = OK or better.

The Most Likely Rule

(1) Rank the outcomes 1,2,3, . . . from least to most desirable. (2) Find the most likely state for each choice. (3) Select the choice with the maximum outcome corresponding to the most likely state.
RESULT: Select choice (CB).

This rule loses its appeal in decision problems where the probability of states is different for different choices since in those cases the maximum probabilities of the choices could be quite different. See Figure 8.

Least Likely Rule

(1) Rank the states 1, 2, 3, 4, . . . from least to most probable. (2) Find the minimum (worst) outcome for each choice. (3) Select the choice with the least probable minimum outcome.
RESULT: Select choice (CB = K/CB)—see Figure 8.

CHOICES	STATES	PROB RANK	OUTCOME	UTILITY		
Keel	Under 8	2	Very poor	-5 (ave. = 2.3)		
	8-12	4	OK	2 (ave. = 4.0)		
	13-16	3	Good	4 (ave. = 1.3)	Acceptable	
	Over 16	1	Joy	9 (ave. = -.66)	Acceptable	Rank sum = 4
CB	Under 8	2	Dream	10 (ave. = 2.3)	Acceptable	
	8-12	4	Very good	6 (ave. = 4.0)	Acceptable	
	13-16	3	Hard	-2 (ave. = 1.3)		
	Over 16	1	Impossible	-10 (ave. = -.66)		Rank sum = 6
K/CB	Under 8	2	OK	2 (ave. = 2.3)		
	8-12	4	Good	4 (ave. = 4.0)		
	13-16	3	OK	-1 (ave. = 1.3)		
	Over 16	1	Poor	3 (ave. = -.66)	Acceptable	Rank sum = 1

Figure 7

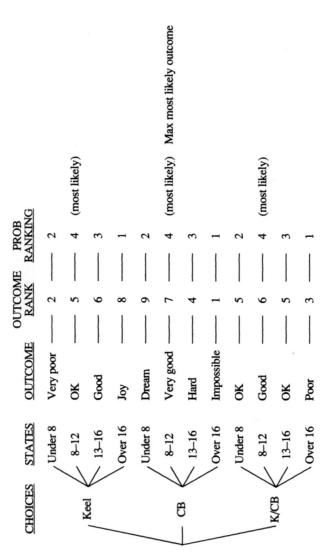

Figure 8

The least likely rule is a version of the maximin rule with probability rankings, though as a conservative rule that seeks to avoid losses, it is inferior to maximin.

Parameters for a Theory of Hyperchoice

The decision as to which decision rule to adopt ought to depend upon a number of factors. These include, first, the type of probability information that is available and how reliable it is. This information can range from nonexistent, to information concerning simply the least or most likely state corresponding to each choice, to rankings of the probabilities of states, to real probability numbers. And the information can be more or less reliable. Finally, the choice of decision rule will be affected by the spread of probability numbers. For example, in the extreme case where all states are equiprobable, rules with no probability component can be employed.

The second consideration involves the type of information concerning the values of the outcomes. While you could use a coin flip decision rule in the absence of any value information, we should stipulate that rational decision rules do not come into play unless there is some value information. The value information can range from simply identifying the least or most desirable outcome for each choice, to judgments of acceptable or unacceptable, to value rankings, to utility numbers. In specific sorts of cases, particular quantities such as numbers of deaths, or numbers of dollars can serve as the value measure. In addition, the choice of decision rule will be affected by the spread of value measures, as is evident by the rules governing when to use maximin as opposed to maximax. Finally, whether you are measuring costs in absolute terms or in opportunity loss or anticipatory regret terms will influence your choice of rules.

Third, consider the costs involved in using one rule rather than another. For example, if the probability information is unreliable, then a decision must be made as to whether a rule not employing probability data should be used or the costs of getting reliable probability data be incurred. To make this determination, a theory of hyperchoice would be extremely useful. Such a theory would give you a rating in percentage points for each rule showing its approximation to the results of the expected utility rule. Bordley (1985) suggests the following procedure for developing a rating procedure for decision rules. Construct a decision problem under risk with specific probabilities and utilities.

Simulate the problem on a computer, running many trials, so that the states occur with the frequencies that their probabilities dictate. Use the EU rule to select the choice, and also use a random selection procedure to select the choice. Presumably, the expected utility of the EU determined choices will exceed the expected utility of the randomly determined choices. Calculate the difference between these two expected utilities. Using the same problem, calculate the expected utility of choosing by some alternative rule and find the difference between it and that of the random choice procedure. You now have two differences, the difference between randomly selected and EU selected choices; and the difference between alternate rule choices and random choices. The EU/random difference should be larger. Divide it into the alternate rule/random difference to get the fraction below:

$$\frac{\text{EU (alternate rule choices) } minus \text{ EU (random choices)}}{\text{EU (EU rule choices) } \quad minus \text{ EU (random choices)}}$$

This fraction will generate a percentage that represents the proximity of the alternate rule to the EU rule. For example, in a specific case the maximim rule may provide 85% of the improvement over random choice outcomes that EU provides. Then the difference between the EU and the alternative rules must be adjusted by the costs of using the EU rule. This gives an idea of when the expected utility of doing what is necessary to use the EU rule is greater than the EU of using an alternative (Bordley 1985).

Finally, one must consider the issue of whether the situation calls for a one-time-only choice, or will be repeated many times. We have discussed elsewhere the question of why it is reasonable to use a rule such as expected utility in situations that are unrepeated. We recommend that the decision-maker look at his choice as one of a life-long approach to decision-making in general. On the other hand, there are certain life or death situations that stand outside of our day-to-day decision-making and are unrepeated. In these situations we can't rely upon random sequences to compensate for losses over the long run, first because the relevant states are not, in fact, a consequence of random factors, and second because the situation will not be repeated. Therefore, in these situations rules like maximin may, in fact, be superior even to the normative ideal of expected utility. The conditions for such a suspension of expected utility need to be investigated, and the simulation approach seems logically unable to perform this investigation.

The following are some rules of thumb for the selection of decision rules.

Rules of Hyperchoice

(1) In instances where probabilities are unknown or unreliable and where the outcome structures are such that one outcome is significantly worse than the others (which are more or less alike), the *maximin rule* is best. As the spread between the worst outcome and the others increases, so also does the rationale for the maximin rule. Extreme spreads would justify the ignoring of probability information.

(2) In instances where probabilities are unknown or unreliable and where the outcome structures are such that one outcome is significantly better than the others (which are more or less alike), the *maximax rule* is best. As the spread between the best outcome and the others increases, so also does the rationale for the maximin rule. Extreme spreads would justify the ignoring of probability information.

(3) In the absence of specific probability information except a reason to believe that the probabilities do not deviate significantly from each other and where the outcome structures do not indicate the use of maximin or maximax, the *greatest average utility rule* is best.

(4) In circumstances that call for the use of the greatest average utility rule but where the outcome value information is confined to rankings, use the *ranking rule*.

(5) In circumstances where information consists in a ranking of the likelihood of the states and a ranking of outcome values, and in which the outcome structures do not provide a strong case for maximin or maximax, use the *weighted ranking rule*.

(6) In instances where the maximin rule is indicated but where anticipatory regret or opportunity losses are the appropriate measures of loss, use the *minimax regret rule*.

(7) In the absence of probability information, and where there is a natural definition for "acceptable outcome" using some external criteria based upon a value analysis, and where the outcome structures do not justify maximin or maximax, use the *approval voting rule*.

(8) In instances where there is a ranking of probability information, and where there is a natural definition of "acceptable outcome," and

where outcome structures do not justify maximin or maximax, use the *weighted approval voting rule*.

(9) In instances where the probability information is limited to knowing the most probable state for each choice, and where outcomes are represented either by rankings or utilities, and where outcome structures do not justify maximin or maximax, use the *most likely rule*.

(10) In instances where the utility information is limited to knowing the worst outcome for each choice, and where the states are represented either by rankings or probabilities, use the *least likely rule*.

Appendix C

Mixed Strategies in 2 × 2 Games

In this appendix we introduce a simple algorithm for finding mixed strategies in 2 × 2 matrix games. You will recall from Chapter 8 that if a game has a saddlepoint, neither side has any advantage in moving from his maximin choice even if he knows for certain that the other side will always select his maximin choice. This is a reason for thinking of saddlepoint games as being stable or in equilibrium. The players will settle on their maximin choices and stay there. The outcome so produced is known as the *solution* to the game.

If games do not have saddlepoints, that means, that the players usually have something to gain by hiding their intentions from the other side and had better mix things up, i.e., use a mixed strategy.

Let us recall the football problem discussed in Chapter 8, reproduced below.

		OPPONENT'S CHOICES		
		NORMAL DEFENSE	RUSH THE KICKER	row minima
OUR CHOICES	KICK	2.7 (−2.7)	1.8 (−1.8)	1.8
	PASS	1.2 (−1.2)	2.4 (−2.4)	1.2
	column minima	−2.7	−2.4	

As we saw earlier, the maximin choice is "kick" for Rows and "rush" for Columns, but the resulting outcome in the upper right is not a saddlepoint. Since once it becomes clear to Columns that Rows intends to choose "kick," he can switch to his normal defense. The primary problem for Rows is to hide his intentions, and this he can do by randomizing his choices through the selection of a mixed strategy.

Von Neumann and Morgenstern demonstrated that in such situations either there is a saddlepoint, in which case a pure maximin strategy will guarantee some minimal amount, or, if no saddlepoint exists, some mix of choices can be found that will provide some guaranteed minimal payoff. In other words, by the choice of the proper mix of choices a player can assure himself some minimal payoff, *no matter what the other party chooses to do*.

Derivation of the Algorithm

In order to use the algorithm we first need to label the cells of our 2 × 2 game as below, where A, B, C and D represent Rows' payoffs in the cells, and A', B', C' and D' represent Columns' payoff.

COLUMNS
PLAYER

		COL 1		COL 2	
ROWS PLAYER	Row 1	A,	A'	B,	B'
	Row 2	C,	C'	D,	D'

What we want to discover is the proportion of time Rows should choose row 1 and the proportion row 2. If we label the proportion of time row 1 should be chosen as p, then it follows that we should choose row 2 in proportion $1-p$. We have relabeled the matrix to include these, as yet, unknown proportions. See top of page 377.

Our problem is to find values of p and $1-p$ that will provide a minimal payoff, no matter what columns does. Now, if the final payoff to us is independent of what the columns' player does, we should receive that payoff even when he chooses column 1 all the time, or column 2 all the time. If he chooses column 1, we will get the value A p percent of the time and the value C $(1-p)$ percent of the time, or

$$\text{Payoff(col 1)} = p \times A + (1-p) \times C$$

COLUMNS
PLAYER

		COL 1	COL 2
ROWS PLAYER	p	A, A'	B, B'
	1-p	C, C'	D, D'

Likewise if he chooses column 2 all of the time, our payoff should be:

$$\text{Payoff(col 2)} = p \times B + (1-p) \times D$$

And, since the payoff will be the same in each case, Payoff(col 1) will equal Payoff(col 2) and therefore:

$$p \times A + (1-p) \times C = p \times B + (1-p) \times D$$

Solving for p gives:

$$p(A) + C - p(C) = p(B) + D - p(D)$$
$$p(A) - p(C) - p(B) + p(D) = D - C$$
$$p(A - C - B + D) = D - C$$
$$p = D - C / A + D - B - C$$

The correct proportions for the Columns' player is found in the same way, but in this case we are looking for proportions "q" and "$1-q$" in which Columns should choose column 1 and column 2, and which will provide a minimal payoff, no matter what Rows does.

COLUMNS
PLAYER

		q	$1-q$
ROWS PLAYER	Row 1	A, A'	B, B'
	Row 2	C, C'	D, D'

Once again Columns payoff should be the same if Row chooses row 1 all the time or row 2 all the time. Therefore:

$$\text{Payoff(row 1)} = q \times A' + (1-q) \times B'$$

Likewise if he chooses Row 2 all of the time, Column's payoff should be:

$$\text{Payoff(row 2)} = q \times C' + (1-q) \times D'$$

And, since the payoff will be the same in each case, Payoff(row 1) will equal Payoff(row 2) and therefore:

$$q \times A' + (1-q) \times B' = q \times C' + (1-q) \times D'$$

Solving for *q* gives:

$$q(A') + B' - q(B') = q(C') + D' - q(D')$$
$$q(A') - q(B') - q(C') + q(D') = D' - B'$$
$$q(A' - B' - C' + D') = D' - B'$$
$$q = D' - B' / B' + D' - B' - C'$$

If each player plays with these proportions, then the expected payoff for each player can then be determined. That payoff is known as the *value* of the game. With the set of formulas so obtained, we can find mixed strategies for any 2 × 2 zerosum game that lacks a saddlepoint.

Let's apply the above formula to our earlier football example, which is reproduced below:

		OPPONENT'S CHOICES		
		NORMAL DEFENSE	RUSH THE KICKER	row minima
OUR CHOICES	KICK	2.7 (-2.7)	1.8 (-1.8)	1.8
	PASS	1.2 (-1.2)	2.4 (-2.4)	1.2
column minima		-2.7	-2.4	

ROWS' PROPORTIONS, $(p, 1-p)$:

$p(\text{row1}) = D - C / A + D - B - C$
$p(\text{row 1}) = 2.4 - 1.2 / 2.7 + 2.4 - 1.8 - 1.2$
$p(\text{row 1}) = 1.2 / 2.1$
$p(\text{row 1}) = 4/7$

$p(\text{row 2}) = 1 - p = 1 - 4/7$
$p(\text{row 2}) = 3/7$

If Rows randomizes his choices in the proportion of 4 to 3 then he can assure himself of some minimal value no matter what Columns does. To determine that value we solve for Payoff(1) so:

$\text{Payoff}(1) = p \times A + (1-p) \times C$
$\text{Payoff}(1) = 4/7 \times 2.7 + 3/7 \times 1.2$
$\text{Payoff}(1) = 2.057$

As a check we solve for Payoff(2), which should be the same:

$\text{Payoff}(2) = p \times B + (1-p) \times D$
$\text{Payoff}(2) = 4/7 \times 1.8 + 3/7 \times 2.4$
$\text{Payoff}(2) = 2.057$

COLUMNS' PROPORTIONS, $(q, 1-q)$:

$p(\text{col 1}) = D - B / A + D - B - C$
$p(\text{col 1}) = -2.4 + 1.8 / -2.7 - 2.4 + 1.8 + 1.2$
$p(\text{col 1}) = -.6 / -2.1$
$p(\text{col 1}) = 2/7$

$p(\text{col 2}) = 1 - p = 1 - 2/7$
$p(\text{col 2}) = 5/7$

Let us now find the value of Column's payoff if he uses the mixture 2/7, 5/7. Since this is a zerosum game it must work out to be -2.057.

$\text{Payoff}(1) = q \times A + (1-q) \times B$
$\text{Payoff}(1) = 2/7 \times -2.7 + 5/7 \times -1.8$
$\text{Payoff}(1) = -2.057$

As a check we calculate payoff(2) for Columns:

$$\text{Payoff(2)} = q \times C + (1-q) \times D$$
$$\text{Payoff(2)} = 2/7 \times 1.2 + 5/7 \times 2.4$$
$$\text{Payoff(2)} = -2.057$$

Given the football example and assuming that the values we assigned made sense, this means that Rows has a certain advantage in this situation and should kick most of time (4/7), but pass fairly frequently (3/7) to assure his maximin mixed strategy value of 2.057 points per play. Columns in the defensive position can minimize his loss using a rush defense most of the time (5/7), but occasionally (2/7) defend against the pass.

An interesting exercise for football buffs might be to gather statistics on passing and kicking in certain situations for your favorite team, set up a matrix representation of your team's circumstances, as we have done here, and solve for the appropriate mixed strategy. Maybe your team follows game theory and doesn't know it? Maybe they have hired a game theorist and you don't know it?

Algorithm for Mixed Strategies in All 2 × 2 Games

Having derived the proper formulas above, we can simplify the steps taken and reduce the procedure to a simple algorithm.

To find the proper mix we follow the steps outlined below:

1. Find the mix of strategies for rows by:

$$p(\text{row 1}) = D - C / A + D - B - C$$
$$p(\text{row 2}) = 1 - p \,(\text{row 1})$$

2. Find the mix of strategies for columns by:

$$p(\text{col 1}) = D' - B' / A' + D' - B' - C'$$
$$p(\text{col 2}) = 1 - p(\text{col 1})$$

3. Find the value of the game for Rows and Columns by:

$$\text{Value(Rows)} = p \times A + (1-p) \times C$$
$$\text{Value(Columns)} = q \times A + (1-p) \times B$$

The *value* of the game is that amount that each player will obtain if he plays using his appropriate mix of strategies, i.e., plays according to his MAXIMIN MIXED STRATEGY. If he uses any other mix of strategies, he may get less, but if he uses the maximin mixed strategy he can guarantee himself at least the value of the game, no matter what his opponent does.

Consider another example:

COLUMNS PLAYER

		COL 1	COL 2	
R O W S	Row 1	2, –2	5, –5	2
	Row 2	3, –3	1, –1	1
		–3	–5	

Here the upper left cell (2, −2) results from the maximin choices of both players, but in this case it is not a saddlepoint since for Columns, −2 does not equal the column minima of −3, even though 2 does equal the row minima of 2. Therefore a mixed strategy is required. Practically, if Rows knows that Columns will play column 1, then he can do better by playing row 2, but since Columns can anticipate this, Columns could shift to column 2 and lose only 1. We find the mixed strategy below:

1. Find the mix of strategies for Rows by:

$$P(\text{row } 1) = D − C / A + D − B − C$$
$$P(\text{row } 1) = 1 − 3 / 2 + 1 − 5 − 3$$
$$= 2/5$$
$$P(\text{row } 2) = 1 − P(\text{row } 1)$$
$$= 1 − 2/5$$
$$= 3/5$$

2. Find the mix of strategies for columns by:

$$P(\text{col } 1) = D' − B' / A' + D' − B' − C'$$
$$P(\text{col } 1) = −1 + 5 / −2 − 1 + 5 + 3$$
$$= 4/5$$
$$P(\text{col } 2) = 1 − P(\text{col } 1)$$
$$= 1 − 4/5$$
$$= 1/5$$

3. Find the value of the game by:

$$\begin{aligned}
\text{Value(Rows)} &= p \times A + (1-p) \times C \\
&= 2/5 \times 2 + 3/5 \times 3 \\
&= .8 + 1.8 \\
&= 2.6 \\
\text{Value(Columns)} &= q \times A + (1-q) \times B \\
&= 4/5 \times (-2) + 1/5 \times (-5) \\
&= -2.6
\end{aligned}$$

The Minimax Mixed Strategy

As discussed in Chapter 8, in zerosum games the maximin and minimax strategy produces the identical outcome. This is not the case in nonzerosum games.

If the game has no saddlepoint, the minimax mixed strategy can be found in much the same way we found the maximin mixed strategy. In that game we chose a mix of choices that minimized our loss. In this case we choose a mix of choices that minimizes the other's gain. We seek a mix of shares that will provide a fixed payoff to *the other,* regardless of what the other does. In the maximin, remember, we sought a mix of strategies that provided a fixed return *to ourselves* regardless of what the other did. As discussed in the text, this will also enable us to find mixed EESs for some 2×2 evolutionary games.

We need first to label the matrix as before, p and $(1-p)$ represent Rows' mix of choices, and q and $(1-q)$ represents Columns' mix of choices.

COLUMNS
PLAYER

		q		1-q	
ROWS PLAYER	p	A,	A'	B,	B'
	1-p	C,	C'	D,	D'

Rows Minimax Mixed Strategy

Rows needs a mix of strategies that will keep Columns value at some minimal level and that is unaffected by the choices Columns makes.

Now if the final payoff the Column's player receives is independent of what he chooses, he should receive that payoff even when he chooses column 1 all the time, or column 2 all the time. If he chooses column 1 he will get the value A' (p) percent of the time and the value jC' $(1-p)$ percent of the time, or:

$$\text{Columns' Payoff(col 1)} = p \times A' + (1-p) \times C'$$

Likewise if he chooses column 2 all of the time his payoff should be:

$$\text{Columns' Payoff(col 2)} = p \times B' + (1-p) \times D'$$

And since the payoff should be the same in each case:

$$p \times A' + (1-p) \times C' = p \times B' + (1-p) \times D'$$

Solving for p gives:

$$p(A') + C' - p(C') = p(B) + D' - p(D')$$
$$p(A') - p(C') - p(B') + p(D') = D' - C'$$
$$p(A' - C' - B' - D') = D' - C'$$
$$p = D' - C' / A' + D' - B' - C'$$

Payoff to Columns if Row uses his minimax mixed strategy:

$$\text{Columns' Payoff} = p \times A' + (1-p) \times C'$$

Column's Minimax Mixed Strategy

We can, using the same logic, find Column's mix of strategies. If the final payoff the Rows player receives is independent of what he chooses, he should receive that payoff even when he chooses row 1 all the time, or row 2 all the time. If he chooses row 1, he will get the value A (q) percent of the time and the value B $(1 - q)$ percent of the time, or:

$$\text{Rows' Payoff(row 1)} = q \times A + (1 - q) \times B$$

Likewise if he chooses row 2 all of the time his payoff should be:

$$\text{Rows' Payoff(row 2)} = q \times C + (1-q) \times D$$

And, since the payoff should be the same in each case:

$$q \times A + (1-q) \times B = q \times C + (1-q) \times D$$

Solving for q gives:

$$q(A) \times B - q(B) = q(C) + D - q(D)$$
$$q(A) - q(B) - q(C) + q(D) - B$$
$$q(A - B - C + D) = D - B$$
$$q = D - B / A + D - B - C$$

Payoff to Rows if Columns uses his minimax mixed strategy:

$$\text{Rows Payoff} = q \times A + (1-q) \times B$$

The Algorithm for Minimax Mixed Strategy in 2 × 2 Games

We give the algorithm based on the above in step form. Remember it cannot be used if the game has a saddlepoint.

1. Find the mix of strategies for Rows by:

$$P(\text{row 1}) = p = D' - C' / A' + D' - B' - C'$$
$$P(\text{row 2}) = 1 - P(\text{row 1})$$

2. Find the payoff to columns given that Rows uses his minimax mixed strategy.

$$\text{Payoff(Columns)} = p \times A' + (1-p) \times C'$$

3. Find the mix of strategies for Columns by:

$$P(\text{col 1}) = q = D - B / A + D - B - C$$
$$P(\text{col 2}) = 1 - P(\text{col 1})$$

4. Find the payoff to Rows given that Columns uses his minimax mixed strategy.

$$\text{Payoff(Rows)} = q \times A + (1-q) \times B$$

Example—Chicken

Let's look at our original version of the chicken game as an example.

DRIVER B

		SWERVE	STAY	row minima
D R I V E R	A SWERVE	5, 5	–15, 10	–15
	A STAY	10, –15	–50, –50	–50
		–15	–50	

Rows Minimax Mixed Strategy

We find the proportion or probability of choosing row 1 or p(row 1) by:

p(row 1) = D′ − C′ / A′ + B′ − B′ − C′
p(row 1) = (− 50) − (− 15) / (5) + (− 50) − (10) − (− 15)
p(row 1) = − 35 / − 40
p(row 1) = 7/8
p(row 2) = 1 − 7/8
p(row 2) = 1/8

$$\text{Payoff(Columns)} = p \times A′ + (1−p) \times C′$$
$$= 7/8 \times 5 + 1/8 \times (− 15)$$
$$= 2.5$$

Columns Minimax Mixed Strategy

Since this game is symmetric we should get the same result for Columns. We do the work for purposes of example.

$$q = D − B / A + D − B − C$$
$$= (− 50) − (− 15) / (5) + (− 50) − (− 15) − (10)$$
$$= − 35 / − 40$$
$$= 7/8$$
$$1−q = 1/8$$

$$Payoff(Rows) = q \times A + (1-q) \times B$$
$$= 7/8 \times 5 + 1/8 \times (-15)$$
$$= 2.5$$

Which is what we would expect given that the game is symmetric.

A little calculation will reveal that no matter how the Columns player chooses, so long as Rows chooses rows 1 and 2 in the ratio of 7/8 and 1/8 or 7 to 1, he will receive a maximum of 2.5. Even if Columns chooses row 2 on every occasion (the competitive "stay" strategy), he will receive 2.5, but, and here is the kicker, Rows will receive -19.375 for using the minimax strategy, which is less than the -15 he could get by using his maximin *stay* strategy and giving in all the time. In other words, Rows can force Columns to some minimal amount, but if Columns chooses he can "punish" rows for using his minimax strategy.

Example—Battle of the Sexes

The scenario for this game is given in Chapter 8, which you may wish to review at this point. You will recall that in looking for a mixed strategy ESS, we can find it by finding male and female minimax mixed strategies.

MALE ANIMAL

			FAITHFUL		PHILANDERER		row minima
F A							
E N		FAST	+5,	+5	–5,	+15	–5
M I							
A M		COY	+2,	+2	0,	0	0
L A							
E L		column minima		+2		0	

Applying the algorithm gives:
1. Find the mix of strategies for Rows (Female) by:

$$P(\text{row } 1) = p = D' - C' / A' + D' - B' - C'$$
$$= 0 - 2 / 5 + 0 - 15 - 2$$
$$= -2 / -12$$
$$= 1/6$$
$$P(\text{row } 2) = 1 - P(\text{row } 1)$$
$$= 5/6$$

2. Find the payoff to columns given that Rows uses his minimax mixed strategy.

$$\begin{aligned}\text{Payoff(Columns)} &= p \times A' + (1-p) \times C' \\ &= 1/6 \times 5 + 5/6 \times 2 \\ &= 2.5 \end{aligned}$$

3. Find the mix of strategies for Columns (Males) by:

$$\begin{aligned}p(\text{col 1}) = q = \quad &D - B / A + D - B - C \\ &0 - (-5) / 5 + 0 - (-5) - 2 \\ &5 / 8 \\ p(\text{col 2}) = 1 - \quad &p(\text{col 1}) \\ = 1 &- 5/8 \\ = 3/8 \end{aligned}$$

4. Find the payoff to Rows given that Columns uses his minimax mixed strategy.

$$\begin{aligned}\text{Payoff(Rows)} &= q \times A + (1-q) \times B \\ &= 5/8 \times 5 + 3/8 \times (-5) \\ &= 1.25 \end{aligned}$$

Since the game is not symmetric, the players here, Male and Female, receive different payoffs using their minimax mixed strategies. This appears odd and somewhat paradoxical in that if males and females receive different payoffs in evolutionary units, it would suggest that in time females will "die out." But that is of course impossible.

The paradox is only apparent, we believe, and is resolved by remembering that a successful mating is equally successful for both the male and female involved. In this hypothetical game created by Dawkins (1976), the payoffs cannot, therefore, represent only reproductive success but the other sorts of costs, in terms of energy expenditure, etc., involved in the game. Remember that in this game the females are competing with females and the males with males. An ESS for females is one that is better than any other strategy, *for females*. An ESS for males is one that is better than any other *for males*.

It appears that in Dawkins' hypothetical mating game, the females have to pay more than males for the same level of evolutionary success. Whether this is true in actual populations remains an empirical question. It should be noted, however, that in most mammalian species we generally think of the female as making a *greater parental investment* in offspring than the male. This is especially so where males do not contribute to the rearing of the young, and, of course, they cannot contribute to its gestation. In many species the male's primary investment seems to be competing with other males for access to females. *C'est la vie.*

Another Example—Hawks and Doves

The scenario for this game (Maynard Smith 1976, Dawkins 1976) is also given in Chapter 8. The matrix is given below:

ANIMAL B

		DOVE	HAWK	
DOVE		+15, +15	0, +50	0
HAWK		+50, 0	−25, −25	−25
		0	−25	

A N I M A L   A

Applying our algorithm:

1. Find the mix of strategies for rows by:

$$p(\text{row 1}) = p = D' - C' / A' + D' - B' - C'$$
$$= -25 - 0 / 15 + (-25) - 50 - 0$$
$$= -25 / -60$$
$$= 5/12$$
$$p(\text{row 2}) = 1 - P(\text{row 1})$$
$$1 - 5/12$$
$$7/12$$

2. Find the payoff to columns given that Rows uses his minimax mixed strategy.

$$\text{Payoff(Columns)} = p \times A' + (1-p) \times C'$$
$$5/12 \times 15 + 7/12 \times 0$$
$$6.25$$

And, since the game is symmetric the same mix of strategies would be arrived at for Columns, who receives the same payoff. As we suggested in the text, this outcome is not as good as the mutually agreed upon choice of (A, A') or (15, 15), but of course there is no way the animals can sit down and agree to cooperate or guarantee such an agreement.

Problems for Analysis

1. Draw up the matrix for the game of matching pennies given in the exercises in Chapter 8. Remember you win a dollar if the pennies match; you lose a dollar if they differ. Determine the appropriate maximin mixed strategy for you and your opponent, using the algorithm.

2. Do the same as in problem #1, but this time assume that you get $1.00 for a pair of heads and $3.00 for a pair of tails. Assume that if the coins differ you lose $1 if you show a tail, but lose $3 if you show a head.

3. Suppose you come to an intersection with a four-way stop sign at the same time as another individual. You think that going first is the best outcome worth 6, going second is second best worth 3. Sitting there, waiting, is third best and worth -5. Going at the same time as the other is worst worth -10, since the street is covered with ice and you will probably crash. Assume the same payoff values for any other driver, i.e., assume the game is symmetric. Depict this as a matrix game. Does it have a saddlepoint? If no communication is possible, what should you do? Suppose you decide to use the minimax (not maximin) mixed strategy. What would it be? If both use the minimax strategy, what is your expected payoff?

Appendix D

Bargaining in Three-Person Games

In this appendix we introduce some very basic principles of 3-person games that shed light on bargaining and negotiations when more than two parties are involved. Many of the principles apply in games with more than 3 persons.

Constant Sum Games and Coalition Formation

As an example of these games let us consider the 1988 elections in Israel. The two major parties, Likud and Labor, both failed to achieve a majority, and a much smaller group of religious parties appeared to hold the balance of power. However, the religious groups seemed to have overplayed their hand, and asked for so much power that Labor and Likud were forced into an uneasy alliance with each other. Nevertheless, many people were surprised by the potential power of the weaker religious parties, which seemed out of proportion to their numerical representation in the population. The following hypothetical experiment should shed light on this problem.

Imagine that you are a subject in an experiment with two other people. You are labeled A, and the others are labeled B and C, respectively. You are also told that you hold 4 votes, B holds 3 votes, and C holds 2 votes. You are instructed that your role in the experiment is to join with one of the others to form a majority that will win a prize of 100 points, but you must first agree about how to divide the 100 points. This is similar to a number of experiments that have been performed, some of which involved actual experiments, others questionnaires soliciting hypothetical responses (Gamson 1964, Chertkoff 1971, Vinacke and Arkoff 1957, among others).

We can think of this experiment as a very simple model of what goes on in parliamentary systems. Once a majority is formed, it obtains whatever there is to be had of government control. Majorities control patronage, important leadership positions and cabinet posts, the direction of domestic and foreign policy, economic and social welfare policy, etc. If one party is given a clear majority by the electorate, they get control and need not seek allies. In many cases, as was the situation in the Israeli election, no party gets a clear majority. In that case two or more parties must join together.

Which parties join will depend in large measure on whether they can come to an agreement on how to divide the goods or utilities that control of the government brings. In the case of the Israeli elections, the religious party demanded control over a wide range of domestic activity and wanted, for instance, to eliminate public transportation and sporting events during the Sabbath.

Most *n*-person games involve two phases: the first involves the formation of alliances, perhaps among powers preparing for war; the second involves playing out the two-party contest that is left. The assumption here is that if something important is at stake, the parties will eventually coalesce into two groups who will then engage in a 2-person contest to determine the final distribution of what is at stake. The theory of *n*-person games focuses attention on the first or alliance-forming aspect of the situation. Two-person theory deals with how to operate once the sides are drawn.

Games of more than two players are usually depicted in characteristic function form. You will recall from Chapter 9 that in a 2-person game, the characteristic function defines what each person can get on his own without cooperation, and what the two acting as a team can obtain. The same principle holds in 3-person games. Below is the characteristic function for the experimental game described above.

$$v(A) = 0 \qquad v(B) = 0 \qquad v(C) = 0$$
$$v(AB) = 100 \qquad v(AC) = 100 \qquad v(BC) = 100$$
$$v(ABC) = 100$$

This may look a little forbidding, but it is actually simple and useful. It tells us that any of the three participants, if they are left out, obtain nothing—they need a partner to get something. Therefore $v(A) = 0$ and $v(B) = 0$, while $v(AB)$, the *coalition* of A and B, receives 100. The coalition where all three join together is called the *grand coalition*, but since this is a constant sum game it cannot get any more than any coalition of two. In most experimental games it is outlawed, since many subjects, wishing to avoid the unpleasant task of excluding someone, may be inclined to form the grand coalition as a way of avoiding playing the game as instructed. That strategy, by the way, does make sense in certain cases. But more on that later.

If we think of the 100 points as "that which is gained by the coalitions," then every constant sum game is of the above form, if we substitute 100 points with x, where x represents "all there is to be gained." The characteristic function would look so:

$$v(A) = 0 \qquad v(B) = 0 \qquad v(C) = 0$$
$$v(AB) = x \qquad v(AC) = x \qquad v(BC) = x$$
$$v(ABC) = x$$

It is also interesting that every 3-person constant sum game through normalization can be transformed into a 3-person zerosum game, but that need not detain us here. In such games two players can get the total amount available, namely x, and a third player cannot add anything additional.

In trying to find a solution, von Neumann and Morgenstern ask us to make two assumptions as to rationality, namely:

(1) The assumption of individual rationality: no individual would join in a coalition and accept less than he can get on his own. This, you will recall, was a fundamental assumption we made when discussing bargaining in 2-person games. In this game nobody should take less than 0.

(2) The assumption of group rationality: no group or coalition will take less than is available to it by concerted action. In other words it will take x, all that is available.

In the case of our experimental game, this means no subject should agree to take less than zero, which seems obvious. The second assumption means that no two-player coalition, once formed, should ever join with a third party to form the grand coalition. If it did so, it would have to give something to the third party to satisfy his assumption #1, that he must get more than 0. If it gave him something, then it would have to violate assumption #2 for itself and accept less than the 100 points it can get on its own. Once a two-party coalition forms in a constant sum 3-person game, a third party adds no value. If he does add some value, then the above characteristic function misrepresents the situation and the game is really not a constant sum game.

The implication of the above is that the solution must be one that ends up with a two-player coalition. But which coalition? In this case it could be any of the 2-person coalitions. Since the game is symmetric, no player has an obvious advantage, and therefore each is equally likely to join with any other.

Suppose you were in such a game and were trying to find some way to assure your membership in a winning partnership. It might occur to you that one way to assure yourself a partner might be to announce that you are happy with only 40 out of the 100 points, and will be glad to form a partnership with the first taker. You would, in your announcement, have been proposing a payoff division or *imputation*. An imputation is a set of payoffs for all participants, including those excluded from the inning coalition. If you joined with B and you got 40 and he 60, your proposed imputation would look so: AB, C: 40, 60, 0. If you joined with C it would be AC, B: 40, 0, 60. In the first case you get 40, B gets 60, and C, since he is left out, gets 0. In the second, B gets 0 because he is left out.

Suppose you joined with B with the imputation AB,C: 40,60,0, and were about to announce it to the experimenter. Consider C's dilemma at this point. He is about to end up odd-man-out with nothing. He might decide to emulate your actions and make an offer to you of a split in which he received only 30: i.e., the imputation AC, B: 70, 0, 30, which is certainly better for both of you, since you get 70 which is more than 40, and he gets 30 which is more than 0. Such a proposal is said to dominate for both players, in that it is better or equal for both. But now B, as the excluded party, may make a similar proposal, say the imputation BC, A: 0, 30, 70, which dominates for B and C. In theory such bidding and counterbidding could go on indefinitely because there is no imputation for two players that couldn't be countered by one that dominates it, at least for one of the parties in a coalition and the excluded party.

In fact, such bidding could go on indefinitely, until all parties exhausted themselves. A rational player might come to realize that only by agreeing to accept 1/2, could he make a partnership with himself as attractive or better than the two others could get by joining with each other. Any arrangement in which, for instance, A took 1/2 will be as good or better than what B or C could get with each other. Either they would have to split equally with each other and take 1/2, or if they did not, then one of them must get less and would be better off going with A. Such a payoff split is said to be stable, and in this game there are three such stable splits or arrangements, namely any one of the three 2-person coalitions where the partners divide the payoff equally. These three form the *stable set of imputations,* which is the von Neumann and Morgenstern solution to the game.

We can illustrate the stable set in a payoff table below:

	PLAYERS PAYOFF		
	A	B	C
COALITION			
AB	50	50	0
AC	50	0	50
BC	0	50	50

In the above, if the coalition AB forms then A gets 50, B gets 50, and C gets nothing. The stable set represents a sort of equilibrium in that in an interminable series of offers and counter-offers, players' offers should tend to converge on the 50-50 split. It has another property in that within the stable set, no one outcome or imputation dominates a third, for *both* players. If personalities are not involved no participant should prefer to be in one of the winning coalitions rather than another, and therefore it qualifies as an equilibrium of sorts. The stable set of imputations is an elusive concept, to be sure, but it has a rather elegant mathematical justification that cannot concern us here. Part of its appeal for us is that in the simple majority game of three persons, it conforms with common sense, as we normally use the term.

Strength in Weakness

Let us recall the experimental game in which A had 4 votes, B had 3 votes and C had 2 votes. As discussed earlier, this situation has been presented to subjects in numerous studies, in both survey form (asking participants how they would act), and in actual experiments where their behavior was observed. Such studies produce a surprising *strength in weakness* phenomenon. People seem to expect that the two weaker parties will unite and that the stronger of the two will receive somewhat more than the weaker in a coalition. For instance, in survey studies most subjects who were asked to think of themselves as B above said they preferred membership with C rather than with A. And in such a coalition B expected to get more of the payoff. Often they used their votes to suggest the appropriate division. Where B held 3 and C held 2, they often suggested a 60-40 split of the winnings. Those in the position of A showed a preference for C with 2 votes over B who had 3.

Many hypotheses have been offered to explain these results. They appear paradoxical in that since any two players form a majority, they should split the winnings equally, as game theory suggests. Some research (Roth 1979) indicates that with extended bargaining, the *strength in weakness* effect tends to fade, as subjects come to recognize the power of the excluded party to make competing offers. Or the paradox can be explained if the subjects *overinterpreted* the experimental situation and thought about it in more realistic terms. After all, votes usually mean something. Those with more stock have more votes and also get more earnings, because they have invested more. In actual political situations, the weaker party may, in fact, be desirable because weaker political parties have fewer members, and therefore can provide more to their constituents per capita, than could larger parties (Riker 1962). In this hypothetical example, assuming votes represent constituents, then B and C can divide the 100 units among 5 members each, obtaining 20 units per capita, whereas a coalition of A and B needs to share the 100 units among 7 members where each gets approximately 14 units. This reasoning, however, suggests that the experimental game might be better characterized as a 9-player game. A proper analysis of such a game is, however, beyond the scope of this book.

The Israeli elections of 1988 appeared, at least initially, to support the strength in weakness hypothesis. But the religious parties asked for too much. If our analysis is correct, the religious parties lost out because they failed to recognize that their weakness provided strength only so long as it could be of advantage to one of the major parties. By demanding too much they were acting like a hypothetical player in a three-person zerosum game demanding more than half of the payoff, and in so doing, assured the other two that they could find a better arrangement with each other. To be sure there were other, complicating factors that, in the end, determined the result.

In an interesting sidelight, Riker (1962) suggests that subgroups will form within any winning coalition whenever it gets too big, and attempt to dump some members to increase the per capita share of those remaining. Riker argued therefore that minimal winning coalitions should be the rule, i.e., coalitions should only rarely get bigger than they need to be to win.

In actual political circumstances, not all coalitions are equally likely. There may be factors external to a game, as depicted in the characteristic function, which are important. For instance in parliamentary systems some parties never join, such as those on the extreme left and extreme right, because to do so would be to deprive them of constituent support. They also have, as it were, an ideological distaste for each other. Therefore, when considering coalitions in such systems, not all potential arrangements are possible.

It would seem best to find a way to represent those values and concerns within the utilities assigned. If a coalition containing a despised party is unacceptable to another party, then the coalition containing both should be assigned zero worth. But if some coalitions provide different payoffs than others, then the game is not, strictly speaking, constant sum.

Standards of Behavior

Von Neumann and Morgenstern suggested that there may be in any group or society certain restraints on the behavior of individuals that limit the extent to which they may exploit an excluded party. If these restraints are accepted by the parties and enforced, they, in effect, become part of the "rules of the game," defining what can and what cannot be done. These are referred to by von Neumann and Morgenstern as *standards of behavior*. In actual parliamentary politics, the losing side retains considerable strength, usually by virtue of constitutional rules or past practice. If they didn't, they would merely go home, since they would have no function. There would be no such thing as a loyal opposition. One reason for these restraints is plain, and that is to maintain the support, however grudging, of the weaker parties' constituencies. Without such restraints political democracy would quickly degenerate into mob rule. There are numerous other reasons for such "standards of behavior," which we cannot discuss in this context.

If you think of three friends who enjoy tennis, an obvious standard of behavior would require that even if any two can play and obtain the utility associated with the pleasure of the game, they will probably rotate playing so as to maintain social harmony. If two players formed a coalition and continually snubbed a third, then clearly they risk threatening a relationship that may have great value outside the context of tennis playing.

Nonconstant Sum Three-person Games

While there are many cases where a third party can add no value once two have joined together, it is far more commonly the case for additional members to bring in some additional value. Any game where one or more of the coalitions provide different payoffs are classified as nonconstant sum 3-person games. If the grand coalition provides more than any of the 2-player coalitions, then everybody can add some value, and the grand coalition makes sense. In fact, it is the only sensible or rational solution, according to the assumption of societal rationality.

Consider the following example. Albert owns a restaurant in a good location, which is currently earning $100,000. He has been approached by a famous chef, Brabent, who claims he can easily help triple profits if he becomes associated with the restaurant. He bases this on his belief that he will attract not only more clients, but more affluent clients to the restaurant, and that therefore prices can be raised. He is currently earning $75,000. Cal is a young, but rising singer-pianist, who currently earns $50,000, and he has proposed to Albert that they form a partnership, since he believes his type of entertainment could considerably improve the business. Suppose he thinks he can bring in at least double the number of patrons. Brabent and Cal figure they could go into business together, but that would require furnishing a restaurant, various start-up costs, etc. All three consult with a leading restaurant accountant who knows the trade well. He gives the following estimates of expected yearly profits, over a five year period, for the different partnerships, including the one in which all three join together. He uses the average for five years since he realizes that different arrangements may take longer to reach their potential than others. Having studied game theory, he lists these estimates in the form of a characteristic function. All numbers are in thousands. Albert is A, Brabent is B, and Cal is C.

$$v(A) = 100 \qquad v(B) = 75 \qquad v(C) = 50$$
$$v(AB) = 300 \qquad v(AC) = 250 \qquad v(BC) = 200$$
$$v(ABC) = 400$$

All three are in negotiations, trying to determine how they should distribute the profits. Brabent points out that he triples Albert's profits and thinks he should get half or $150,000. He thinks it would be useful to bring in Cal who adds another $100,000, but doesn't like Cal's proposal to take $75,000. Cal claims it wouldn't be worth his while for less than that. How to decide what is reasonable, and what is fair?

As in 2-person bargaining it is useful to normalize the characteristic function to see the value each person adds. We do this just as we did in the 2-person case. You might want to review that section now, if you have forgotten it.

$$v(A) = 100 - 100 \qquad v(B) = 75 - 75 \qquad v(C) = 50 - 50$$
$$v(AB) = 300 - 100 - 75 \quad v(AC) = 250 - 100 - 50 \quad v(BC) = 200 - 75 - 50$$
$$v(ABC) = 400 - 100 - 75 - 50$$

which with a little calculation gives the following normalized characteristic function:

$$v(A) = 0 \qquad v(B) = 0 \qquad v(C) = 0$$
$$v(AB) = 125 \qquad v(AC) = 100 \qquad v(BC) = 75$$
$$v(ABC) = 175$$

This gives us the additional value, which is added in the various arrangements. It is typical of many human endeavors that value is added by cooperative engagements. But we still have no clear way of determining a sound division. Any arrangement in which each got what they can get alone and each partnership of two, once formed, got at least what it could get without a third party would satisfy the conditions of individual and societal rationality. How much each member got in such an arrangement after that would depend on bargaining ability, and other factors.

The Shapley Value

Is there some arrangement that could be said to be fair? Perhaps the idea of a value-added division that we used to define fairness in the 2-person case can be useful here. In fact one possible solution is based on that reasoning, namely the Shapley (1953) value. In the 2-person case, we allotted one half the value added by a partnership to each player. That made sense because no partnership was possible without both participants. Here such an approach would make sense for the two-member coalitions, but it ignores the differences in bargaining power that players have by virtue of alternative arrangements. Also, in the case of the grand coalition, the value a player adds depends on when he enters the coalition. The Shapley value solution assumes a completely random sequence of coalition formation.

To work it out we first look at the two-member coalitions, which can each form in two ways. These are listed below, as is the value added by the player who enters last, and the expected added value assuming the random sequence.

Sequence of Formation	Value Added	By Player	Prob	Expected Value-added
A B	125	B	1/6	20.8
B A	125	A	1/6	20.8
A C	100	C	1/6	16.6
C A	100	A	· 1/6	16.6
B C	75	C	1/6	12.5
C B	75	B	1/6	12.5

In other words if the sequence of coalition formation were totally random, then 1/6 of the time A would add 125 or an expected value-added of 20.8 when he joins with B. 1/6 of the time he would add 100 when he joins with C, for an expected added-value of 16.6.

Once the 2-player coalitions have formed there are three ways the grand coalition can form.

Sequence of Formation	Value Added	By Player	Prob	Expected Value-added
A B C	50	C	1/3	16.6
A C B	75	B	1/3	25
B C A	100	A	1/3	33.3

A partner's expected contribution is therefore the sum of his expected contributions to all the coalitions he can join. For A, this is 20.8 + 16.6 in the two-member partnerships, and 33.3 in the grand coalition for a total of 70.8. Similar calculation will reveal that B's expected value is 58.4, and C's expected value is 45.8.

The Shapley values found in this way will always sum to the total in the grand coalition. In order to determine the actual payoff we need to add these values to the original individual values. We reproduce the original version of the characteristic function below:

$$v(A) = 100 \qquad v(B) = 75 \qquad v(C) = 50$$
$$v(AB) = 300 \qquad v(AC) = 250 \qquad v(BC) = 200$$
$$v(ABC) = 400$$

In the grand coalition that pays 400, Albert should get $100 + 70.8$ or 170.8. Brabent should get 133.4, and Cal 95.8. These figures represent their initial position alone and their various expected contributions to the coalitions that form, assuming they form randomly. Interestingly, if we used the Shapley value to determine a solution to the 3-person zerosum case it would give each player 1/3, which of course is the long-term expected payoff in that game. Also if a situation is completely symmetrical it will provide equal payoff to all parties, which it must if it is to be considered *fair*.

The Core

Consider the following characteristic function:

$$v(A) = 0 \qquad v(B) = 0 \qquad v(C) = 0$$
$$v(AB) = 8 \qquad v(AC) = 8 \qquad v(BC) = 8$$
$$v(ABC) = 10$$

This is a nonconstant sum game. What is a possible solution? Let us assume that all 2-person coalitions are equally likely and assume that the AB coalition forms. And since the game is symmetric among the 2-person solutions, it resembles the constant sum case, and a reasonable division would be the 50-50 split where A got 4 and B got 4. If they are, as a team, approached by C who seeks membership, they should, as rational players, welcome his membership. But what should be get? The answer is that the bargaining between AB and C, is bounded only by 0, which is the least C can obtain (under the assumption of individual rationality), and 2, which is the maximum he can obtain (unless AB violates the assumption of group rationality).

Where the division will settle is dependent, as usual in such cases, on bargaining ability, etc. If you consider that all 2-player coalitions are equally likely, a very large number of imputation sets is possible. Furthermore, in such a game it matters very much which coalition forms first, and who is initially excluded. In that regard, its dynamics are very much like the constant sum case in that someone is bound to be slighted in some way.

Consider the following, very different situation.

$$v(A) = 0 \qquad v(B) = 0 \qquad v(C) = 0$$
$$v(AB) = 4 \qquad v(AC) = 4 \qquad v(BC) = 4$$
$$v(ABC) = 10$$

In this case, the most a player can expect in a 2-member coalition is half of 4, or 2. Once such a coalition forms, it must bargain with the excluded party who brings an additional value of 6. Such a game is said to have a *core* in that it is possible for the assumption of group rationality to be satisfied simultaneously for all potential coalitions. The division 3,3,4 would satisfy as would the equal split where each receives 3 and 1/3. Games with cores are very different from those without. Notice that here, the order in which coalitions form is less important, and no party need be slighted. If anything the excluded party in games with cores has an advantage in that he has so much to add. He is a star of sorts.

Universal Veto Power—Unanimity Rule

Consider three high school students whose car has broken down. They need $.25 cents to make a phone call to get help. Suppose they jointly hold a winning lottery ticket for a school event, but must be present to claim the $100 prize. With a phone call they can get to the event in time. John has $.10, Philip had $.10 and Mary has $.05. Suppose further that they have started to bicker about how to divide the winnings. Is there any basis upon which to decide? We can represent this in characteristic function form so:

$$v(A) = \$0 \qquad v(B) = \$0 \qquad v(C) = \$0$$
$$v(AB) = \$0 \qquad v(AC) = \$0 \qquad v(BC) = \$0$$
$$v(ABC) = \$100$$

In this case, no 2-member coalition can get anything, all three members' contributions are necessary. This is an extreme case where the *core* is very large. Based on individual rationality, any payoff arrangement where each player gets more than zero is acceptable as a solution. Furthermore, any payoff to any 2-player coalition of more than 0 satisfies the rule of societal rationality for the two-member groups. Finally to be a solution, all that is available (in this case $100) must be realized. In this case the solution, according to von Neumann and Morgenstern, would be the grand coalition with any distribution of the $100. In other words, the solution would be the imputation set in which A, B, and C each got something, but any arrangement would satisfy.

This reflects the fact that the third member to join the grand coalition is the one who adds all the value. And since any member can choose to be the last to join, each has veto power over the group's success. Such a situation is equivalent to a *rule of unanimity* in any organization. Needless to say, if there are no clear-cut standards of behavior in such situations, chaos will reign, and just as often the prize will be lost due to the various claims of each member who holds a veto over the group's actions. If they choose the Shapley value, they would divide the winnings equally, after returning each person's coin.

Monopoly Veto Power

Suppose a boy has a box of nails and is approached by two others with hammers. They have been offered $10 to repair a fence. A is the boy with the nails, B and C the boys with the hammers. Assume only two boys are needed for the job. We can depict this in characteristic function form so:

$$v(A) = 0 \qquad v(B) = 0 \qquad v(C) = 0$$
$$v(AB) = \$10 \qquad v(AC) = \$10 \qquad v(BC) = 0$$
$$v(ABC) = \$10$$

In this situation, A has a monopoly position and can demand any payment for his assistance. A must be in a coalition if it is to gain anything, and since B and C can assure nothing with each other, neither has much bargaining power *vis à vis* A. Whatever B offers to give A, C can better it, and such an outcome will dominate for C and for A. Suppose B offers A the payoff division AB, C: 7, 3, 0. C can then offer the imputation AC, B: 8, 0, 2, which is better for A and for

C, and better than anything B can offer C. The only thing that limits A's power are the other things B and C can do if A fails to provide them with sufficient return. If they have no where else to turn, then A is powerful indeed. Clearly monopolies require regulation, or standards of behavior if they are not to become grossly exploitative.

One interesting possibility in the above is one where B and C form a union and agree to refuse to entertain separate bids from A and agree to share their returns equally. In such a case they *as a team* have as much power as B. Of course, if there are many people with hammers who haven't joined the union, then their cooperation will not do them much good.

There is an enormous richness to the work on *n*-person game theory. This appendix was designed to highlight some of the ways it can be used to better conceptualize multiparty negotiations. If it has whetted your appetite for more—good. There is a virtual feast for those who wish to pursue it. Good places to start are Luce and Raiffa (1957), Rapoport (1970), and Shubik (1975, 1982).

Bibliography

Adams, Ernest, and Fagot, Robert. 1959. "A Model of Riskless Choice." *Behavioral Science* 4: 1–9.

Anderson, Craig A.; Horowitz, Leonard M.; and French, Rita D. 1983. "Attribution Style of Lonely and Depressed People." *Journal of Personality and Social Psychology* 45: 127–36.

Arkes, Hal R., and Blumer, Catherine. 1985. "The Psychology of Sunk Cost." *Organizational Behavior and Human Decision Processes* 35: 124–40.

Aronson, Elliot, and Mills, Judson. 1959. "The Effect of Severity of Initiation on Liking for a Group." *Journal of Abnormal and Social Psychology* 59: 177–81.

Asch, Solomon E., 1955. "Opinions and Social Pressures." *Scientific American* 193: 31–35.

Bandura, Albert; Ross, Dorothea M.; and Ross, Sheila A. 1963. "Imitation of Film Mediated Aggressive Models." *Journal of Abnormal and Social Psychology* 66: 3–11.

Bar-Hillel, Maya. 1982. "Studies of Representativeness." In *Judgment under Uncertainty: Heuristics and Biases*. Edited by Daniel Kahneman, Paul Slovic, and Amos Tversky. Cambridge, England: Cambridge University Press.

Baron, Joan, and Sternberg, Robert J. 1987. *Teaching Thinking Skills*. New York: W. H. Freeman.

Baron, Jonathan. 1988. *Thinking and Deciding*. Cambridge, England: Cambridge University Press.

——. 1985. *Rationality and Intelligence*. Cambridge, England: Cambridge University Press.

Black, Max. 1962. *Models and Metaphors*. Ithaca, N.Y.: Cornell University Press.

406 Bibliography

Bordley, Robert F. 1985. "Comparing Different Decision Rules." *Behavioral Science* 30: 230–39.

Brahms, Samual and Fishburn, Peter, 1978. "Approval Voting." *American Political Science Review*. 72: 831–47.

Brown, Roger. 1986. *Social Psychology*. Cambridge, England: Cambridge University Press.

Chertkoff, Jerome M. 1971. "Coalition Formation as a Function of Differences in Resources." *Journal of Conflict Resolution* 15: 371–83.

Clough, Donald J. 1984. *Decisions in Public and Private Sectors*. Englewood Cliffs: Prentice Hall.

Coombs, Clyde H.; Ralffa, Howard; and Thrall, Robert M. 1950. "Some Views on Mathematical Models and Measurement Theory." In their *Decision Processes*. New York: Wiley.

Davidson, Donald, Suppes, Patrick and McKinsey, John. 1957. *Decision Making: An Experimental Approach*. Stanford: Stanford University Press.

Dawes, Robyn. 1988. *Rational Choice in an Uncertain World*. New York: Harcourt Brace.

Dawkins, Richard. 1976. *The Selfish Gene*. London: Oxford University Press.

Dreyfus, Herbert, and Dreyfus, Stuart. 1986. *Mind Over Machine: The Power of Human Intuition and Expertise in the Era of the Computer*. New York: The Free Press.

Edwards, Ward, and Newman, J. Robert. 1982. *Multiattribute Evaluation*. Beverly Hills: Sage Publications.

Ellis, Brian. 1968. *Basic Concepts of Measurement*. Cambridge, England: Cambridge University Press.

Ellsberg, Daniel. 1968. "Classical and Current Notions of Measurable Utility." In *Utility Theory: A Book of Readings*. Edited by A. N. Page. New York: Wiley.

Elster, Jon. 1979. *Ulysses and the Sirens: Studies in Rationality and Irrationality*. New York: Cambridge University Press.

Festinger, Leon. 1964. *Conflict, Decision and Dissonance*. Stanford: Stanford University Press.

———. 1957. *A Theory of Cognitive Dissonance*. Evanston, Ill.: Row Peterson.

Fisher, Roger, and Ury, William. 1981. *Getting to Yes: Negotiating Agreement without Giving In*. Boston: Houghton Mifflin.

Frank, Robert H. 1985. *Choosing the Right Pond: Human Behavior and the Quest for Status*. New York: Oxford University Press.

Ferguson, George A. 1966. *Statistical Analysis in Psychology and Education*. New York: McGraw-Hill.

Gamson, William A. 1964. "Experimental Studies in Coalition Formation." *Advances in Experimental Social Psychology,* edited by Leonard Berkowitz, vol. I. New York: Academic Press.

Gamson, William A., Fireman, B. and Retina, S., 1982. *Encounters with Unjust Authority.* Homewood, Ill.: Dorsey Press.

Giere, Ronald. 1979. *Understanding Scientific Inference.* New York: Holt, Reinhart.

Green, Paul E., and Wind, Yoram. 1973. *Multiattribute Decisions in Marketing.* Hinsdale, Ill.: Dryden Press.

Hammond, Kenneth R.; McClelland, Gary H.; and Mumpower, Jeryl. 1980. *Human Judgment and Decision Making.* New York: Praeger Publishers.

Harvey, John H., and Weary, Gifford. 1985. *Attribution: Basic Issues and Applications.* Orlando, Fla.: Academic Press.

Hession, Enda. 1977. "The Application of Multiattribute Utility Models to Some Uncertain Decision Situations in Areas of Business and Public Policy." In *Decision Making and Change in Human Affairs.* Edited by Helmut Jungermann and Gerard de Zeeuw. Boston: D. Reidel Publishing Company.

Hicks, John R. 1956. *A Revision of Demand Theory.* Oxford: at The Clarendon Press.

Hofstadter, Douglas. 1985 "The Prisoner's Dilemma, Computer Tournaments, and the Evolution of Cooperation." In *Metamathematical Themas.* New York: Basic Books.

Hogarth, Robin M. 1983. *Judgment and Choice.* New York: Wiley.

Howard, Ronald A. 1980. "An Assessment of Decision Analysis." *Operations Research* 28: 4–27.

Janis, Irving. 1983. *Short-Term Counseling.* New Haven: Yale University Press.

———. 1972. *Victims of Groupthink.* Boston: Houghton Mifflin.

Janis, Irving, and Mann, Leon. 1977. *Decision Making: A Psychological Analysis of Conflict. Choice and Commitment.* New York: Free Press.

Jevons, William Stanley. 1957. *Theory of Political Economy.* New York: Kelley and Millman.

Jukes, Thomas H. 1989. "Apocalypse and Apple Pie." *The Wall Street Journal* (letter to the editor) April 7.

Jungermann, Helmut, and De Zeeuw, Gerard, eds. 1977. *Decision Making and Change in Human Affairs.* Boston: D. Reidel Publishing.

Kahneman, Daniel; Slovic, Paul; and Tversky, Amos. 1982. *Judgment under Uncertainty: Heuristics and Biases.* Cambridge, England: Cambridge University Press.

Kahneman, Daniel, and Tversky, Amos. 1979. "Prospect Theory: An Analysis of Decision under Risk." *Econometrica* 47: 263–91.

Kahneman, Daniel and Tversky, Amos. 1972. "Subjective probability: a judgment of representativeness." *Cognitive Psychology* 3: 430–454.

Kant, Immanuel. 1985. *Foundations of Metaphysics of Morals*. Translated by Lewis White Beck. New York: MacMillan Publishing.

Keeney, Ralph, and Raiffa, Howard. 1976. *Decisions with Multiple Objectives*. New York: Wiley.

Latane, Bib, and Darley, John M. 1970. *The Unresponsive Bystander: Why Doesn't He Help?* New York: Appleton-Century-Crofts.

Lewin, Kurt. 1935. *Dynamic Theory of Personality*. New York: McGraw Hill.

Lichtenstein, Sarah; Slovic, Paul; Fischhoff, Baruch. 1978. "Judged Frequency of Lethal Events." *Journal of Experimental Psychology* 4: 551–8.

Luce, R. Duncan, and Raiffa, Howard. 1957. *Games and Decisions*. New York: Wiley.

McCall, Robert B. 1986. *Fundamental Statistics for the Behavioral Sciences* 4th ed., New York: Harcourt Brace Jovanovich.

MacCrimmon, Kenneth, and Wehrung, Donald. 1986. *Taking Risks*. New York: Free Press.

Maynard Smith, John and Price, G. R., 1973. "The Logic of Animal Conflict." *Nature* 246: 15–18.

Maynard Smith, John, 1976. "Evolution and the Theory of Games," *American Scientist* 64: 41–45.

Michalos, Alex C. 1967. "Postulates of Rational Preference." *Philosophy of Science* 34: 18–23.

Milgram, Stanley. 1974. *Obedience to Authority*. New York: Harper and Row.

Mill, John Stuart. 1882. *Utilitarianism*. London: Longmans Green and Company.

Mullen, John D. 1979. "Does the Logic of Preference Rest upon a Mistake." *Metaphilosophy* 10: 247–55.

———. 1970. "Michalos' Postulates of Rational Preference." *Philosophy of Science* 37: 618–19.

Nash, John F. 1953. "Two Person Cooperative Games." *Econometrica* 21: 128–40.

Nemeth, Chalan. 1979. "The Role of the Active Minority in Intergroup Relations." In *The Social Psychology of Intergroup Relations*. Edited by William Austin and Stephen Worchel. Monterey, Calif.: Nelson Hall.

Nisbett, Richard E.; Borgida, Eugene; Crandall, Rick; and Reed, Harvey. 1982. "Popular Induction: Information Is Not Necessarily Informative. In

Judgment under Uncertainty: Heuristics and Blases. Edited by Daniel Kahneman, Paul Slovic, and Amos Tversky. Cambridge, England: Cambridge University Press.

Nisbett, Richard, and Ross, Lee. 1980. *Human Inference: Strategies and Shortcomings of Informal Judgment.* Englewood Cliffs: Prentice Hall.

Payne, John. 1982. "Contingent Decision Behavior." *Psychological Bulletin* 92: 382–402.

Perkins, David N. 1987. "Thinking Frames." In *Teaching Thinking Skills.* Edited by Joan Baron and Robert Sternberg. New York: W. H. Freeman.

Pruitt, Dean G. 1981. *Negotiating Behavior.* New York: Academic Press.

Raiffa, Howard. 1982. *The Art and Science of Negotiations.* Cambridge, Mass., Harvard University Press.

———. 1968. *Decision Analysis.* Reading, Mass.: Addison Wesley.

Ramsey, Frank Plumpton, 1931. *Foundations of Mathematics and Other Essays.* New York: Harcourt, Brace & Co.

Rapoport, Anatol, Guyer, Melvin J. and Gordon, David G. 1976. *The 2 × 2 Game.* Ann Arbor: University of Michigan Press.

Rapoport, Anatol and Chammah, Albert M., 1969. *The Prisoner's Dilemma: A Study of Conflict and Cooperation,* Ann Arbor: University of Michigan Press.

Rapoport, Anatol. 1970. *N-person Game Theory: Concepts and Applications.* Ann Arbor: University of Michigan Press.

———. 1969. *Two-Person Game Theory: The Essential Ideas.* Ann Arbor: University of Michigan Press.

Rescher, Nicholas, 1983. *Risk.* Lanham, Md.: University Press of America.

Riker, William H. 1962. *The Theory of Political Coalitions.* New Haven, Conn.: Yale University Press.

Ross, Lee, and Anderson, Craig A. 1982. "Shortcomings in the Attribution Process: On the Origins and Maintenance of Erroneous Social Assessments." In *Judgment under Uncertainty: Heuristics and Biases.* Edited by Daniel Kahneman, Paul Slovic, and Amos Tversky. Cambridge, England: Cambridge University Press.

Roth, Byron M. 1979. "Competing Norms of Distribution in Coalition Games." *Journal of Conflict Resolution* 23: 513–37.

Savage, Leonard J. 1951. "The Theory of Statistical Decision." *Journal of the American Statistical Association* 46: 55–67.

Schelling, Thomas C. 1984. *Choice and Consequences: Perspectives of an Errant Economist.* Cambridge, Mass.: Harvard University Press.

———. 1960. *The Strategy of Conflict.* Cambridge, Mass.: Harvard University Press.

Shapley, Lloyd S. 1953. "A Value for n-Person Games." In *Contributions to the Theory of Games, vol. II. Annals of mathematical studies.* Edited by H. W. Kuhn and A. W. Tucker. Princeton, N.J.: Princeton University Press.

Shaughnessy, J. Michael. 1981. "Misperceptions of Probability." In *Teaching Statistics and Probability.* Washington, D.C.: Yearbook of the National Council of Teachers of Mathematics.

Shoemaker, Paul. 1982. "The Expected Utility Model: Its Variants, Purposes, Evidence and Limitations." *Journal of Economic Literature* 20: 529–63.

Shubik, Martin. 1982. *Game Theory in the Social Sciences: Concepts and Solutions.* Cambridge, Mass.: MIT Press.

———. 1975. *Games for Society, Business, and War: Toward a Theory of Gaming.* New York: Elsevier.

———. 1971. "The Dollar Auction Game: A Paradox in Noncooperative Behavior and Escalation." *Journal of Conflict Resolution* xv, 1. 109–11.

———. 1964. *Game Theory and Related Approaches to Social Behavior.* New York: Wiley.

Simon, Herbert A. 1957b. *Models of Man: Social and Rational.* New York: Wiley.

Sowell, Thomas. 1984. *Civil Rights: Rhetoric or Reality.* New York: William Morrow.

Stigler, George. 1968 "The Development of Utility Theory." In *Utility Theory: A Book of Readings.* Edited by A. N. Page. New York: Wiley.

Stevens, Stanley Smith. 1946. "On the Theory of Scales of Measurement." *Science* 103: 677–80.

Swap, Walter C., ed. 1984. *Group Decision Making.* Beverly Hills: Sage Publications.

Taylor, Shelley E. 1982. "The Availability Blas in Social Perception and Interaction." In *Judgment under Uncertainty: Heuristics and Biases.* Edited by Daniel Kahneman, Paul Slovic, and Amos Tversky. Cambridge, Eng.: Cambridge University Press.

Thorngate, Warren. 1980. "Efficient Decision Heuristics." *Behavioral Science* 25: 219–25.

Tversky, Amos. 1972. "Elimination by aspects: a theory of choice." *Psychological Review* 79: 281–99.

Tversky, Amos, and Kahneman, Daniel. 1985. "The Framing of Decisions and the Psychology of Choice." In *Behavioral Decision Making.* Edited by George Wright. New York: Plenum.

———. 1973. "Availability: A Heuristic for Judging Frequency and Probability." *Cognitive Psychology* 5: 207–32.

———. 1971. "Belief in the Law of Small Numbers." *Psychological Bulletin* 76: 105–110.

Vinacke, William E. 1959. "Sex Roles in Three Person Game Theory." *Sociometry* 22: 343–60.

Vinacke, W. Edgar and Arkoff, Abe, 1957. "Experimental Study of Coalitions in the Triad." *American Sociological Review* 22: 406–415.

von Neumann, John, and Morgenstern, Oskar. 1947. *The Theory of Games and Economic Behavior*. Princeton: Princeton University Press.

Von Winterfeldt, Detlov, and Edwards, Ward. 1986. *Decision Analysis and Behavioral Research*. Cambridge, Eng.: Cambridge University Press.

Weldon, J. C. 1950. "A Note on Measures of Utility." *Canadian Journal of Economics and Political Science* 16: 229–32.

Wright, George. 1984. *Behavioral Decision Theory*. Beverly Hills: Sage Publications.

Index